HABITAT, ECONOMY

AND

SOCIETY

*A Geographical Introduction
to Ethnology*

by
C. DARYLL FORDE

A Dutton **dep** *Paperback*

NEW YORK
E. P. DUTTON & CO., INC.

This paperback edition of

"HABITAT, ECONOMY AND SOCIETY"

First published 1963 by E. P. Dutton & Co., Inc.
All rights reserved. Printed in the U.S.A.

C. DARYLL FORDE has been Professor of Anthropology at the University of London since 1945 and is the Director of the International African Institute.

HABITAT, ECONOMY AND SOCIETY was first published in the United States in 1949. The text used in this Dutton Paperback is that of the fifth edition.

PREFACE

THIS book is intended as an introduction to the ethnography and human geography of non-European peoples. It deals with the economic and social life of a number of groups at diverse levels of cultural achievement and in different regions of the world, and with the rise of new crafts and organizations in the growth of civilization. An attempt has been made to write it in a manner free from unnecessary technicalities suitable both for the more general reader and for study in the later school and earlier university years. Broad facts and generalizations about 'peoples in many lands' are quite often taught to young children, but the specialization of later studies has tended to exclude any further consideration of the subject. While the development of geography as a school and university subject has sometimes involved cursory attention to the races of man and the life of 'primitive' peoples, some general knowledge of ethnology and sociology, and even of the great epochs in the growth of civilization have not become the requisites of a liberal education. The main body of anthropological thought has been neglected as being a specialist discipline.

This has had unfortunate consequences. The student both in school and at the university has as a rule acquired any knowledge of the broader facts and problems of human civilization only in connexion with the adaptations of the more complex civilizations to their present physical environment, while those made by simpler societies and the relation of such adaptation to other cultural processes have been largely ignored. This has tended to produce an unbalanced view, not necessarily because physical conditions have been declared to be of paramount importance, but simply because other factors have remained unknown or but vaguely apprehended.

University teaching in anthropology which should correct this bias has indeed begun to develop in recent years, but it has so far played relatively little part in undergraduate studies, and the results of new developments in theory and of investigations in the field do not pass beyond the research seminars and the reports of learned societies and institutions.

It is hoped therefore that this book may be of value not only to the professed student, but to all who are interested in the rich diversity of human efforts for economic and social satisfaction in cultures foreign to the modern Western world.

The method here adopted is as far as possible inductive. By the description and analysis of a number of different peoples a body of relevant information is built up which, it is hoped, will create interest and focus attention on the major problems which arise. In the last part of the book some of these problems are dealt with and, by reference back to the peoples studied, an attempt has been made to achieve the objectivity necessary in an introductory study.

From the ethnological point of view the studies are incomplete in so far as they concentrate on economic life and fail to deal, except incidentally and by allusion, with the religious and ceremonial life of the peoples concerned. This omission has been deliberately made and for several reasons. In the first place I have written for those with little or no previous knowledge of ethnology, to whom brief summaries of ritual and belief would, apart from a lengthy critique, have little meaning. Further, my object has been to deal with the broad features of economic pattern and to consider their relation to physical environment, to social organization and to major factors in the growth of civilization. Nearly all the fundamental cultural processes may be exhibited in this way, and the inclusion of esoteric material, while considerably increasing the length of the individual studies and distracting attention from the general theme, would not have contributed substantially to the main purpose. Moreover, religion and ritual may frequently have little genetic relation to the broad elements of economic and social life. In any living culture, it is true, the two categories are inevitably interwoven and so are intimately related in daily life. Belief and ceremonial are adapted to, and sometimes turned into new channels of development by economic and political stimuli; and it is also clear, as will be seen, that religious concepts may deeply affect economic and social development and may limit or even prevent adaptations that are obviously possible. Nevertheless, the power of ceremonial, magical practices and fundamental religious attitudes to transgress economic and political boundaries on a large scale is, I believe, undeniable and the wide field of investigation that they afford cannot be considered here.

It may be thought that I might in a few instances have dealt with peoples who are less familiar as topics of general and popular ethnography. But the real significance of a people not, for our purpose, diminished by general familiarity, and have endeavoured to consider aspects that are not usually emphasized in the general literature. Again it might appear that I have inconsequently passed over a people for whom we have modern and detailed studies in favour of another concerning whom our knowledge is less abundant and precise. This is, however, due to real difficulties: either, for instance, that adequate description and analysis would have involved discussions of special problems which could not adequately be dealt with within the framework of this survey, or at the particular stage of the book to which the people would relate, or again that the objective data on habitat, craft and economic life are really lacking, despite the size and modernity of the work.

Each chapter on a particular people has been made as self-contained as was consistent with the general aim of the book, but it has not been possible to write them all according to any uniform plan. I have attempted, rather, to emphasize salient characteristics, to concentrate on aspects of economic and social life that are well illustrated among a particular group, and above all to convey something of the special genius of a particular culture. A few of the studies are necessarily curtailed by the lack of detailed material, but these briefer sketches have been included because the people concerned are of considerable theoretical importance.

It is obvious that, apart from the few sections in which I have been able to rely to some extent on my own observations, I have been primarily dependent throughout on the field surveys and studies of others. While I have refrained from annotating the text, the sources of material and references to particular topics for each chapter will be found at the end of the book. These notes in each case express my great indebtedness to the workers concerned, several of whom have been kind enough to criticize my drafts. I wish for this and other valuable advice to thank in particular Professors A. L. Kroeber, R. H. Lowie, V. G. Childe, H. J. Fleure and E. G. R. Taylor; Drs. Clark Wissler, D. Jenness, W. Ivens, G. Slater and R. Olson; Sir Percy Sykes, Miss I. T. Kelly; and Messrs. J. H. Driberg and J. Hornell.

I am also indebted to the following for kind permission to reproduce or to use for drawings illustrations in their publications: the American Museum of Natural History, Dr. Wissler and Professor Lowie for figures 13, 14, 16–22, 24, 26–36, 42, 43 and 104; the Bureau of American Ethnology and Professor Franz Boas for figures 46–9, 52, 54–5 and 79–82; the Royal

Anthropological Institute for figures 74–8, 105 and the frontis
piece; the Museum of the American Indian, Heye Foundatio:
for figures 37–9, 57; the University of California Press fc
figures 11–12; the United States National Museum and Professc
Boas for figure 25; the Liverpool University Press for figure
5, 6 and 8; the University of Minnesota Press for figures 83–5
the American Geographical Society and Professor Alois Mus
for figures 97–8; the Geographical Association for figure 9(
the Field Museum, Chicago, and Dr. R. Linton for figure 7(
the Clarendon Press for figures 67, 69 and 95; the Oxfor
University Press and Dr. Gilbert Slater for figures 87, 89 an
91; Messrs. Constable Ltd., for figures 58–9; Messrs. Hutchinso
Ltd. and Dr. Paul Schebesta for figures 4 and 7; Messrs. Kega
Paul, Ltd. and Dr. W. Ivens for figures 66 and 68; the Gylder
dalske Boghandel Nordisk Forlag and Professor Mathiasse
for figures 44–5, 50–1, 53 and 56; Sir Percy Sykes for figure
100 and 102; Dr. Paul Leser for figures 88 and 107–8; an
Dr. W. Ivens for figure 65. My thanks are due to the Wellcom
Historical and Medical Museum and to Dr. L. W. G. Malcolı
for permission to draw specimens for figure 63.

I am grateful to Mr. Anthony Brown for the care and ski
with which he prepared from photographic material many (
the line drawings which illustrate the text, and also to Mr
Alexander Murison and to my wife for much help in th
collection of material and for reading the proofs.

C. DARYLL FORDE

ABERYSTWYTH
March 1934

NOTE ON WORLD MAPS IN FIGURES 1 AND 2

It may be of use to explain the curious shape of the map graticules used for the World Maps, figures 1 and 2. In order to avoid the gross exaggeration of extra-tropical areas involved in the Mercator projection and of the distortions of shape produced in the Mollweide Equal Area projection, especially when the Pacific Ocean is to be shown in the centre of the map, I have drawn the two land hemispheres on separate Mollweide graticules. By interrupting that for the Old World in the southern hemisphere it has also been possible to show the greater part of Oceania without serious distortion of shape. My thanks are due to my colleague Mr. W. E. Whitehouse for help in preparing the graticules.

C. D. F.

CONTENTS

PART I

FOOD GATHERERS

PART II

CULTIVATORS

PART III

PASTORAL NOMADS

PART IV

HABITAT AND ECONOMY

ILLUSTRATIONS

CHAPTER I

INTRODUCTION

I F an aboriginal Tasmanian family, miraculously surviving in the mountain forests and with no previous experience of Europeans, could be induced to watch a cinema film of our everyday life they would doubtless regard it as an amazing, incomprehensible, and rather terrifying sight. We lived in a land very similar in its scenery and climate to their own island; but every morning, so far as they might understand, we left a cliff face by a small hole, entered hard and shiny houses which moved over the ground, went into another great cliff-house, and climbed inside to a small chamber into which light came from another hole covered by a slab of rock through which you could be seen. All day and all the week, it seemed, we took no steps whatever to obtain food except to ask for it in other large structures which were apparently full of nothing else. In the evenings, if it were summer, we played with other people, hitting a ball into marked squares across a net, or moved with peculiar gait round and round, each male embracing a female in a crowd of similarly embraced couples, while noises emerged from a square drum-like object which nobody manipulated to make it play. Yet the magical purpose of this ritual remained quite obscure. Our magical beliefs might be detected in visits to a man who tapped us all over and finally gave us a small white square which, when taken to another magician, was exchanged for a transparent box of magic fluid. All this time we gathered no fruits, had no personal stores of food, hunted no animals. From similar views of the countryside the Tasmanians would slowly understand that some of our fellows did produce food, but that their efforts were so amazingly prolific that the great mass of the people could live packed together in large settlements, occupying themselves all day long making all sorts of unnatural objects move, clang and clatter, despite an obvious freedom to sit about in some quiet spot to tell and hear stories, sing songs or gamble. If the scenes were various enough the natives would discover storytellers, gamblers and community singers, but for a long time many of our activities would seem incredible and meaningless.

Yet despite the wonders, absurdities and indecencies which they observed, they could have no doubts that our bodies were essentially like their own, and that we depended on food obtained from plants and animals, although we apparently had a magic which made the plants grow as abundantly as we wanted and the animals herd together as tame as dogs wherever we put them, ready to be slaughtered at will. They could see that tools were cunningly fashioned from trees and stones that were dug up from the ground: in a word, that we used the resources of the same earth as themselves, that we had regulations of conduct some of them similar to their own, and, like theirs, sometimes broken.

If then the same film were later shown to a Samoyed in North Siberia, a Melanesian, an East African negro, an Indian *ryot* in an isolated Deccan village, these people would, in roughly that order, recognize more and more in our way of life as similar to their own. The Samoyed would be amazed at the Tasmanian's ignorance of domestic herds, the Melanesian at the Samoyed's ignorance of agriculture, the East African at the Melanesian's lack of metal tools, the Indian at the East African's lack of carts and his failure to use his beasts for burden and plough.

Even to-day, when European practices are penetrating to the remotest corners of the continents, there still remain great contrasts in the basic economy of peoples in different lands ; similarly, there is a wide range in the scale of their social grouping, from independent family groups to large confederacies of tribes and powerful states. Five hundred years ago, before the Great Age of Discovery opened, the relative isolation of these different ways of life was far greater, so that the records of travellers and explorers, from Marco Polo to Philby, have continually added to our knowledge of the varieties of human life, custom and belief. With the accumulation and comparison of ethnographical records we advance slowly towards a fuller understanding of the underlying factors and processes.

Attempts at such understanding and explanation are by no means modern. The very Tasmanians with whom we began would probably return with what we should call a rationalized account of our life, and would try to explain it to their fellows in terms of their own life and experience. Since ancient times records and opinions have accumulated, and various causes have been invoked as the reasons for the differences between the lives and customs of different groups of mankind. These fall into a few major groups of causes. Quite early a connexion was sought between the characters of men's bodies and their social and economic life—in other words, race was thought to explain many differences, generally because the different races were believed to have different qualities of mind and temper, so that some lagged behind while others climbed a ladder of progress. But serious difficulties are encountered in any thoroughgoing racial explanation. People of apparently similar race have lived very different lives and vice versa; moreover, a single racial group has occupied a very different position in the social and economic scale at different times. At one period the leaders of civilization were of one race, at others of another.

Often in opposition to the racial explanation there has been explanation by the physical environment, that is, according to differences in climate and vegetation which lead men to one kind of activity, type of society, and even of religious belief in one region, and to different activities, social institutions and beliefs in other regions. Despite the intimate relation between human activities and the conditions and resources of the physical world, there are clear limits to this explanation, for in regions closely similar in relief, climate, and vegetation sharply contrasted types of human life are to be found. The Tasmanian who was so amazed and confounded by the pictures of our life occupied an island of closely similar climatic type; yet he would find far fewer puzzles in the life of collecting peoples in the heart of the equatorial jungle of Malaya despite the sharp contrasts with his cool Pacific home.

Other students have in consequence reacted against environmental explanation. They have pointed out that the tools and weapons, the ways of obtaining food, the ceremonies and beliefs of any one people are rarely their special property and were probably not first discovered or used by them, and that their environment only helped to decide whether they should or should not adopt a practice which had become known to them. Any given tool such as the poisoned arrow or, at a higher stage, the plough, is shared by many people and can be used under widely different physical conditions. Man can be divided into great groups according as these do, or do not, use certain tools. But the peoples who use the plough are not necessarily more intelligent than those who do not. They may merely have had an opportunity of learning how to make and use it from some other people. And although with a different set of tools or social customs one people may reach a far higher level than another group which is without them, it does not follow that the first people are of superior race or live in a better environment. In other words, knowledge has spread

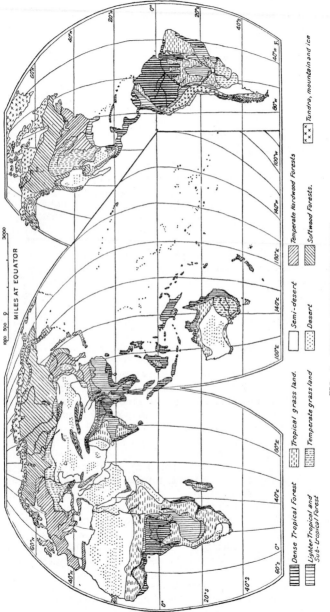

FIG. I. WORLD VEGETATION BELTS

MILES AT EQUATOR

Dense Tropical Forest

Lighter Tropical and Sub-Tropical Forest

Tropical grass land.

Temperate grass land

Semi-desert

Desert

Temperate Hardwood Forests

Softwood Forests.

Tundra, mountain and ice

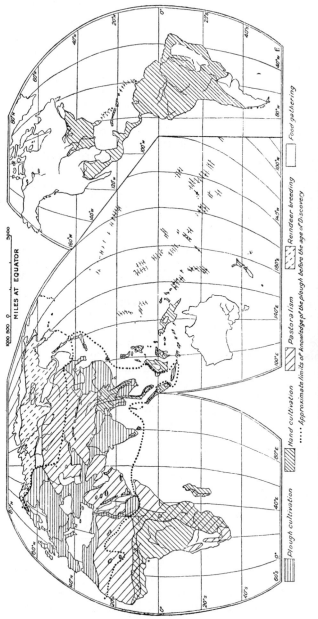

MILES AT EQUATOR

Plough cultivation   Hand cultivation   Pastoralism   Reindeer breeding   Food gathering

..... Approximate limits of knowledge of the plough before the age of Discovery

FIG. 2. WORLD DISTRIBUTION OF DOMINANT ECONOMIES

widely over the earth from very early times. Such advances as the cultivation of plants and the working of metals after discovery by one people have been handed on to others in ever-widening circles. A similar spread can be seen going on to-day: farm tractors made in the United States are being introduced into the semi-arid grasslands of Turkestan, and the children of pastoral nomads are learning how to use them. But before the development of the railway and steamship, still more before the appearance of riding animals and ocean sailing, the spread of arts and crafts from any one centre was much slower and the range was more limited than in the Western World of to-day; barriers that are now merely a nuisance and an expense were then almost unsurmountable.

This spread or diffusion of knowledge and culture is obviously a most important process in changing the lives of people and the details of its operation have been much discussed. Diffusion does not proceed automatically to the areas environmentally best suited to it or to the peoples most receptive: distance and accident play an important part. And again, mere proximity does not inevitably mean that a people will adopt the practices of their neighbours or of immigrants. Many hunting groups in the forests of Africa and south-eastern Asia have lived for generations on the outskirts of villages of cultivators. They will steal agricultural produce or trade for it, but they grow none themselves. North Chinese peasants spreading northwards to dispossess cattle nomads will raise no beasts, save for ploughing, and will drink no milk and make no butter or cheese. Moreover, the changes in the life of any people do not consist solely in simple additions to their stock of knowledge or belief from time to time, according to their external contacts, nor is their acceptance of one practice or the rejection of another to be decided only according to whether it suits their physical environment. This is permissive only.

Furthermore, social practices of great consequence are relatively indifferent to the physical environment. Slavery is found in the Congo forests, in the Arabian desert and on the forested coasts of British Columbia. Some students have therefore urged that the vital problem for study is the relation of any one element to the rest of the life of a people. They insist that the spread of crafts and customs are but contributing factors, the movements of the raw materials, as it were, out of which human life is built up. Social change is not a mechanical addition or subtraction but the integration of the new among the old. Every advance, therefore, depends on the pre-existing pattern and must fit into it, and in doing so an intrusive lement will probably undergo changes itself, so that any practice however similar in its general character will play a different part in the general life of each separate people. The metal-workers or smiths, for example, have very different social positions in different parts of the world: among some peoples they are a privileged class, among others they are outcasts. These contrasts have important effects on the part that metal-working plays in the economic and artistic life of the people.

It is clear that both the spread of knowledge and customs from one people to another, that is *diffusion*, and the part any element plays in the life of a people, that is its *functional relations*, are extremely important in influencing the final pattern of human life in any one region or among any group. These active cultural factors operate on the relatively static materials of race and physical environment. In order to appreciate these matters it is necessary, however, to obtain a fairly full and balanced picture of actual peoples. By considering as a whole the life of a number of tribes, grouped provisionally according to their way of life, but ranging from occupants of equatorial forests to those of arctic tundra, some of the relations between the trilogy, habitat, economy and society will be explored.

PART I

FOOD GATHERERS

CHAPTER II

THE SEMANG AND SAKAI: COLLECTORS IN THE MALAYAN FORESTS

IN Further India a great tongue of land projects into the
equatorial seas. This peninsula of Malaya is a mountainous
country whose core rises in great ranges to summits of
seven and eight thousand feet, trapping the monsoonal air
streams and increasing the heavy equatorial rainfall. The
climate is hot throughout the year, and even the highest slopes
have only occasional cool spells. The driest month is wet and
more than a hundred inches of rain fall over a great part of
the country, so that a mantle of dense vegetation extends from
the mangrove swamps of the coasts to the very summits of the
mountains.[1]

Mohammedan Malays, Chinese and Europeans have penetrated deeply into the peninsula, especially in recent times,
but the aboriginal population
survives little changed in the
interior. There are scattered
through the forests on the
slopes of the ranges two
peoples who differ in physique
and in their way of life even
from the most backward
Malays. They are the Semang
and the Sakai.

Small groups of Semang
are found in the hill country
of the great mountain ranges
in both British territory and
in southern Siam. Their
general appearance is that of
dwarfed negroes. The men
are well under five feet tall
and the women shorter,

FIG. 3. SEMANG AND SAKAI IN THE
MALAY PENINSULA

but their bodily proportions are not distorted. With dark

[1] Apart from clearings effected by Malays and Europeans a jungle of lofty
trees with a dense undergrowth of canes and a tangle of creepers clothes both
the river valleys and the slopes of the ranges.

brown skins, very broad noses, staring eyes, sometimes thick-lipped mouths, and lacking beards but with short black hair so curly that it forms little spiral tufts all over the head, they have obviously many similarities to the negroid stocks of Africa and the western Pacific Islands, and are therefore referred to as negritoes.

The Semang, save where occasionally they have interbred with Malays and adopted their habits, raise no crops and have no domestic animals, but are dependent on the wild products of the forests. And since, although vegetation is abundant, it is characteristic of the equatorial forests that few plants and trees of the same kind grow together in close proximity, the Semang migrate continually save for short natural harvests, and rarely stay more than three or four days in one place. The resources of any one locality are necessarily limited and will not support a dense collection of people, so that the individual groups of Semang are small. A band of twenty or thirty persons including children is a large one.

But a negrito group does not roam aimlessly and at will throughout the interior jungles of Malaya. Each group, which is usually a large family of parents and grown children with their families, has its small traditional territory of some twenty square miles, over which its claim to the especially valuable fruits of certain trees is recognized among its neighbours. For hunting and collecting of roots it is free to wander over the lands of neighbouring groups, but it always returns to gather the heavy green prickly fruit of the tall durian trees in its own territory. Since the group must gather its daily food as it travels, movement is slow, and it does not cover a wide extent of territory: five or six miles would be a fair day's travel. Within any given locality a number of groups are in fairly frequent contact, but beyond a radius of twenty to thirty miles encounters are very rare. Thus there arise small agglomerations of groups which from their frequent contacts maintain a similarity of speech and feel some sense of community, while a few miles away the dialect may change so markedly that intercourse is difficult and we have entered the sphere of another collection of groups. These agglomerations can hardly be spoken of as tribes, for they have no set organization and do not act consciously as a body. Their character and size is a function of the limited mobility of each component group.

The group alone is a fairly definite and independent unit. In choosing a camp site it generally follows the oldest man, and beyond the recognition of his wisdom there is no authority and no system of leadership. Tools and ornaments belong to their

lividual owners. Food indeed is often shared within the
oup, but not with other groups. When a man mates at about
ghteen years he usually chooses a woman from a neighbouring
iit, and often goes to live with his wife's people for a year or
o, but later returns to bring up his family with his parents.
It is difficult to realize the narrow bounds within which the
e of an individual is passed. Throughout his life a man will
main with a handful of his kin. From time to time he will
counter for a few days other groups of similar size. Very

FIG. 4. A SEMANG SHELTER
(*After Schebesta*)

rely will he go far afield, and few strangers cross his path.
he knowledge and opinions of his elder relatives are the only
iews he hears. This limited range of contact and stimulus
of fundamental importance in understanding the stability
nd slowness of change among the simpler societies of man.
A camp is usually made in some small natural clearing in the
rest or beneath an overhanging ledge of rock. The shelters
f the encampment are abandoned every time a move is made
nd are improvised again at the next halt, for they are easily
uilt with the large leaves of the many palm trees available in
ie jungle, although they vary in elaborateness, from a screen
f a single palm leaf to a group of interconnected shelters

enclosing a large space and set up on more frequently visit
sites. In a typical camp group there will be from six to
dozen shelters, generally arranged in a circle or oval. Ea
shelter is made by the mother for her husband and childre
Three or four stout sticks are driven into the ground in
line, sloping over towards the central clearing, and support
by forked struts or held in position by fibre strings pegg
in the ground. The outer side of the sloping stakes is th
closely thatched horizontally, working from the bottom
the top. Rattan leaves are used, and each is folded on i
midrib to give a double thickness of fronds. This slopi
thatch-like wall is adjustable, and its angle is raised or lower
according to the weather. In stormy weather more foliage
heaped on outside and held in position by branches. Benea
it, their heads to the back, raised couches are built to lift th
occupants from the damp earth and vegetation. They a
made of split bamboos and raised at one or at both ends wi
a thick tree branch or a strut supported by forks. A fire
built on one or both sides of the couch. Fire is obtained
rubbing together two pieces of dried cane or by running
piece of rattan to and fro round a strip of cane. The slown
of this method is increased by the humidity of the climate,
that fire is maintained continuously if possible and genera
carried from place to place with torches of bamboo or of dri
'ropes' of damar resin which is collected in the higher rang
and wrapped in dried leaves bound with rattan.

The Semang depend mainly on vegetable food, hunting a
fishing only when in need or as opportunity arises. They gath
a wide range of berries, nuts, pith, leaves, shoots and especia
roots and tubers, of which the long tuberous growths of t
wild yams are the most important. They are recognized
their leaves and dug up, sometimes from a depth of two
three feet with long sticks whose points have been hardened
the fire. This is mainly women's work, but the men may he
The produce is usually carried by the women in matwo
baskets of split rattan or bamboo, strapped on their backs li
rucksacks. Little can be stored or preserved, so that the par
must forage daily. The main meal of the day is usually ma
towards sundown, but they eat also in the early morning, a
have frequent 'snacks'. Several tubers, and especially the w
yams, which are almost a staple, and some fruits like that
the perah tree contain poisonous juices which are ingeniou
removed in various ways. The yams, for instance, are put
soak in river or swamp and then rasped with a length of prick
rattan, squeezed in a matting bag, and dried over the fi

thers are pounded to a pulp, mixed with ashes or lime, and
eamed. Food that is not eaten raw is usually boiled in tubes
it from long lengths of green bamboo, which withstands the
ames long enough to cook the food.

At certain seasons of the year a number of fruits, such as
urian and mangosteen, are available in abundance, and at this
me the group repairs to its own territory to gather this rich
pply and feast. The durian harvest is by far the most
nportant. This fruit is a large and rather bitter-tasting pulp
ntained in a thick rind which is covered in spines. The whole
uit may weigh several pounds and when ripe falls to the
ound beneath the tall trees. The durian trees are owned by
dividuals and passed on to their children. Although the
arvest is usually shared within the group, it would be most
nproper to pick another's durians, while the taking of durians
om the territory of another group would lead to serious
uarrels and violence.

The hunting of the Semang is sporadic and confined to
latively small game. The large carnivores, tiger, panther
nd leopard, and the elephant, are dreaded and avoided. Rats,
quirrels, birds, lizards, and occasionally monkeys and wild
gs are the usual game. Apart from a heavy hardwood stake
ith a fire-hardened point the bow is their only weapon. It is
simple curved wooden bow, made from a length of pliant
ngset tree branch, tapering at each end and strung with
new and bark fibre. The bamboo for once will not serve.
he branch is scraped down with rough stones and sharp
ivers of bamboo to a length of five or six feet and a diameter
about an inch at the grip. The arrows, nearly a yard long,
ave a heavy wooden tip fitted into a bamboo shaft equipped
ith two rather useless feathers. The arrow-tip is poisoned
ith *ipoh*, a vegetable poison obtained from the gum of the
as tree. These trees, which grow only sparsely except at
gher altitudes, are owned by individuals who frequently have
make long journeys to obtain a supply of the poison by
ashing the tree bark and heating the sap over the fire until
forms a dark, sticky paste. The poison when fresh is almost
stantaneously fatal to birds and small mammals, and will
ll monkeys and wild pig in a few minutes. For the larger
ame the juice of a poisonous creeper which is still more
owerful is often added to the *ipoh* paste. Until recently the
mang had no dogs, and those they now possess are of very
tle use in the chase. Game is also snared in simple noose and
ring traps, and birds are limed with the sticky sap of wild fig
ees smeared on splinters of bamboo, which adhere to their feet.

Although women never hunt, they join in fishing when
group comes down to a large river. Small fry are caught
bamboo scoops and larger fish are speared with the point
leaf stem of a large palm. Where the water is shallow a par
may drive the fish upstream towards the waiting spear-me
Although simple fish-traps are made, no dams or weirs a
built, and it is doubtful if the waters are ever poisoned.
Semang groups appear to concentrate on fishing for their foo
supply. Rivers are crossed and sometimes travelled for sho
distances on improvised rafts of lashed bamboos, but no cano
are made

FIG. 5.   A SEMANG GROOVED BAT FOR BEATING BARK
CLOTH.   MAI DARAT; BATANG PADANG, SOUTH PERAK
SCALE, ABOUT ¼
(*After Annandale and Robinson*)

Like their food-supply, the clothing of the Semang is su
plied mainly from the vegetation of the surrounding fores
Both men and women wear girdles and necklaces of leaves
the shiny black strands from a common fungus in the fores
and of the rock vein creeper. These are regarded as charm
not as clothing, though frequently a girdle or loin-cloth
made of bark cloth strips. The bark of a wild breadfruit
upas sapling is pounded until it can be easily removed from th
tree by two encircling cuts and one vertical one. The inne

bark is then washed and drie
and hammered out with woode
cudgels, or coarsely groove
bats, until it forms a strip
yard or so in length. Bar
cloth is not known among othe
negritoes in south-eastern Asia
but it is widely used by culti
vating peoples both there an
in the Pacific, and it is there
fore possible that the Seman
acquired it but recently by con
tact with the Savage Malays
The possession of a specialize

FIG. 6.   A SEMANG WOMAN'S BAM-
BOO COMB.   MABEK, JALOR
SCALE, ¼
(*After Annandale and Robinson*)

tool for its manufacture strongly suggests this. One of the mos
characteristic features of the women's dress is the wooder

comb with long teeth, which is cut from a segment of bamboo and is decorated with incised patterns which magically protect the wearer against disease.

It will have been noticed that the bamboo is of service at every turn as tool material among the Semang. The pliancy and toughness of the wood, the sharpness of its cut edges and its tubular noded form adapt it for many uses, from cooking-vessels and arrow quivers to matting and knives. A fire-hardened blade of bamboo will cut ordinary bamboo itself and keep its edge for a considerable time. Pliant rattan canes and woods for digging sticks, bows and spears almost complete their tool materials. Wooden mortars are sometimes made by burning out a hollow in an available bole or trunk of a fallen palm tree. Animal bones are scraped down to make awls, but stone tools, although used, are very undeveloped. The splitting and scraping of wood is generally done with rough, shapeless stones picked up at need and thrown away again. Indeed it is doubtful whether an archaeologist finding the remains of a Semang hearth after the wooden tools had rotted away in the hot, humid climate, would in the few rough stones recognize a human industry at all.

The Semang are not the sole representatives of their race. Negrito peoples are found in isolated groups scattered widely through south-eastern Asia. The Aëta peoples of the Philippines, the Kubu of Sumatra, and the Toala of Celebes have very similar economies, although hunting plays a greater part in the life of some Aëta groups, who organize drives against stockades and pitfalls constructed for larger game, including wild buffalo.

There is, however, a people whom we must consider briefly, since they exhibit important contrasts. They are the Andamanese. They differ from the secluded interior peoples like the Semang and Aëta in that they were found in sole occupation of an island territory. The Andaman Islands are an interrupted prolongation of the Arakan Yoma, the great north to south mountain chain of western Burma, and lie about two hundred miles from the mainland. In its fundamentals the economy of the Andamanese does not differ from that of the Semang. There is, however, some degree of economic specialization between the coastal groups and those of the interior. On the shores a rich harvest of marine life, and in particular the turtle, is to be gathered; in the interior, in addition to the wild fruits and small mammals, the bush pig is extensively hunted, and considerable barter, which takes the form of exchanging gifts, has developed between the coast and the interior communities. The Andamanese encampments, although formerly no larger or more elaborate than those of the Semang, appear to have been in general more permanent. A community often remains several months in one place, and usually has a headquarters to which it returns in the drier season from December to May. Eight to a dozen open shelters with sloping roofs, very much like those of the Semang, and each occupied by a man and woman with their young children are grouped round a small clearing, which is used for dancing and feasts. Very often, however, a larger and more permanent structure is erected: a rough frame of posts or of arched boughs covered with palm thatching to provide a place of general assembly. The large middens or rubbish-heaps of shells and other refuse which have accumulated round these hamlets make it clear that they must in some cases have been occupied, even if intermittently, for many years.

The Andaman youth has to undergo a long series of food-privations as he approaches manhood, one after another of the staple and favourite foods being forbidden him for a year or more at a time, and a ceremonial feast has to prepare him before he may safely eat them again. This deprivation of food to the young, which results in the older and often less active people securing a larger share, accords with the general tenor of Andaman society, in which respect for the old is instilled into the young in many ways.

But apart from these specializations, some of which may be considered to result from more favourable physical circumstances, there are other and more surprising features of Andaman life. Some of their material equipment is considerably more elaborate than that of the other negritoes. The coast peoples build large and shapely canoes, some of them equipped with outriggers; for pig-hunting they use a harpoon, while their bows are of a complicated S form, reminiscent of a type known in some parts of Melanesia. More remarkable, they are known to have made useful if rather rough decorated pottery for several generations before the British occupation of the islands, in the middle of the nineteenth century. The dead among the Andamanese are treated elaborately. Unlike the Semang and Aëta, who merely expose or bury the body and leave the spot, the Andamanese exhume the corpse after a long mourning, and the bones, particularly the skull, are preserved by the relatives.

These and other practices of the Andamanese set them off from the other south-east Asiatic negritoes and raise important problems. In the first place, it is important to notice that the

Andamans lie at no great distance from the Nicobar Islands and from the continental mainland. As we shall see later, the sea affords far less of a barrier to primitive man than might at first be supposed and ocean travel, be it deliberate or involuntary, has the special characteristic that the voyagers may be carried over great distances without any serious cultural change during the journey. Unlike a group which may wander slowly on land for some generations, coming into contact with many peoples, sea voyagers may acquire nothing on the journey, and often, owing to the difficulty of return, may remain to implant their knowledge and practices in the new territory. If, of course, the movement is prolonged over many years or even generations, and involves movements back into the homeland, the situation becomes more complex and bears more similarity to complicated land migrations. There is, however, abundant evidence of modern castaways and of primitive peoples who have made long sea journeys, encountering new peoples, among whom they settled and lived. Indeed the aboriginal Andamanese themselves must almost certainly have reached their islands by water, since the sea barrier was already in existence before the probable emergence of modern man.

If we consider these points in relation to the peculiarities of Andaman life we must ask immediately whether those features, which are additional to the typical negrito life, have not reached them as a result of occasional incursions. The Andamanese appear in general to be of a homogeneous negrito stock, but such movements would not substantially modify the racial composition of the population. In describing the Semang the modifications which occur among some groups as a result of adopting practices, such as rice-eating or the use of new weapons, which have been learned from neighbouring peoples, have not been discussed. The modifications of Andaman life are probably of the same kind and are due to the same causes. This becomes even clearer when we learn that the use of outrigger canoes and also a cult of the skulls of the dead is found in the adjacent Nicobar Islands whose inhabitants have a still more complex culture.

We have now to return to Malaya to consider briefly another people, the Sakai, who are found south of the Semang and usually at lower levels in the densely forested valleys and plains, although the territories of the two peoples interpenetrate a good deal.

In some districts they have interbred extensively with Malays or negritoes, but where mainly pure in race the Sakai contrast strongly with the negritoes in appearance. Although but little taller they are of more slender build and their skin colour is often quite light; their heads are long and narrow, unlike the small, rounded negrito head, and their hair, though black, is long and only slightly wavy. But their life in general is very similar to that of the Semang, although their habitations are more elaborate and they return to them more regularly. They build rather flimsy rectangular huts, walled with bark strips or plaited palm fronds and roofed with gabled thatch of palm

FIG. 7. A SAKAI PILE DWELLING
(*After Schebesta*)

leaves; some are over twenty feet long and hold several families, but others are quite small. More remarkable is their elevation above the ground, which undoubtedly affords considerable protection both against damp and wild beasts. The larger huts are raised a yard or two above the ground on piles or the trunks of large trees, and are reached by a notched trunk, while the small huts may be perched high in the branches of a tall tree. The encampment is often further protected by rough stockades of felled trees. Raised dwellings are used by Savage Malay cultivators who occupy the outer fringes of the Malayan jungle, with whom the Sakai are often in close contact, and it is not improbable that the Sakai huts are made in imitation of these and are not part of their earlier culture.

In their hunting the Sakai exhibit another great contrast. They use the blowpipe and not the bow. The blowpipe is a tube some eight to twelve feet long made from a particular and rather rare bamboo. The internodes of this *Bamboo wrayi* are often as much as six feet long, and two of these placed end to end, covered and held in position by a hollowed length of stouter bamboo whose knots have been bored or punched out, provide the long, straight and smooth tube which is essential for this weapon. Where bamboos with closer knots have to be used, several tubular sections are carefully fitted end to

FIG. 8. SAKAI HUNTERS
(*Based on photographs in Annandale and
Robinson*)

end, bound together, and covered with a casing of another longer bamboo, split lengthwise, smoothed and bound tightly to the inner tube. The light darts, only a few inches long, are made from the mid-rib of a palm frond scraped down to the thinness of a knitting-needle and notched near the point to break off in the wound. The point is smeared with *ipoh* poison, like the Semang arrow, and is set in a blunt cone of soft wood or pith whose base fits the tube. When inserted in the gun a wad of fluffy fibres from the leaf bases of palms is placed behind to prevent leakage of the air-pressure when the hunter raises the tube and blows his dart with a skilfully controlled breath. This weapon, whose aim is fairly accurate up to about seventy-five or a hundred feet, is, however, inferior to the bow both in range and force. It is nevertheless the favourite means of hunting among the Savage Malays, and has been adopted by some Semang groups in contact with them or with the Sakai.

The blowpipe is widely used in south-eastern Asia. It is used by the negrito Toala in Celebes, but, although Sakai blow-guns are among the finest, is not confined to purely hunting peoples. At present we do not know whether it was a discovery of the hunters and has been adopted by cultivators like the Savage Malays or whether the reverse is true: it presents the same kind of problem as the bark cloth of the Semang.

It has long been realized that racially the Sakai are allied to the Australian aborigines, and other australoid peoples are found in south-east Asia. These include the Vedda of Ceylon and the Kubu of Sumatra. In economy and in the size of the effective unit many Australian groups hardly reach the level of the Sakai. They have no blowgun and the bow is only known in the far north, where, like the outrigger canoe, it is an import from New Guinea. Many Australians are, however, skilful workers in flint, and they exhibit specializations in their social and religious organization which raise some of the most important problems in ethnology.

We should at this point observe that the food-gathering peoples of south-eastern Asia are not all members of the two race types so far encountered. The Punan of interior Borneo, for instance, rank closely with the Sakai in their economic and social life. They are hunters who use the blowpipe and lack the warlike practices and large communal houses of the settled cultivating tribes. But in physical type they are hard to separate from the latter; they are clearly of the Malay type, probably a blend of Mediterranean or Brown race and Mongoloid stocks, and sharply distinct from the negrito and australoid.

Before concluding this chapter it is necessary to refer briefly to the equatorial hunting peoples of Africa, since there are similarities not only in physical environment but also in racial type with the negritoes of south-east Asia. Contrary to popular belief, the Congo forest is not exclusively occupied by dangerous and elusive pygmies: by far the greater part of the area is occupied by agricultural negro tribes (see Chapter X). But there are considerable tracts of country in which the uncleared forest is occupied by pygmy groups, especially the Ituri Forest along the Semliki river in the north-east and to the north of the lower Congo in the southern Gaboon. They are also found in the Kasai valley in the south and extend sporadically across to Uganda. They live in small family groups in relative isolation and move about continually. They hunt with the bow and poisoned arrows, and some groups have dogs, but their food-supply is often derived mainly from plants, insects, and smaller game.

On the whole, however, they live in much closer relation with the settled cultivators than do the Semang and Sakai, and this area is famous for the development of 'silent trading' between the pygmies and the negroes. Many pygmy groups are tacitly attached to a negro village and have an understanding for the barter of game for agricultural crops. After a successful hunt the negritoes enter the banana groves of the villagers, gather fruit, and hang suitable meat in its place; the villagers when needing game will also lay out agricultural produce in an accustomed place for the hunters, who will in due course bring to that place a portion of their bag.

CHAPTER III

THE BUSHMEN: HUNTERS IN THE KALAHARI
DESERT

THE term Bushmen (*Boschimänner*) was given in the seventeenth century by the Dutch settlers to the diminutive hunting peoples with whom they early came in contact in South Africa. In appearance they show many points of resemblance to the negritoes that we have been concerned with in the previous chapter. They are of similar stature and have negroid facial features, but they lack the projecting mouth, thick everted lips, and wide-open eyes characteristic of both negro and negrito. One of their most well-known physical peculiarities is the tendency, especially among women, to steatopygy, i.e. the excessive development of fatty tissue on the buttocks. As a race they are sufficiently distinctive to make it doubtful whether they can be closely related to the negrito pygmies, except in so far as both are variants of a common stock, most numerously represented by the larger negroes.

To-day the Bushmen, apart from isolated and dependent individuals, are found in the barren inhospitable country in the north-west of the Union, in South-west Africa, and in adjacent territories to the north. Indeed, it is as hunters in the tropical scrub and desert lands that they claim our attention. But they were not in the past restricted to these barren lands. Bushman groups are known from historical records and archaeological evidence to have exte.ided formerly far north and eastwards into Basutoland, Natal, and Southern Rhodesia. The existence of a related speech among hunters in eastern Tanganyika Territory and the sporadic occurrence of Bushman types among the negroid populations of the East African highlands, suggest that these people have moved obliquely across Africa from the tropical highlands to the south-west. The distribution of characteristic implements and wall-paintings in southern and eastern Africa confirms this view.

When the Dutch settlers arrived to invade their hunting-grounds the Bushmen were already giving way before the pressure of other African peoples. Down the eastern coast-ands and along the central plateau of the present Southern Rhodesia, Transvaal and Bechuanaland, Bantu-speaking negroes were advancing and establishing their farms and driving their live stock to pasture in the open country. Similarly, from the south-west another people, the Hottentots, closely related to the Bushmen in race and speech but distinguished from them in having learned and adopted the herding of cattle and goats from more northern peoples, had invaded former Bushman territory and had already appropriated extensive pastures in what is now South-west Africa and the western and southern parts of Cape Province. The continuance of Bantu advance and the destruction of the southern Bushmen by European settlers has to-day reduced surviving settlements of fairly pure and independent Bushmen living their old life to a relatively small area in northern South-west Africa and Bechuanaland. There may not be many more than six thousand still in existence.

During this period of retreat their life has been considerably impoverished and modified by frequent dependence upon Hottentots, Bantus and Europeans. Indeed the best-preserved groups are frequently among those most influenced in this way. In order to portray the essential characteristics of Bushman life we shall consider not one alone of the four divisions into which they have been linguistically divided, but the records, both past and present, of individual groups in various parts of their territory.

South Africa is a great plateau about three to six thousand feet high, with massive ranges in the east. Its climate is subtropical, and except in the extreme south-west it is a land of summer rains. These are abundant in the eastern half and result in dense forests on the eastern mountains and coastlands, fading westwards into parkland, which, with the diminishing rainfall, degenerates into expanses of tall grass, thorn scrub and ultimately bare sandy and stony deserts. Beyond the forests, rainfall is everywhere uncertain, and uncertainty reaches a maximum in the Kalahari and the Namib desert coast. The Kalahari itself, stretching from the Orange river to the Okavango swamps and Lake Ngami in the southern borders of the Congo basin, is a land of ephemeral streams. The average rainfall figures of twenty inches in the north and east and only eight inches in the south-west give no clue to the wide variations from year to year. Permanent water is found only in depressions of the stream-beds and on low mud-flats or pans cutting the water-table. In the richer parts and in the better years there is a cover of tall grass broken by thorny trees and stunted baobabs, but elsewhere there are only patches of the short 'Bushman grass' and scattered euphorbia trees, with groves of acacia marking the high-water level along the stream-beds. But even in the driest parts a few leguminous and bulbous plants flourish, especially the famous Bushman 'melons', *tsama* (*Citrullus vulgaris*) and *naras*, which lie like pale balloons on the sandy surface, and are sought by man and beast for the water in their succulent interiors.

The forests and grasslands of Africa are unique and renowned for their wealth of large game. This is not consequent on the vegetation alone. The reason for the contrast with similar areas in the Americas and Australia, for example, is to be sought in the disposition of land and sea at critical periods of the earth's history, when the numerous herbivores and carnivores appeared, developed and spread over wide areas. Many species of antelope both large, like the great kudu, and small like the duiken and steenbok, are found in great numbers in southern Africa. Other herbivores are the giraffe, ostrich zebra, elephant, rhinoceros, hippopotamus and quagga, upon which prey a large number of carnivores—the lion, leopard wildcat, lynx, hyena and jackal. An extensive supplementary diet is also provided by the many small animals, ants, lizards frogs, bees and locusts.

With this wealth of animal life, water and not food is the problem of settlement in the drier country. The European can obtain water from great depths, but the simpler peoples are restricted to surface supplies. Most fundamental is the sharp seasonal contrast. In summer should the rains prove normal the streams fill, grass, succulents and shrubs spring up in abundance, and the game spreads widely over the country But the hot summer sun rapidly dries up the supplies of water and scorches the grass, and in the dry winter season only a few pools are left and the edible vegetation has rapidly shrunk The beasts, although individuals can in extremity survive for weeks on naras melons alone, concentrate in huge numbers round the permanent water-holes. This seasonal rhythm is less all-compelling to the Bushmen. The edible fruits are less abundant than in the equatorial forest, but the animal food supply is far richer and more easily taken Hunting plays a greater part than the gathering of plants, but it involves close conformity to this seasonal alternation of widespread abundance followed by migration of game to a few favoured spots Thus the territory of a Bushman group which may at first sight seem large may be only just adequate for the winter season; it must, above all, contain permanent water sources or which both beasts and man depend. Trespass across tribal frontiers is dangerous unless previous relations are friendly and the arrival is frankly announced, and there is often a neutral zone between the territory of one group and that of its neighbours. As among the Semang, the sole effective social group among the Bushmen is a small band of people usually related by blood or marriage and varying from twenty to a hundred in number. The adjacent groups in a district will speak a single dialect, and a common descriptive name, e.g. the River People, suggests some sense of their contiguity. But the individual groups rarely gather in one place or plan any co-operative action unless there is a sudden abundance of game in the wet season, when two groups may join in a drive over a wide tract of country. Each maintains a strict autonomy within its territory. Individuals and small parties may pass from one band to another. A man may take his family to visit his parents-in-law and remain with them for some time. Small parties make brief trading visits to barter food and skins for weapons and ornaments. A hunter may follow wounded animals into neighbouring territory, but he must visit the band and share his game, otherwise, if caught, he will be attacked. But these movements are irregular and individual. No permanent alliances are formed, and continued trespass or killing from whatever cause will lead to a feud involving whole bands which may be perpetuated by sporadic encounters over several generations.

The four major divisions into which the Bushmen are often divided are dependent on the four dialect groups into which the entire range of Bushman speech can be divided. They are in no sense political units.

The Bushman band and its territory, then, is a miniature realm; it consists of a number of families, each with its own huts, and only at the dry season are these families likely to be united in the vicinity of a water-hole. In the rainier season they scatter over the territory which they hold in common and hand on to their descendants. Moving several times a year whenever the local food supply gets scarce, their encampments are selected by the senior male, who lights a fire before the women begin to build the shelters. These are half domes of light sticks perhaps four feet high, interlaced with twigs and thatched with grass. The floor is scooped out and covered with grass and the fire pit set in front. In inclement weather further segments of the dome may be added and the entrance thus narrowed to afford greater protection. (Fig. 9.)

Each family produces its own food. The women collect the

roots, berries, grubs, insects and small game like tortoises,
frogs, iguanas and lizards, as well as the essential firewood and
water, setting out daily in small parties with their digging
sticks and loose hide shoulder cloaks which serve as receptacles.
The digging stick, where the ground is hard, is often tipped
with horn and weighted with a bored stone wedged into
position. Water is collected and brought into the camp in
ostrich egg-shells or dried bucks' stomachs, for the Bushmen
always camp several miles from their water-holes, especially
in the dry season, lest they disturb the game which comes to
them. The men also go out almost daily to hunt, and unless
they are following wounded game return for the main evening
meal. The hunting methods vary with the season and the

FIG. 9. A BUSHMAN CAMP

prey. Usually a man goes out alone or with his son or other
relative whom he is training, and a dog. He moves, with bow
and poisoned arrow, towards a water-hole or salt lick frequented by his quarry where he stalks or ambushes his game.
The hunter creeps up to leeward and endeavours to approach
as closely as possible, since the range and impact of his arrows
are not great and the quarry is swift. The southern Bushmen
are very skilled in the use of disguises, and imitate the cries
especially of the young animals. Arrow poisons are variously
concocted from plant juices, snake sacs and the dried bodies
of certain grubs and spiders, but they are none of them instan-
taneous and many hours may elapse before the animal falls
exhausted, so that long pursuits are generally necessary. The
hunter following the spoor of the wounded animal must reach
it before the hyena or the vulture snatches his prey.

Success in hunting is ensured by magical observances, which
vary in different parts of the country. In the south, for
example, flesh of a slow-moving animal should be eaten when

wounded game is followed. In the north-west the ashes of the
burnt flesh of desirable game are rubbed into cuts on the face
and body of the aspiring hunter, but this scarification is not
practised elsewhere.

When, as in the wet season, large game can be driven into
the treacherous mud-flats, where they are easily mired, or
when, as during the height of the drought, they shed their
hooves, animals can be run down on foot and finally disabled
with the knobbed throwing stick.

Individual hunters will also construct snares and traps.
Among the northern Bushmen small buck and occasionally
larger game are taken in baited nooses attached to bent
saplings or stakes, and elsewhere timber or stone falls are
arranged which collapse on the animal which takes the bait.
Poisoned drinking-places are frequently prepared at the height
of the drought in the western and more desert areas. The pool
or water-hole is itself fenced off, and a mud basin prepared
alongside is filled with water into which poisonous euphorbia
branches are thrown and weighted down.

But snaring plays a far smaller part than true hunting.
Moreover, with the great wealth of fast-moving but gregarious
herbivores, there is opportunity for more effective action than
that of the single stalker, and at suitable times when a large
bag is required the whole of a Bushman group will combine in
a drive which is carefully prepared beforehand. Fences of
logs and brushwood are built across a valley floor, openings
being left at which large pitfalls are dug. The beaters move
out in a wide sweep on the higher ground coming in from
windward to drive the game before them to the fence. Close
by each opening hunters conceal themselves to despatch the
animals as they fall into the pits. These fences, sometimes
extending for miles across a valley, are recorded by several
early travellers in Bushman country. Large pitfalls, sometimes four yards long and deep, floored over with a thin layer
of brush, are also constructed by the group along a track down
to a water-hole.

Every man hunts or gathers for his own immediate family,
and he can and does establish private property not only in
what is brought in, but also in resources found and left for
gathering at a later date. This is usually done by sticking an
arrow in the ground close to the bees' hive, nest of ostrich
eggs, or patch of roots which the discoverer wishes to preserve.
The arrow by its individual marking establishes the identity of
the owner. Similarly, caches of food and water in ostrich egg-
shells are sometimes made. Should a family in extremity find

such a cache and use it they must trace the depositor and inform him lest he seek to avenge the theft. But when any large game is brought into the camp it is in fact generally shared. The hunter usually keeps the valuable hide and sinews and directs the division of the meat.

The crafts of the Bushman are in general few and simple but they show an ingenious use of the limited resources of their region. Wood provides the material for most of their weapons and tools—for their bows, throwing sticks, spears, and fire drill—while shredded bark twisted on the thigh affords cordage. A straight, light, tubular material for their arrow shafts is found in the reeds which fringe the water-holes. These reeds are also used as sucking-tubes in times of drought, when water can often be slowly drawn up from a few feet below the dried bed of a lake or stream.

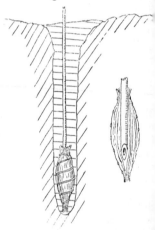

The dominance of game in their economy ensures a fairly abundant supply of hides, bone and sinew. The two last are of great importance—affording the bone arrow foreshaft and the tough bowstring. The leg bone of an ostrich or giraffe, split, scraped and ground down to a point provides the best arrow-tip. The hides themselves, especially buckskin, are used for clothing and bags. The clothing of a Bushman is scanty.

FIG. 10. BUSHMAN GRASS FILTER AND TUBE FOR SUCKING WATER

A man wears a triangular loin-cloth whose point is drawn backwards between the legs; a woman wears a squarish front apron hanging from a waist belt, while older women sometimes wear an apron at the back as well and suspend it from the shoulder. But the most important item of female attire is the cloak or *kaross*. It is both a garment and a hold-all. When it is tied at the right shoulder and at the waist, the baby, the food and the firewood are all held in its folds on the daily journey back to the camp. Men also often wear a light cloak over the right shoulder and covering the back; among some groups skin caps and tough hide sandals are worn.

Where traded iron goods are not numerous the Bushmen are skilled flint-workers, making a variety of tools, from scrapers for wood and hides to points for their arrows and drills. The southern Bushmen in Cape Colony formerly made rough pottery with tubular handles but the forms and distribution of this pottery have caused it to be generally regarded not as a discovery of their own but an introduction from the north-east.

The large eggs of the ostrich not only provide water-bottles, which are carried in netting bags, but also the material for the famous Bushman beads. The shells are broken into small chips. These are bored, shaped to rough discs and finally tightly strung and ground down on a grooved stone slab until the string is smooth and cylindrical. These beads are more popular and widespread than any other ornament. They have been made for many generations and are found in archaeological deposits of early Bushman remains. Made only in certain districts, they are the most important element of barter between individuals, being exchanged for hides and for products obtained outside Bushman territory, such as iron knives and spearheads, millet, and especially tobacco. For there exists an extensive if unorganized system of barter which reaches to the Bantu tribes in the north, in whose direction honey, wax, feathers, ivory, skins and beads are passed on from person to person for these foreign products.

Although the surviving Bushman groups to-day occupy an arid environment and serve as a type of hunters in semi-desert scrublands, there is no reason to believe that the fundamental patterns of their life were substantially different when they occupied the richer grasslands to the south and east. The need for water and the seasonal rhythm may be more strongly marked among the Kalahari survivors, but those factors existed already. Nor is there any indication that the Bushmen of the richer territories had a more complex social life. The density of population over a given area, and the size of the territorial groups, may have been somewhat larger, but this, although probably intensifying social activity, did not involve any important contrast with the bands of the Kalahari to-day.

CHAPTER IV

THE PAIUTE: COLLECTORS IN THE GREAT BASIN

IT will be instructive to compare with the Bushmen the peoples of somewhat similar economy who occupy the arid plateaux of the Great Basin in western North America in rather higher latitudes.

In the lee of the great ranges of the Sierra Nevada there lie, between the Columbia and Colorado rivers, a series of semi-desert upland basins at a general level of three to four thousand feet. Only the mountain masses to the west and east which rise above eight and nine thousand feet receive an adequate precipitation, and these are snow-covered for a considerable part of the year.

The summers are surprisingly hot for the latitude and elevation. Shade temperatures of more than 100° F. are recorded at altitudes of over five thousand feet. The average temperature for July at that height may be over 70° F., while the floors of the lower depressions may reach amazing temperatures. The highest recorded maximum for North America comes from Death Valley in the south-west of this area where the mean July temperature is actually 102° F. The winters, on the other hand, are bitterly cold. Ten or more degrees of frost may continue for several weeks, and records of 60° below freezing point have been obtained in the more northerly parts. The light thunder-showers of summer are not extensively supplemented by winter snow, and away from the mountain ridges the total rainfall nowhere exceeds ten inches. Most of the streams depend on the high mountain snows, and many only reach the basin floors in spring, to be lost there in the sands and gravels or to flow into shallow salt lakes.

This great tract of semi-arid territory, some two hundred thousand square miles in area, is therefore more extreme in its climatic variations than south-western Africa. The relief is also much stronger, so that the vegetation zones lie closer together. Dense coniferous forests clothe the high bordering ranges, while thinner woodlands of pines and juniper are found on the many smaller ranges rising above six thousand feet which subdivide the Great Basin and run in a generally north-south direction. Below the mountain forests a belt of grassland occupies the lower slopes, and on the basin floors is replaced by patches of bunch grass, sage brush and other scrub. The vegetation is, moreover, often interrupted by wide tracts of barren alkali—the dried floor of a salt lake—or stretches of stony gravel.

This country was until quite late in the nineteenth century virtually untouched by Western civilization. It was sparsely inhabited by small groups who are generally referred to collectively from their territory and speech as the Plateau Shoshoneans. Although large tracts are now occupied by cattle

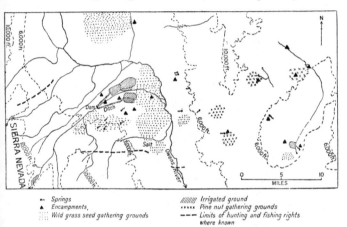

FIG. 11. SKETCH MAP OF THE TERRITORY OF A NORTHERN PAIUTE BAND
IN OWEN'S VALLEY
(*After Steward, simplified*)

ranches and smaller areas by irrigated farms and mining centres, the greater part of this country in the states of California, Nevada, Oregon and Utah has remained largely unchanged by the brief century of American occupation. Much of the aboriginal life of the small native communities has survived to the present time, especially among the Northern Paiute, or Paviotso, who occupy the open valleys east of the Sierra Nevada in north-eastern California, Nevada and southern Oregon.

The largest unit in Northern Paiute society was a band of a hundred or so people who occupied a common territory of about fifty to a hundred square miles. During the winter the band congregated in one or two fairly large and semi-permanent settlements, but in spring it broke up into family groups which scattered over the territory. Among some of the Nevada bands individual families claimed rights over particular springs, streams and resources of seeds and roots, but more usually all families wandered freely in the territory of its band. Most of the movements were up and down the slopes of the surrounding ranges and the distances covered were small.

The commonest form of winter dwelling, known as the 'wikiup' was a conical structure with a central fire pit and smoke-hole. Juniper, where available, afforded good poles for the frame and stout bark strips for the covering, and these supplies were often carried great distances. Elsewhere willow

FIG. 12. NORTHERN PAIUTE REED HUT
(*After photographs by Steward*)

poles were covered with dried brush or matting made from dried tule reeds or tall grasses.

In the winter settlement a sweat house was usually erected near a stream. Among the more north-easterly groups in northern California and Nevada it was merely a small domed shelter covered with grass or skins. Hot stones were placed inside and water was poured on these to produce a hot, steamy atmosphere in which the men sweated before plunging into the river. This sweating was believed to have medicinal value, but it also had strong religious associations. In Owen's Valley the sweat house was a more considerable structure, resembling that of central California, and heat alone, from a central fire pit, was used for sweating. It was the largest and most substantial building in the camp and was used as a meeting-house by the men and as a dormitory by the youths.

During the warmer half-year these settlements were generally deserted for unwalled shades with flat, square roofs of grass and brush supported on four poles or, more usually, for circular and semicircular wind-screens built up with stakes and matting or brush against which sand might be piled on the outer side. The fireplace was set within the curve and the sleeping places round the walls. Neither the winter settlements nor the smaller summer camps appear to have had any definite plan.

Large game was not abundant in the Great Basin, and vegetable foods, insects and small animals were the main diet. The seeds of numerous grasses and a large range of berries were gathered, while bulbs and wild roots were dug with pointed sticks. The hard seeds of tall grasses such as porcupine and wild rye were gathered on the valley slopes. The more luxuriant rice grass grew around marshy depressions on the basin floors. Sunflower seeds were especially valued. The seeds of the ubiquitous sage brush were little used, save in times of great scarcity, on account of their bitter taste. Seeds were also regularly stolen from stores gathered by rats and squirrels. Wild onions and clovers were eaten raw. Tiger lily and spike rush bulbs were dug up in large quantities.

In Owen's Valley several groups took advantage of favourable conditions to irrigate patches of ground. The growth of bulbous plants and grasses is patently more luxuriant wherever abundant water reaches them, and this was achieved artificially by diverting from their narrow channels the snow-fed streams flowing down from the Sierra Nevada. In spring, before the streams rose with the snow-melt, a dam of boulders, brushwood and mud was thrown across a creek where it reached the valley floor. Above the dam one or two main ditches, sometimes more than a mile long, were laboriously cut with long poles to lead the river water out on to the gently sloping ground over which it was distributed in minor channels. Smaller dams of brushwood and mud were made as needed to concentrate the flow of water in any particular direction. Sometimes two or more main ditches were cut and different tracts were watered in successive years. After the harvest the main dam was pulled down, so that with the reduced flow of late summer and winter the stream could resume its natural course. All the men in a group joined in the construction of the dams and in the clearing of the channels, and all women were free to gather on the irrigated ground. There was, however, no attempt at planting or working the soil, and none of the cultivated plants grown to the south of the Colorado were known. It would appear unlikely that irrigation could have been introduced from outside apart from any knowledge of cultivation or

cultivated plants, and there is no archaeological evidence of
the former existence of agriculture in this area, so that this
watering of wild plants may have been an entirely native
device (see fig. 11).

In most districts a considerable harvest of pine nuts was
gathered in the wooded ranges in the late autumn. The cones
were beaten from the trees and heated so that the nuts could
be removed and packed in bags. The crop varied considerably
from year to year, and when it was particularly good many
groups would remain on the ranges all through the winter to
accumulate a large surplus of a food which, with its thick shell,
would keep well for a year or longer. Towards the south in the
lower-lying land there was an abundant harvest of the sweet
and nutritious pods of the mesquite tree, whose long roots
could reach subsoil water. Grasshoppers, lizards and tortoises
were obtainable during summer. Like the Bushmen the
Paiute regarded a swarm of grasshoppers as the occasion for
a great feast. A wide circle of beaters swept them into a
central pit, and they were consumed in enormous quantities,
boiled and roasted, while the surplus was pounded into a paste
and dried for storage.

Gathering was women's work, although men would help,
particularly with the pine-nut harvest where there was tree
climbing to be done. The women went out daily in small
parties. Seeds they gathered with small, fan-like beaters of
open basketry, with which the grasses were beaten against the
mouth of a small collecting
basket. This was from time to
time emptied into the conical
burden basket, supported on the
back from a forehead band. The
seeds were later winnowed and
parched—that is, dried out by
shaking up with live coals—on
shallow basketry trays. Finally
the hard seeds, nuts and other

FIG. 13.   NORTHERN PAIUTE
GRINDING SLAB AND MULLER
(*After Lowie*)

food were crushed and ground on flat, square grindstones with
a cylindrical stone muller.

One of the salient characteristics of Paiute economy, and a
feature in which they contrast not only with the equatorial
Semang but also with the Bushmen, is their extensive storage
of food. The lack of vegetable food during the late winter and
spring and the scanty products of the chase were met by gathering a surplus at other seasons. Ground seeds were dried in
cakes. Berries were dried whole or pounded. Pine nuts and

roots were packed away in skin bags. These supplies were accumulated in large grass-lined pits dug at the winter settlements.

Although squirrels, gophers, rats and, above all, rabbits were fairly abundant, larger game was rare and difficult to hunt in the Great Basin. Winter was the main hunting period, and the larger groups at the winter settlements made possible a more effective attack on the slender resources. Although the objective was often only the humble rabbit the communal hunt was the climax of Paiute social life, during which neighbouring camps joined forces and celebrated their success with dances and gambling contests. In each winter camp there was usually a leader referred to in modern days as the 'Rabbit Boss'. He directed the party, which might be several dozen or even fifty strong. A given hunt would last ten days or a fortnight. Each day the party set out for a new tract of country. In a suitable place fibre nets about four feet high and a hundred or more feet long were set up in a semicircle. The rabbits were driven towards the nets from a wide valley tract by converging groups of beaters and were clubbed or shot while entangled in its meshes. The nets were often re-erected several times a day, and a wide range of country was covered, during ten or fourteen days' intensive hunting.

The so-called antelope, or wild goat (*Antilocapra americana*) was more elaborately hunted. A large circular area was enclosed with a sage-brush fence, or by frequent mounds of brush and stones. A converging avenue of brush led to this enclosure. The party which had located an 'antelope' herd headed it in the direction of this pound. As the animals entered the lane its fencing was fired and the frightened creatures rushed on to the enclosure, where they were driven round and round until, exhausted, they fell easy victims to heavy sticks. But antelope herds were not numerous in this country, and they were not easily lured or driven into the pounds. The difficulty of the hunt was reflected in the ceremony which should precede it. When the pound had been built men and women gathered in the circle. Women wearing antelope head-dresses imitated the cries of the animal, songs were sung and sticks rasped to charm the herd to approach and enter willingly. A few active men then went out disguised in antelope head-dresses, and, taking advantage of the great curiosity of these animals, lured them close to the pound so that they could be driven in by the main body.

Duck, mud-hen and geese were often hunted by parties on mountain lakes. Each hunter built himself a raft-like canoe of tule reeds four or five feet long, and the group formed two parties which surrounded the birds and drove them into nets erected on stakes fixed in the lake bottom.

Only the more skilful and enduring went out to stalk the bigger game. Mountain sheep and deer, although sometimes driven into pounds or rounded up by burning the grass, were more usually hunted by individuals and small parties in the higher ranges. The former, particularly valued for its hide, sinews and horns, quite apart from meat, occupied difficult mountain country, and had often to be cornered on precipitous ledges. Knowing that the sheep always fled to the summits when disturbed, hiding-places of piled stones were sometimes built there. In them a few hunters lay concealed, while a party of beaters drove the sheep up from below. The deer hunter usually went out alone with his dog. Finding his quarry, he had then to run it down relentlessly, perhaps for several days, until he could get close enough to shoot it; he would then have to carry it painfully home on his back.

Decoys were used also, both for duck and deer hunting. For the one a stuffed duck was floated on reeds to induce others to settle near the hunter's ambush. For deer an antler head-dress was often worn to facilitate close approach to the animals. The Paiute dogs were a small breed and few in number. Although they were of some value in hunting, they were not used to carry packs or drag burdens.

The hunter's weapon was the bow and arrow, and every man made his own. Although good bow woods were available, they were usually reinforced with a backing of sinew strands or strips of mountain sheep horn attached with fish glue. Bows were also made entirely of horn by splicing two sheep horns together. The arrow shaft of a light berry stem was fitted with a fore shaft of heavier greasewood, and for large game a barbed point of chipped obsidian was attached. Poisons were obtained from snakes and the dried spleen of deer, but they were not rapid in action.

The relative importance of game in the economy of the Plateau Shoshoneans varied. Among the Northern Paiute hunting skill was highly esteemed, and the product of the communal and individual hunting expeditions might be considerable. But it dwindled southwards as game became scarcer in the low-lying and more desert country, until among the Shoshonean Cahuilla, to the west of the Colorado river, hunting had almost no place. Here in true desert country mesquite pods, the fruits and stems of yuccas and cacti and a few grasses were practically the sole resources.

Fish were caught in the streams and mountain lakes. They were stupefied in dammed pools by dropping in a mash of poisonous leaves. They were shot with unfeathered arrows, which often had a two-pronged point of hard wood. Two-pronged spears were used to catch fish lured to the bank at night with torches. Double-barbed hooks of deer bone were used with lines, and ordinary conical burden baskets were drawn through shallows or set below dams.

These peoples were truly omniverous. No single staple dominated their food-supply. Although the pine-nut harvest was highly valued, there were other equally important resources, and the failure, partial or complete, of any one could generally be compensated by more intensive gathering of another. So that although they exploited an impoverished region with a rude economy they were nevertheless very rarely faced with a serious dearth of food-supply. They probably knew less of real famine than wealthier and more specialized hunters like the Indians of the Plains, whose economy was so largely dependent on the normal abundance of a single animal, and to whom an unexpected animal migration might mean starvation. Food was obtained by a few simple methods which involved little skill or danger, and only a strenuous effort. Patience and a rough flexibility rather than long experience in specialized techniques were the qualities that were demanded of the successful provider.

The crafts of the Paiute are remarkable and contrast with those of the Bushmen. In some directions they are cruder; in others they are much more specialized. Like the Bushmen they made extensive use of animal hides, although the supply was more limited. Tanning processes were more elaborate and varied with the intended use of the hide. The unpromising skin of the rabbit was pressed into valuable service. The skins were removed almost entire and each was cut into a single long, narrow strip which might reach almost ten feet in length. These strips were twisted together, stretched out to dry and then looped or knotted together to form a long rope, which was wound over a simple frame as a continuous warp. The warps were then knotted together at frequent intervals with sinew or fibre cords to produce one of the most characteristic objects of the hunting peoples of north-western America—the rabbit-skin blanket, a warm wrap and a great protection against bleak winter conditions. For an average blanket about five feet square thirty to fifty jack rabbit skins were needed. Similar blankets were made of sage bark cords when rabbit skins were lacking.

Apart from winter cloaks of animal skins, and small hemispherical caps of basketry the Paiute often went naked, although women might wear rough aprons of milkweed fibre, shredded bark or antelope hide and the men a breech clout and leggings of buckskin when travelling over rough country. Soft-soled deer hide moccasins were worn and circular snowshoes, consisting of a wooden frame and crosspieces of bent willows, were used for winter travel on the snow.

But the most elaborate craft of the Basin peoples was basketry. Fine basketry is characteristic of most of the western peoples of North America, and in general it was developed among non-agricultural groups. The open basketry for light carrying baskets, seed beaters and so forth, was usually twined, but sturdier trays and bottles which were to hold water were made by coiling a continuous band of flexible rods, binding each coil to the one below in the manner of our own raffia table mats. Split willow twigs were the fundamental materials, and patterns were carefully worked by introducing other materials of darker colour or by staining the willows. Some of the Paiute groups in Owen's Valley made pottery, but the others could boil only by dropping red-hot stones into baskets full of water. Basketry water-bottles were proofed by dropping in lumps of pitch and hot stones, so that when shaken up the melted pitch adhered to the inner walls.

From obsidian, which occurred in considerable outcrops in this region, knives and arrow-points were chipped. An obsidian knife five or six inches long was carried by every Paiute in a small fibre bag which hung at his waist and also contained his fire-making kit—a hardwood drill and a softwood hearth, with depressions in which the drill was twirled. Since, however, fire-making was laborious, slow torches of closely braided fibre were usually carried on journeys.

Any couple might marry so long as blood relationship could not be traced and many men took their wives from other families in their own band. On mating, the man normally joined his wife's family and remained with it for some time, so that hunting ability was frequently a great advantage to the suitor. But when he had children of his own the man usually took his family back to the

FIG. 14. NORTHERN PAIUTE FIRE-MAKING KIT SHOWING HEARTH AND COMPOSITE DRILL
(After Lowie)

camp of his own parents and remained with them. A second wife, often a sister of the first, would sometimes be taken.

Although the relations between bands were usually friendly, quarrels over hunting and gathering rights fairly often developed in times of stress. These were usually short-lived brawls in which the intruders were attacked with stones. Although there were no specialized weapons of war the Paiute protected themselves in more serious fighting that occasionally broke out with rough hide armour, a double layer of stiff hide covering both trunk and face and provided with eye slits.

Although similar in general character and organization Paiute society, reflecting the detailed conditions of the Great Basin, exhibits very different specializations from that of the Bushmen. Game is scarcer and co-operation is more necessary to attack it. Vegetable food plays a much greater part. The long, severe winter is met by storage of supplies on a scale unknown among the Bushmen who, despite the great environmental contrasts, are closer to the Semang in the day-to-day character of the food quest.

.   .   .   .   .

The economy of the Basin tribes did not end abruptly at the mountain borders. In the eastern Basin indeed, among the Ute and Shoshoni, many practices of the Indians of the western Plains filtered in, and no sharp line of demarcation can be set between the two areas. To the west again there was little difference in economy between the two slopes of the Sierra Nevada. Moreover, a food-gathering economy of very similar type dominated the whole of central California. But central California is a richer land and the cultural patterns were more specialized. With a more lavish food basis it was possible to elaborate both craft and custom to a greater degree. While there was much variation in detail among the major tribal groupings of central California a brief glance at the life of the Yokuts who occupied the southern, San Joaquin, section of the Great Valley of California will serve to call attention to the salient contrasts. A varied but fundamentally vegetable food-supply is again characteristic but other important food plants were available in this milder climate, namely the acorn and the buckeye nut. The acorn provided the daily food of the greater part of aboriginal California. Oaks are not indeed available everywhere. The territory of the more southern Yokuts groups on the floor of the upper part of the valley, in the rain-shadow of the coast ranges, is in parts little less arid than the Great Basin itself. But groves were to be found here along the watercourses and throughout the foothill country,

while the more northern parts were well wooded. Large stores
of acorns were gathered by every household and ground to
meal with a stone pestle in a wooden mortar or on a smooth
bedrock surface in which a deep hollow was pecked and slowly
smoothed and deepened by wear. The tannin was leached
out usually by pouring considerable quantities of hot water on
meal spread out in a large depression in a pile of sand. This
meal cooked as a gruel by stone boiling in a large basket
corresponded to the mush of grass seeds among the Paiute,
and was the staple food at almost every meal. The poisonous
buckeye nut was rendered harmless in the same way. Gathered
roots, insects, fish, small animals, snared waterfowl and pigeons
and occasionally deer, antelope and elk relieved the monotony
of the acorn mush.

The greater and more varied food wealth of the region
permitted a greater stability, of which full advantage was
taken. The winter villages of the Yokuts were more elaborate
affairs than those of the western Basin tribes. The houses,
although lightly built of reed matting, were more permanent
and spacious. Several groups built long, gabled communal
structures, in which as many as a dozen families had each its
own entrance and fireplace. The Yokuts group was generally
larger than a Paiute band. It occupied a smaller area and was
far more integrated. Characteristically there would be probably
about two hundred and fifty persons in a group holding a
territory of some three hundred square miles. It had a genuine
if miniature tribal organization. Each of the fifty or so groups
of the Yokuts had its own name, dialect, and above all, its
territory.

Rarely more than two days' journey from end to end
in any direction, it was considered as belonging to the tribe
as a whole. There was usually a main village site in each
territory, which was continuously occupied over many generations.

Most marriages were between members of different groups,
and although the Yokuts reckoned descent paternally, the
husband lived with his wife's family in its village.

But in addition to the tribal organization there was another
element which profoundly affected their social life. The
Yokuts as a whole, fifty or so little tribes making a total of
perhaps fifteen to twenty thousand people, considered themselves divided into two divisions, the Upstream and the
Downstream people. These were not geographic divisions,
however; each was represented about equally in every tribe
and village, and membership was passed on from father to

child. Certain animals were symbolically associated with each division, of which the Eagle and Bear are the most important among the Upstream people and the Coyote and Falcon among the Downstream people, and the peculiar intimacy, usually referred to as totemism, which individuals felt for the animals of their group is indicated by the fact that they referred to them abstractly or collectively by the word used for their only domestic animal, the dog. A man inquired of another not 'To which division do you belong?' but 'What is your dog?' These two divisions or moieties served to divide each community for many activities. There were formal games between the two sides. Each had a distinctive body paint. They mourned each other's dead. But, most important of all, only persons belonging to opposite moieties, no matter from what tribe they came, could marry. This rule even extended to marriage with members of a neighbouring people to the north, the Miwok, who had a similar system. In other words, a man need not take his wife from another group or tribe, but he had to mate outside his moiety. The totemic moiety was the exogamous unit.

Among the Yokuts there were definite leaders of the tribal group of whom wise judgement and lavish bestowal of food and property were expected. But the tribal chiefs, and perhaps the headmen of individual communities, inherited their positions and prestige from their fathers and received presents from the community with which to give feasts. Among some Yokuts tribes there appear to have been two chiefs, one for each moiety, but the chief of the Downstream division, which seems always to have been considered superior, was apparently the more important.

For the bestowal of gifts and for certain forms of barter the Yokuts used strings of shell beads whose value was calculated according to units of length, measured on the hand. In more recent times, at least, they obtained the shells by long expeditions into alien territory on the Pacific coast.

Many other elements of Yokuts life—their use of rough pottery, their mourning rites, the initiation of young men and other ceremonial rites—serve to contrast these central Californian people with their more impoverished counterparts in the Great Basin. In some instances the added elements which make their society more complex can be shown by comparative study to have resulted from the northward expansion of crafts or customs from other peoples. But although it is unlikely or doubtful whether the more complex elements are local growths, the fact that they have taken root among these people is a point of great importance. The fundamental condition which has made this possible is the greater wealth of their material environment, which permitted at the hunting stage a denser and more stable population and a greater leisure from the daily round of food collection.

CHAPTER V

THE BLACKFOOT: BUFFALO HUNTERS OF THE
NORTH AMERICAN PLAINS

I N the heart of the North American continent, between the eastern forests and the great mountains and plateaux of the west, there stretches a belt of elevated grassland rarely more than five hundred miles wide, but extending northwards from within a few miles of the Gulf of Mexico over fifteen hundred miles into central Canada. The rainfall in this area, in the lee of the western mountains and far from the eastern shore, is insufficient for forest growth. Thunder-showers in summer and still more uncertain falls of rain or snow in winter fail to raise the annual fall above twenty inches on the eastern margin, while it may fall below ten inches in the west. Groves of cotton-wood and willow spread westward as tongues up the valleys of the Mississippi tributaries, and occupy damp hollows on the Plains, while pine clumps cover the summits of the ridges and the foothills of the Rockies. But the greater part of the great belt of rolling country is treeless and covered only with grass—taller and more luxuriant in the east and fading into scrubland in the west.

Owing to the great range from north to south the severity of the climate varies considerably. In the south snow is hardly known. The winters, although, as in the heart of all great land masses, cold by contrast with the tropical summers, are short, and the cold spells brought by northerly winds soon give way to milder weather. But in the north the mean temperature may remain below freezing for three or four months of the year, when severe gales whip up the thin snow cover in driving storms. The land warms rapidly in the early spring, however, and the summer season is hot with brilliant sunshine, interrupted by occasional showers.

These great prairies of North America were the natural home of great herds of herbivorous animals, and particularly of the American bison, popularly called the 'buffalo'. The buffalo was not confined to the open grassland. A woodland species, described by the sixteenth-century explorers, extended far into the forested country on the north and east. On the

Plains, however, they were far more numerous, moving in great herds over the country which they shared with the smaller deer and 'antelopes'. The herds migrated slowly; they did not range widely, and their movements were very persistent extremely hardy, they could easily weather blizzards which would kill domestic cattle. Keeping closer in the lee of the mountains in winter, the same herds moved along the same routes from one natural pasture to another, until they trod out great lanes of habitual migration. The bison is extremely gregarious, and only by accident would an individual be separated from the herd of perhaps a thousand head or more in which it customarily moved.

In these western grasslands with their great animal herds there developed a human economy and society—that of the Plains Indians—remarkably adapted to these limited but rich resources and uniform in both social custom and material culture. But before Europeans themselves had penetrated more than the fringes of the area, or knew much of its native life, they were responsible for the introduction of a domestic animal which considerably modified the native culture. It is probable that during the first explorations of the Spaniards into the southern Plains in the sixteenth century a number of escaped or abandoned horses reached these open lands, where they found a region of unlimited pastures and few natural enemies. They multiplied rapidly, and their numbers were frequently added to by others from the frontier settlements of Spanish territory. In the meantime the southernmost Plains tribes, from their intermittent contacts with the Spanish explorers and frontier settlements in the seventeenth century were introduced to a use for these new animals which offered enormous advantages in their bison-hunting life—the art of horse-riding. From that time the acquisition of horses, whether by theft or barter from the Spaniards or by catching those which had run wild on the prairies, became a main objective of the Indians, and the new knowledge spread rapidly northwards, together with copies in native materials of the heavy saddles of the Spaniards. For the next two centuries, before they lost their independence, the Plains tribes became a horse-riding people with greatly increased mobility and mutual contacts.

The introduction of the horse did not basically change the culture of the western Plains, but it widened the range of activities, greatly increased success in hunting and provided a wealth of food and leisure and a form of personal property which gave impetus to a wide range of modifications. It also reversed the cultural relations of the buffalo hunters to the

ultivators farther east. When in the eighteenth and early
nineteenth centuries explorers and traders entered the Plains
from the east in greater numbers, they found these people
were everywhere skilled riders, among whom raiding and the
stealing of horses from one another was a main occupation of
the able-bodied men of the tribes. The environmental limitations of the Plains, save in the western fringe along the Rocky
foothills, are, however, less severe than has been generally
assumed. The progress of archaeological investigation is re-
vealing the important fact that agriculture was more widespread in pre-horse days than in historic times and extended
several hundred miles west of the Missouri river. The horse
gave the ascendancy to the western nomadic hunting peoples,
and the cultivators were either driven out or abandoned their
more settled life and more advanced culture for the rich rewards
of buffalo hunting.

The Plains were not occupied by peoples of a single origin
or linguistic stock, and almost all the tribes had linguistic
relatives of very different modes of life outside the Plains area.
Some of them, like the Algonkian-speaking Cheyenne of the
Upper Arkansas river country, are known to have entered the
region in post-Columbian times from the forest country south
of Lake Superior, where they had lived a settled agricultural
life, and they are an outstanding example of the rapidity with
which a people can transform their way of life and social
institutions. Adopting the customs of one after another of
the tribes with whom they came in contact during their south-
westward migration, they abandoned settled houses and
cultivation, together with much of their former social and
ceremonial life, becoming, in two centuries or less, a typical
Plains tribe.

Along the moister eastern margin of the Plains the agricultural practices of the eastern woodlands of North America
had spread up the great river valleys, and crops of maize and
pumpkins were grown. Thus a belt of eastern tribes combined
an agricultural life in settled villages during part of the year
with a nomadic hunting life on the surrounding grasslands for
the rest. But the more western tribes depended entirely on
the natural resources of the Plains, and in their exploitation
of its greatest wealth, the herds of bison and antelope, wandered over the country in hunting groups forming temporary
camps of hide tents. Typical hunting tribes of the western
Plains are the Blackfoot, occupying territory now lying on
either side of the Canadian border in Alberta and Montana,
and to the south the Crow, Assiniboine, Arapaho, Cheyenne,

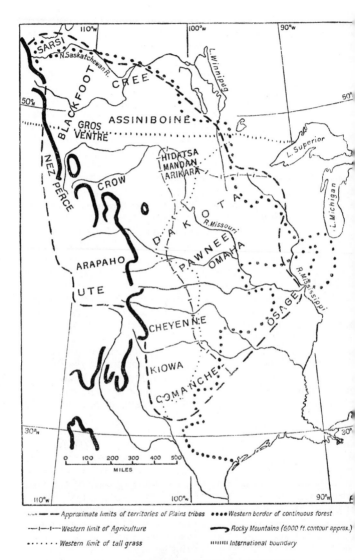

Legend:

---·--- Approximate limits of territories of Plains tribes   ●●● Western border of continuous forest

---I---I--- Western limit of Agriculture   Rocky Mountains (6,000 ft. contour approx.)

······· Western limit of tall grass ||||||| International boundary

FIG. 15. SKETCH MAP OF THE GREAT PLAINS
(*Tribal distributions after Wissler, Goddard and Jenness*)

Kiowa and finally in the plains of present-day Texas, just east of the Rio Grande, the Comanche. In horse days their numbers were considerable and there might be five thousand or more people in a single tribe.

The Blackfoot, whose territory lay towards the northern margin of the region beyond the range of aboriginal maize growing, are one of the most typical of the Plains peoples. Their native life, substantially unchanged until the extermination of the buffalo in the eighties of last century, has been perhaps more completely studied than that of any other group. Blackfoot country lay immediately east of the Rockies, between the north and south branches of the Saskatchewan river, although some of the southern groups ranged as far as the Missouri river. This area is by no means one monotonous plain. Lying at a general level of three to four thousand feet it slopes gently up to the foothills of the Rocky Mountains. The tracts of rolling grassland are broken, especially in the west, by stretches of rough country and by low hills and steep-faced buttes clad in pine and spruce. The main rivers and tributary streams flow below the general level in bottom lands flanked by low but steep bluffs.

Although these northern hunters, a relatively tall people, were not sharply distinct from neighbouring Indians, the hawk-like visage which is popularly associated with the Plains tribes was not frequently found among them. Indeed, in skin colour and cast of countenance they looked more mongoloid than was common.

In historic times the Blackfoot were divided into three independent tribes which, although believing in a common origin and maintaining friendly relations, had each its own territory, tribal organization and ceremonial. These three tribes, which may once have numbered over ten thousand, were the Blackfoot proper or Northern Blackfoot, whose country lay around and to the west of the present town of Edmonton; the Blood, the second group, to the south of these; and farthest south-east, mainly around the present site of Calgary, the third division, the Piegan.

The conditions of hunting buffalo differed considerably at the various seasons of the year. The grass on the north-western Plains sprouts in the late spring and for a few weeks is green and rich. It remains in fair condition for another month, but dries out in the later summer, so that only parched tufts remain for the rest of the year, and, as the condition of the Blackfoot horses often showed, the winter feed was often very poor. The buffalo and other game reacted to these conditions.

During the late spring and early summer they congregate in enormous herds, migrated along established routes to the richest pastures and fattened on the fresh grass, coming into prime condition from June to August. But in the autumn and winter, when feed was scarcer and less nutritious, they scattered more widely, forming smaller herds, and were compelled to shift more frequently from place to place. These considerations affected not only the methods of hunting but the distribution of population. While there was every advantage in the formation of large groups in summer for organized attack on the great herds, in the winter season there was need for the separation of the people into smaller groups scattered widely over the country.

Thus, as among other Plains peoples, the Blackfoot tribe formed effective units for only that part of the year when abundant food and the opportunities for large-scale communal hunting favoured concentration. For the rest of the year they were divided into a considerable number of smaller groups which did not, however, lose their identity during the summer season. These smaller groups or bands were fundamentally economic and social units, camp groups adapted to the requirements of the winter. Each had its delimited territory. Streams, ridges of high ground and other natural features were agreed upon as boundaries between the lands of adjacent camps. The nucleus of such a band was usually a number of male relatives and their families, but it was by no means exclusive; individuals or families from other bands, unless they were undesirable for some special reason, might join them. The remnants of a camp group that had suffered misfortune, or a man who had quarrelled violently with his relations, would join another band and, since habitual residence and participation in group affairs was the only essential condition, such new-comers soon became recognized members and might rise to leadership in the band. An individual was responsible to his band. Every member contributed to any penalties another might incur, and would defend him against attack even if guilty of murder. A woman usually went to live with her husband's group on marriage, and the children were considered as belonging to the father's band, but exceptions were fairly common. A man might have several wives but polygyny was probably rare in early times, save in the case of a few influential individuals. The bands of Blackfoot were thus essentially camp groups of relatives mainly connected in the male line, but often including connexions by marriage and even strangers.

The bands of Blackfoot and other tribes of the northern Plains were more definite and formal in their organization than the family camps of the Paiute described in an earlier chapter, but band membership and camp group did not always correspond at any particular time. Members of other bands could and did join camp groups without seeking or acquiring membership of the band of which it was mainly composed. Moreover, a large band might, with increase in numbers, separate into two or more encampments, which would, however, for a considerable period consider themselves members of the same band. The situation can probably best be summarized by saying that the winter camp groups of related families tended continually to express their economic and social individuality as named bands, but that the situation was modified by processes of accretion and division more rapidly than was reflected in the nominal constitution and membership of the bands at any one time. Among some tribes of the northern Plains the bands had, in recent times, more importance as political and ceremonial groups during the summer tribal camp than as economic and social units during the winter; but it is possible that they are survivors of former economic units that had been disrupted, with the result that people were now camping irrespective of their band affiliations.

The number of bands and the size of each probably varied considerably over long periods. There were over twenty among the Piegan and only six among the Northern Blackfoot shortly after the middle of last century. Each had its own name, which, as so often in Plains names, referred to some real or imaginary peculiarity of the group such as: Solid Topnots, Sharp Whiskers, Short Necks, Lone Fighters, Seldom Lonesome, They Don't Laugh, Skunks, etc. Some band names are common to all three Blackfoot tribes and appear to have been fixed for a long period.

The bands had no formal chiefs, but social leaders who acquired general authority in virtue of their qualities and energy. Skill in the organization of hunting and raiding, with generosity and fairness in all dealings, were the qualities looked for in the leader of a band. During the summer season, when the tribe united, the more outstanding leaders of large and powerful bands were accepted as tribal leaders, among whom one usually stood out as pre-eminent. This tribal leadership often remained in the hands of one band, and often of one family of that band, for several generations. But the tribal leader could not act effectively without the approval and support of the others. Although not formally elected the duties and procedure of both band and tribal leaders were in practice quite precise. They were guardians of the welfare of the band or tribe and preservers of the peace; they arbitrated in all disputes, gave instructions for the strategy of the hunt and on the details of migrations and encampment. For matters of great importance several leading men from each group were called in to form a wider council which might be safely relied on to express the general will.

For the winter season each band or camp group retired to a traditional tract of territory in which it had one or more favourite sites. Sheltered valleys and hollows, affording if possible some timber cover, were sought as a protection against the severe gales. Group hunting played a prominent part in the winter season, although the group was smaller than in summer, and the buffalo were driven into pounds large enough to hold a hundred head or more. Scouts from the camps reconnoitred the established trails in their neighbourhood on the look-out for herds. These were not readily scared, but in the days before the horse they moved far more rapidly than the hunters. When a herd was reported in the vicinity of the camp individual hunting was strictly barred lest the animals be prematurely driven off by the ineffective attacks of single hunters and so prevent a large meat-supply being obtained for the group. An individual or a small group of men could only with difficulty approach closely to a herd, and even then it was no easy matter in early days to inflict a serious wound with a stone arrow-point on a beast with the tough hide of the buffalo.

Ingenious contrivances were, however, devised to reward co-operative action, and in the winter season the pounds were the most important. In the days before the horse they were probably in use throughout the year; but with the horse the large summer herds could be more easily surrounded in the open than before. The Blackfoot pound was usually constructed at the foot of a steep cliff, usually the natural bank of a stream bottom. The walls were built of logs, brush, earth or rock; they had to be high and close, but not necessarily very strong, for the buffalo rarely charged them unless they could see a way through. From the top of the bluff above the pound two splaying lines of brush heaps or rock piles, each a few yards apart, were built out for a quarter of a mile or more. At the bluff end the piles were larger and closer, and might for a short distance form a continuous fence. The strategy of the hunt was to entice the herd between these converging lines, so that they could then be driven down the lane to stampede over the cliff, falling injured into the pound below. The ounds were permanent constructions repaired from year to ear as required, and every camp constructed several in the icinity of favourite buffalo lanes. When a herd had been eported within a mile or two of a suitable pound a man with pecial skill set out, after appropriate ceremonial, covered in buffalo skin and wearing a buffalo head as a mask. He loved cautiously towards the herd, attracted its attention by is movements and moved slowly in the direction of the ound, hoping to entice the herd to follow. He was assisted y a number of active men who approached it from the far ide, and by disturbing it also tried to edge the animals in the irection of the pound. This enticement and driving was by o means easy and there were many failures. Calm days when cent did not carry or a light wind was blowing in the direction f the pound were most favourable. With good fortune the erd in time began to follow the decoy, breaking into a trot as e increased his pace, until they came within the converging nes of brush piles. These had in the meantime been manned y all available persons in the camp, who rose from conceal- lent as the buffalo came abreast of them, and shouting and aving their hide robes frightened the herd into a stampede s the decoy slipped to one side. In their headlong rush the ntire herd of perhaps more than a hundred animals fell over ne bluff, and those that were not killed or injured by the ll circled round in panic while the best marksmen shot them rith arrows or struck them down with stones and cudgels.

Where suitable bluffs were not to be found the Blackfoot onstructed a more elaborate pound, which was the standard ype for the Plains Cree and Assiniboine in the smoother ountry to the east. A large, circular corral of logs and brush- ood was built. The walls were about eight feet high, save or the place where the lines of brush piles converged on it. Iere there was a gap several yards wide, to which led an nclined causeway of logs rising gently from the ground and eaching a height of about four feet at the entrance to the ound. This causeway was fenced along the sides, and the uffalo, when driven down between the wings, mounted the ridge and were forced to jump into the pound beyond. When ney had entered, the men nearest at hand mounted the cause- ay and rapidly covered the entrance gap with poles, brush nd skins.

When in later times horses were available, herds could be rought to the pounds from several miles distant. By riding longside a herd at a few hundred yards' distance it was ossible for a small party of horsemen to guide it very readily

in the required direction. After the killing the entire cam
flocked to the scene, flayed and cut up the animals, leavir
nothing behind but a pile of surplus horns. Men, women ar
children and dogs were all given a load to carry back, an
before leaving, nooses were often set at small holes in tl
fencing to catch wolves, foxes and badgers, which were soc
attracted to the scene.

If the buffalo failed to appear on their accustomed rout
the hunters were compelled to go out, individually or in sma
parties, to seek them farther afield. When snow lay sma
parties could often drive a number into the deeper drifts, whe
they floundered helplessly and were held at bay by huntir
dogs, until the hunters came up to attack at close quarte:
with lances and clubs. Skilful hunters, wearing disguis
and imitating the movements of the buffalo or wolf, cou
often approach close to a herd and wound animals with arrov
without scaring the rest of the herd. Bulls often turned o
the wounded, and the hunter could thus induce a fight, durir
which he could shoot down the preoccupied beasts.

If a fairly large party could surround a small herd on a sti
day it was possible to close in on them unnoticed until tl
hunters were able, by yelling and waving their large robes, t
prevent them breaking away. The buffalo would rush aroun
in a circle until exhausted, when they could be wounded,
not killed, by arrows, and finally attacked at close quarters.

Although the buffalo provided by far the greater part of th
food-supply of the Blackfoot other game was not entirel
neglected. Antelope were formerly as abundant on the Plain
but they were smaller and fleeter and figured far less cor
spicuously in hunting. Yet their hides were greatly value
for women's clothing and soft bags, and when they were neede
for these purposes a hunt was organized to drive them betwee
lanes, as with the buffalo. But for antelope a pit was cor
structed instead of a pound. This was usually at the end of
high, angled fence of brush and concealed from the animals b
a low transverse fence over which they leaped. Clubbers la
concealed in shallow trenches by the brush fences and struc
down the antelope as they fell into the pit or tried to escap
Mountain sheep were prized both for their meat and larg
curving horns. They were hunted in winter in the foothill
being cornered on rock ledges or driven over precipices.

The surrounding of buffalo in the open was most effectiv
in the summer season, when they moved eastwards to th
flatter country and formed larger herds. Rich reward resulte
from successful hunting, but that success depended on th

ctive marshalling of considerable bodies of men. It was
the great summer hunt that the various bands assembled
a tribal camp. As the spring progressed the bands joined
into a few major groups, and finally at an appointed season
whole tribe converged on the summer camp, where for a
weeks intensive hunting was followed by feasting and
emonial.

he summer hunting depended essentially on surrounding
buffalo with all the available strength of the tribe. In
days before the horse, which made the surround so much
ier, large pounds were probably used in summer as well. The
ular picture of a party of Indians on horseback circling con-
ously round a stampeding herd into which they shoot their
ws represents the conditions of later days. When a herd
been reported by the scouts a plan of attack was arranged
the hunters were divided into a number of parties, which,
g by different routes, surrounded it from all sides. To
in the great herds more effectively the parched grass was
etimes fired on the windward side. After they had acquired
ses the surround was far more easily effected and animals
ch broke away could often be run down. Still later in the
eteenth century, when muskets were obtained by barter
h traders who had come west across the Mississippi, hunting
smaller parties played an increasing part. But long before
there had grown up a number of strict rules regulating
munal hunting which were found among almost every
e throughout the Plains. When a considerable herd was
he vicinity individual hunting was strictly barred, and it
a public duty to report it to the tribal leaders so that a
munal hunt might be arranged. This regulation and
edure was controlled by one or more of the men's societies.
or the tribal assembly in summer a great camp circle was
ned. The tipis were set up three or four deep in a circle of
aps half a mile in diameter with a wide opening on the
. Each band camped as a group in a traditional position
he circle.

early every man among the Blackfoot was a member of
ociety which performed dances and ceremonies, and also
ed as a group in the organization of the encampment and
rations during the summer season. In each of the three
ckfoot tribes there were several of these societies—from
to a dozen or more—which collectively embraced all the
of the tribe and were known as 'All Comrades'. Each
ety had its own name, songs, dances and ranks. Its
bers were of about the same age and experience but they

did not remain in the same society throughout. Every fo
years or so they transferred their rights of membership
younger men and themselves obtained the rights to the socie
next senior. These transfers, although generally made at t
same time during the summer camp, were, however, individu
transactions, the junior man making a payment of rob
weapons or horses for the regalia and rank within the socie
to the man whose place he wished to take. The latter th
belonged to no society until he proceeded to purchase memb
ship in the society above from an individual who was rea
to sell.

Thus, once every four years as a rule, all the men save t
oldest changed their society for the one next senior, wh
the youths joined the lowest for the first time. The societ
as a whole, therefore, fell into a graded series, through whi
each individual passed as through forms at school. As
school, individuals did not always start at the bottom, a
one or two might skip a grade later on or stay behind beyo
the normal period. Moreover, a few old men became honora
members of the more junior societies and acted as instructc
while one or two young men were admitted to the sen
societies to serve as messengers and helpers of the old and l
active majority.

In each of the three divisions of the Blackfoot the sen
societies corresponded closely with each other, with simi
names and relative order, but the number and names of t
junior societies showed greater differences, probably becar
they were formed in more recent times after the three divisic
had separated or lost their former close contact. Amc
the Piegan division the names and order of the societies at t
end of the last century were: Pigeons, Mosquitoes, Brav
All-Brave-Dogs, Front Tails, Raven Bearers, Dogs, Kitfox
Catchers, and, most senior, the Bulls. This system of grac
societies was a special development which had spread amc
some of the northern Plains tribes. Among other tribes t
societies remained at an earlier stage without official gradi
or provisions for systematic transfer.

Apart from the ceremonies and dances, which probal
loomed largest in the members' eyes, the functions of t
societies were mainly to maintain order and co-operative act
in the camp during the communal hunt and migrations of t
summer seasons. For the rest of the year they were in abeyar
and the members were scattered among the various ban
When the bands assembled in the spring, the leaders of t
societies conferred with the band chiefs, who outlined th

proposals for camping sites and routes of travel, and selected two or three of the societies to undertake the various duties for that season. While these were nominally under the control of the chiefs their duties were so well known that they generally acted on their own initiative. The leaders of the chosen societies pitched their tipis in a group in the centre of the camp circle. The members patrolled the camp in turn during the night. They punished recalcitrant offenders against public welfare by beating and destruction of property. Some went ahead when a march began to select the precise site of the next camp, while others superintended the column of march. The societies were also mainly responsible for knowing the position and movements of the buffalo herds and for organizing the tribal hunts. In any emergency the chiefs could call upon one or more of them to deal with the situation. They could not, however, act until they were called upon to do so. The changing membership, coupled with the rivalry of one with another and the short season of their activity, averted any tendency to the permanent seizure of power by one or all of these societies.

The summer camp was the occasion for great ceremonial activity. A host of feasts and ceremonies followed the short period of intensive hunting, in which large stores of food were accumulated. With appropriate ritual and after due payment of hide robes and horses, 'medicine bundles' of magical objects and the formulas necessary for their effective use were often transferred from one man to another. The societies performed their special dances and rituals, and if the time for purchase and transfer of society membership was due, great triple tipis were built in which the lengthy ceremonies of exchange were held. Finally came the great annual ceremony of the Sun Dance at which individuals and the tribe as a whole sought power and well-being in a protracted ritual that lasted a week or more. The camp circle broke up shortly after this and the bands moved away in the direction of their winter quarters, which mostly lay farther to the west in the rougher foothill country. With the disintegration of the camp there ended also any real authority of the tribal leaders and councils.

The buffalo which so dominated the activities of the Blackfoot supplied them with more than meat. Almost every part of the animal was used. The hide was dressed with the hair left on to provide heavy winter robes; thinned and with the hair removed, it was the material for shirts, leggings, moccasins, tent covers, bags and receptacles of every kind. Cut into strips it furnished ropes and lines. The hair was used to stuff pillows and later saddles, and to decorate garments, shields and quivers. The back sinews were used for thread and string and, attached with glue made from the hooves, as a backing

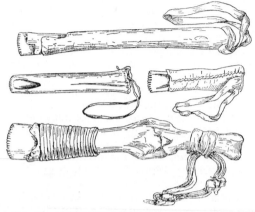

FIG. 16. BLACKFOOT TOOLS FOR FLESHING HIDES
(After Wissler)

for the wooden bows to give greater strength and elasticity. The horns were softened by boiling and shaped into spoons and ladles, and the bones fashioned into tools for the dressing of hides.

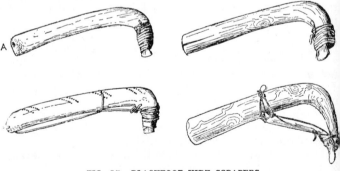

FIG. 17. BLACKFOOT HIDE SCRAPERS
LENGTH OF *A*, 35 CM.
(After Wissler)

The Plains Indians hunted more continuously and energetically than the Paiute, and, unlike them, left the dressing of the skins to women, whose more restricted gathering activities eft them more leisure for this work. Hides were prepared in two forms. Tough, stiff rawhide, used for shields, large packing cases and, in later times, moccasin soles, was obtained by pegging out the skin and laboriously scraping off all flesh, fat and muscle tissue with a heavy bone tool with a toothed end. The skin was then left to cure, bleach and harden in the sun for some days, after which it was scraped again and shaved down to an even thickness with a stone adze bound to a curved handle of wood and bone. It was then ready for use.

But for clothes, tipi covers and many other uses a supple

FIG. 18. **BLACKFOOT HIDE SHIRT**
LENGTH 84 CM.
(*After Wissler*)

soft finish was needed, and this was obtained by treating the rawhide still further. An oily mixture of animal brains and fat was rubbed well into the hide with a smooth stone and left in the sun until it dried out. It was next soaked with warm water and rolled up for a few days and then vigorously rubbed over with a rough stone and sawed to and fro through a loop of twisted sinew or across a taut rope until it was dry and supple and ready for use.

Men's shirts and women's dresses were made with two soft tanned elk or cow buffalo hides, joined shoulder to shoulder with an opening for the neck or, for women, attached to a

yoke which covered the shoulders. They were then elaborately
decorated with strips of weasel skin and with patterns painted
on or worked with dyed strips of the quills of porcupines and
birds. On journeys and in cold weather leggings of soft hide
suspended from a waist belt were also worn.

The cover of the conical tent or tipi was also made of soft
buffalo hides. When spread out on the ground it formed an
approximate semicircle, which for an ordinary tipi of later
times had a radius of thirteen to eighteen feet and required
rather more than a dozen skins. The designing of a cover was
skilled work, and its sewing with sinew and a bone bodkin

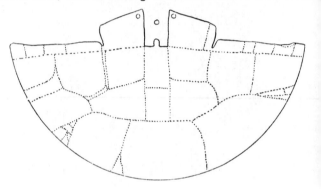

FIG. 19. PATTERN OF A SKIN TIPI COVER
(*After Wissler*)

was laborious. When a new one was required the woman
gathered a store of food and invited a large group of friends
and relatives to share in the work, for the tipi was the woman's
property, first given her by her family on marriage and always
erected by her. The frame was of pine or spruce poles obtained
in the foothills. Four poles, tied together near the tops with
sinew in a secure tipi knot, were first set up in a pyramid. Half
a dozen more were then set between these to form a circle.
The last pole was securely lashed at several points to the centre
line of the hide cover, which was then raised in position at the
rear of the frame, and drawn round from either side to be
pinned together down the front. The poles were then adjusted
until the cover was drawn tight all round and finally pegged
down to the ground, or weighted with stones. Two projecting
tongues of the cover now hung limply down at the top. Through
holes or in pockets in these the ends of two longer poles were
thrust so that the flaps stood out as 'ears' which could, by

adjusting the poles, be set wide apart, leaving a clear smoke-hole in fine weather or be drawn together to exclude wind and rain or to retain heat at night after the fire had died down. The doorway was a mere slit, often worn oval by use and covered with a hide curtain outside. In recent times the usual tipi was about fourteen feet in diameter and about ten feet high, but some were occasionally over twenty feet and required more than forty skins for their covers. Before horses were available to assist in transport the tipis must, however, have been considerably smaller.

On the inside, a wall or lining strip of hide, four or five feet high, hung vertically from the poles to which it was lashed.

FIG. 20. A BLACKFOOT ENCAMPMENT

This excluded ground draughts and provided convenient cup-board space within. The fire-place, surrounded by a ring of flat stones, was set below the smoke-hole, usually a little in front of the centre, since the poles of the back sloped more steeply than the front. Ceremonial objects and trophies were placed at the rear behind a second fire-place at which sweet grasses were burned in rituals. The couches of the owner and his wife were on the left side of the entrance, children and dependants sleeping on the right. These couches were of dried grass or twigs covered with soft buffalo hides, and at the head, and often the foot of each were back rests for reclining during the day. These were flexible triangular supports of willow stems arranged horizontally, threaded with leather thongs suspended from a tripod of wood and pegged down at the head of the couch. Over them soft dressed skins were thrown. Both the outside of the tipi and the inner curtains were often

decorated with painted geometrical patterns, or had recorded
on them in a series of pictographs exploits of their owner.

Hides were also a primary raw material for the household

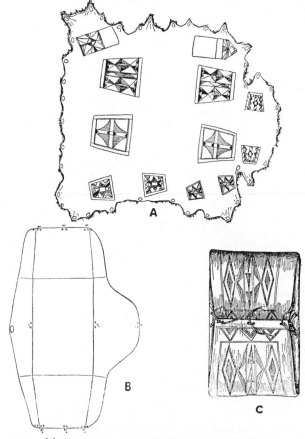

FIG. 21.   (a) A DRESSED HIDE, 160 CM. LONG, PREPARED FOR CUTTING
OUT PARFLECHES AND BAGS, THE DESIGNS HAVE ALREADY BEEN PAINTED;
(b) A PARFLECHE PATTERN SHOWING STRING HOLES; (c) A FOLDED
PARFLECHE, LENGTH 65 CM.
(After Wissler)

utensils of the Blackfoot. Carrying and storage bags were
made of rawhide. The smaller ones were sewn up, but the most
characteristic receptacle for large stores of food was the large,
flat, rawhide envelope generally known by the trapper's term

parfleche. It was rectangular in shape, a yard or more in length, and deep flaps were folded over the rectangle from each side and lashed together when the contents had been placed in position The top flaps of the parfleche were carefully decorated with symmetrical geometric patterns, which were very uniform in general style for the Blackfoot as a whole and distinguishable from the equally standard styles of other Plains tribes. Cylindrical rawhide cases, with long fringes of fur or soft hide, often hung from the back-rest tripods in the tipi and contained ceremonial objects. Elaborately decorated bags were made from the skins of smaller animals to hold the pipe outfit, which played an important part both in hospitality and ceremonial. Water buckets were made from buffalo paunches and stiffened with willow rings to keep them distended when hung from a hook.

Hide thongs and covers were used in hafting hammers for breaking up small wood and bones, and for cudgels and war clubs. For the first a handle of flexible willow was wrapped round the groove pecked in a suitable stone and the whole, save for the hammering face, covered with green hide cut to shape and sewed tight with sinew. As it dried the hide shrank and hardened, making a stout and rigid casing for the tool. For war clubs the stone head was often wrapped and sewn in a similar cover and swung loosely from the end of the handle to which the hide was attached.

Although wooden dishes were occasionally made by burning out and adzing down the knots of the willow trees, the horns of buffalo and mountain sheep provided the most convenient receptacles. Knives of chipped stone were skilfully made, but buffalo bones, especially ribs, were used for cutting all softer materials.

Fresh paunches and hides were used as vessels for stone boiling meat and soups after a kill of buffalo. The hide was either depressed in a hollow in the ground or supported round the margins with short stakes. Cured hides were not suitable for this purpose, and since they had neither pottery nor stone vessels most of their food was roasted.

Although fresh meat was theoretically obtainable throughout the year, there were often considerable periods in which no herds were found or successfully attacked, and there was always the risk that herds forsaking their established trails might desert a tract of country for long periods. Serious famines could and did occur long before the buffalo were slaughtered wholesale by white hunters at the end of last century. Since, however, the communal hunting of the Plains yielded a very abundant meat-supply after a successful hunt, there was opportunity to devise means for storing large quantities. After a hunt the store of meat was cut into thin strips and dried in the sun on wooden frames. When dry the meat was slightly roasted, pounded to a mince, mixed with fat and then packed and sealed with a covering of tallow in large bags or parfleches that in later times often contained a hundred pounds each and consumed the meat of two buffaloes. This is the pemmican so well known from the accounts of early explorers and traders. The finest pemmican was made from the choicest cuts pounded and mixed with marrow fat and dried berries. Large stone-lined pits were built near the winter camp in which these food-supplies could be stored, secure from the attacks of carnivores and rodents.

While meat was the main food of the Blackfoot and other Plains tribes, wild roots and berries were not neglected, and a considerable variety was gathered by the women during the year. The various harvests often controlled the precise location of the camp. In the spring a valuable root, known as *pomme blanche* to white trappers, was obtained in large quantities with digging sticks. In the country nearest the Rockies the camas bulb, a food staple among the northern Plateau peoples, was obtained in summer. Several kinds of berry and the wild choke-cherry were harvested in the autumn. The surplus was in each case dried and stored or mixed in the pemmican.

Although the Blackfoot depended entirely on natural products for their food they did, like many other Plains tribes and other hunting peoples, cultivate one plant—tobacco. A plot of ground near the winter camp was cleared and the soil raked over early each spring and the tobacco seeds planted ceremonially by a party of men. The plot was visited occasionally by one or two men during the summer, who had to make long journeys for the purpose and bring back samples of the growing plant. The crop was gathered when the camp returned to winter quarters in the autumn. This tobacco smoked in pipes of soft and easily worked stone played a very important part in Blackfoot and all Plains ceremonial. Although the plant was very hardy and grew with so little care, it had to be sown afresh each year to maintain the supply. The significance of tobacco planting among the Blackfoot and other western peoples in North America is considered later (see p. 255).

The migration of the individual camp groups and of the tribes as a whole involved frequent transport of the entire household. The dwellings and utensils of the Blackfoot were mostly of a light and portable character, but, although they were few compared with those of a sedentary people, the tipi with its contents formed a large load. The advent of the horse made possible a considerable increase in the weight of the household property that could be transported and tipis became larger and more luxurious. But even in pre-horse days the Indians of the Plains had devised means for transporting a considerable quantity of material. Although heavy burdens were carried on the back, a great deal was transported by the dogs, of which every woman kept two or three or more. Small burdens could be carried in bags slung across their backs, but they could drag a much greater weight than they could carry, and for this purpose the Plains peoples used a drag-frame known as the *travois*—two splayed poles two or three yards

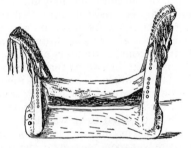

FIG. 22. A BLACKFOOT SADDLE
LENGTH, 34 CM.
(*After Wissler*)

long lashed together—which was harnessed on the shoulders of the dog, and carried a netted hoop or platform of slats attached to the two poles behind the animal. When the horse was introduced the same device was enlarged to carry much heavier loads. This drag-frame was well suited to the relatively smooth and open country in which the Plains people lived. They had no sleds or toboggans, and the travois appears to be an indigenous development which remained limited to their own culture area. It is probable that it originated with the poles of the tipi itself, and it was frequently improvised from tipi poles in later days, but the Blackfoot also made well-finished travois which could not be taken apart for use as poles.

With the introduction of the horse, saddles and trappings were made. The heavier wooden saddles used mostly by women followed closely the design of Spanish saddles, of which they were translations into wood and rawhide, the wooden frame being held rigid by a cover of rawhide, which was shrunk

on to it. For the chase men used light pad saddles of soft hide
stuffed with hair.

Some Plains tribes made coracles of buffalo hide stretched
on willow frames, with paddles to cross deep rivers, but the
Blackfoot contented themselves with improvised rafts of poles
and buffalo hides, which they propelled by swimming whenever
they were compelled to take loads across rivers. The difficulty
of swimming horses across wide rivers, especially the Missouri
seems to have had an important effect in retarding the spread
of the horse in the northern Plains, and may in part account
for the fact that the Blackfoot and other northern Plains tribes
appear to have obtained most of their horses, in earlier days,
from the Plateau peoples to the south-west.

The appearance of the horse not only made the successful
hunting of the buffalo far easier: it permitted the increase in
size and comfort of the tipi and the amount of household goods
that could be transported. It also fostered, from the very
manner of its introduction, a tradition of raiding which came
to dominate Plains life in the two centuries of prosperity before
the extinction of the buffalo. The use of these valued 'elk
dogs' spread so rapidly largely because they were continually
being stolen from the horse tribes by those who did not already
possess them. Once acquired there was no strict limit to the
number that could be maintained, for although the winter
feed was poor, there was room for a great increase in numbers.
Thus the acquisition of horses became a main objective of
every able-bodied man. But the Indians appear to have
acquired very little skill in breeding, and the horse supply
was dependent on the capture and taming of those that had
run wild and on those stolen or obtained by barter from
white men. The demand for horses was thus not easily
satisfied, and systematic raiding of the horses of enemy tribes
was the regular method by which young men acquired them.
Horse raiding was the essential basis of Plains Indians' warfare in the historic period. We have no means of knowing
the conditions in pre-horse days, but although it is by no
means certain that the warlike habits of the Plains Indians
are all of recent development, there can be no doubt that they
received an enormous impetus from the appearance of the horse.
The status of an individual depended very largely on his
personal courage as displayed in raids, and elaborate conventions grew up as to what constituted brave deeds, for which
the French trapper's term *coup*, or blow, has come into use.
The native weapons of the Blackfoot were the sinew backed
bow and arrow and a circular shield of thick rawhide from the

neck of a buffalo hide. Heavy wooden lances were also used extensively by some tribes in horse days and may have been copied from Spanish models. Plains warfare but rarely involved pitched battles, or, indeed, save where specific motives for revenge existed, the serious reduction of the enemy's strength. Horses, not killing, were the reasons for going 'on the war-path'. A small party set out on foot to the enemy's territory, taking only their weapons, sleeping robes and a small store of dried meat. If possible they crept up to an enemy camp, cut loose the horses and drove them off. Conflict followed only if they were discovered or pursued. Among the Blackfoot the capture of an enemy's weapons ranked highest as a deed. Among some other tribes, where the counting of coups was more formally elaborated, the touching of an enemy ranked first, with the capture of weapons and horses as subsidiary deeds. Coups could, among some tribes like the Cheyenne, be counted by several persons on a single enemy, and they ranked in strict order of touching, irrespective of who actually wounded or killed him. These deeds, recorded in picture writing on tipi walls and buffalo robes, constituted a sort of heraldry. Whenever a man was called upon to play a part in a social or ceremonial function he first recounted his deeds.

Alternating periods of friendship and strife were the relations of the Blackfoot to other tribes, but, like other Plains tribes, the Blackfoot had traditional enemies like the Cree, Assiniboine and Crow, and also allies, such as the Sarcee and less permanently the Gros Ventre, against whom the elders forbade the young warriors to raid. The frequent contact of tribe with tribe, whether in war or peace, was facilitated by the development of elaborate gesture symbols, or 'sign language', which was uniform over wide areas, irrespective of the fundamental differences in speech.

Rank among the Blackfoot depended not only on military prowess but also on the possession of 'medicines', that is, of rituals, and the objects necessary for their performance, which would ensure the success of some project or desire, be it health, a journey, a raid, a hunt or another ceremony. The 'medicines' were owned by individuals and transferred from one to another for payments. These were, however, not primarily commercial transactions, but their full consideration cannot be undertaken here. The ritual apparatus was usually wrapped in bundles of otter or some other valued skin. While most older men possessed some medicine the owners of the 'medicine pipe bundles' were the senior and most entitled to respect. On the rank of their medicine depended the place at a feast, the order of speech at meetings and many other matters of precedence, all of which were observed most scrupulously. Rigid rules of etiquette and ceremonial procedure affected all sides of the social life of the Blackfoot and gave it a highly formalized aspect, characteristic of the Plains and surprising among a people of apparently simple economy.

But the Blackfoot and other Plains Indians are a hunting people among whom special conditions existed. They had a very rich source of food supply in the bison herds. Between the periods of intensive hunting they had considerable leisure, which on account of their nomadism could be applied only to a limited extent to arts and crafts, and appears to have been devoted largely to the elaboration of ceremonial which affected every aspect of their life. They occupied a very wide tract of open country, across which travel was easy, so that every tribe made many contacts with its neighbours on a wide front and over what were, for a food gathering people, very large areas. Finally, they had acquired a domestic animal from a higher civilization which gave them unusual opportunity for satisfying their need and opportunity for mobility. The western Plains thus form a very large area of surprisingly uniform and complex culture of hunting peoples diverse in origin, among whom new concepts and fashions spread with great rapidity to the limits of the area, but nearly always stopped short where the mobile hunting life was itself arrested.

CHAPTER VI

THE NOOTKA, KWAKIUTL AND OTHER FISHING PEOPLES OF BRITISH COLUMBIA

ON the north-western American coast lands from Yakutat Bay, lying below the great St. Elias Range in southern Alaska, to Humboldt Bay in northern California, a remarkable and distinctive civilization flourished, little changed by the activities of the white fur traders until the present century. In the last fifty years the economy of these peoples has been increasingly modified by white civilization, but the surviving population to-day, although often centred round Canadian and American fish canneries or lumber camps, has retained much of the original culture. Although there were many minor variations in different parts of this coastal region which extended from 60° N. to nearly 40° N. over a distance of some fifteen hundred miles, there was an underlying unity based on particular ways of exploiting and using the special resources of the area. All these peoples depended almost entirely on the sea and rivers for their food-supply. They lived in settled communities of considerable size, built large and substantial houses with the forest timbers, and regarded the acquisition and lavish display of wealth and property as the criterion of social importance and success.

This culture, set off in so many ways from the rest of North America, was most elaborately developed in the northern area from Vancouver Island and the mouth of the Fraser river to south-eastern Alaska. South of the straits of St. Juan de Fuca the particular natural conditions of the rich resources fade out, and in northern California the native life was hardly more than a pale reflection of the richer culture to the north.

This northern Pacific coast in many ways recalls the shores of western Scotland and of Scandinavia. The extensive and geologically recent subsidence of this mountainous country has allowed the sea to flood the lower parts of deep, glaciated valleys. Fjord-like inlets penetrate a hundred miles and more far into the land between great blocks of highland which rise abruptly from the water and culminate in lofty mountains. Former coastal ranges have been cut off by narrow straits from the

present mainland to form intricate chains of islands. There
are innumerable smaller islands flanking the mainland, while
among the larger outlying islands are Vancouver Island, three

FIG. 23. THE PEOPLES OF THE NORTH WEST COAST
(*Distributions after Boas, Goddard, and Jenness*)

hundred miles long, and the Queen Charlotte Islands, of which
the two largest together reach a length of one hundred and
eighty miles.

Behind the shores of the mainland the coast range of British
Columbia rises rapidly to great mountain masses of more than

ve thousand feet, from which long, steep-faced promontories
un out to cut off the deep inlet of one drowned valley from
ıe next. Innumerable mountain torrents drain into the inlets,
ıt surprisingly few large rivers provide valley routes to the
ıterior. Between the great Fraser valley, at whose entrance
ancouver stands to-day, and the Skeena river, with its modern
ort, Prince Rupert, five hundred miles farther north, not a
ngle river breaks through the coast range to reach the sea.
he shorelands are therefore cut off from easy communication
ith the interior, and, what was of more immediate importance
ɔ its native inhabitants, even short journeys from one part to
ıother were far more easily effected by water than by travelling
verland across the lofty spurs that cut off one valley from
ıe next.

In climate too the Northwest Coast can be compared to
estern Britain and Scandinavia. Westerly air streams bring
ımp mild weather, while a branch of the warm Japanese
ırrent turning northward along this coast is comparable to,
not quite so effective as the Gulf Stream drift that moderates
ıe climate of north-western Europe. Winter frosts are of
ıort duration, and snow does not lie for any length of time
the lower levels. The high mountain backing induces very
ɩavy rainfall, especially during the winter months of the
ar, when the westerly winds are strongest. On the seaward
ɔpes of Vancouver and Queen Charlotte Islands and of parts
the mainland, the annual rainfall reaches one hundred
ches, the greater part of which falls in the heavy downpours
autumn and winter. Fogs and mists are common at these
ısons, but the summer is drier and sunnier than on the coast
ıds of north-western Europe.

This damp and mild climate makes possible the most luxuriant
·est growth in North America. Tall, straight-trunked ever-
ɩens such as spruce, hemlock and cedar often over two
ndred and fifty feet high, clothe the mountains for several
ɔusand feet and reach right down to the shore. Ferns of
ıazing size and impenetrable thickets of shrubs, themselves
en as large as ordinary trees, cover the ground. The great
aight-grained red and yellow cedar trees with trunks often
rard and more in diameter provided the most valuable and
·st easily worked timber.

Although elk, moose, deer and mountain sheep were fairly
merous in the forests of the mainland and on some of the
nds, the wealth of the sea life was so great that these peoples
ended almost solely upon it. Halibut, cod and herring were
en at sea, while throughout the summer runs of migrating

salmon swarmed up the inlets and often literally filled the river on their way to their upstream breeding grounds. In sprin the candlefish or olachen, a small fish about nine inches long from which an edible oil could be extracted, ascended the rivers In the sea, preying on the abundant fish shoals, were great se mammals—whales, sea-lions, sea-otters, seals and porpoises.

In language the peoples of this region belong to widel divergent stocks, branches of which in some cases extend fa into the interior. But the social and economic life varie remarkably little in its salient features and was moreover cor fined to the immediate coast lands. Relatively few isolate elements have penetrated into the interior. The south-eas shores of Vancouver Island and the opposite mainland wer occupied by peoples of Salish speech. Linguistic relatives (these Coast Salish extended into the interior in the Fraze and Columbia basins as far as the barrier of the Rocky Mou tains. In north-western Vancouver Island and the adjacer mainland nearly as far north as the Bella Coola river were th Kwakiutl proper. Two divergent Kwakiutl dialects extende north to Douglas Channel and the Kitamat river, but thes groups were more closely related in the details of their soci and ceremonial life to another Salish-speaking people—th Bella Coola, who occupied the deep inlets of Burke and Dea Channels. The Nootka of the western side of Vancouver Islar were in speech remotely related to the Kwakiutl, but th northern peoples, the Tsimshian of the Skeena and Nass river the Haida of Queen Charlotte Island and the Tlingit of th archipelago and coast lands of south-eastern Alaska forme separate language groups. (See fig. 23.)

All had the characteristic broad face, narrow nose and da brown skin of the American Indian, but they were no mo homogeneous in race than in language. The Kwakiutl we remarkable for a great length of face and a large hooked nos The more northern peoples, especially the Tsimshian, were, (the contrary, extremely broad in face with small, often conca noses. Among several groups the head was artificially deform in infancy by tight bandages and strapping to cradle boards.

This Northwest Coast area was thus occupied by peoples various origins whose common culture is one of the mo specialized in North America and perhaps the most advanc found among any non-agricultural people.

Although they were sedentary in the sense that permane village sites were occupied for several generations, as inde the great shell middens near certain sites still testify, a villa community did not occupy its main settlement througho the year, but moved as a body, or in a few large groups, to a number of sites, each occupied in turn for a short period every year to exploit its special resources.

The main village, at which the largest and most elaborately ornamented houses were erected, was occupied during the more leisurely winter season, during which fishing almost ceased and the preparation of tools, canoes and other equipment occupied the time between the preparation of feasts and ceremonies. From the spring until the autumn, however, this settlement was frequently deserted for long periods, and temporary camps were established at the various fishing and collecting sites. Where, as nearly always, these could be reached by water, the wall planks of the winter houses were often dismantled and lashed across pairs of canoes to provide both a deck for the transport of goods and the material for building temporary houses at the new site. Suitable main posts were often erected at such places and used from year to year for the framework of these dwellings.

The difficult nature of the mountainous country which reached right down to shore, inlets and rivers, together with the rich resources of the sea and streams, concentrated settlement along the narrow waterfronts.

The permanent villages were nearly all close to the sea, with ready access to fresh water and a landing beach, but sheltered

FIG. 24. A HAIDA VILLAGE
(*Based on photographs by Swanton*)

from storms. The houses extended in a long line facing the water. The larger villages had thirty or more houses, sometimes laid out in two rows and containing a population of several hundred. In front of the houses there was a wide, levelled street, often supported by an embankment of heavy logs from which steps led down to the beach. Large platforms were often erected in front of each house. Supported on a framework of poles and on the embankment of the street these projected over the beach.

The houses varied in detail among different groups, but all had two essential features. First, they were of great size and each one housed a number of families, the number of inmates varying from a dozen or so in a smaller house some forty feet square to more than a hundred in the largest structures of the Nootka and Coast Salish which were several hundred feet long. Further, they all consisted of a massive and permanent framework of heavy timbers, which often endured for many generations, and an outer shell of planking which was not only renovated as required and sometimes destroyed at the death of the house owner, but was also taken down and transported to different sites during the seasonal migration. There were two main styles of building, the pent-roofed and the gabled. The houses of the Coast Salish and most of the Nootka groups were rectangular pent-roofed structures from forty to sixty feet wide and sometimes several hundred feet long. The framework consisted of two parallel rows of massive oblong pillars fifteen to twenty feet tall, hewn from cedar trunks. One row, generally the rear among the Nootka, was taller than the other, to give a gentle slope to the roof planks which lay on stout rafters spanning the pillars. The great cedar planks which covered the roof and walls were two or three feet wide and several inches thick. Those on the wall were lashed in position horizontally to overlap like weather boarding. The roof boards ran down the slope and were adzed to a curved section and overlapped. Lying alternatively concave and convex, like the tiles on a Chinese pagoda, they provided a freely draining waterproof roof.

Some Nootka, however, adopted the more elaborate and imposing style of the northern peoples who built gabled roofs. This type of house was square in plan and from forty to sixty feet long on each side (fig. 25). The entrance lay on the side facing the beach or river's edge and the gable ran from front to back. There were generally two long main poles often two feet in diameter and lying parallel two or three yards apart resting on short cross-beams, each again supported by two massive carved uprights two feet or more in diameter and some fifteen feet tall, erected within the house a few feet from the front and back walls. Rafters ran from the supports of the side walls across the roof poles, while the uprights of the front and back walls projected to provide supports for lighter poles crossing the rafters and supporting the planking of the roof. The wall planks of the Kwakiutl and Haida houses, at least in recent times, were very massive and ran vertically from the ground to the eaves.

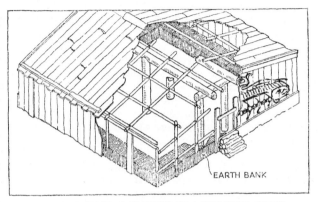

EARTH BANK

FIG. 25. ISOMETRIC DIAGRAM OF A KWAKIUTL HOUSE
(*Based on plans and elevations by Boas*)

Earthen banks some six feet wide, about a yard high and faced with planking ran along the inner walls of all houses. On these the bedding and stores of each family were laid out. In the south, matting partitions separated the various family sections in the winter season, while the more northern peoples commonly built on the platforms little gable-roofed sleeping cabins, themselves miniature houses. Among the Haida the floor was often excavated several feet and a tier of two or three timber-work platforms was erected round the walls to provide sleeping quarters and storage space.

Enormous posts carved with animal crests of the house owner were often erected in front of each house, especially among the Haida. Crests were also painted as enormous figures across the house front. In both styles the entrance was often through the gaping mouth of a monster (figs. 24 and 36).

These great houses, like the other woodwork of these peoples, were entirely executed with stone, shell and bone tools, and were made possible by the valuable qualities of the great red and yellow cedars. Durable but soft to work, the great trunks split readily along the straight grain. Long planks could therefore be obtained by driving in rows of bone wedges across the base of a fallen tree. The Kwakiutl sometimes wedged planks from the living trees, while the Nootka would fell even the largest. But the use of heavy planking demanded a massive framework. Lacking all knowledge of the pulley, a large party of men was needed for the building of a new house, for which the great posts had to be set in position by simple leverage, balancing and propping.

Although animal skins were available and these people showed great skill in many crafts, they made no attempt to devise well-fitting garments. In this the Pacific coast as a whole is to be contrasted with the rest of the continent. Neither the tailored fur garments of the Eskimo nor the hide shirts and leggings of the Plains are found here. Men wore a loin-cloth of deerskin and women a bark fibre apron, and both went barefoot. A thick waterproof cape of cedar bark matting gave protection against heavy rain. In winter, when the weather was damp and inclement for long periods, blankets of cedar bark or fur were thrown round the shoulders as required. Apart from ceremonial costumes the only articles of attire on which ornament was lavished were basketry hats.

Halibut, cod and salmon were caught in the coastal waters with hook and line, and hooks of special and ingenious forms, of bent wood and bone, were devised for the different fish. Halibut, for which the best grounds were several miles off the coast, were caught in large numbers from March to June with set lines attached to floats or with weighted hooks on long lines trolled behind slow-moving canoes. Cod were speared in deep water after being lured to the surface with a bait of live herring or a spinning lure.

When the herrings came close inshore in March and May, entering the bays and inlets to spawn, they were caught in nets, or, if the shoals were dense, could be taken from canoes with a 'fish rake', a long, flat-sided pole fitted along the sides with many sharp bone points. Moving this quickly through the shoal the fisherman could transfix several herrings with a single sweep. Leafy hemlock branches were often sunk with stones on shallow bottoms, where the herrings habitually spawned. The spawn itself was then collected from these branches to be dried and stored for food.

Sea mammals, especially porpoises, sea-otters and seals were harpooned from canoes, especially in the spring. The Kwakiutl, who took many porpoises, used a two-pronged harpoon. Each prong had a detachable barbed head tied to a common line. The sea-otter, to-day almost extinct on account of the high value placed on its magnificent skin by the fur traders of last century, was very swift and wary. It was pursued in light canoes. If found sleeping on the surface a sea-otter could sometimes be harpooned and immediately dragged aboard. More usually it had to be pursued for hours before the hunters had the good fortune to find themselves near enough to shoot with bows on some occasion that it rose to breathe.

Sea-lions and seals were more usually harpooned and clubbed when they were ashore among the rocks early in the year.

While whale meat was everywhere prized, most of these peoples depended on occasional animals washed into shallow water by storms or stranded on a beach. The Nootka and a few tribes to the south hunted the whale, and round this bold and dangerous task much magic centred. The chief whale harpooner in a Nootka village inherited his position and submitted to many restrictions on his food and behaviour. Before the whaling season, which began in April, he retired for some weeks to a special shrine of his predecessors and ancestors. Painting his body red and wrapped in a sea-otter skin the leader selected his crews from the bravest and most skilful men. They set out in a number of canoes, each holding seven or eight men, and paddled out far from land seeking a whale.

The stout head of the whaling harpoon had a triangular shell point and barbs of antler. This was wedged on one end of a heavy yew shaft ten feet or more in length, but detached itself when thrust home. To the harpoon head a line of whale sinew many fathoms long was tied, and along it at intervals, near the head, a number of inflated seal skins were attached. The chief harpooner directed his crew to bring the canoe into close quarters with the whale. Risking at every moment a flip of the great tail that would have smashed the canoe to pieces, they manœuvred until the harpooner, in the bow, was within striking distance of the whale. When struck the whale plunged away, carrying with it the line which was hurriedly cast off from the canoe. Following in its wake the harpooners of the other canoes were now free to attack the whale whenever it rose to the surface. Pierced with many harpoons and prevented from diving or escaping by the trailing lines of inflated skins, the great animal was slowly exhausted by its wounds and struggles and could at last be safely approached and despatched. The hunt was by no means always successful. The whale quite often broke away before it was seriously injured, carrying harpoons and lines with it. If successful the hunters attached further seal skins to the carcase and it was towed home by the whole fleet of canoes.

But the several species of salmon furnished the largest and

most assured portion of the food-supply, and on them these peoples mainly depended. While some were fished from canoes along the shore with baited hook and line or caught behind dams built at the mouths of tidal rivers, for the main salmon catches the Northwest Coast peoples took advantage of the great seasonal 'runs' when the salmon ascend the rivers in huge numbers to spawn in the upper reaches. The various species ascend at different times and runs succeed one another from March until nearly the end of the year, spring (March–June) and autumn (August–September) being the most important seasons. At the height of a run, narrow sections of a river were sometimes literally filled with salmon in the finest condition, struggling upstream. At such places they could be speared and even hooked out of the water several at a time with gaffs. Usually, however, it was more effective to dam part of the river and catch the ascending fish in traps. Rocky narrows which offered opportunities for such constructions were selected and stout weirs of logs and stones, too broad and high for the fish to leap over, were built. In narrow gaps were set fish-traps constructed with cedar slats or willow rods and of many patterns adapted to particular circumstances (fig. 27). The Kwakiutl also used dip nets and seines of nettle fibre cord in their salmon fishing.

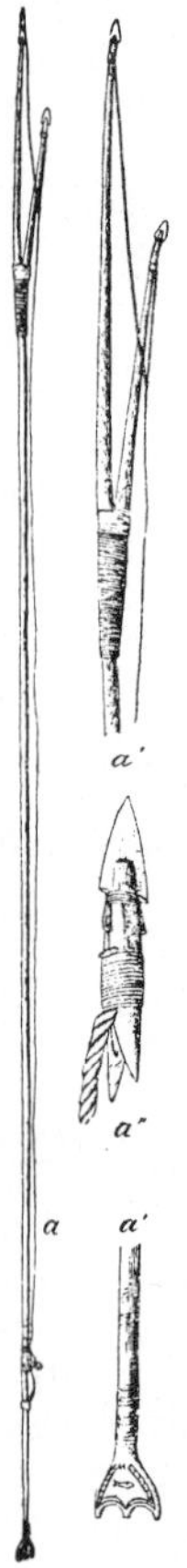

The values of particular sites, the times at which they could most profitably be exploited and minute details of the habits of the various species of salmon were all thoroughly known. The Nootka practised a unique device to ensure their salmon supplies. If the run on a particular stream began to fail they actually re-stocked it, obtaining spawn from another river at the breeding season and carrying it back in moss-lined boxes to start a new generation in the depleted stream.

Although salmon were of major importance in the economy of these people they were not caught at inland river sites by all groups. Some, lacking good river sites or attracted by other resources, remained on the coast during the periods of the salmon runs and bartered the product of their sea fishing for salmon obtained by others. On the other

FIG. 26. A KWAKIUTL TWO-PRONGED SALMON HARPOON, SHOWING DETAIL OF PRONGS, DETACHABLE HEAD (a´) AND BUTT (*After Goddard*)

hand, some groups, especially among the Tsimshian, occupied sites many miles up the rivers and had no coastal territories. These in turn were dependent on barter for sea produce.

The candlefish ascend the rivers in the middle of March, and for six weeks great catches could be made daily in great bag nets extended and held open between piles driven into the river bed. On the Nass river, where the candlefish were particularly abundant, this fishing often began before the river

FIG. 27. A KWAKIUTL SALMON TRAP FOR NARROW STREAMS
(*After Goddard*)

ice melted and piles had to be driven through it. The work was often both difficult and hazardous, for as the ice broke up and floes were carried rapidly downstream the nets were often carried away while canoes capsized and were smashed by the running ice.

After they had been allowed to decay for a week oil was extracted by boiling the candlefish in huge wooden troughs or in canoes heated by dropping in red-hot stones. This oil, rising to the surface and squeezed from the boiled fish, was a most important addition to a diet which consisted so largely of smoked and dried fish. Candlefish were caught in large quantities on relatively few rivers, and, moreover, large runs did not occur every year. But since it did not deteriorate rapidly, considerable stores of oil were accumulated in favourable years and there was a very extensive trade in this commodity. It was transported over long distances not only by canoe along the coast but also overland by the 'grease trails', some of which ran far into the interior and afforded opportunity for barter with the hunting peoples.

Shell-fish and edible seaweeds along the shore were collected by women. Although relatively unimportant in good years they afforded a most valuable reserve of food after a poor fishing season.

Intense fishing activity was confined to the summer half of the year, during which large stores of fish were accumulated. After the season of sea fishing for herring, halibut and cod, a group of families migrated upstream to their salmon weirs. The women were busily engaged throughout in preserving the fish, splitting them open and drying them on racks over fires.

The game of the forests was often neglected if not despised as a source of food, and some of these peoples had a definite aversion to meat, but deer, elk, mountain sheep, goat and bears were hunted, and for the first large drives were organized among the Nootka and Kwakiutl. The wool, skins, horns and sinews were the main objective, and venison was eaten only when other foods were scarce. Strong yew bows were used for hunting, but the sinew backing widely used among the interior hunting peoples of western America was not adopted here.

During the later summer the rich harvest of berries and roots was gathered by the women. Preserved in various ways these provided a much-needed vegetable element in their diet. Tracts of ground, rich in these wild products, were claimed as private property, and payment was demanded of those outside the owning household for gathering in its territory. Camas, the bulb of a wild hyacinth, and an important food staple among the peoples of the interior, was also obtained in large quantities by the more southern coast peoples who bartered large supplies to groups to the north. Patches of the wild clover root were enclosed in stone fences by Kwakiutl women, each of whom had her individual plot which she kept weeded to encourage a good growth. Nettle leaves, roots of bracken and edible seaweed were also gathered. The leaves of a plant whose identity is uncertain, but which presumably had a narcotic effect, were dried and mixed with lime for chewing, after the manner of coca chewing in South America and areca-betel chewing in Asia and the western Pacific (see pp. 141 and 191).

he patches on which it grew were regularly visited and cleared
f other vegetation, and the plant itself was sown and culti-
ated by the Tlingit and Haida. It has been generally stated
aat the plant was a tobacco. There is, however, no actual
vidence of its identity with any of the cultivated tobaccos of
boriginal America.

Since both food getting and travel were done almost entirely
y water, seaworthy canoes were of great importance, and
essels of different sizes were constructed for various purposes.
ll were dug-out canoes, hollowed out of cedar trunks. The
orthern peoples, including the mainland Kwakiutl groups,
ften fitted tall, V-shaped bow and stern pieces to their canoes
ig. 24) which projected high above the water, and breasting
ie waves facilitated navigation in heavy seas. The canoes of
ie Nootka, the Salish and the Kwakiutl of Vancouver Island
ad high-pointed prows, but the stern pieces were lower and
in vertically into the water. On the rivers punt-like 'shovel
ose' canoes which could more easily be poled were used, and
uth of the Columbia river this was the only form that was
ade.

Among the Nootka when a new canoe was required a large
ee near the water was felled and split in half with wooden
edges. The selected half was charred with fire to lighten
ie work of rough hollowing with stone and elk-horn chisels
nd heavy stone mallets. It was floated back to the winter
uarters, where the canoe builder carefully adzed down the
alls, producing an even tooling on the finished surfaces which
as greatly admired. When the sides were sufficiently thin
ie canoe was filled with water, and this was heated by dropping
ı hot stones. The softened hull could then be spread to give
beam greater than the width of the trunk from which the
anoe was hewn, and strong cross-pieces were inserted to
aintain the shape. This operation required very careful
idgment, and since a gust of cold wind might split the hull
om bow to stern, a shelter of matting was erected around the
anoe to prevent any sudden drop in temperature during the
ork. The prow and stern pieces were made separately and
shed on with nettle fibre cords through holes bored with
ird-bone gimlets and the whole elaborately painted with
presentations of the owner's crest. The work on a canoe
roceeded surprisingly fast, for the straight-grained cedar was
asily worked, and a skilled canoe builder could finish a hull
ı a month or so.

The Nootka and the Haida were the most skilled canoe
uilders, and on them the surrounding peoples depended for

their larger craft. The largest Haida canoes were nearl
seventy feet long and could carry a crew of a hundred me
In these craft they made voyages of many hundreds of mile
frequently visiting the mainland, and even travelling as fa
south as Vancouver Island. Cedar trunks large enough fc
these great canoes were restricted to a few localities, and bot
trunks and finished canoes were often traded over considerabl
distances. Large canoes could be built only by wealthy indiv
duals who could command both the material and heavy labou
involved.

Sails of bark matting or light slats of wood were sometime
used, especially for the double canoes spanned by house plank
that were contrived for the migrations to summer camp
Sails were unknown elsewhere in North America, and it i
probable that here the device was a modern one, suggested b
the ships of the early European explorers.

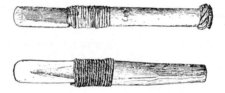

FIG. 28. KWAKIUTL CHISELS WITH BONE BLADES
(*After Goddard*)

While wedges and chisels of stone and bone were used wit'
stone hammers and long-handled mauls in the rough work c
felling trees, splitting off planks and the first shaping of canoe
and carved beams, the adze was the essential tool for th
smooth finishing and carving of objects. Hard stone pebble
and large shells were laboriously ground down to form fla
blades. The larger adzes, for heavier work, weighed severa
pounds and were grooved to take the lashings which boun
them to wooden handles of various shapes (fig. 29).

Pottery was unknown in this region and, apart from burde
baskets and small dishes and spoons of mountain sheep hor
receptacles of all kinds from large storage chests to cookin
utensils were made of wood. While platters and small foo
bowls were often hollowed out and carved from a single piec
of alder wood, rectangular vessels and chests were carpentere
from boards. The sides of a box were usually made from
single length carefully measured to fit the base. Bevelle

grooves were cut on the inner side at each of the intended corners, and these were steamed one by one for bending to the required angle (fig. 31). The two ends of the board which

FIG. 29. NOOTKA HAND ADZE
WITH BLADE OF STONE
(*After Goddard*)

FIG. 30. KWAKIUTL OIL DISHES
HOLLOWED OUT OF ALDER WOOD
(*After Goddard*)

met to form the last corner were joined by pegs or lashings of spruce-root fibre passing through bored holes. The bottom was similarly attached by pegging or sewing, and the cords

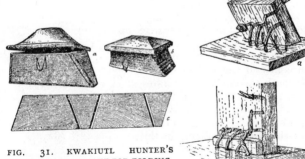

FIG. 31. KWAKIUTL HUNTER'S
BOXES AND BOARD CUT FOR FOLDING
TO MAKE A BOX
(*After Goddard*)

FIG. 32. A KWAKIUTL METHOD
OF JOINING BOARDS BY SEWING
(*After Goddard*)

binding these edges were often concealed in deep grooves.

Bowls and boxes, unless intended for rough use, were usually elaborately carved in low relief with the grotesque conventionalized animal figures characteristic of Northwest Coast art.

Elaborate masks were also carved in wood and painted for use in ceremonials. Although limited to the simplest tools, these people developed an amazing skill in wood-working of all kinds.

While basketry played far less part here than among the peoples of the interior, twined work reached a very high

FIG. 33.   KWAKIUTL WOODEN VESSELS : LEFT, URINAL;
RIGHT, WATER BUCKET
(*After Goddard*)

standard in both technique and decoration among some groups, especially the Tlingit and Salish.

Along the Copper river in Tlingit territory nuggets of pure copper were found in a natural state and, as among the Copper Eskimo of Coronation Gulf and the Indian peoples of the south-eastern United States, they were hammered into a variety of objects. Copper knives and ornaments were made, but the greater part of the copper available in this area appears to have been beaten into flat shield-like ceremonial objects two or more feet long, with a ı-shaped rib on the lower part and an incised or painted design above (fig. 34). These 'coppers' had a very high value in terms of sea-otter skins, blankets or other bartered goods, and were the proudest possessions of wealthy chiefs, who never-

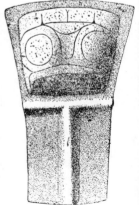

FIG. 34.   A COPPER: DESIGN,
HORNED OWL
(*After Goddard*)

theless broke them up and even threw them into the sea in their displays of rivalry.

The inner bark of the cedar was woven into bags, pouches, belts, capes and blankets, on a simple frame in which the warp strands hung loosely from a horizontal bar. No heddles or shuttles were employed and the woof had to be passed over and under each strand with the fingers. This weaving was therefore technically very simple and more akin to matting, while the frame cannot be regarded as a true loom.

The wool of the wild mountain goat, which was hunted and killed for this purpose, was also used for these matting blankets by most of these peoples. Separated from the hair and twisted into yarn between the palm of the hand and the thigh the wool was dyed black and yellow by boiling in decoctions of hemlock bark and moss. But since the supply depended on the hunters' luck this wool could be obtained only in small and uncertain quantities and was often eked out as a facing to a core of cedar bark. The very simplicity of the manufacture in which every weft strand was inserted with the finger made it possible to work most intricate patterns. In early times these were mostly geometrical, but in the fur-trading days of the nineteenth century, when the sudden increase of wealth afforded greater leisure and led to elaboration of ceremonial life, decorations hitherto used in painting and carving on wood were copied by the women of some Tlingit groups on to the blankets. These 'Chilcat' blankets, although only a recent product, afford an interesting instance of the transfer of a dominant art style to another material and also of the invasion of a female craft by styles derived from the wood-carving art of the men. The manufacture of the Chilcat blankets entailed so much time and labour that they were used only for ceremonial purposes. Only the wealthiest could acquire them, and they were traded far down the coast of British Columbia.

The weaving of the Salish groups on the lower Fraser was technically more elaborate. They raised a breed of small white woolly-haired dogs which were shorn to provide a more regular, although still limited, supply of wool. These dogs were used for no other purpose and were kept in folds, often on small coastal islands, so that the breed should not be spoiled by crossing with that of the common house dogs. The Salish used a simple weighted spindle in the making of yarn and the weaving frame was also more elaborate. It consisted of two horizontal rollers set between uprights and adjusted to give a tension to the continuous warp which passed round them. The warp did not, however, run spirally round the rollers. A tight cord or stick was set horizontally between the rollers, and over this the warp was looped back, so that when the cylinder of fabric was completed the stick or cord could be withdrawn and the blanket would separate into a single piece without cutting. This ingenious device was also used inland higher up the Fraser valley and in the interior of Washington. It is unknown elsewhere except in South America along the eastern foothills of the Central Andes, on the Venezuelan and Guiana coasts and probably in Peru. It is, however, possible that it was used in former times in the south-eastern

FIG. 35. FRONT AND BACK OF A DECORATED BOX.
MOON AS A BIRD (ABOVE) ; MOUNTAIN GOAT (BELOW)
(*After Goddard*)

United States, and despite its widely scattered distribution in recent times this form of weaving may have reached the Northwest Coast from the far south.

The art of the Northwest Coast peoples, based essentially on the representation of animals and mythical creatures adopted as crests by the noble families, was one of the most remarkable in the New World. Although one or two salient features of a particular animal, such as the curve of an eagle's beak or the dorsal fin of a 'killer' whale were always shown and gave a clue to the identity of the animal, the forms were often distorted beyond recognition by any one unfamiliar with the convention.

The animals were frequently given human features while the proportions and positions of limbs were changed to suit the shapes of the particular objects on which they were carved and painted. On cylindrical and sometimes on plane surfaces animals were shown as if split from the back and spread out into two profiles joined only in front (fig. 35).

The great 'totem poles' of the Haida displayed their owners' crests, which were often combined in a sequence implying the mythological origins and social connexions of the family (fig. 36).

Despite the wealth of resources and the relatively dense population no extensive political organization was developed in this area. The settlement group or village was the largest coherent unit. Each so-called 'tribe' of the Northwest Coast had in fact little unity beyond a community of language and similarities in the details of custom and ceremonial. Moreover, a village might itself be riven by feuds between members and adherents of powerful and rival families or larger groups, clans or moieties.

A few noble or chiefly families formed the core of every village. Such a family possessed property, including rights to fishing, hunting and collecting grounds, which were the foundations of its wealth and enabled it to maintain its claims to a variety of social and ceremonial privileges. These privileges were of a most varied character. They included for example the right to initiate and to perform a particular and prominent part in a ceremonial, to wear a particular mask and to carve as crests

FIG. 30. HAIDA TOTEM POLE (LEFT) AND MEMORIAL COLUMN
(*After Goddard*)

on its house front or posts, on its canoes and chests, representations of certain animals and monsters claimed as ancestors and insignia of the family or clan. The value of all these non-economic privileges depended, of course, like European heraldic devices, on the esteem in which they were held by the rest of the community which had no rights to them. The relative value of a crest or song depended largely on the display of wealth that the particular owners could make. According to native beliefs each noble family originally had its own settlement, but, as a result of war and migrations, several had come to live in one place. On each noble family a number of commoners and slaves were dependent, and the whole group occupied one or more of the large plank-built houses. A noble family in one village often had close relations of the same lineage or extended family in other settlements and with them shared many names, crests, social and other privileges in common.

Although the nobles married among themselves the commoners did not form a sharply separate caste, but were often cadet branches of lineages which, through failure to inherit fishing and hunting grounds or social and ceremonial privileges, were dependent on their wealthy and distinguished relatives.

The property and privileges of a noble family might be many and various, and sometimes included ceremonial and property rights in several villages. These could be, and often were, passed on separately to different descendants. Ownership was not, however, a purely individual matter. Many crests were the common property of all members of the family, while other and more particular rights were exercised by an individual as representative trustee for his close relatives, ancestors and descendants. Among the Nootka indeed it was the youngest member of a noble line who theoretically exercised the privileges of the family.

Since the public acceptance of a social privilege depended on giving a large feast at which it was adopted, privileges could readily lapse, although they had been nominally inherited, if the heir lacked the wealth to provide the required festival. At the same time a relatively poor man ranking as a commoner on account of his lack of titles could if he acquired the means to give feasts, as frequently occurred in early days of white settlement and fur trading, assume some title which noble relatives had not validated in a feast. By lavish display and gifts he and his descendants might then raise their rank to the most eminent in the village. The nobles and commoners were not therefore two sharply distinct castes, nor were the nobles a close group in which all had equal prestige. From the richest noble with the most extensive fishing grounds and most resounding titles to the commoner who had received from a noble relative in gratitude some small right to hunt or fish independently in a particular place, there were many gradations. Usually the high-born were rich and a wealthy parvenu in fur-trading days could not acquire the prestige of an aristocrat. But the grading of rank was unstable, prestige was rapidly whittled away if the wealth with which a family displayed its rank were seriously diminished. Thus the noble families within a single village and those of neighbouring settlements were in continual rivalry each to establish its greater prestige. To rest on one's laurels was but to admit the greater glory of another. And it is for this reason that the famous ceremonial feasts or *potlatches* of the Northwest Coast Indians had such compelling importance.

The chiefs or heads of noble families had each a following of relatives and commoners, on the size and solidarity of which their wealth and authority depended. This gave them influence and a power to command, but no general authority beyond their personal prestige. Formal political organization was conspicuously absent. A chief was in the first place master of his own considerable household, that is the relatives, close and remote, who lived with him and the dependent families of commoners and slaves. If he were head of the senior or most powerful branch of a lineage which had members in several villages these gave him allegiance and supplies for maintaining the prestige of the whole lineage. If, further, his family was the most numerous in the village or controlled the richest fishing sites he was usually recognized also as leader of the village. In every case he acted for the members of the group whose prestige was bound up with his own. If he raised his rank in relation to neighbouring rivals by giving great feasts and presents his group as a whole, be it household, lineage or village, or all three, gained in respect. If, however, he were insulted or degraded the group was correspondingly put to shame. Since the chief symbolized the prestige of those he represented, he could depend on the industry and self-sacrifice of his followers in supplying labour and materials for the preparation of the ceremonial feasts.

Every important social event demanded a lavish ceremony: the birth of a child; the ceremony when a girl reached puberty; the burial of a relative; the assumption of a predecessor's rank and titles; the building of a new house: these and many minor events were all the occasion for ceremonial feasts. For them large stores of food and gifts were accumulated in advance. New carvings were made to represent the crests of the feast-giver, who generally assumed a new name and in a dramatic

performance, for which elaborate masks and costumes wer
worn, enacted mythological events connected with hi
titles.

At these feasts, generally referred to in the Chinook jargor
used by the early traders, as *potlatches*, the invited guests wer
elaborately announced in turn and seated in strict order c
rank. The giver of the feast made presents of sea-otter skins
blankets, coppers and even canoes. While some of these wer
for services, the greater part were gifts made to the guest
according to their rank. Although the glory of munificenc
was everywhere paramount, the obligations of repaymen
played a prominent part, especially among the Kwakiutl. Th
acceptance of gifts at a feast there involved an obligation t
repay them with considerable interest when the guest in tur
gave a feast. A Kwakiutl would sometimes borrow materi
beforehand, again at high interest, in order to increase th
lavishness of his gifts at the feast. Careful record was ker
by official tally-keepers of all these gifts which were practicall
forced loans, and the extent of all obligations was publicl
known. Farther north, however, the repayment obligation
and the idea of interest were unknown.

Property was also destroyed. Canoes and coppers were ofter
deliberately broken, slaves were sometimes killed and valuabl
olachen oil would be squandered by pouring it on the fire unt
the leaping flames set the roof timbers on fire. By some or a
these means the feast-giver challenged his guests to greate
orgies of destructiveness.

Renown depended on the frequency and lavishness of thes
celebrations. To give them at all a man must have acquire
titles which he could publicly display. These were inherite
in various ways among the different groups: among th
Nootka from both paternal and maternal relatives at wil
among the northern peoples, where marriage was regulated b
maternal exogamous divisions into clans and phratries, inheri
tance passed in the maternal line, usually from a man to hi
sisters' sons, while among the Kwakiutl, where names an
crests as well as territories were usually secured in marriag
and held in trust by the son-in-law for his children, an ambitiou
man endeavoured to marry well and often. In fact, if
daughter were lacking an heir might go through a form c
marriage with his predecessor's foot in order to acquire an
perpetuate the titles! Among the Bella Coola, where th
titles of rank were also obtainable through marriage,
man would endeavour to 'marry' his daughter to severa
men of position in quick succession, even before she reache

puberty, so that titles acquired by these marriage ceremonies all accrued to his grandchildren regardless of their actual paternity.

To acquire territorial rights and to secure a following by showing evidence of initiative, ability and generosity were, however, as important as the inheritance of honorific titles. The last were of little value unless they were made the occasion of frequent display, and for this the labours of willing supporters was essential. Ability and leadership appear to have counted almost as much as inherited rank in enhancing the prestige of an individual and of his group.

Everywhere there was a tendency for families of high rank to intermarry in order to concentrate territorial possessions and social positions; and if a member of the aristocracy was to avoid the shame of marrying beneath him, his choice was often limited to a few individuals. Two head chiefs among the Tsimshian are known to have married each other's sisters over many generations.

Nobility on the Northwest Coast was not therefore a permanent status expressed in rigid forms, but the relative standing attained by the inheritance of a considerable number of independent privileges which might be independently transmitted from one generation to the next.

Captives taken in warfare among these peoples were kept in slavery. A captive was not, however, counted as a slave until a year or so had passed, so that his kinsmen might have time to ransom him. Slaves were allowed to marry only among themselves, and their descendants continued indefinitely as the property of the owning family. Although in their daily lives they suffered little hardship, and were no less well fed and sheltered than the mass of the people, the surplus of their labours was amassed by their masters, who had, moreover, complete power over their lives. Socially they had no position and were treated as chattels. Former rank or wealth could make no difference to the fate of a slave if there had been no opportunity for his own people to buy him back. Slaves were valuable both as a source and an indication of the wealth of their owners. To kill a slave at a feast was thought to display power and carelessness of property. But they might also be freed on such occasions and for similar motives. Slaves were often killed to accompany the dead at the funerary ceremonies of their masters, and among the northern peoples a slave was usually killed and buried under a main post at the ceremony attending the construction of a new house. One of the secret societies of the Kwakiutl formerly killed slaves for cannibalism in its ceremonies. At *potlatches* and marriage feasts slaves were sometimes given away.

While the limited intercourse between distant areas restricted slave-trading, there was extensive barter of slaves in some areas, especially in the south, where powerful Nootka settlements raided weaker groups on Vancouver Island and the mainland, bartering their captives elsewhere for such goods as blankets and candlefish oil. Slaves were frequently sold to distant peoples whence escape was impossible, and in the nineteenth century Salish slaves from the lower Fraser region were found in large numbers among the Tlingit in southern Alaska, where the proportion of slaves to the total population rose in some districts as high as one-third. Every man of rank considered the possession of a slave family essential to his position, while the head of a noble lineage often had many in his household.

Within the range of any village group there was a considerable number of districts and sites visited in turn for sealing, fishing, gathering and hunting at different seasons of the year. Places at which seals congregated along the coast in spring; portions of the rivers particularly suited to the erection of salmon weirs; tracts on which there were rich harvests of berries and roots and forest ranges frequented by deer, elk and mountain goat; all these were known, highly valued and claimed as the property of clans and families. Among the northern peoples who had a matrilineal clan organization most of these lands formed part of a wider clan territory, and ownership could only be inherited within the clan. Such a territory usually passed here to a close maternal kinsman and most often to a son of the former owner's sister. But even where, as among the Tlingit, there were such subdivided maternal clan territories, individuals also held lands in their own right which they sometimes passed on to their sons so that the clan membership of the owner changed. But clan rights were largely conventional. Others were rarely refused permission to hunt or gather if it were requested, though the owning clan or family had the prestige of granting that permission. The value of rights over these territories followed from the need to accumulate large quantities of food for the feasts and ceremonies in which the noble families established their rank and prestige. Dependent families and slaves were not thereby reduced to poverty or semi-starvation They exploited the territories of the wealthy families on which they were dependent and were fed from the produce, but the surplus was accumulated by the owner alone, unless he chose to permit other families to use his territories, sometimes in return for payment. Strict delimitation of productive land was therefore characteristic of this region and unsanctioned trespass was vigorously resisted. Moreover, as a result of complex movements over long periods the lands of a clan or family might be remote from its village, while the lands surrounding that village might belong to others. Captain Cook said of the Nootka that nowhere in his several voyages did he meet with any people who had such strict notions of exclusive rights to everything their country produced.

Despite the importance of slaves and the disputes between settlements for valued hunting and fishing territories the peoples of the Northwest Coast did not set great store by military prowess. The wealth of resources and the intensity of economic competition between the chiefly families appear to have concentrated the energies of the settlements on the exploitation of their territories. The villages were too busy in summer for military expeditions, while in the winter season travel, especially by sea, was far more difficult. Although the acquisition of surplus stores of food and goods for use in ceremonials and feasts was the primary objective of every noble household, the plundering of settlements by powerful rivals does not appear to have developed to any great extent. The chiefs of large settlements did, however, often restrict the trading activities of weaker neighbours. They refused the passage of canoes through their coastal waters and thus monopolized the barter along a considerable coastal area.

Long-continued rivalry between chiefs of neighbouring settlements was also liable to flare up into open hostility which, once begun, might continue intermittently for many years. Revenge for a killing, even if accidental, was often taken indiscriminately on the next individual or group of the offender's settlement. This sporadic fighting was by no means restricted to conflicts between members of different language groups. The difficulties attending a long expedition, especially, perhaps, the problem of obtaining food-supplies, restricted the range of hostile movements. The large Nootka settlements along the west coast of Vancouver Island appear to have been more frequently in conflict among themselves than with the Kwakiutl and Coast Salish settlements on the far side of the island and on the mainland.

Where, however, the bellicose chief of a large settlement was able to invite or compel the assistance of his weaker neighbours, considerable war fleets occasionally assembled and attacked villages fifty to a hundred miles away. Although small quantities of booty, such as sea-otter skins and also the heads of slain enemies, were brought back from a successful attack, the humbling of the enemy and the destruction of his village appears always to have been the main objective. War leaders were chosen for their valour and resourcefulness irrespective of rank. If successful, however, such a leader acquired both prestige and the means to give feasts and presents, which enhanced his position.

Attacks were made before dawn, and the crews of the war canoes were usually carefully organized, each crew being assigned to a particular house in the enemy's settlement. Some bore the brunt of the fighting, others carried brands to fire the houses and ropes for binding captives to be carried off as slaves.

At times of unrest timber stockades were sometimes erected round safe retreats, but the main villages remained unfortified. Bows, heavy spears and flat paddle-shaped clubs were used in fighting, and warriors often wore armour. Heavy, sleeveless war shirts and even frocks which reached to the ankles were made of elkhide, sometimes of double thickness and stout enough to resist arrows and even spear-thrusts. In the north armoured waistcoats were made with rods or slats of wood arranged vertically and laced close together. With wooden neck pieces, reaching to the eyes and thick hide helmets, the warriors were well protected against native weapons. This rod armour appears to have been introduced from the North Pacific coast of Asia, where it was widely used in former times.

It will readily be seen that the system of competitive ranking and obligatory feasts among the Northwest Coast peoples was an enormous stimulus to the intensive exploitation of natural resources and to the elaboration of crafts and arts. The great accumulations of food and goods continually astonished the early explorers, while the lavish ornament, especially in wood carving, has enriched the museums of the world and made the 'totem pole' one of the most popularly known of ethnological specimens.

A natural wealth of food-supplies and materials made the system possible, but without the system, which can by no means be regarded as their inevitable consequence, such intensive exploitation of the resources would probably not have occurred. As will be seen, the Tasmanians and Fuegians bear witness that cool, temperate forested coast lands were not inevitably well exploited by savage man, and if it be argued, that these areas are less rich in marine life it remains true that the differences of cultural level are far greater than those of the natural resources. Moreover, the fishing folk of the north-east coast lands of Asia, despite their rich resources and the many indirect contacts with Chinese civilization, failed to exploit their territories so successfully, or to develop so intricate a social and ceremonial organization and so elaborate an art as the splendid, if flamboyant, product of the peoples of the Northwest Coast.

We must therefore recognize that, whatever its origin and despite the economic waste it sometimes involved, the competitive and even mercenary cast of society among these peoples raised their economy to a unique level among the food-gathering peoples of the world.

The Pacific coast lands of South America corresponding in latitude to British Columbia, although generally so similar in physical conditions, present a profound cultural contrast with the Northwest Coast. Coastal subsidence of the mountainous and glaciated land has resulted in a similar configuration and topography. In southern Chile, from Puerto Montt southwards to Cape Horn at latitude 56° S., a belt of islands separated by intricate channels fringes the mountainous and indented coastline. The westerly winds and cyclonic storms of the 'Roaring Forties' result in a cool temperature and very humid climate. Rainfall is over fifty inches everywhere on the coast south of 40° S. and rises to over a hundred inches on the mountain slopes, and on account of the enormous expanse of open ocean the climate is more stormy and severe than in corresponding latitudes on the Northwest Coast. The waters of the cold Antarctic current which branches to north and south on meeting the coast rarely rise above 50° F., and lower the temperature of the ocean winds whose high humidity makes the far south one of the cloudiest regions of the world. Overcast skies and sea-mists are characteristic throughout the year. The winds of the westerly air streams are almost always high and squally, and in the winter season these become the severe and prolonged gales for which the Cape Horn passage has always been notorious.

The dense forest associated with these damp, cool, temperate conditions begins at about 40° S. and extends right down to Tierra del Fuego. It is in many parts even more impenetrable than on the Northwest Coast, but its composition is different; evergreen and deciduous beeches are the most characteristic trees, and there is a dense undergrowth of smaller trees, fungi and mosses. The tangle of growing vegetation and fallen trunks is often as dense as equatorial forest. The tree limit is reached at three or four thousand feet on the slopes of the southern Andes, and many glaciers reach the sea from the great snow-fields above the forests in latitudes several hundred miles nearer the Equator than on the Northwest Coast.

Into the northern part of this forest zone cultivating peoples of central Chile had penetrated as far as Chiloe Island. The Araucanians of the woodland area of central Chile, unlike the inhabitants of the comparable North American area of 'Mediterranean' climate and vegetation in California, had not remained at a food gathering level of economy, but had been profoundly influenced by the higher civilization of the central Andean highlands. The settled Araucanians occupied considerable villages of stone or plank walled houses with thatched roofs. They cultivated maize, quinoa, potatoes, sweet potatoes and beans, making use of the Andean streams to irrigate the drier lands of the inner valleys. Some reared a variety of domestic llama. Their weaving and pottery, both of high quality, showed strong influences from the Peruvian highland. The culture of the Araucanians, as reflected in the relative importance of agriculture and in the finish of their crafts, appears to have been considerably poorer in the forested zone south of 40° S., while their first occupation of Chiloe Island may have taken place in post-Columbian times.

South of the agricultural Araucanians, however, there is a sharp break in economy and cultural level; a division which has not been obscured by the southward diffusion of a few Araucanian elements which will be considered later. Over the whole area from Guaitecas Island to the far south of Tierra del Fuego there is a great uniformity in the details of the culture of the fishing peoples of this forested coast land. Three distinct language groups are found: the Chono who extend south to about the Gulf of Peñas, the Alakaluf reaching as far as the Brecknock Peninsula and the Yahgan whose settlements were scattered along the shores of Beagle Channel and the southernmost islands. Among all these peoples settlements were scattered, small and transitory, material equipment was meagre and showed almost no technical or artistic elaboration

Their dwellings were small domed or conical huts of sticks covered with grass and ferns. Their food-supply was derived in the main from the abundant marine life of the shores and coastal waters, and included fish, seals, otters, whales and shellfish. Of these the last, especially mussels, were the staple diet, as the great shell middens testify. The Alakaluf and Yahgan are said to have attacked whales at sea with harpoons on occasion, but this was probably very rare. Shell-fish were collected by the women and sea-fish and seals were hunted by the men with stone-headed spears and simple barbed harpoon points of bone loosely wedged on to ordinary spear-shafts.

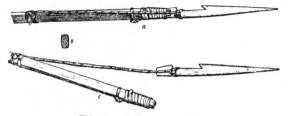

FIG. 37. YAHGAN HARPOON
(*a*), ASSEMBLED FOR CASTING; (*b*), SECTION OF SHAFT; (*c*), POSITION WHEN DRAGGING THROUGH WATER. LENGTH OF HEAD, 10 IN.
(*After Lothrop*)

Fish-hooks and traps were unknown, and the Chono alone made large nets of bark fibre cord; fishing was therefore restricted to spearing with the aid of weirs at the mouths of streams.

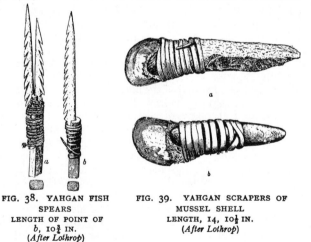

FIG. 38. YAHGAN FISH SPEARS
LENGTH OF POINT OF *b*, 10¾ IN.
(*After Lothrop*)

FIG. 39. YAHGAN SCRAPERS OF MUSSEL SHELL
LENGTH, 14, 10½ IN.
(*After Lothrop*)

For fishing and travel bark canoes were used. Three large strips of the thick bark of one of the varieties of beech were removed and roughly shaped with shell knives. These were sewn together and lashed to numerous ribs and cross struts to form a fairly seaworthy, but very leaky, canoe from twelve to twenty-four feet long, pointed at both ends. Among some of the Chono groups three thick pine planks were similarly used to construct a more durable flat-bottomed canoe, equally rudely shaped and leaky. More elaborate plank-built boats were constructed from laurel wood by the southern Araucanians, who also used this timber for their houses. The Chono, like the Araucanians, knew how to make polished stone axes, which were few among the Alakaluf and unknown among the Yahgan, and it would appear most probable that the Chono plank boats are reproductions in timber of the widespread bark canoe made possible by the acquisition of polished stone tools. Dugout canoes were made by the Araucanians, but these were not copied by the Chono, and in the absence of stone adzes were beyond the scope of the Alakaluf and Yahgan.

The plant food, although rather limited in character, was not fully exploited. The nutritious wild celery was apparently neglected and gathering was largely restricted to a few edible fungi, which were dried and stored in caches together with surplus fish, seal meat and blubber, during the seasons of plenty. As for meat, land animals were very little hunted and the bow and arrow, although known, was scarcely used by many groups despite the fact that the Ona, on the Atlantic side of Tierra del Fuego and in south Patagonia, were skilled hunters of the wild guanaco on which they depended mainly for food.

The culture of the southern Chilean coast becomes richer towards the Equator as more Araucanian elements come in. In this it contrasts with that of the north-west coast of America, where the specialized sea culture fades southwards into the more generalized economy of central California. The southward diffusion of Araucanian elements, such as polished stone tools, the use of timber planking, the growing of potatoes and even maize, and the weaving of bark fibre, had modified the life of the Chono and had in some cases penetrated sporadically among the northern groups of Alakaluf, but few of these higher elements had reached their limits of expansion. These southern peoples remained virtually isolated and had also stagnated at a cultural level which had probably already been established several thousands of years ago. The Yahgan and Alakaluf are in every way inferior to the Haida and Tlingit. They present a striking contrast to the Northwest Coast peoples in their failure to elaborate a material culture adapted to relatively rich resources and to achieve a commensurate stability of settlement.

Still more limited in their cultural equipment were the native peoples of another temperate forest area, the aborigines of Tasmania. This small island of about twenty-six thousand square miles also lies in the south temperate zone of the westerlies and has a wet, windy, oceanic climate, generally similar in type to those of the areas already discussed. The island is also mountainous; high ranges rising to five thousand feet are found in the west, and, save in the north, the shores are broken up into a maze of peninsulas and islands. The deep drowned inlets and sounds of the south and east are in many ways similar to the coastal features of British Columbia and southern Chile. The heavy rainfall of over a hundred inches a year on the windward western side results in a dense temperate forest which has many resemblances to that of southern Chile and includes several almost identical tree species, notably both evergreen and deciduous beeches. Woodlands of eucalyptus gums and tree ferns clothe the plateaus and ranges of the east, and only in the more sheltered and drier lowlands of the north and the north-eastern interior is more open country found.

As a result of the early isolation of Australasia the fauna was limited in type, but there was no lack of game. Opossums and squirrels lived in the forests, and several species of kangaroo, wallaby and wombat, together with the emu and smaller game, were found in the more open woodlands. Swans bred in the inland lakes and many sea-birds along the coasts. In the coastal waters many edible species of sea-fish and both whales and seals were plentiful; along the shores oysters, mussels, limpets and crayfish, some of them of great size, were extraordinarily abundant. The fish of the rivers and the many mountain lakes made up for their small size by their numbers.

Tasmania undoubtedly offered considerable resources to a food-gathering population, and the British Columbians would have lived well there. But it was in fact occupied at the beginning of the nineteenth century by some two thousand people whose crafts were ruder and more restricted than those of any known members of the human race. Though we may consider the southern Chileans to have neglected many of the available resources of their habitat, the Tasmanians lagged still further behind. Their equipment was very scanty and unspecialized, and in general showed less development than that of the Malayan Semang. They had no bow and used a short, heavy tapering stick both for throwing and clubbing: no bone or stone points were made for hafting to their spears, which were no more than long saplings with the butt end burned to a point and hardened in the fire. Their only other wooden tool was a heavy pole, flattened at one end, with which

the women prised up roots and dislodged shell-fish. Roughly
worked flakes of chert were extemporized to cut and scrape.
Neither pottery nor tight basketry existed and unworked
scallop shells off the beach served as their only cooking-pots.
The women appear to have made the more elaborate utensils,
the coarse baskets of reeds and bark twine in which they
gathered shell-fish, and the rafts—cigar-like bundles of eucalyptus bark with two smaller bundles to form the gunwales—
some of which were more than fifteen feet long, and, although
not watertight, were satisfactory enough floats for use along
the shore. Bladed paddles were unknown and these rafts were
punted or paddled with long poles. The men rounded up
kangaroo and wallaby by burning the brush, but they appear

FIG. 40.   TASMANIAN WINDBREAKS
(*After Peron*)

to have neglected the marine life almost entirely and shell-fish
alone were seriously exploited. Women gathered these and
even on occasion stalked basking seals, but they had no nets,
no lines, no weirs. Scaled fish were not caught and appear to
have been avoided as food for magical reasons.

Tasmanian shelters—low, unroofed windbreaks made with
sheets of bark or boughs—were even more inadequate than
those of the Fuegians. The small Tasmanian bands, each
usually less than fifty persons, were scattered over the country
in temporary camps which often broke up into family parties.
This separatism was reflected in their speech, which, although
of a single stock, showed great variations within short distances and has been divided into four main languages each
with nearly two dozen dialects.

The mental indolence and lack of foresight so often attributed
to the Fuegians would appear to be a still more marked characteristic of the Tasmanians. That such apathy existed can
hardly be doubted, but these peoples were also isolated in areas
with little or no contact with other peoples. In any case, the
bracing climate of the stormy westerly zone to which the
vigour of west European peoples has so often been attributed
failed to stimulate any important development of their culture.

CHAPTER VII

THE YUKAGHIR: REINDEER HUNTERS IN THE SIBERIAN TUNDRA

THERE survive in north-eastern Siberia a few remnants of a once-numerous people who, until pressed from the south and west by herding peoples, maintained a purely hunting economy under climatic conditions probably more severe than anywhere else in the world. They were reduced to

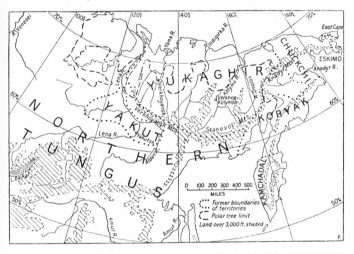

FIG. 41. SKETCH MAP OF EASTERN SIBERIA, SHEWING THE DISTRIBUTION OF NATIVE PEOPLES
(*After Jochelson, Bogoras and Shirokogoroff*)

a few thousand at the beginning of the nineteenth century, and many have now joined groups of reindeer herders and adopted many of their customs. These northern hunters are the Yukaghir, who once occupied the east Siberian tundra north of the mountain arc of the Verkhoyansk and Stanovoi Mountains and survive along the southern tributaries of the Kolyma river above Verkhne Kolymsk.

Unfortunately no detailed account of the economy, equip
ment and crafts of these people is available, but the records of
Russian explorers and the study of their social and ceremonial
life made by Jochelson afford a general picture. They occupy
the country to the north of the Verkhoyansk Mountains which
is drained northwards to the Arctic Ocean by the Kolyma,
Indigirka, Yana and other rivers. The severity of the winter
freezes all water surfaces for seven or eight months of the year.
In the heart of a great continent, exposed to the Arctic and
cut off by mountains to the west and south the winter temperatures in this area are the lowest in the world: at the mouth of
the Yana river the mean January temperature is more than
40° F., and at Verkhoyansk more than 70° F. below freezing,
while the lowest recorded temperature just south of Verkhoyansk was −90° F., or 122° of frost. There are only seventy
to eighty days in the year that are free of frost, and during
this short period, although there is often almost continuous
sunshine and the weather is often sultry, the soil thaws only
to a depth of two or three feet. The rivers are ice-free for only
about one-third of the year. On account of the cold and the
high latitude rain and snow falls are actually small, but snow
lies throughout the nine months' winter and is piled into deep
drifts by the Arctic gales. As temperatures rise towards the
end of May, snow and ice melt on every hand. In the flat
Kolyma basin, since the frozen subsoil is impervious, the low-
lying country becomes a vast stretch of lake-studded marsh
traversed by innumerable stream channels and land travel
becomes almost impossible. The hardy northern trees, stone
pine, larch, birch and alder, clothe the mountain slopes and
the more southerly country at their feet with fairly close forest.
A few spread northward down the more sheltered river valleys,
but save for occasional dwarf birch and the Arctic willow which
creeps along the ground the northern plains support only a
scanty vegetation of sedge grasses, mosses, lichens and low
berry-bearing bushes. These burst suddenly into life when
the short summer begins and support the animals, which then
move out over the tundra in surprising numbers. The polar
hare, elk and reindeer and great flocks of geese, duck and
ptarmigans appear almost miraculously to be preyed upon by
the wolverine and sable as well as by man. In the forest to
the south the black bear, musk deer, squirrel and mountain
sheep are found. Although salmon are rare a large number of
other fish ascend the rivers in spring for long distances, returning to the sea in the late summer before the rivers freeze again.
  The herds of wild reindeer are by far the most important

source of food and skins for the Yukaghir. The wild reindeer are but little smaller than the east Siberian horse. They migrate seasonally on either side of the forest border. In winter most of the herds seek the shelter of the wooded country, where they find carpets of lichens in the openings of the forest. though one variety remains on the tundra throughout the year. Reindeer will eat twigs, fungi and shrubs, but the lichens, particularly the species popularly miscalled reindeer moss, are their favourite and only abundant food. With their sharp hooves and strong forelegs they can scrape away the snow to surprising depths to uncover the vegetation, while in summer, splaying out their movable toes, they can move easily over marshy ground that could not support other animals of their size. When the rich carpet of mosses and lichens springs up after the thaw on the tundra the woodland reindeer migrate northward, where they can find some relief from the great swarms of mosquitoes which torment all animals in summer on the forest border.

The Yukaghir are mongoloid in race. They are a short thickset people with flat but rather narrow faces, small snub noses, yellow-brown skin colour and coarse straight black hair. Their clothes are of reindeer and other furs. A sack-like coat of reindeer hide reaching to the knees, with long sleeves and tail, is the main garment, and during the colder spells two or more hide coats with the fur left on are worn one above the other. A long front apron of hide also hangs down from the neck; the lower part is usually decorated with elaborate trimmings of variously coloured fur and hair. Leggings and long boots are worn by both sexes. They move and camp in small groups of families which rarely exceed one hundred persons in all and are often smaller. Individuals rarely marry outside their group.

Each band has its own hunting and fishing grounds, to which it returns every year. Some spend the summer on the tundra and retreat southwards in winter to the margins of the forest. For winter travel they use light birchwood sleds drawn by small teams of domestic dogs. The runners are held by a number of half hoops of bent birchwood on which a flat frame is lashed for carrying loads. These dogs sledges are rarely more than five feet long. Although they can be used on smooth mossy ground after the snow has melted, the marshy conditions in summer often make land travel extremely difficult and small dugout canoes hollowed out of poplar trunks and crude plank boats are used on the lakes and streams at this season. For transport on the main rivers larger rafts are made by tying larch poles together. The winter camps are moved two or three times between October and May to hunt the game of fresh tracts of forest. With sinew-backed bows and, more recently, firearms, they hunt the reindeer that have also retreated south, and make expeditions into the forested uplands for elk, musk deer and mountain sheep. The best hunting periods are in autumn and spring, for in the depths of winter

FIG. 42. A YUKAGHIR SUMMER CAMP
(*Based on photographs by Jochelson*

the reindeer herds are very wary. Lanes of widely spaced stones or posts are set up and the animals are driven down these by parties of beaters towards the hunters in ambush at the far end. In spring reindeer and elk are more easily run down and bogged when the snow begins to thaw.

In April before the thaw sets in the Yukaghir of the Upper Kolyma basin begin to move northwards out over the tundra to live there for the few summer months mainly by fishing and snaring of ptarmigan and swamp fowl on the marshes. Fibre nets are set in the streams and a kind of pike common to the tundra rivers is taken with a bone gorge on a sinew line. There are two fishing seasons, one in late spring when many fish are ascending the rivers, the other fairly late in summer when they are returning to the sea. The surplus from the spring fishing must be dried if it is to be preserved, but the stores accumulated during the later period will keep fairly well right through the cold winter, and, in fact, the Yukaghir prefers his fish slightly putrefied. Berries, such as wild currants and raspberries, lily bulbs, the inner bark of the larch, the juice of the red poplar and other wild food plants are gathered at this season by the women.

Towards the end of October the movement south to the winter quarters is once more begun. Throughout the year these groups live in conical tents of light poles covered with reindeer skins, cruder versions of the hide tipi of the North American Plains, which they pack on the dog sleds and rafts when moving from place to place. Birch bark, the common material for tent covering among the true forest peoples farther south, is rarely used by the Yukaghir. It is scarce on the northern margins of the forest and is less readily transported and set up. For winter covers the fur is left on the hide and the lower part of the tent is banked up with snow for greater warmth.

But other Yukaghir groups living nearer the Arctic coast in the lower Kolyma basin remain in the tundra throughout the year and reverse the régime that has just been described. They do not approach the sea, but winter along the lower reaches of the rivers in small villages of pit dwellings excavated a few feet and covered with timber and sods. In early spring they move a hundred miles or more upstream with their dog sledges before the thaw, to live a wandering life in skin tents, hunting the reindeer, elk and other animals which they encounter at this season on the tundra. Before the short summer is over they slowly descend the rivers again in dugouts and rafts taking fish and waterfowl on their route. They return to their winter quarters in late autumn with a store of dried meat and fish with which they eke out the scanty products of the winter chase, when only the tundra reindeer herds remain and small game like the polar hare and the tundra carnivores, the wolverine and sable, can be snared.

The 'old man', the ablest of the elders in every group, who presides at ceremonials and festivals, has considerable authority over its members. He selects the fishing sites and assigns each family to its proper place; he sends hunters out in different directions; and for the seasonal migrations, when the group breaks up into small family units travelling by different routes, he selects the meeting places. The produce of hunting and fishing are not kept by individuals but are handed over to the 'old man', whose wife distributes it. Tents, nets and boats are the property of the group or, more occasionally, the family, and personal property is practically restricted to clothing and individual hunting weapons.

The young men are severely trained for the difficult and exhausting task of reindeer hunting, for a herd once disturbed moves off with great speed and must be followed relentlessly for days if a kill is to be made. If ambushes are impossible some part of a herd is separated off and chased at the run over many miles until the exhausted animals can be approached more closely and brought down with arrows and spears. The leading hunter of the group, like the 'strong man' who organizes the defence of the group or its territory, attains and keeps his position only by the display of great bravery, strength and resourcefulness. The big hunts in the spring take place after long rituals in which the spirit protector possessed by every kind of animal is cajoled into permitting a kill.

During the summer several Yukaghir bands frequently join together for festivals at which there are games and trials of strength between the young men and of magical power between the shamans or magicians. Serious dispute and fighting between Yukaghir groups has been rare, but there has long been enmity against the Tungus and Koryak herders of tame reindeer in the south and east. The herders have invaded Yukaghir hunting territories while they in turn have attacked the domestic herds. Captives taken in fighting are made to work for the group, and the men in particular are humiliated; they are compelled to do women's work, to load up sledges and clean fish and are excluded from all hunting.

The Yukaghir are to-day a fast disappearing remnant, and nearly all of them have now joined adjacent reindeer herding peoples, particularly the Tungus, who will be considered later. They are, however, of far greater significance than their mere numbers would suggest, for they are representatives of the most primitive economy in north-eastern Asia, to which the domestication and herding of the reindeer have since been added nearly everywhere. Among them are found the only examples of exclusively food-gathering communities in Arctic Asia. Their movements accord with the sharp seasonal and geographical changes in the availability of food-supply in which reindeer and river fish are the most prominent elements.

CHAPTER VIII

THE ESKIMO: SEAL AND CARIBOU HUNTERS
IN ARCTIC AMERICA

CIRCLING nearly half the globe along the Arctic coast of North America, fringing the ice cap of Greenland in the east and reaching across to the Asiatic shore of the Bering Straits, there stretches one of the most extensive, uniform and at the same time one of the most specialized primitive cultures in the world. Similar activities, weapons, tools, crafts and social customs are found among all the Eskimo of this northern zone. The cultural homogeneity is matched by a unity of race type and language which is equally marked. The Eskimo, or Innuit, betray in their flat, broad faces and coarse black hair an undoubted kinship with the American Indians to the south and with the mongoloids of north-eastern Asia. They are short and thick-set, from five feet two inches to five feet four inches in height, sallow skinned and with dark brown eyes, often narrow slanting lids, showing the Mongolian fold. But on account of special peculiarities, of which unusual long-headedness is one of the most outstanding, they must be distinguished from the majority of the Indian peoples of northern America.

Recently, however, an Indian population closely similar to some of the Eskimo in race type has been identified among the Chipewayan living in the vicinity of Lake Athabaska.

The Eskimo dialects from Greenland to East Cape in Siberia belong to a single stock. No relation has yet been found between their speech and those of other peoples, far or near, except the kindred Aleuts of the South Bering Sea. Equally remarkable, the variation over this immense distance is very small, and is only of the order of difference of that between the Germanic tongues. Rasmussen, in his famous journey through the whole length of Eskimo territory, was able to understand something of every dialect he heard. This relative uniformity of speech over such enormous distances—a great contrast with Arctic Asia—suggests that the dispersion of the Eskimo along the immense Arctic frontier is very recent. But since it is known that peoples of Eskimo culture have occupied these areas for perhaps two thousand years it is possible that earlier and more divergent dialects have been submerged by a recent expansion.

The culture is most characteristically developed around the shore of Baffin Land and the northern parts of Hudson Bay in latitudes 65° to 70° N. In this central area, as throughout the Arctic zone, the long northern winter of shrunken days and

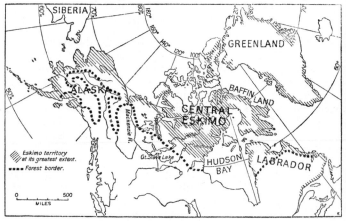

FIG. 43. SKETCH MAP OF ESKIMO TERRITORY
(*Distribution after Steensby and others*)

prolonged darkness is followed by a brief summer, when the hours of daylight are equally prolonged, the radiant heat then has considerable warming power, the ice floes melt and open water flanks the shore. In the vicinity of the Arctic circle there is about a month of continuous daylight at midsummer, while at midwinter the sun is above the horizon for only an hour or so.

Although the mean annual temperatures fall well below freezing, the winter cold is actually less intense than in the hearts of the northern continents, as in the lower Mackenzie Basin in Canada, and above all in the interior of north-eastern Siberia. A hundred Fahrenheit degrees of frost may occur on individual days, and in severe winters the mean January temperature may fall below —50° F. in the Arctic Archipelago, but —30° to —35° is a more usual value on the coasts, and temperature falls inland   The severity of the Arctic winter lies not only in its long duration, but in the shortness of the daylight hours. There are no trees to break the force of the strong winds, and violent blizzards occur, which make it impossible to leave shelter for days. The air is always damp and thick mists are frequent in the calmer periods.

For only two or three months in the year does the mean temperature rise above freezing point. But during this time, although air temperatures are kept down by melting snow and the resulting spread and evaporation of ice-cold water, there is a bodily sensation of warmth from the radiant heat of the sun. As the days shorten again and the sun's path runs ever closer to the horizon the coastal waters freeze over, drifting ice is annealed to the main mass and a skirt of winter ice produces a temporary extension of territory over which the northern hunter may wander. For these ice floes are only superficially barren; beneath them in the unfrozen waters marine life goes on and the sea mammals maintain breathing holes through the ice.

The distribution of floe ice plays a very great part in determining distribution of winter settlement. On open shores exposed to strong currents and to high prevailing winds from the north-east, the pack ice of the polar seas is heaped up by the early winter gales into great ridges of overriding blocks before the floes of winter ice which form on the coastal waters have had time to consolidate. So they remain throughout the winter a tangle of miniature ranges, gullies and ravines, across which travel on foot is slow and by sledge impossible. But in sheltered bays and fjords the floe ice develops as a smooth and level skirt, a newly added coast plain which offers great mobility to the Eskimo sledge and dog team and conceals beneath its surface a rich reward for the hunter.

The Eskimo families congregate in early winter in settlements along the shore, or on the floe ice; here they remain until March or April. Only then with longer days and the approach of spring do they begin to scatter. The hunting of one animal, the seal, by narrowly restricted means, dominates the winter activity. The seals feeding fairly close inshore are compelled to establish breathing holes through the floes. These they scratch as the ice forms in late autumn, and are able to maintain through the winter, because the cover of drifting snow retards the formation of a great thickness of ice. These holes, concealed though they may be by a thin covering of snow, can be scented by the Eskimo dog. The hunter scraping away a peep-hole can tell if it is in use, since there will then be but a thin ice film or none at all. Replacing the snow cover and leaving a tell-tale pointer of bone which will move when the seal thrusts up its muzzle, the hunter has to wait in the raw cold of the short arctic winter day. Every seal will usually have a number of blow holes which it visits in turn at intervals throughout the day; the vigil at any one hole may therefore last several hours before the seal appears. When the pointer moves and the hunter is sure that the muzzle of his prey is squarely below the hole he raises the harpoon and thrusts it into the muzzle of the beast. The detachable head is embedded firmly in the flesh and the seal skin or sinew line runs out as the seal plunges madly away. The Eskimo plays it carefully, tires it and finally, hacking at the ice to enlarge the hole, drags the exhausted animal to the surface.

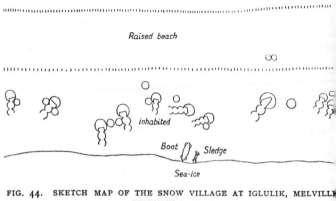

Raised beach

inhabited

Boat   Sledge

Sea-ice

FIG. 44.   SKETCH MAP OF THE SNOW VILLAGE AT IGLULIK, MELVILLE
PENINSULA, 1922
SCALE, I : 1000
(*After Mathiassen*)

This is what is known to the Eskimo as *maupok* hunting literally 'he waits'. In parts of Greenland the more elaborate *ituarpok* method is found. Two holes, one or both made by the hunters themselves, are used. At one a man spies, and entices the seal with bait while the harpooner stands over the other and at the given signal strikes through this hole at the seal below. *Maupok* hunting has the great advantage that good light is not necessary. The pointer above the seal hole can be watched in a twilight in which the stalking of game would be quite impossible. In favoured stretches the seals are abundant, and the hunter has great skill in recognizing a hole likely to be visited shortly, but to be in reach of a good hunting ground within the space of the short daylight the camp must usually be established on the ice itself, for the hunter can rarely use his sledge or travel safely more than a few miles from the settlement. Since it is difficult to obtain supplies for more than a few days ahead in winter, a period of severe blizzards or even fogs may bring a camp to the verge of famine. Death by starvation is a constant danger in the winter season.

The seal provides not only food but fuel. Wood is not available and seal blubber is far superior as fuel to the fat of the caribou, which is hunted in the summer. It burns more readily and clearly and gives out much greater heat. With the onset of the severe cold the need for fuel is probably paramount in the change over to seal hunting and the neglect of the remaining caribou.

By about March, as the days lengthen and lanes of open water form, the families begin to scatter to hunt the seals in open water or to stalk them as they lie basking on the surface at their breathing holes and on the edge of floes. The seals now congregate in much larger numbers. Their young are born and families lie basking in the warming sunshine. Early spring is the great opportunity for stalking or *utoq* hunting. Leaving his sledge and team, the hunter advances with a hunting dog until he sights a group of seals. Creeping along the ice, his head camouflaged in a sealskin cap, he advances so close that with a sudden leap he can rush on them and thrust his harpoon into the laggard of the group. *Utoq* hunting can for a brief season yield a far greater reward than the slow watching at the holes, and a skilful hunter may take several seals in a day. But after a few short weeks the floes begin to crack up, breaking into a number of slowly melting islands.

In Baffin Land and along the northern shores of Hudson Bay the hunting method again changes. At the widening lanes a more varied game is now at hand, whales migrate north to this region and walrus are more abundant; a throwing harpoon is used to strike the animals in the water while the skin-covered canoe—the *kayak*—takes the place of the sledge as a means of transport and is used to bring in the harpooned beasts.

During this period of abundance large stores of seal blubber are packed in hide bags and stored in pits on the shore beneath solid rock cairns, to protect them from the wolverines and foxes.

At this season the concentration on sea mammal hunting was formerly less complete, for that slow moving arctic herbivore—the musk ox—was found in considerable herds on the northern mainland and islands. A musk ox herd does not migrate seasonally, and the animals are far slower than the caribou to the south. They could be run down and kept at bay by dogs so that the hunters might dispatch them with lances. These slow breeding clumsy animals, whose flesh is greatly relished, are no match for the Eskimo, and their numbers are apparently soon reduced wherever they are hunted intensively. With the introduction of firearms the herds have been so severely diminished nearly everywhere that they are no longer an important or reliable source of food. The polar bear, a truly arctic animal which hunts on the pack ice, is also taken in spring when it comes close to land in pursuit of the young seals. It is pursued by sledge and brought to bay by releasing the dogs.

By midsummer the snow cover has melted on land and the stunted vegetation sprouts, and the hunting of land animals becomes important. The Eskimo turn their backs abruptly on the sea and, moving up a valley from the shore, come out upon the low inland plateaux. Moving inland they seek the large herds of caribou, the American variety of reindeer, which range far north across the tundra, feeding on the summer growth of mosses, lichen and small shrubs. Some herds migrate before the breaking of the ice to the islands of the Northern Archipelago and they cross to Baffin Land in large numbers. Considerable herds remain on the tundra throughout the year, but in winter they scatter widely and are very difficult to approach. In summer, although individual hunting with the bow is common, the herding habits of the caribou encourage group hunting, and the families which have scattered in the spring unite again before moving inland. Summer camps are established near the heads of wide valleys which give easy access to the narrower ravines and uplands. The herds move northward at this season, travelling as much as two hundred miles from their winter grounds, and have persistent habits in their migrations. They often take the same route for many years and vary little in the times of their movements. At the beginning of the season the animals can often be driven on to marshy ground with a thin ice covering where hunters may easily run them down. But the favourite and most successful of the hunting methods is a drive into a lake or river where spearmen lie ambushed in kayaks and paddle rapidly into the herd, spearing them as they swim. Among the Eskimo east of Melville Peninsula kayaks are far more extensively used in summer and on the rivers and estuaries than on the waters of the sea coast. Or, again, the caribou may be driven from the hills into a narrow valley towards a line of bowmen concealed in hollows and behind bushes. Parallel lines of small stone or sod cairns are often erected, fictitious beaters reducing the numbers required for the drive, and serving to hem in the herds and direct them to the ambushes.

Besides caribou smaller game are taken. Wolves and hares are caught in traps and snares, while the large summer flocks of duck and geese and other birds which migrate north to breed in the Arctic are struck down with light spears propelled with a spear thrower, or taken in whalebone nooses.

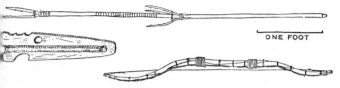

ONE FOOT

FIG. 45. ESKIMO BOW, BIRD LANCE AND SPEAR THROWER
(*After photographs by Boas and Mathiassen*)

Fishing plays an almost equally important part in the summer activities. Salmon trout are the chief catch. In June, shortly after the ice has melted, the mature fish migrate up the rivers to the lakes, while the two-year-old fry descend to the sea soon afterwards. The fish often move in such vast shoals that they choke the waters and can be speared wholesale with the ingenious trident spears which grip the impaled fish and draw them from the water. At other times they are caught in bag nets or trapped behind weirs in the estuaries with the ebb of the tide. The Eskimo also use hook and line and make ivory minnows for use as lures.

During the summer a number of edible berries and roots and vegetable material for other uses are also carefully collected by the women. But these are obtained only in relative small quantities, are luxuries, and do not add very substantially to the diet.

The summer settlements are encampments of small seal or caribou skin tents of a peculiar shape, with a ridge pole and a semi-conical rear. Variants of this single type are found throughout Eskimo territory from Greenland to Alaska.

At the close of the summer season the Central Eskimo groups return to the shore with a considerable store of food. This early winter season is often an interval when there is no hunting, for there are very few caribou near the coast after the beginning of November, while the ice does not bear until December. But there is usually abundant stored food, and it is a period of plenty and comparative leisure, the time of festivals and short journeys. Some groups then occupy permanent stone and earth houses, repaired and renovated as required and occupied from generation to generation. They are the real focus of the group, and their sites represent a nice adjustment to the various needs of building materials, accessibility to smooth floe ice in

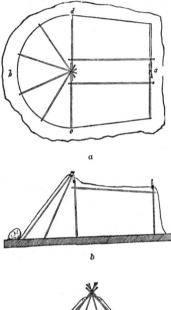

winter and to the interior rivers and lakes and hunting grounds in summer. In plan they are essentially similar to the igloo and will be described later. But new houses of this type have not been built for generations except on South-ampton Island and parts of Baffin Land. In many places they have fallen into complete ruin and are avoided by the Eskimo of to-day, who pass direct from their skin tents, which they use as late as possible, to the snow igloos of winter.

While the typical Eskimos of the central area pass the winter hunting on the ice floes some groups on the Canadian barren lands, to the north-west of Hudson Bay where the autumn caribou hunting is richer, remain on land throughout the winter, living on their stores of venison sup-plemented by the chase of caribou. Most of these never visit the sea at all and use caribou tallow instead of sea blubber for light and heat.

FIG. 46. PLAN AND SECTIONS OF SUMMER TENT USED AT CUMBER-LAND SOUND
(*After Boas*)

In the life of the Central Eskimo there is thus a marked seasonal rhythm and clear-cut separation of the economic activities of the long winter season and those of the short summer. The separateness of summer and winter occupations is recognized and enforced by a number of regulations. The sea mammals are fundamentally the more important, and manifest their dominance in myth and custom. The great mythological heroine of the Central and Eastern Eskimo is Sedna, from whose chopped-off fingers the seals and walrus were created. She lives at the bottom of the sea, controls the animals and when angered wreaks her vengeance with storms and withholds the seals and walrus. No activities connected with the caribou may be undertaken during the period of seal hunting. If clothes are to be made from the summer's store of caribou hides, sealing must wait until they are finished. Caribou meat may not be cooked and eaten in an igloo on the winter ice.

The régime here described is characteristic of the Eskimo tribes for many hundreds of miles throughout the central mainland and archipelago. Proceeding south-east and west from this central zone, however, there are gradual changes in climatic conditions, and above all in the character and period of ice formation, which is accompanied by a modification of this seasonal rhythm. In western Alaska, in Labrador and west Greenland the winter shortens, the sea is open for longer periods and the ice floes are less extensive. The igloo disappears and the hunters alone move out over the ice on short journeys, returning to their families which remain on the coast in winter pit dwellings.

Still farther southwards and towards the limits of Eskimo settlement, in southern Alaska, south Greenland and southern Labrador, the winters grow less severe, sea ice is less and less developed and ceases to be an important factor in the winter conditions. In these sub-arctic areas the winter régime is modified. Although the population remains by the shore hunting the same animals, it must now be done on open water and boats are necessary. Here the kayak is used throughout the year in sea hunting, and has been adapted and developed into a most efficient hunting vessel from which seal and walrus are harpooned. For the movement of a party, however, and for the capture of larger prey, especially the whale, another vessel is used—a broad-beamed open boat. This is the *umiak*, or 'woman's boat', which is also used in northern Alaska and Hudson Bay. The summer movement inland is, however, maintained, except in Greenland, where the ice cap restricts settlement to the shore and the economy becomes entirely littoral. But the shore is less completely deserted in sub-arctic Labrador and Alaska and a considerable proportion of the community may remain behind, especially in the west where the summer walrus hunting and whaling offer great reward. With the decline of ice floe hunting the sledge and dog team loses its importance, and on the west coast of Greenland it finally disappears just north of the Arctic circle.

After this review of the fundamental elements of Eskimo economy the characteristic features can be considered in more detail. The Eskimo to-day probably number less than forty thousand, and the great majority of them are in the more southern parts of Greenland and Alaska, where their life has been considerably modified by the influence of white whalers, traders and missions. Although the Eskimo, like the other hunting peoples so far considered, can be divided into a number of fairly large divisions or tribes each of which speaks a single dialect, the smaller group occupying a single coast settlement and hunting over a traditional territory is the true social unit. These villages may be from ten to thirty miles apart, thinly strung out along the shores, and although mutual visits are frequent the wider division does not function as a political body, and its similarity of dialect, a result of proximity and fairly frequent intercourse, is often its only expression of unity. In the central area from Coronation Gulf to Baffin Land there are probably only four to five thousand Eskimo in communities varying from thirty to five hundred in number. The households of a settlement are mostly related, and individuals usually marry outside their group. A man may have a wife in more than one settlement and thereby acquire the right to hunt in the territories of several groups. Authority is confined to the matter in hand at a given time, and leaders of hunting parties and expeditions are selected according to their skill and knowledge in particular things. The only otherwise influential individual is the sorcerer, or witch doctor, whose powers are considered supernatural. In hysterical trances his body is entered by spirits, who denounce wrongdoers and foretell the fate of the sick and hungry.

In the late spring and early summer, after coming off the ice and before the caribou hunting, individuals and small parties often undertake long journeys, travelling as much as two hundred miles out and back in a single season. When journeying to a really distant place several hundred miles away the traveller will frequently remain there for the rest of the year to return in the following spring. Reckoning distances by 'sleepings' and directions from prevailing winds, keeping their course by sun, stars or in thick weather by wind—in a calm mist they wisely refuse to travel—the Eskimo acquire a wide knowledge of the land for many hundreds of miles. When a man wishes to travel far abroad he consults another better acquainted with the country who can often draw him on dried gut a map of surprising accuracy. Marking in main points whose relative directions are known and perhaps verified by view from a commanding position, the details are filled in with great care. Distances and the configurations of coast lines over an area of more than a hundred miles in any direction are often shown with such clarity and precision that the map can be readily recognized alongside a white man's chart. Extensive intercommunication between groups and tribes is thus maintained, and although some difficult sections as between the Mackenzie River and Coronation Gulf are but infrequently traversed, all are ultimately linked along this vast stretch of fifteen thousand miles of coast line.

Although the days of the moon-months are sometimes exactly counted and the names adjusted by omission when they begin to deviate too much from the season in which they customarily fall, yet years are reckoned only for a span of two or three into the past and future.

The most striking fact of Eskimo culture is the elaborate nature of their habitations, implements and weapons. Far from the primitive character of their economy and the severity of their environment resulting, as might have been expected, in a low grade material culture, they make use of some of the most elaborate devices known among primitive men, and their implements show amazing qualities of resourcefulness and ingenuity. First and foremost, apart from occasional driftwood at the northern estuaries, they lack almost everywhere the wood which is so invaluable a material for most peoples of lowly economy; bone, stone and hide, and even snow and ice must take its place.

The permanent houses on the shore occupied by some groups are ovoid or rectangular in plan, three or four yards across, with a long, narrow entrance passage. The passage and a central aisle in the chamber are excavated in the ground, but the floor of the aisle stands about a foot higher than the passage to exclude cold draught. The bedding is laid out at the back, the sides being reserved for cooking and stores, one for each of the two families that usually occupy a house. Around the circumference of the chamber and for a few feet along the outer passage, a walling of stone or sods rises to a height of five or six feet. This is covered by rafters of whalebone rib or, occasionally, of driftwood, set lengthwise and lashed to a curved rib in front. The curved front rib provides a space for a gut-skin window immediately above the inner end of the passage. The rafters are covered with a double layer of seal skins with moss between. (See fig. 47.)

The snow igloo closely follows the plan of the stone house, but the large blocks of snow, cut from a drift of fine grained compacted snow with a bone or ivory knife, are laid spirally and sloping inwards to build up a dome without any scaffolding. Each block is rapidly and skilfully cut out by eye to fit in its place with the right slope and to afford a firm foundation for

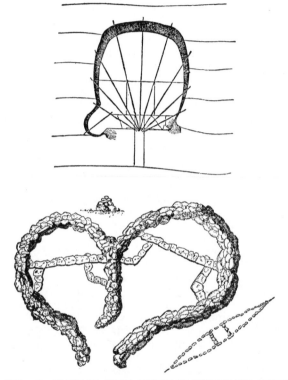

FIG. 47. PLANS OF STONE HOUSES IN CUMBERLAND SOUND
THE ONE SHOWN ABOVE WAS OCCUPIED BY THREE FAMILIES
(*After Boas*)

later courses. The final key block in the dome is lowered into position from outside. Any crevices are tightly packed with snow and the main structure is complete. With use during the winter cold its solidity increases, for the meltings on the inner walls are soon frozen again to solid ice. For long occupation the chamber may be four or more yards in diameter and three yards high. Side ledges and a rear platform are built of snow on a plan similar to that of the stone house. These are covered with moss and skins to prevent extensive melting of the snow. An ice or gut-skin window is again set above the exit tunnel, which may be sub-divided into a number of small domed or vaulted sections for stores, while the exit of the outer tunnel has a sharp angle bend to exclude blasts of

FIG. 48. SKETCH AND SECTIONS OF SNOW HOUSE OF DAVIS STRAIT
(*After Boas*)

cold air. In some areas the main chamber is lined with skins held in position by sinew cords passing through the walls of the dome and held by toggles. A considerable air space is left between the skin ceiling and the snow roof. With such a lining and an air exit hole in the roof a temperature of ten to twenty degrees above freezing can be maintained without serious melting of the igloo, since there is always cool air between it and the interior. While such a house is carefully

FIG. 49. SECTION TO SHOW INTERIOR OF SNOW HOUSE
NOTE SKIN LINING, GUT SKIN WINDOW, SMALL ENTRANCE
TO SIDE CHAMBER AND LAMPS AND KETTLES ON THE
SIDE PLATFORMS
(*After Boas*)

constructed and takes time to build, a temporary igloo about two yards in diameter can be built in an hour or so by a single man or small party while on a journey and camping for the night.

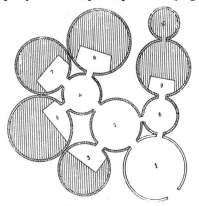

FIG. 50. PLAN OF GROUP OF CONNECTED SNOW HOUSES
(*After Mathiassen*)

Where several families are camping together a large chamber is often built as a meeting place for singing and dancing and

tch doctors' exhibitions, while several dwelling chambers
ilt around are connected to it by galleries. (See fig. 50.)
The lack of timber, the fuel so obvious in other regions, is
et by using the animal fat so abundantly provided by the
ubber of seals. This is burned with a row of moss or cotton-
ass wicks in a shallow tray hollowed from the soft soap stone
ich has often to be obtained by barter from great distances.
od when not eaten raw is boiled in a deep rectangular kettle
so carved from soap stone and suspended from a horizontal
le or supported on a four-legged frame above the lamp.
othing and other goods which need to be dried are placed
a netting tray set over the kettle. Even at the mouth of
e Mackenzie River and for several hundred miles to either
le where there is an abundance of driftwood brought down
om the forests by this great northern river the Eskimo,
though they build timber houses, nevertheless use blubber
mps despite the abundance of timber for fuel.
The clothing of the Eskimo is supplied mainly by the product
the summer chase, for caribou hide is warmer, lighter and
ore supple than seal skin. Where caribou fail, as among the
lar Eskimo of Smith Sound in north-west Greenland, polar
ar fur affords clothing for severe conditions. Eskimo gar-
ents are no shapeless wraps. They are carefully cut out and
ilored on established patterns for men and women. For
otection against water and damp, waterproof suits of gut
e made. Clothing is made by women. It is finely stitched
th sinew thread and often beautifully finished with border
rips of contrasting colour. To protect their eyes against the
ntinual glare of snow and ice during the spring on the coast
e Eskimo wear slit goggles of ivory.
For winter travel on ice and snow and even on smooth
ossy tundra in summer the Eskimo use sledge and dog team.

FIG. 51. IGLULIK DOG SLEDGE
LENGTH, 3.53 M.
(*After photograph by Mathiassen*)

e sledge, built of whalebone, or of wood where available,
lashed together with hide thongs through holes made with
rotating stone-tipped bow drill. Guiding handles of antler

are often made. The traces and harness are of hide. Th
runners, from five to fifteen feet long, are made of wha
jaw-bone, of wood shod with ivory or whalebone strips, or eve
of frozen hide. The Arctic snow is often soft and powder
In it runners will stick as if in sand unless their surfaces a
very smooth and friction thereby reduced. Ice provides suc
a surface, but a layer of ice will not adhere firmly to wood
bone. The runners are therefore shod with a layer of froze
mud, moss or even seal's blood to which ice does adhere closel
On to this, before setting out on a journey water is squirte

FIG. 52. CENTRAL ESKIMO DOG IN HARNESS
(After Boas)

from the mouth and smoothed over as it freezes. Each de
pulls on a separate hide trace which is attached above t
rump to a harness of hide strips passing under its fore-lim
and round its chest. They fan out in front of the sledge, ea
dog picking its own way across the irregularities in the sno
The dog teams require great skill in handling. Each forms
small society on its own, and dogs can be introduced into
separated from a team only with difficulty. The strongest an
most spirited dog has the longest trace and is allowed to run
few feet in advance of the rest as a leader, while the weak
and more unruly elements are kept nearer to the sledge. If t
dogs are not accustomed to one another a team is almo
unmanageable. They must know their leader and his authori
is almost unlimited. When the dogs are fed he takes the choi

morsels; when two of them quarrel he bites both. The shaggy Eskimo dog is of a single breed throughout the entire range of the culture. The ordinary team to-day consists of five or six dogs, and in considering the economy of the Eskimo the need for feeding these dog teams must always be borne in mind. For them as well as the family the hunter must supply seal meat throughout the winter. Before rifles were introduced the Eskimo could not support the large dog teams that are found to-day and few families had more than two or three dogs.

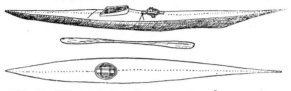

FIG. 53. TWO IGLULIK KAYAKS, 19 AND 18 FEET LONG
(*After photographs by Mathiassen*)

But for summer hunting on rivers, lakes and the coastal waters the kayak is their indispensable vehicle. On a canoe-shaped frame of whalebone or wood a cover of seal skins is tightly bound with thongs. The top is entirely covered save for an oval man-hole in which the hunter sits and manipulates his double paddle. A number of rests and thongs are arranged to hold the hunting equipment.

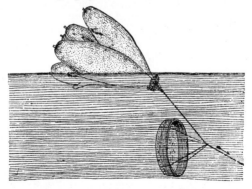

FIG. 54. SEAL BLADDERS AND HIDE HOOP ATTACHED
TO HARPOON LINE FOR TIRING LARGER BEASTS
(*After Boas*)

In Alaska and Greenland the *umiak*, or woman's boat, is used not only on journeys but for hunting larger animals, especially the whale. The umiak is similarly skin covered, but it is wide and open and propelled with long single paddles. In the central area to the west of Hudson Bay as far as Coronation Gulf the Eskimo have no umiaks.

The Eskimo harpoon is one of the most remarkable and ingenious of primitive weapons. Details of construction vary with the particular purpose but in general it consists of five essential parts:

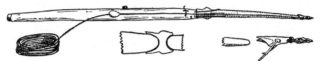

FIG. 55. CENTRAL ESKIMO HEAVY WALRUS HARPOON SHOWING
DETAILS OF HEAD AND SECTION OF SOCKET
(*After Boas*)

(1) A stout wooden shaft of four to five feet.
(2) An ivory head rammed tightly on the shaft with a socket on its upper surface into which fits:
(3) A fore-shaft of walrus tusk one to three feet long. This is bound by thongs to the main shaft but can swivel through a small angle in its socket.
(4) The harpoon head of bone, now provided with an iron blade, socketed to fit on the end of the fore-shaft. The head is designed to turn in the flesh of the wounded animal and so hold it when trying to escape.
(5) The harpoon line attached through lateral holes in the point and then drawn tightly down and round an ivory knob midway along the wooden shaft. The rest of the line lies coiled at the hunter's side.

For seal hole hunting thrusting harpoons and for sea hunting throwing harpoons are used. In either case, when the point strikes home the fore-shaft bends over sufficiently to release the point and the wounded animal is played on the line, which is allowed to run out. For the easier tiring and capture of larger animals in sea hunting inflated seal bladders and a hide-covered hoop are often attached to the harpoon line. The first prevent the animals diving while the hoop attached to lie across the line of pull sets up a resistance which the harpooned animal has to overcome and is thereby more quickly exhausted. The fish and bird spears are similarly ingenious and carefully finished weapons. Before the introduction of firearms the swifter land animals, and especially the caribou, could only be taken with spear or bow and arrow. The bow is made usually of three sections of wood or caribou antler strips rivetted and bound together in various ways. It is reinforced with strands of sinew lashed to the outer face and forms a very powerful weapon. (See fig. 45).

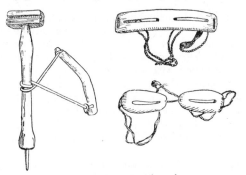

FIG. 56. IGLULIK BOW DRILL (LEFT) AND IVORY
SNOW GOGGLES
(*After photographs by Mathiassen*)

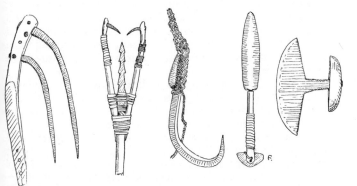

FIG. 57. ESKIMO IMPLEMENTS OF NATIVE COPPER FROM CORONATION
GULF
(ON VARIOUS SCALES). FROM LEFT TO RIGHT: GAFF HOOK OF ANTLER WITH
COPPER PRONGS FOR ATTACHMENT TO A LONG POLE; FISH SPEAR WITH COPPER
BARBS AND CENTRE BARB OF ANTLER; COPPER FISH-HOOK ON SINEW LINE;
SNOW-KNIFE IN ANTLER HANDLE; WOMAN'S KNIFE WITH WOODEN GRIP
(*After photographs by Cadzow*)

The efficiency of Eskimo bone work is largely dependent on the possession of a bow drill. The shaft is held firm by gripping the mouthpiece in the teeth while the bow is moved to and fro across the body with one hand to rotate the drill whose stone or metal point bites into the wood or bone. The same drill is sometimes used for fire making. A hard willow point is rotated in a driftwood board with a tinder of dried moss. But many Eskimo groups more frequently made fire with a strike-a-light of flint and iron pyrites.

The Eskimo in the neighbourhood of the Coppermine River, which enters Coronation Gulf, have taken advantage of the nuggets of pure copper which are exposed on the surface in several places. Pieces of the soft metal have been broken up and then hammered with stone to fashion chopping knives of distinctive shape. The use of native copper has also been noticed on the Northwest Coast, where the objects made are very different.[1] In far north-western Greenland there is one of the few large deposits of telluric iron. This native metallic iron was also used by the Eskimo of that district and fashioned into knives and points.

The origin of the Eskimo and their way of life has probably been more discussed than the similar problems of any other primitive people. Apart from a great deal of loose speculation much comparative study based on recent field investigations has been devoted to Eskimo questions. The fantastic theory that the Eskimo are lineal descendants of the later cave hunters of Europe, based as it was on an inconsistent medley of alleged racial and cultural parallels has been finally dismissed, and some of the stages in the development of this northern culture have been clearly established.

It is first of all necessary to realize clearly that although Eskimo culture is basically similar over a wide range, the distribution of special features affords important clues to the development of their economy. Some elements are universal. Such are the bow and arrow, salmon spear, ridge pole tent and the caribou hunting methods, all concerned with summer land activities; the harpoon, and also the kayak, which is absent among the Polar Eskimo of north-western Greenland alone. More restricted are a group of elements or traits which are found only under truly Arctic conditions and slowly disappear towards the south-west and south-east. Among these are the dog sledge, the snow house and ice hunting methods. Finally in the sub-arctic margins of the Eskimo area to west and east where these disappear we find on both sides modifications which are equally lacking in the central area. The most important of these are

---

[1] Beaten copper ornaments were also widely made from native copper in the south-eastern United States and the metal was bartered over considerable distances. The smelting of copper from ores was quite unknown north of southern Mexico.

specialized forms of kayak and hunting equipment associated with sea hunting and the umiak.

The first important question is the relation of the peripheral sub-arctic culture to that of the central and Arctic. In the central area all the characteristic methods and implements of the Eskimo are found. Moreover, the types of implements and weapons such as the kayak and harpoon are simpler here, while in Alaska and southern Greenland they are further elaborated in relation to local needs or have degenerated. The development of the sub-arctic sea kayak from the central Eskimo river kayak can be traced in great detail. One group of sub-arctic activities cannot, however, be interpreted in this way. This is the hunting of large sea beasts, especially the whale, from the big open boat. The umiak is not used in parts of the central area where the shortness of the seasons of open water renders it, like the elaborated sea kayak, almost useless, but it is of great importance both in south-western Alaska and southern Greenland. Whale fishing in open wooden boats is, moreover, extensively practised by the littoral peoples of the north-eastern shores of Asia, and expeditions into Eskimo water could readily have introduced this boat to the western Eskimo, who may have reproduced it in skin, the material of their kayaks. The use of pottery, and other special features among the Alaskan Eskimo point strongly to such Asiatic contacts. To account for the appearance of the umiak in Greenland it must be assumed that the new boat type was carried eastwards and was used sufficiently for a time by central peoples, for it to become known in the east, where again it could serve a very valuable purpose. The so-called Thule culture of the central area, which has now died out but has been recovered by archaeological investigations, included a number of elements not found to-day in the centre, but common to Alaska and Greenland and forming a link between them. Cogent reasons for considering the sub-arctic cultures as in the main derived from the Arctic have also been shown by Boas in a comparative study of myth and legend.

The next point to consider is the relation of the little groups of Caribou Eskimo of the Barren lands to the Arctic Eskimo on the one hand and to the northernmost Indian peoples of the forest-tundra fringe on the other. Some close similarities can be found between the economy of the Indian caribou hunters, the Barren Ground Eskimo and the summer activities of the Arctic Eskimo. That all make drives of animals towards ambushes may not be of great significance, since this, as will already have been realized, is widespread among hunting peoples and is probably a very ancient device, but the use of snow-shoes by the Caribou Eskimo and by some groups in the central area, the close similarity of the type of salmon spear, the formation of caches and treatment of hides are important parallels. Still more remarkable, the winter fishing through holes in the river ice practised by the northern Indians is essentially similar to the *maupok* and *ituarpok* methods of Eskimo seal hunting. This has led to the suggestion that the Arctic Eskimo may be a Canadian tundra people who have migrated north to the shore and adapted their life to conditions there. The recent demonstration of the racial similarity of some of the Eskimo to some of the northern Indians on the tundra border to-day would seem to favour this view. But the Arctic Eskimo possess many implements and devices absent among any Indian group, and which cannot be ascribed directly to environmental adaptation. These include the dog-drawn sledge (as opposed to the Indian man-hauled toboggan), the bow drill, the skin-covered kayak, the double paddle, the socketed harpoon, tailored clothing, the blubber heating lamp and many others. Since it can be shown that several of these are found in north-eastern Asia, it would appear that not only the umiak and other features of the western sub-arctic culture are of Asiatic origin, but that many important Arctic traits derive thence as well.

The investigations of ancient and deserted habitations at many sites from Greenland to the Asiatic shore have proved not only that the essential culture of the Eskimo has been in existence for perhaps two thousand years, but also that it is to-day impoverished in certain areas, especially to the west of Hudson Bay, as compared with a former time when the people were more effective hunters of sea mammals. Although there is abundant and widespread evidence of this earlier phase, known as the Thule culture, no trace has yet been found of a stage when hypothetical forerunners of the Eskimo came to the Arctic shores from the Barren grounds of Canada. More-over, a possible forerunner of the Thule culture has been found at sites on islands in the Bering Straits. That the dog sledge, harpoon, bow drill, large open boat, tailored clothing and several other devices were derived from Asiatic contacts is generally admitted. It still remains unknown, however, whether these elements were later additions to an early and still unknown Eskimo culture, native to North America, or whether they were introduced into arctic North America and Greenland by early Eskimo spreading eastwards from the Asiatic shore and the Bering Sea.

PART II

CULTIVATORS

CHAPTER IX

THE BORO OF THE WESTERN AMAZON FOREST

THE Boro are a group of more than ten thousand South American Indians living in some fifty separate and independent settlements, but speaking closely related dialects of a single language. They occupy a tract of country only a degree or so south of the Equator and about five thousand square miles in extent, in the region where the frontiers of Brazil, Peru and Colombia meet in the heart of the Amazon jungle. It lies between the Japura and the Putumayo or Issa Rivers, large tributaries of the Upper Amazon.

The natives of the western Amazon basin have the essential physical characters of the American Indian, brown skin, straight black hair and medium stature, but there are considerable variations in detail from group to group. The Boro are in general lighter skinned than their south-western neighbours, the Witoto, who are also shorter and more heavily built. Both are broad in face and generally mongoloid in features. What little body hair they have is removed from time to time by smearing on rubber latex, which on drying is pulled away, bringing the hairs with it. The women cut or singe their hair to a long bob, but most men wear it uncut, hanging loosely down the back.

The floor of the Amazon basin is one of the greatest alluvial plains in the world. Opening out westwards between the mountainous massifs of the Guiana and the Brazilian highlands, it extends for over two thousand miles from the Atlantic to end abruptly at the foot of the eastern flank of the Andean ranges. These rise steeply in less than a hundred miles from only five hundred feet to altitudes of over ten thousand feet above sea-level. A fan of great rivers descending from the surrounding highlands and swollen by the equatorial rains has filled the basin to great depths with alluvium. River mud and decaying vegetation have been slowly built up in great thicknesses of soft black soil. The plain itself is largely the product of the ancestors of the Amazon and its great feeders which have filled the shallow sea of an earlier geological time with thick deposits weathered from the slopes of the Andes and the

Guiana highlands. Thus an enormous lowland has been built up, most of it still less than five hundred feet above sea-level. Although the lower Amazon flows through undulating country the upper basin is a smooth plain whose eastward slope is perceptible only in the sluggish movement of the rivers. Below the foothill country the plain is completely stoneless until the lower Amazon valley is reached, for the underlying rock is almost nowhere exposed and fine silt alone is carried by the slow-moving rivers.

This great lowland area extending nearly ten degrees to either side of the Equator is strongly heated by the high sun throughout the year. Shifting its position with the march of the seasons there is a focus of greatest heat and rising air into which breezes blow from all directions. The strongest and most important air stream is the current formed by the converging trade winds of the Atlantic which blow up the relatively narrow valley of the lower Amazon almost throughout the year and bear a constant supply of ocean moisture. But within the upper Amazon basin above Manaos, winds are more variable, and in the west the irregular breezes change their normal direction with the movement of the centre of greatest heat.

After the hottest period towards the end of the year, there follows a period of calms and the months of heaviest rain. Mean temperatures actually vary but little from month to month, and the difference between dawn and afternoon on a single day, often 10° to 15° F., is greater than the mean variation from season to season. The great humidity of this equatorial lowland prevents intense heating of the land, and temperatures, although always warm, are rarely torrid. June is the coolest month, and at this time when occasionally a cold south-west wind blows down from the Andean plateaux, there may be a sudden chill and, within a few hours, a fall of more than 15° F. below normal temperatures. Although some years are as a whole definitely colder than others, the mean daily temperature in general remains between 80° and 85° F. throughout the year. For seven months, from November to May, with maxima in January and March, the heavy rains fall. Then for five months there is a less rainy, but by no means dry, season. Although for a week or two in the year there may be no rainfall, at other times showers occur almost daily. Clouds roll up before dawn and again in the afternoon, and rain falls. Mists shroud the rivers both in the early morning and evening. Nothing is ever dry: land and air are continually saturated.

From the mountainous regions which flank this basin and

receive even greater precipitation flow the great feeders of the
Amazon. The Issa is more than a third of a mile wide at its
junction with the Amazon, and farther upstream, where it
passes through southern borders of the Boro territory, it is
already nearly two hundred yards across. The heavy rainfall
in the first half of the year in the basin itself and on the slopes
of the Andean and Guiana highlands causes the rivers to rise
steadily from ten to twenty feet between February and June,
after which the water-level falls away to a minimum in October.
This annual flood is not turbulent, for the country is flat and
the watercourses are enormous, but it inundates wide stretches
of riverine lands and causes the collapse on a prodigious scale
of steep river banks cut in the soft muds and clays. The
Kahuanari River, which flows through the heart of the Boro
country to join the Japura is, however, liable to very sudden
floods after heavy rains. It sometimes rises as much as twenty
feet in a single day.

This enormous plain, intersected by many great rivers and
innumerable tributary streams, is covered without a single
extensive break over more than two million square miles, by
dense equatorial forest. The damp heat and the rich alluvial
soil, fertilized by the decay of the vegetation itself, promotes
the proverbially luxuriant growth of equatorial forest in which
the dense foliage of the taller trees forms a roof of vegetation,
while beneath flourishes a dense undergrowth of palms, bushes
and creepers.

In this monotonous tangle the wider rivers provide almost
the only continuous openings to the sky and avenues of easy
passage. The forest rises from the water's edge and within a
few yards every bearing is lost in the dense bush. Creepers of
many kinds and of every size, from huge cables to thin cords,
loop from tree to tree, pushing up to the sunlight and knotting
the undergrowth into impenetrable thickets. Lichens and
mosses cover the tree trunks. The spines of the palms which
grow in the shade of the loftier trees, the thorns of climbing
plants and the attacks of ants and flies add to the difficulties
of travel in the forest. Communication over any considerable
distance is forced on to the waterways.

The Boro, like all other peoples of the Japura River region,
occupy small clearings in the forest, which are made by
laboriously burning down the trees in some relatively open tract.
In such a clearing, rarely more than a few hundred yards or
so in any direction, some fifty to two hundred individuals have
their habitation and cultivated plots. The group does not live
in scattered huts but occupies a single large house, sixty to

seventy feet long on each side and thirty or more feet high. The forms of the communal houses of the west Amazon tribes vary in different areas. Those of the Boro are square in plan with rounded corners, and rise to a high transverse ridge pole. Large trunks, twenty to thirty feet high, obtained by burning down tall forest trees, form the main supports of the roof; cross beams and rafters are lashed to them with creepers. Folded palm leaves, closely set in split bamboos are tied to the framework in an overlapping thatch a foot or more in thickness. The sloping roofs are brought down to within almost a yard of the ground and the low vertical walls are similarly thatched or covered with matting. In these large

FIG. 58. A BORO SETTLEMENT
(*Based on photographs by Whiffen*)

and lofty houses, which from within resemble nothing so much as a circus tent, the whole group lives. Each family of man, wife and children has its own fireplace close against some part of the wall of the communal house, where utensils and possessions are kept and the sleeping hammocks are hung close above the fire. Among some other Amazon tribes each family screens off its quarters with matting partitions. The central area is kept clear as a place of assembly and dancing. There are no deliberate openings for light or ventilation in the house and the doorway is merely a small covered aperture in the low wall. Light and air filter in through the same cracks in the thatching which permit the smoke of the fires to be slowly dissipated.

Outside the house there is usually an open space or dancing

ground, and beyond it, at the far end of the open space and in adjacent smaller clearings, is the cultivated ground.

Settlements are nearly always situated well away from the main rivers and often at some distance from the stream used for water and bathing. Here the occupants are more secure against both flood and the attacks of enemies and also insect pests which are particularly bad near the river banks. The path to the stream is never straight and open, but is made deliberately tortuous and is usually interrupted by a stretch of uncleared jungle through which those who know it can pick their way by a zigzag route.

These laboriously made clearings and the large communal houses, which demand a great deal of time and effort for their construction, are not, however, occupied for any length of time. The houses once built are rarely repaired, and after a few years, when the thatch begins to leak, when the gardens lose their fertility, and when, moreover, the site of the village begins to be known by hostile groups, the place is abandoned. A new clearing is made a few miles away, a new house is built and fresh plots are laid out for cultivation.

The Boro have no domestic animals. They do not even keep dogs, although these are found among most Amazon peoples. The men hunt the wild game of the forest, but this is relatively meagre and elusive; the main dependence is on agriculture. The heavy labour of forest clearing and the rough digging of the ground with a wedge-ended stick is done by the men, but the rest of the agricultural work and the preparation of food is the duty of the women. The plots appear to be regarded as the property of the men, but ownership, as distinct from labour, is of little significance and the question of inheritance scarcely arises since a clearing is only of value for a few years.

Apart from the larger plot owned by the chief of the settlement, which is usually in the main clearing, the cultivated areas are scattered in a number of isolated patches in the surrounding jungle. Most of them are within a mile or so of the house, but others may be as much as a day's journey away, and their owners sometimes build and live in temporary huts nearby during the planting season.

When a new patch of cultivation is to be made, the larger trees are felled by burning and the small growth hacked down with stone axes at the end of the wetter season. The axes of the Japura peoples are square-ended wedges of polished stone, grooved near the butt for hafting with fibre and pitch to a stout stick. This rough tool is used for clearing brush, for splitting wood in building the houses, canoes, and for a dozen miscellaneous tasks. Stone axes are rare and treasured possessions, passed on from generation to generation and often accredited with magical properties. For the country is completely stoneless and a lost axe can only be replaced on some infrequent and uncertain opportunity for barter. Thus, being so poor in stone and lacking all knowledge of metals, the Boro make nearly all their implements of wood and bone, while boring and scraping tools can be more easily improvised from sharp animal teeth.

The tree stumps left on a clearing soon decay or are reduced by the swarms of ants. When the rains have slackened the undergrowth and creepers are burned out by starting a number of fires which often smoulder uncertainly in the equatorial dampness. The ground is then roughly broken by the men with heavy wooden stakes and clubs, and in this wilderness of charred trunks and uneven ground the women go out in parties to plant the crop with simple digging sticks. The same tool serves as spade, hoe and rake in their struggle to combat the quick growing wild vegetation that threatens to stifle their plants. Planting can go on throughout the year, but there is a main harvest from the sowings made during the heavy rain season. Cultivated ground is exhausted after only two or three harvests and a new plot must then be cleared. The old patch may be revisited for survivors of formerly cultivated plants and for wild fruits, but it is not tilled again.

The most important crop raised is manioc, from the roots of which cassava is prepared. Several species of manioc grow wild in the forest, but the cultivated varieties yield larger tubers. The first tubers can be dug about eight months after planting, though some kinds are allowed to develop in the ground for two or three seasons before they are dug. Manioc is propagated by replanting cuttings from the old growth each in a separate hole. Other root crops, especially yams and sweet potatoes, are also grown in smaller quantities, while pumpkin seeds are planted and then left to propagate themselves. Peppers, beans, pineapples and a few fruit-bearing trees are also grown. Little maize is cultivated by the Boro and their neighbours, although it is much grown by other Amazon peoples, despite the unsuitability of this sub-tropical cereal to the damp equatorial climate.

The most important crops after manioc are, however, the stimulants—coca and tobacco. The coca shrub is difficult to raise and receives much attention in its early stages. When new bushes are needed seed is planted when the heaviest rains begin, and with good fortune these produce a bushy shrub growing to a height of five or six feet, which, after eighteen months, bears its narcotic fruit for thirty to forty years. Coca is planted and tended by the men and the narcotic is forbidden to women, but tobacco, which is similarly forbidden to women, is nevertheless planted and prepared by them.

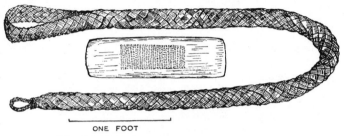

ONE FOOT

FIG. 59. BORO CASSAVA GRATER AND SQUEEZER
(After photographs by Whiffen)

The manioc tubers which go on developing for several seasons vary from a half to several pounds in weight and are dug for food as they are required. Little or none of the crop is stored, either dried or cooked, in the houses. Although sweet manioc grows wild it is little used and the most important and productive species — *Manihot utilissima*—contains poisonous quantities of prussic acid in its juices. To extract this the roots are sliced, soaked for a day or more with a piece of rotten manioc, which promotes fermentation in the rest and frees some of the poisons. They are then grated on an oval wooden board closely set with small projecting palm spines. The grated manioc is then tightly packed in a squeezer—a long, finely meshed cylinder of plaited palm bark seven or more feet long. One end of the cassava squeezer is attached by a loop to a convenient rafter in the house. A stout stick is fixed at the other end, and on this the woman sits, bearing down with all

FIG. 60. AN AMAZONIAN CASSAVA SQUEEZER
(From description by Whiffen)

her weight, so that the contents of the cylinder are compressed and most of the juice pressed out. The pulp, after being left to dry, is powdered by hand into a flour; this is heated in a platter and frequently stirred to remove more volatile poisonous matter. After this lengthy process the flour is kneaded with water and lightly baked on a clay dish to form a tough, leathery cake of unleavened bread. The water squeezed from the manioc is boiled till it thickens to paste, and seasoned with peppers and fish this is used as a sauce for cassava. Among some peoples this manioc water also affords a meat preservative but this process is unknown to the Boro and their neighbours who must eat their game soon after it is killed. Manioc leaves are also boiled and eaten as a vegetable after being pounded very fine and seasoned with such fish, worms and insects as happen to be available.

Honey is an important ingredient in drinks prepared for feasts and is collected from hollow trees and branches where bees make their nests, while the Menimehe, the northern neighbours of the Boro, set up hollow trunks in the thatch of their houses for bees to swarm in.

The women make pottery, netted hammocks and most of the basketry. The more elaborate and decorated pottery made by a few Japura river peoples is bartered over considerable distances, but plain bowls and dishes are made by all groups. Selected clay from the river bank is mixed with wood ashes. The pots are built up in coils and baked by covering them with hot ashes and slow burning fuel. Larger receptacles, used especially for intoxicating drinks at dances and feasts, are roughly shaped out of bark or hollowed wood. The Boro, like most of the northern peoples of South America, sleep in hammocks. These are rectangles of netting of palm or other fibre cords stretched by two sticks and slung less than a yard from the ground by ropes tied to convenient house posts. They are made on a simple frame of two upright posts round which a long cord is passed to and fro with intervals of an inch or two between each strand. Cross cords running vertically are then knotted in position. Finely patterned leg and arm bands are also knotted with the fingers without any frame or even warp and woof bands. Fine matting is made, but true weaving is unknown. Bark cloth is the only other clothing material.

Basketry of simple shapes but of fine quality and much of it worked in intricate patterns is made with bark strips, cane and palm leaves, by both men and women. Large, durable baskets slung on the back from a head band are used by the women for carrying back food from the plots, and the hunter quickly contrives a basketry sling from the leaves of surrounding trees to carry back any game he may take in the forest.

Although aware of the adhesive properties of the latex of rubber trees and vines the Japura peoples have not acquired the special uses to which it is put by some upper Amazon tribes, who make from it elastic rings, hollow rubber balls and syringes. They do, however, use it to cap their drum sticks.

The hunting and trapping of wild game is the daily task of men. There is a considerable variety of wild life from tapir, peccary or bush pig, ant-bear and sloth, to the numerous species of rodents, small monkeys and birds—parrots, macaws, toucans, egrets and so on—and reptiles, but no species is abundant and hunting is impeded by the closeness of the vegetation. The hunters are, however, extremely skilled in identifying tracks and anticipating the movements of game. Their detailed knowledge of the forest life and their ability in deducing extremely precise information from scanty tracks have amazed European explorers. In hunting the larger animals, especially tapirs, light spears are effective up to a range of about thirty yards. The hunter carries several of them, some ready to hand and others in a bamboo case. The spear, made of the hard wood of a particular palm, tapers towards the butt; it is scraped smooth, like other wooden weapons and utensils, with the file-like jaw of the pirai fish and polished with rough-surfaced leaves. The short head which holds a poisoned spine of bamboo is made separately and bound on to the shaft. Pits floored with poisoned stakes and concealed by brushwood are dug across frequented tracks, and drives are often made by a party of men who beat up the game, forcing it to cross a line of these pits. Deadfalls of logs are set across tracks in the forest to trap anything from a rat to a jaguar which may pass that way.

But by far the most important weapon is the blowpipe, similar in form and principle to the south-east Asiatic weapon, with which light poisoned darts are shot at the birds, monkeys and other animals in the trees. The Boro blowpipe is from eight to fourteen feet long. Smaller ones are made of reeds, but most are made in two pieces from a small palm which has a hollow stem an inch or two in outer diameter. Half sections of the pipe are made from separate stems, which, by splitting, scraping and rubbing, are made to fit exactly when they are bound together from end to end with fibre or bark. The bore, about a quarter inch in diameter, is polished by pulling through strings to which sand has been made to adhere with gum; the outside of the tube is coated in gum or wax. A mouthpiece of

vegetable ivory or other wood is fitted to one end and a small
projecting bone is fixed about a foot from the mouthpiece to
serve as a sight. The darts of palm leaf stem are about nine
inches long and no thicker than a match. They are carried in
a small grass-lined bamboo quiver to protect their delicate
points. To this quiver is attached a small gourd containing
a supply of fluffy down from the seed capsules of the wild silk-
cotton tree, with which each arrow is tufted before insertion
into the tube. This tuft provides the airtight plug and steadies
the flight of the dart, which can be shot accurately by an expert
to a mark a hundred and fifty feet away. The smallest birds
can be hit at fifty feet. Although blunt darts are sometimes
used to stun small birds the points are usually sharpened and
partly cut through to break off in the wound.

Still more important is the poisoning of the tip, for the
wound inflicted by these light darts is in itself slight. The
Amazon Indians prepare the most effective poisons of any
savage people. The most important is the famous curare, a
poison which completely paralyses its victim within a few
seconds. This is made by a complicated recipe, greatly
treasured and passed on from father to son, in which the sap
of the *Strychnos toxifera* is the most important ingredient.
Putrefying animal matter is also used in the preparation of
other poisons. The Boro are not among the most skilful
poison makers, and they, like many others, obtain much of
their supply from a few groups such as the Andoke who are
especially skilled in the manufacture of the most potent forms.
Poison is usually carried in a small pot, hung from a necklace
ready for smearing on the points of dart or javelin.

Although there are many fish in the rivers, the Boro pay
less attention to them than many of their neighbours who
use trident fish spears, nets and traps and baited fish-hooks
of bone and palm spines. But the most general way of taking
fish on a large scale is by poisoning, with pounded babasco
root, the waters of a section of river above a weir of wattle
fencing which prevents the dead and drugged fish from drifting
away downstream. Babasco acts with great rapidity on all
but the largest fish, but does not affect their use for human
food.

In a Boro community the only large meal of the day is at
sundown when the bag of game has been brought in and the
cassava bread is baked. For the rest, the Japura river people
drink an infusion of herbs on rising, eat some cold cassava
bread or dip into the stock pot after bathing, and during the
day eat only such of the many wild fruits as they come across

Each family has its stock pot, strongly seasoned with peppers, which simmers almost continually over the fire and is constantly replenished by miscellaneous grubs, fish and offal as well as most of the larger game. At the evening meal the men eat their fill first, each at his own fire. The unmarried youths contribute to the large pot at the chief's hearth, and are fed there from that pot and with cassava bread prepared by his wife and female dependants.

The fires are kept continually burning and the three long logs pointing to the centre are pushed in as they burn away. The peoples to the north of the Japura can make fire and kindle tinder by rotating a reed in a piece of notched wood, a slow and difficult process in the humid and equatorial forest. But the Boro and other Japura peoples are to-day ignorant of any method of firemaking, and whenever individuals leave the house on a lengthy expedition they take smouldering torches of resinous wood some two feet long which can be blown into flame when required.

Coca is used habitually by the Boro and many Amazon peoples, as well as by the inhabitants of the Andean plateau to the west. The leaves of the plant which contain the cocaine are dried over a fire and then pounded up in small wooden mortars with lime obtained by burning certain palm leaves, baked clay that is scraped from beneath the hearth and some powdered cassava flour. The resulting powder is carried in a bark pouch worn round the neck. From time to time a quantity of the powder shaken into a leaf is shot into the mouth, where it forms a ball of paste from which the cocaine is gradually absorbed in the saliva. These people acquire a remarkable tolerance for the drug, which enables them, when taken in considerable quantities, to go several days without sleep, food or drink.

Mineral salt is unobtainable by the Boro and neighbouring peoples except by occasional and indirect barter from great distances. Small quantities of salts are obtained by burning certain saline plants. It has been suggested that this deficiency of salts accounts for the frequent practice of eating certain earths, and particularly clay scraped from beneath the hearth.

Although tobacco is smoked by some of the western Amazon peoples, those in the neighbourhood of the Japura river only prepare it in the form of a paste, which they lick. The leaves are soaked and pounded in a mortar. Some cassava starch is added to stiffen it to a dark pasty fluid which is kept in small pots made from a hollowed nut-shell. Through the small opening is dipped a stick from which the tobacco liquid is then licked. Tobacco is used both privately and ceremonially. At the meetings of all the adult men of the community when they discuss public affairs and settle disputes the tobacco pot is passed round before every decision; all who agree with the spokesman dip a stick in the pot and lick it and the discussion continues until a strong majority opinion for some course is obtained. The dipping of sticks into each other's pots is also used to emphasize and bind an agreement between individuals.

Loin-cloths worn by the Boro men are made of bark cloth, which is also used for various wrappings. The fibrous inner bark of several wild trees provides the material, which is stripped off in narrow lengths some two yards long; these are soaked in the river and beaten out with a grooved wooden mallet. Some of the neighbouring peoples wear aprons over their loin-cloths and others long shirts of bark cloth. A few plait strips of it tightly round the trunk to form rigid stays, which are claimed to increase the force of the expiration in shooting with the blowpipe. The women, as so frequently elsewhere in the Amazon basin, go completely naked save for patterned bands of hand-knotted fibres bound tightly round the calves; these are apparently purely ornamental. For the elaborate dances, however, they paint their bodies in intricate designs of several colours and wear necklaces and girdles of seeds and bartered glass beads, while the men have large and gaily coloured feather head-dresses. Ornamented plugs of wood and shell are generally worn by both men and women in the ear lobes and the lips.

In every house there is a pair of large signal drums or slit gongs, similar in principle to those of south-eastern Asia and Melanesia. There is an elaborate code common to all Boro settlements. Complicated messages and instructions are sent out and can be clearly heard over a radius of ten miles and more. These gongs are always used in pairs and in two sizes. Two trunks of hardwood about six feet long and up to two feet in diameter are felled and trimmed and squared off. A narrow slit with larger openings at each end is then made lengthwise down the trunk. Through this with borers of animal teeth and red-hot stones the interior is laboriously hollowed out. One end is hollowed less than the other so that the shell varies in thickness and distinct notes are obtained from the two ends of a gong. The smaller 'male' gong gives higher notes than the 'female'. They are slung from convenient rafters in the house and the drummer stands between them striking rapidly with a rubber-headed mallet. The signal gongs are occasionally used at the bigger dance feasts, but small playing drums of hollowed palm trunks or bamboo, with drumheads of taut monkey skin, are the more usual accompaniments of the flutes and pan-pipes at festivals.

For river travel dugout canoes sometimes reaching twenty feet in length but little more than a foot wide are burnt and hewn out of cedar, laurel and other suitable trunks. After the tree has been laboriously felled and cut to length by hacking holes at several points round its girth and splitting off pieces by wedging and levering with the stone axe, a fire is kindled along the log. The burning embers are scraped away as the fire eats deeper into the trunk, and while the wood is still hot the sides of the canoe are spread with stretchers, which also produce an upward curve at bow and stern. A community rarely has more than one or two of these dugout canoes, which require a considerable amount of labour and skill for their production, although little attention is devoted to ornamentation and fine finish. They are hidden by the river bank at the customary landing place, and the large elongated paddles are stored in the house. They are used for occasional journeys for feasting and barter at neighbouring settlements and by war parties. A smaller and improvised craft is made as need arises by individuals. The trunk of the bulge-stemmed palm is easily felled and split; the soft pulp within the hard bark can be removed with the hands if need be, and after stiffening the ends of the bulging section with clay, a serviceable coracle is available for short journeys. Although the waterways, in sharp contrast to the jungle, provide lines of easy movement, the peoples of this region are not great water men. No distant trading expeditions are made, nor, apparently, do many communities congregate for festivals. Barter is sporadic and between individuals. Foreign goods are but slowly and casually passed on from hand to hand as occasion arises. The tendency is to secrecy and isolation as displayed in the site of the house, rather than to embrace the opportunities for extensive travel on the calm and ramifying waterways. Save on rare occasions each community appears to keep very strictly to its territory.

Each Boro settlement, like those of neighbouring peoples, is an autonomous unit. As a people the Boro are in no sense an organized tribe. Their unity of speech, custom and even physical type results from the propinquity and intermarriage of the many small autonomous settlements of fifty to two hundred persons, into which they are divided. A few large settlements may consist of two or more communal houses in the same clearing or within short distances of one another, but these are rarer than smaller communities with but a single house. The individual settlements are the only ones to which a real political and social unity can be ascribed. But while only an exceptional individual or a serious danger effects co-operation between them, and although mutual hostility sometimes develops, there is in general however a definite sense of friendliness and community of interest among the Boro settlements as a whole, and this is true of the other language groups in the region. Each community has its own leader or chief who has a general but vague authority in group affairs, organizes defence and warfare and, by acquiring all captive women and feeding all unmarried youths in return for their hunting bag, has a larger household than the ordinary individual. Although chiefly authority usually descends from father to son in a single family it is nearly always subject to popular assent.

The other individual who stands out by virtue of his special functions is the medicine man. His knowledge of magic and his danger to all who would harm him allow him to travel into the jungle for his special purposes when other men nearly always arrange to move in small parties for their better protection. The medicine man is distinct from the chief or social leader of the community, and his powers are usually transmitted to a son, whom he instructs. He claims by his magic to identify the source, usually one of a number of traditional enemies, of any misfortune which overtakes the group. To the accompaniment of the most hysterical excitement he performs faith cures and extracts the magical substances which cause the sicknesses of individuals. In a bag of bark cloth or animal skin he carries his special rattle and a miscellaneous collection of objects such as a claw from a giant condor, a string of hard quartz beads, bored with great skill and labour, which are endowed with great magical power, and above all a pearl shell cup which he talks to in curing and uses to draw out the evil influence affecting his patient. The chief and the medicine man often wear more elaborate necklaces of animal and human teeth. The large teeth of the jaguar, whose form it is believed he can assume, are most commonly worn by the medicine man.

A man remains throughout his life with the community in which he was born, but he must take from another settlement the wife that he brings to live with his own group. The settlement group is therefore a stable patrilocal and exogamous unit. It is not constantly being broken up and re-founded, and there is a continuity of descent from the fathers to the sons who remain in the settlement, while the women leave to mate with men in other settlements. Within the group all children are thought of, and call themselves 'brothers' and 'sisters', just as all their elders are to them relatives of their parents.

The Boro community is therefore in effect a patrilineal exogamous clan. Moreover, the clans, unlike those among many other peoples where the members of any one clan are scattered, here form autonomous territorial and social units. Each clan community has a name which all its members take and pass on to their children. Each recounts the alleged deeds and wise sayings of its earlier generations. All this deepens the feelings of common descent and encourages the sense of unity.

The strange and widespread custom of 'couvade' whereby the father takes to his bed at the birth of a child and must observe many restrictions as to his diet and conduct, is elaborately developed in tropical South America. While a Boro woman will go off to dig in her manioc patch on the very day after her child is born, her husband must remain in his hammock for a month or more. While the mother had to avoid animal food before the child's birth, the father now assumes this taboo and for a period may not even touch or manufacture any weapon or article connected with the hunt.

Fighting between settlements of the different language groups, and even occasionally between settlements of the same speech is common in western Amazonia, but the motives, extent and duration of the attacks are rather obscure. Every community among the Boro and surrounding peoples regards the territory for several miles from its house and plantations as its own hunting and gathering ground. Although the settlement is shifted every few years the new site is never far distant from the old and remains within the traditional territory. Even in this dense jungle, it is claimed, boundary marks and fences are sometimes set up, while stream courses are often used to delimit territories. But apparently invasion of territory for economic reasons rarely occurs, and is not in itself a necessary cause of fighting. It is skill and patience, not increase of land, that are required to maintain the food-supply.

Long-continued hostility between certain peoples and groups nevertheless appears to be characteristic. The Boro and their immediate neighbours the Okaina and Resigero are united in a common hatred of the Witoto, who occupy a wide tract of country to the south-west. This is not associated with any significant difference in culture, for the Witoto are closely similar to the others in customs and way of life. Nor is there apparently any idea of permanent subjugation.

Neither the Boro nor any other group have any effective tribal organization, and conflicts are between small bands from one or a few temporarily combined communities. Nevertheless, attacks are long deliberated, and parties set out through the forest to wait in ambush until they can rush the enemy settlement when all its inmates are asleep or are preoccupied with a feast. No settlements are fortified, and, apart from occasional pitfalls constructed in times of special danger, each relies on the secrecy of its trails in the dense jungle. The most important weapons are those for hand to hand encounter. A flat sword about a yard long is made from tough and heavy ironwood with which to strike at the thighs of an opponent and bring him down so as to smash his head with the long, heavy club, which is also used as a quarterstaff. Spears, heavier than the hunting javelins, are also used in fighting, and the flat sword serves to ward them off, for the Boro and most of their neighbours do not carry the circular tapir hide shield used by some of the peoples farther north. The bow, which is used but little for hunting, is more effective than the blowpipe in fighting. Simple bows of various woods and arrows with poisoned tips of hard palm wood are carried by all war parties.

Prisoners are taken and are carried off by the victors in these encounters; the adults are killed and eaten at the dance feast which celebrates the event. Captured children too young to escape and so betray the settlement to the enemy are, however, handed over to the chief, who brings them up as members of his household in which they serve. These captives, in whom the community takes great pride as evidence of successful fighting, are in some sense slaves of the chief, but they soon come to be reckoned full members of the group. When adult they marry at their own choice and set up their own hearths in the house.

The ceremonial cannibalism practised at the feast which follows a successful fight must undoubtedly keep alive the spirit of revenge and the tradition of hostility, but there does not appear to be any express ritual demand for human victims as sacrifices in connexion with agriculture or other activities. Nor can the cannibalism be seriously assigned to a shortage of other meat or to a perverted desire for human flesh. Only small portions of the limbs of victims are eaten, and the rest is discarded as unclean. The skulls are often suspended as trophies in the house, but the Boro and other Japura peoples do not preserve the heads of their victims, as do the Jivaro in the far west and other tribes to the south of the Amazon main stream. The cannibalism of this area appears to be a faint echo of more elaborate ceremonial practices elsewhere.

The physical conditions of the Amazon forest would appear to be as adverse to cultural development as any tropical region in the world. Men live in small communities surrounded by dense forest, with but intermittent contacts one with another. But the isolation and low cultural level must not be exaggerated. Agriculture is known and practised everywhere, and besides the raising of roots native to the region, foreign plants, especially maize and beans, have been introduced, have spread throughout the region and are used almost everywhere. In post-Columbian times the banana has similarly spread to the most remote districts. The social group is far larger than among hunting peoples in equatorial areas, such as the Semang, while agriculture and large communal houses afford more stable food and shelter. With few exceptions, including pottery and dwellings, however, their crafts are but little more advanced; a consideration of these peoples leaves a general impression of cultural poverty. One cannot speak of tribes and tribal life. No cohesion exists among the many settlements of a single language group. There is very little differentiation in their simple crafts, and the elaborate trading and organization of markets characteristic of many African forest cultivators is entirely lacking. The Congo peoples would use waterways like those of the Amazon to overcome the difficulties of land travel. Fleets of canoes would cover great distances along the rivers. Political as well as economic combinations would have been effected. But the Amazon peoples merely slink along rivers; a small party in a single canoe travels warily to revenge some hostility asserted by the medicine man, or to obtain their mates in some adjoining and friendly community. Neither the limitations of resources such as the rarity of stone, nor even the remote and difficult nature of the country would seem wholly to account for the impression of cultural stagnation in this region. A few fundamental crafts such as cultivation and pot making, and the building of substantial dwellings—most of them probably introduced from outside at unknown times— have been adopted and organized in a parochial and isolating social life deeply tinged with fear of the evil magical power of all other men. It is a society in which the germs of further development seem to have been effectively killed.

CHAPTER X

THE YORUBA AND BOLOKI: HOE CULTIVATORS
IN THE AFRICAN FORESTS

THE peoples of the great forested areas of Equatorial Africa that occupy the Congo Basin and the Guinea coast lands are cultivators. Food-gatherers are a negligible minority who often depend on the agricultural peoples for part of their food-supply.

Although there is a fundamental and underlying unity in both the economy and social organization of the many autonomous groups living in this vast region, the elaborations of various crafts, the division of labour and the development of political organization differ greatly in various parts. Everywhere root crops are grown, but in some areas millet and banana cultivation are more prominent. Among some peoples cultivation is left almost entirely to the women; elsewhere, the men are highly skilled farmers. The political unit ranges from a small village of a few hundred people occupying a clearing in the bush to great native states with a population of more than a million and elaborate systems of government and tribute. In a general way male cultivation, the raising of millet and the development of large states is characteristic of the northern margins of this area, especially in West Africa, where the intrusions of northern peoples from the savanas have stimulated the elaboration of political organization and the specialization of arts and crafts. Yet, on the other hand, there are great native states on the Lower Congo, while the tropical forests of the Guinea coast still shelter small isolated village groups. The cultural history of this great region is little known, and no attempt to reconstruct it will be made here. The economy of a great West African native state, that of the Yoruba-speaking peoples, will be considered in some detail, since it exemplifies the great achievements of the negro peoples of forest Africa. Brief comparisons with a Bantu people of the central Congo—the Boloki—will afford an opportunity for observing the diversity to be found in this region.

In West Africa many small, independent tribal groups may be found, but a great part of the area is occupied by a few large native states, such as Ashanti, Yoruba and Edo, in which economic specialization and political integration are very advanced. The Yoruba-speaking peoples, who occupy the greater part of south-western Nigeria, number about two millions. Their territory of nearly forty thousand square miles

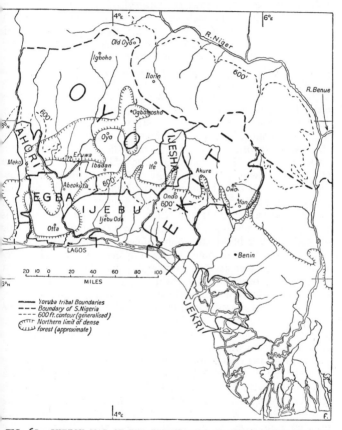

FIG. 61. SKETCH MAP OF THE TERRITORIES OF THE YORUBA TRIBES

extends from the Guinea coast, west of the Niger delta, two hundred miles inland to the Middle Niger where that great river is flowing south-east to join the Benue. There are considerable differences of dialect between the sub-tribes which have varying degrees of political and cultural independence.

The more eastern were in recent centuries under the control of the famous Edo kingdom of Benin, but the greater number owed their allegiance to the Alafin, or priest chief, of the largest group, the Oyo. The population is distributed in hundreds of small villages and several considerable towns. There are about two hundred and fifty towns or large villages with a population of over one thousand each, and fifteen towns of over twenty thousand people, while Ibadan, the largest native city in tropical Africa, has a population of nearly one hundred and fifty thousand or, if the farming suburbs be included, of nearly a quarter of a million. These people afford therefore a fair example of the great negro states which European adventurers of the sixteenth century were astounded to find on the west coast of Africa and along the Lower Congo river.

The Yoruba are as a whole fairly typical West African negroes. Although only about five feet six inches in stature their legs are often long. They are rather heavily built and very muscular. Their characteristic skin colour is a rich chocolate brown, and their kinky hair, which does not grow very long is usually close cropped. Beneath a narrow, high forehead the face juts out in marked prognathism with a flat nose, very wide nostrils and thick, everted lips. The chin is narrow and retreating. There are, however, many individuals of more slender build and more refined countenance.

The coast land of south-western Nigeria is low-lying and swampy. Parallel to the mainland a number of long, flat islands have been linked together by great accumulations of sand and mud swept into position by the strong Guinea current, so that a series of shallow, interconnected lagoons separates the mud flats of the mainland from the open ocean. The modern port of Lagos is situated at the only considerable gap in this coastal barrier which merges into the Niger delta in the west.

The low-lying coast land is, however, narrow. From twenty to sixty miles inland the country rises fairly steeply to a plateau of twelve to fifteen hundred feet. This upland of hard, igneous rocks, which separates the coastal plain from the middle Niger valley, is diversified by low ranges of hills and isolated eminences. Many small rivers flow southward in the direction of the general tilt, and fall in rapids to the coastal plain and lagoons.

The climate of this region is hot and wet for it lies within six and nine degrees of the Equator and immediately north of the warm waters of the Gulf of Guinea. But there are marked seasonal variations. During the summer half year, when the air streams flow landwards from the Gulf, land temperatures are high, and the average for most months is well over 80° F. This is also the wet season. Heavy rains fall from April to July and lighter rains, after a short pause, from August to October. These are periods of cloudy skies and stifling, damp heat. But during the rest of the year the prevailing winds are from the north-east, bringing air from the Sahara, which is cool at this season and always dry. From December to February these northern winds, known as the 'Harmattan', are very strong. Average monthly temperatures fall to 65° F. and for short spells are much lower. The length of the dry season increases inland and towards the north often lasts for five months.

The rain-bearing winds of early summer and autumn do not blow directly onshore, and the rainfall is far less than in the country to the east of the Niger, where coast and plateau curve south. On the coast land seventy to a hundred inches of rain may fall every year, but on the plateau the amount rapidly falls below sixty inches, and is less than fifty inches in the north-west.

Dense tropical forest is confined to the more humid areas of the coastal plains and the southern plateau. The brackish tidal waters of the lagoons are fringed with mangrove swamps and behind them lies the tall rain forest in which lofty smooth-barked evergreen trees and palms of many varieties rise through the dense undergrowth to heights of over two hundred feet. But on the plateau, as the rainfall diminishes north-wards and the dry season becomes longer and more complete, the forest gradually thins and stretches of tall grass diversify the country.

Although considerable tracts of forest land extend as far north as the bend of the Niger, they are increasingly confined to bottom lands, and the evergreen giants such as mahogany and teak are replaced by the deciduous baobab and locust trees. The tall grass is rank and green during the rainy season, when it may reach a height of twelve feet, but it withers down in the dry season and can be burnt off.

The coastal forest belt was until recently less densely settled than the plateau. The Yoruba did not advance into this tract until fairly recent times, and the clearings for fields and townships have made little impression on the luxuriant vegetation. On the plateau, however, centuries of cultivation in which land has been cleared by burning have reduced much of the forest to scattered patches of woodland.

Surrounded by these extensive clearings are the villages and towns. The dwellings are rectangular buildings with saddleback

gabled roofs. Walls four to eight feet high of solid clay are
built up of successive layers, each of which is packed in
position moist and allowed to dry out in the sun before proceeding with the next. The roofs, supported by tall posts, are
heavily thatched with leaves or grass, and the eaves, held up
by carved posts, are carried out far beyond the wall on the
front to cover a wide raised verandah. Sun-dried clay is an
unsuitable building material in a wet climate. Its use, like
much else in Yoruba culture is probably due to influence from
the north, where the great walled towns and flat-roofed houses

FIG. 62.   ENTRANCE TO A LARGE YORUBA COMPOUND

of the grasslands are built entirely of this material. The
Yoruba have, however, retained the thatched roof of the forest
culture and build overhanging eaves and verandahs which
protect the walls from disintegration in the rains.

The houses of related families are usually built in continuous
groups of four or more to enclose a square compound reached
through a single gateway. On the outside they present a
blank expanse of clay walling, and their entrances and the
verandahs stretching continuously from one house to the next,
face the compound. Inside the house are clay benches and
couches covered with skins. The walls are hung with utensils
and weapons, while food stores hang from the roof. There is
no hole above the fire pit, and smoke must find its way slowly
out through the door or the gaps between wall and thatch.
The rain-water flowing from the inner slope of the roofs,
especially where it is concentrated at the corners of the compound, is caught in large pottery butts and used for household

purposes. Special yards, like Roman impluvia, surrounded by steep pitched thatching are also built in the compounds to catch water.

All the larger villages and towns are surrounded at some distance from the compact group of compounds with a wall and outer ditch. Beyond them is often a belt of uncleared forest, which formerly, in time of war, reduced the risk of sudden rushes on the village by attackers and also afforded a retreat in case of defeat. Heavy wooden gates are provided at convenient points of access and each is in charge of an elder, who is responsible for its upkeep and defence and for collecting tolls payable by traders to the chiefs of the various quarters of the town.

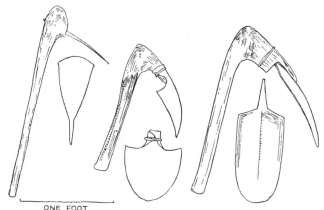

ONE FOOT

FIG. 63. NATIVE HOES FROM SOUTHERN NIGERIA
(*After specimens in the Wellcome Museum*)

Cultivation is the main activity of the Yoruba, as indeed of all the peoples of West Africa in the forest and wetter savana zones. The division of agricultural labour in West Africa is very variable. Among some peoples, especially among the semi-Bantu tribes in the East, it is, apart from the clearing of heavy bush, entirely women's work; but among the Yoruba and many other of the more western peoples almost all cultivation is in the hands of men. Digging sticks and large iron hoes are their only implements. The hoes are rectangular blades nearly a foot long and seven or eight inches broad, with a socket or tang at the base to take a short wooden handle set at a sharp angle. As agricultural implements they are far superior to the digging sticks of the Boro and, wielded by men, they turn up the soil to a much greater depth.

To prepare new plots in the forest belt, trees and brush are felled during the later rains and the short dry period, while in the more open country to the north the grass is burnt off in the dry season. Land can be farmed for longer periods in the forest belt where the same plot is tilled for two periods of five or six years, with a two or three year interval of fallow between. After that it is abandoned and will not be used for cultivation for another twenty years. But on the grassland a plot is exhausted after three or four years' cultivation, although it can be brought back into use after a comparatively short interval of four or five years. Thus the rapid exhaustion of field plots in the absence of any fertilizer other than the ashes of the original burning compels the abandoning of farms and the frequent clearing of new tracts of land. Among the Yoruba, where there are great concentrations of population in large villages and towns, the farmland may therefore lie a considerable distance from the settlement, so that while every household endeavours to maintain a few plots near at hand some of its members must often leave the main settlement for weeks at a time during important seasons of planting and harvest, while others, often serfs of wealthy families, remain permanently in small hamlets or isolated houses.

Yams are everywhere the food staple, and the main care of the cultivator, except in the driest northern parts. Several varieties are grown, and they are planted at different times, so that yam harvests succeed each other throughout the year. The heads of the ripened yams which have been stored for planting are set in flat, circular mounds of prepared soil about a foot high and two feet across, and the vines when they sprout are carefully trained on sticks. Between the mounds pumpkins and other plants are grown. Maize often ranks as the second crop in the forest country, but millet, which was the only grain cultivated before New World plants were introduced by the Portuguese, remains the most important in the grass country with its scantier and more uncertain rains. Cassava, the other great American food plant introduced into Africa, has only recently been adopted by the Yoruba. Bananas are the other important food. Ground nuts are grown in the north and rice is known but little cultivated in the coastal area. A large variety of beans, peas and flavouring plants are raised in smaller amounts.

Towards the end of the dry season the old plots are weeded. Some new land is cleared of trees and grass by burning and the ashes scattered over it as a fertilizer. Yam mounds are then carefully built of well-pulverized soil and are often protected with straw to reduce evaporation. For this heavy work the cultivators of neighbouring plots often unite to work successively on the lands of each member, but if a man cannot then get sufficient labour for clearing dense bush he offers a feast to those who will come to help or may give a present to the village chief in return for the services of his retainers. With the first rains the earliest yams are planted, and then, with the heavier rains, millet and corn, gourds and more yams. Two months of heavy rain follow, during which the plots must be continually hoed clear of weeds. In the 'little dry season' of about a month the first yams are dug and harvests of maize, millet and ground nuts are gathered. Second sowings are made in expectation of the later rains in the stormy months of September and October, and these are harvested in December. The yams to be used for seed are not dug until December, and their heads, or the entire roots if small, are stored in the house or surrounded with ashes in a mound to protect them against white ants. The yam harvests are often stored in the fields until they are required, for they must be kept in waterproof sheds on racks, each tuber separate from its neighbour; millet and maize are usually carried home to be stored in the heat and smoke of the roof over the fire.

Although the agricultural harvests among the Yoruba are many and abundant, they by no means complete the vegetable products, and two of the most important—palm oil and palm wine—are obtained from wild forest trees. The fruit of the oil palm is gathered by men, a slow and arduous task, for many of the palms are more than fifty feet high, and since they are a natural growth they are scattered irregularly through the dense forest. These trees are always spared when clearing land and are owned both singly and in groves by individuals who can maintain their claim though others cultivate the land on which they stand. The thick red oil is prepared by the women who boil the fruit after removing the tough rind and then press, beat and re-boil it several times until as much oil as can be extracted by this crude method has been skimmed off. Palm oil is used in the preparation of nearly every dish and is burned in pottery lamps for lighting. Wine is made by fermenting the sap of the raffia palm. The trees are tapped for this purpose and gourds attached below the incisions to catch the juice; when they are abundant, however, trees are often felled so that the 'cabbage' of young leaves at the top may be cut off and the sap drained out. The kola nut, which is the equivalent of the betel mixture of south-eastern Asia, is both a food and a stimulant and is gathered from wild and planted trees in the tropical belt.

Live stock are of little economic value. Domestic pigs are generally lacking and are not eaten. A poor breed of small black goat, far inferior to the brown goat of northern Nigeria, and a few head of non-humped cattle are to be found in most villages. The cattle, which appear to be immune to the tsetse fly, are something of a mystery, since all other native west African stock are of the humped zebu type; they may, however, be descendants of cattle introduced by the Portuguese in the fifteenth century. But before this time other domestic animals had arrived overland from the north. Chickens are raised, and both the flesh and eggs are eaten, but they are of more importance for sacrifices and divination.

The Yoruba formerly kept horses, but used them only for military purposes. Their cavalry gave them a great advantage over neighbouring peoples in the south.

The few chickens and goats kept by a household can often provide only an occasional supply of meat. But the activities of the Yoruba farmers are so continuous and the land often so closely settled, that save for short periods in the dry season they have little opportunity for the long expeditions generally necessary for successful hunting of such game as hartebeest water buck, eland and antelope. Where, as in the south eastern Yoruba country, game is still abundant in the un cleared bush, hunting has become the work of specialists, who do little else and obtain other products by bartering their surplus. These hunters form independent guilds whose mem bers act in concert under the direction of a leader who plans the expeditions and commands great respect and obedience In some places the hunters form separate villages or compounds in villages and nearly always marry among themselves. The guilds of different areas often form associations and provide mutual hunting privileges in their territories.

Fish are obtained in great quantities both on the coast and along the rivers but this again is largely a specialized activity The coastal villages do little but fish, dry their produce and trade it for agricultural produce from the interior. The inhabitants of riverine villages maintain rights over defined stretches of river whose fishing they supervise. The specialist fishermen and any others who want to fish must hand over a definite part of the catch to the village chiefs. Yoruba fishing is not as elaborate as that of the Ijaw of the Niger delta, whose catches are traded far inland in Ibo and Edo territory, but they use several of the same types of traps, nets and lines adapted for different conditions of river or shore.

The coast people also produce the greater part of the salt supply by burning mangrove leaves or roots. The ashes are placed in closely woven baskets through which water is slowly filtered and then evaporated away by boiling in pots to leave a crust of brine. This is collected and packed in tightly woven baskets of screw pine leaves.

The control of land among the Yoruba is dominated by two fundamental concepts. In the first place, the land belongs to the people both in a narrow and in a wider sense. It belongs to the Yoruba not only in the sense that existing generations have rights by occupation. The ancestors of the people continue to dwell in the soil and descendants acquire the right to use it by virtue of their descent. More particularly, the lands of a town or village belong to the people of that village past, present and future, and finally, the tracts exploited by individual families are in a very special sense the lands of those families to whose descendants in perpetuity they belong. In the farm plots dwell the souls of the ancestors and earth spirits who have a special care for the interests of the particular families. There is, in short, a strongly religious element in the occupation of the soil. An outsider may use land only on sufferance and his descendants can but slowly acquire permanent rights in it. Land is never sold outright.

This position is commonly formulated by ascribing the ownership of land to individuals of authority. The territory of a tribal group belongs in theory to its paramount ruler, but at the same time the lands of a district within that territory are said to belong to the chief of that district, while the lands of a village or a town are in the control of its headman or chief. Finally, the head of a household controls the farmlands of his family, and the individual cultivators, such as the younger brothers and sons of the elder of the family, have plots at their own disposal. These rights operating one within another might appear to afford many opportunities for friction, but disputes are rare since nominal ownership is not considered as giving individual and exclusive rights with complete powers of alienation. The paramount ruler, the chief of a town or a village and the head of a family may redistribute lands within their charge, but they are acting as arbitrators as need arises to meet the demands of growing population or to utilize the lands of dwindling families. They can neither sell such lands nor build up personal estates.

The second basic concept in land tenure is that the effective occupant is entitled to continued use. No one may be dispossessed of his plots by his elders, village chiefs or tribal rulers while he makes use of them. So long as the trees planted and walls built remain standing no one may take over any land without the consent of those who planted or built them. This is not merely a surprising scrupulousness over personal property. Quite apart from the spiritual danger of appropriating land whose indwelling spirits may prove hostile, land in itself has little intrinsic value. Its productive capacity depends entirely on the arduous toil of planting and hoeing that is put into it, and after a few years any plot must be abandoned for long periods until its fertility is restored. Every year some is abandoned, and new plots must continually be cleared, for no cultivator can let all his lands reach exhaustion at the same time. Such a system neither requires nor permits strict personal ownership of every acre of farmland present and potential within reach of a settlement.

The head of a family may, while he lives, redistribute his lands from time to time among the sons or other dependants according to the needs of their households, and when he dies the lands, like other property, pass in the first instance to his children. Nearly all of them usually go to the sons on whom the cultivation has already devolved. The father often declares his wishes as to the occupation of various plots, giving most into the hands of the eldest son, but the heirs are really trustees for their own descendants and have probably been cultivating the plots that they nominally inherit for many years before their father's death. If a brother inherits because there are no adult sons he accepts at the same time the responsibility for the welfare of the dead man's dependants and for the later provision of land for sons who have yet to grow up.

Redistribution of land outside the limits of a village or quarter of a town is but rarely needed. Between villages there are often belts of bush country in which hunting and collecting rights are enjoyed by all villages bordering on them. Where, as in a few districts in recent times, the bush has been progressively cleared from two or more sides, boundary disputes do arise and are eventually settled by lengthy discussions between the chiefs of the towns or villages concerned.

Although sale and purchase of land does not exist, gifts of land to unrelated individuals and families can and do occur. Such gifts are made in perpetuity, and once given may not be decently taken back or claimed by the heirs of the donor, so that it is possible by handing over land to retainers and friends to deprive blood relatives of lands if serious quarrels and hatreds develop in the household. But in practice, since a man can only effectively occupy as much as he or his slaves can till, the sons have acquired control when they take over the working or supervision of some of their parent's land.

Large and powerful families collect round them retainers whom they provide with good farming land. Such land remains in the control of the family, which receives yearly presents from the produce as an acknowledgment of its title, but any territory that a retainer clears for himself from the virgin bush is his own to be disposed of as he wills. Slaves cultivate land for their masters, but they are often left practically free to farm as they will, provided they regularly supply an agreed amount of agricultural produce.

Inheritance of property and position is patrilineal among the Yoruba, but there are traces of a former and indeed fairly recent dominance of matrilineal succession. A man counts as his immediate family, those 'born together', his nearest relatives on both the maternal and paternal sides; but his relations through the mother are considered closer, and it is they, including all that live or are remembered, who form the wider group of relatives or lineage to which he belongs. The mother and the first wife of all authorities from king to compound headman have great influence and are treated with respect. A wife's property is under her exclusive control: she leaves it to whom she wishes and, since women do the greater part of the petty trading, she is often wealthier than the men of a household, particularly in clothes, ornaments and currency.

A group of related families usually lives in a single compound under the leadership of a headman, who bears the same title, *bale*, as the rulers of towns and districts. The head of a compound is its executive and legal authority, responsible for the good conduct of its inmates to the head of a village or town quarter. He exacts penalties for offences within the household, and must protect all inmates against unfair treatment. His first wife shares his authority as mistress of the compound and is relieved of all menial tasks. The headman is usually the senior man in the largest and wealthiest of the families. When he dies one of his sons or brothers assumes office subject to the general approval of the families of the compound.

The occupants of the compounds of a town quarter or of a small village are often interrelated. Such a group is not exogamous although the marriage of near kin is prohibited.

Slaves formerly constituted a considerable proportion of the population, but they were not a depressed and impoverished caste. A master made serious efforts to keep them happy and contented, for they were valuable property. In the larger settlements they lived in the master's compound and were not superficially to be distinguished from its junior families. Many of them occupied hamlets from which they cultivated their owner's land and were often given some of their own. They were obliged only to supply a certain amount of agricultural produce and to render war service. Slaves were obtained by capture in war and by the purchase from other districts of criminals and insolvent debtors. When sold into slavery for crime or debt a slave rarely remained in his own district but was taken elsewhere. They were allowed to acquire property and to redeem themselves. Those that were engaged in trade handed over only a portion of their profits, and often became richer than their masters, whose protection they would lose if they bought their freedom. The trusted slaves of chiefs were often state officials with great authority. A freeman's children by a female slave were considered free.

Slaves had, however, no legal rights; they could be killed by their owners as sacrifices, as scapegoats or for offences they might have committed, and they could be sold at pleasure. The European slave trade, which greatly increased the value of slaves as marketable property, led to the development of raiding for their capture and to the cruelties involved in export. But before this time the slave population, both the humble cultivators and the important officials, appears to have been contented and relatively secure.

As a security against a debt a man can pawn himself or one of his relatives. The status of a pawn is legally quite distinct from that of a slave. The pawn has to perform certain specified services for the creditor; these services pay the interest on the debt, but the pawn cannot release himself from the obligations until the capital itself is repaid or a suitable substitute is offered.

The political structure of the Yoruba state is elaborate but flexible. The priest-chief, or Alafin, resides in Oyo, the capital city of the largest of the tribal divisions. He performs the great magical ceremonies or rituals on which the prosperity of the people and state depend. Yoruba rituals are most elaborate. A hierarchy of anthropomorphic gods from the vague Sky Spirit, the native gods of towns and the divine patrons of crafts to the tutelary spirits of individual families were formerly worshipped with elaborate and barbarous sacrifices of animals and slaves. The Alafin and the other great tribal chiefs are themselves divine. On death their divinity is transferred to carved effigies set up in shrines.

The royal court is an elaborate and intricate organization of ministers and officials, and the Alafin himself is virtually confined to the palace except on the few occasions each year when he performs a public ritual. He is selected by the great chiefs of the Oyo tribe, who remain his advisers and derive their power and influence from the large districts of which they are the leaders and spokesmen. Each is ruler of one of the larger towns with its dependent villages, though preoccupation with affairs in the capital often compels them to delegate many of their functions to sub-chiefs. The chiefs at court supervise the king's actions throughout and are ultimately responsible to the people for his wise conduct. Abuse of sovereignty which menaces public welfare or creates widespread disaffection is the signal for the deposition and forced suicide or exile of the king. The Alafin is also compelled to commit suicide if his health fails, for his vigour is essential to the welfare of the State. The gift of parrot's eggs is the delicate medium through which the chiefs convey to the Alafin their decision that the time has come for him to take his life. The eldest son, although he is closely associated with the king and sometimes takes his place in public ceremonial, never succeeds his father. He and a number of other relatives, wives and slaves, were formerly put to death at the obsequies of the king, whose successor is selected from a different branch of the royal family.

The executive and legal authority of the chiefs over their own district is generally similar to that of the king over the territory as a whole. But the Alafin has the right to, and can, if there is sufficient backing among his other advisers, depose any of the chiefs and can override any executive or legal decision made by them.

The Alafin of Oyo, although nominally paramount over all the Yoruba tribes, has, since the end of the eighteenth century, had little authority outside his own section of the Oyo tribe, which has, however, a population of nearly one million. Although his religious prestige extends throughout Yoruba territory and his performance of the great national ceremonials is believed to be essential to the welfare of all, a number of other sacred rulers, each with distinctive title, like the Awa of Owo, ruler of the Ekiti tribe, and the Awni of Ife, ruler of the south-western Oyo and of the sacred city of Ife, are virtually independent. They are the guardians of their own tribal shrines and the performers of the great rituals of their own people. Moreover, a section of the Yoruba in the north is included within a Moslem Fulani Emirate, and the more eastern Yoruba tribes were formerly subject to the ruler of Benin, himself a descendant of one branch of the Yoruba royal family.

Executive and legal authority is in the same hands in an overriding series from compound headman through village chief and district chief to the king. Each issues regulations and laws in accordance with custom, hears and gives judgment on disputes. Every offence save flagrant murder is in a sense a civil one since no action can be taken until a plaintiff appears. Every litigant conducts his own case, producing evidence, marshalling witnesses, appealing to relevant cases heard before, often speaking with great skill and sometimes with more ingenuity than veracity. Since all cases are heard in public and are one of the main entertainments of the people, the judge, although he has power to punish any disturbance during the hearing, is sensitive to public opinion and realizes that his reputation depends on fair dealing and on his ability to reconcile disputants.

A dispute will generally be heard in the first instance, and if possible settled, by the headman of the household concerned. If one or both of the litigants is dissatisfied he may take it successively to the village chief, the town chief of the district and finally to the king. But at every hearing a fee must be paid to the judge by the litigant who loses his case.

No systematic taxation is levied by the chiefs. They are, however, able to demand the labour of their people for limited periods to undertake public works, such as the clearing of roads and the building of town walls and sacred places. Any one wilfully avoiding this duty may be fined, but a man may by private agreement send a substitute in his own place.

A chief's lands are usually cultivated by the people of his district. Those close at hand do the actual work or provide slave labour, while outlying districts provide food-supplies to maintain the workers.

There is an established method of popular deposition of any district or town chief who loses public respect and approval. A mob is formed which parades the town night after night singing derisive songs and throwing sand and stones at his house. Unless the offending chief can mend his ways and regain some of his prestige within three months he is compelled to commit suicide or leave the country, for his dependants will rarely dare to protect him further, and a select band will rush his compound, killing the offender and all others who resist and selling his relatives and dependants into slavery.

The political and legal actions of chiefs and rulers are, however, greatly restricted by the power and prestige of a secret society known as the Ogboni (the Elders). Although it claims the protection of the Earth goddess and conducts funeral and other rites on behalf of its members, the activities of this society are mainly political. There are lodges of the Ogboni in nearly every village and town quarter. Membership is confined to the heads of important families, and these are graded according to their prestige and their payments to the society. Within a lodge and within the society as a whole there is great solidarity and all proceedings are kept strictly secret under the most severe penalties. The Ogboni thus forms an oligarchy which arrogates to itself the power of deciding any serious question and of instructing the chief concerned as to the policy and action to be pursued. The Ogboni lodges hold secret courts at which they try any persons reported to have offended against the society or its members. Disputes between members rarely come before the public courts but are nearly always settled within the society. When the demands of an Ogboni lodge are refused it proceeds to intimidate the offending family, village or chief, calling upon other lodges to assist if need should arise.

Society organization is also characteristic of both religious and economic life. There are two great religious societies—the Oro and the Egungun, of which the former is in most districts the more influential. Each has its deity, with whom the souls of all departed members unite on death to form a body of spirits worshipped by the society. A man joins the society that his ancestors belonged to and worships them largely through the society. Elaborate funeral rites are conducted when a member dies, and, at an annual festival lasting several days, the dead of recent years are commemorated and their support is supplicated for the living. The Oro has also certain political power and formerly had the duty of executing individuals convicted by the Ogboni. Membership is in both cases confined to men on the payment of fees and giving of pledges. Women are confined to the houses during the annual ceremony of the Oro, when the bull-roarer from which it derives its name is whirled in the streets, and none of its secret ritual held in sacred groves in the bush may be witnessed by non-members.

In the economic sphere the various groups of traders and hunters belong to guilds, to which individuals are admitted on payment of fees and acceptance of the rules of the guild. Any one who attempts to engage in the trade of a guild without being admitted to membership can be fined and will have his goods confiscated.

Benefit clubs are also formed in the villages. The members each pay a certain sum of cowrie shells into a common pool, which may then be borrowed as a whole in turn by the individual members.

Although initiation rites have lost much of their social significance the youths of a Yoruba village or town quarter are organized under the care of an elder man for rituals and games, and the age mates comprising such a group retain a vague solidarity throughout their lives.

War was formerly conducted on an elaborate scale with regimented troops and cavalry. At the end of the eighteenth century the Alafin of Oyo was able to muster an army of a hundred thousand men. Attacks on weaker neighbours, especially on the coast, were made almost every year in the dry season to keep the forces in trim and to gain plunder. But in historic times the Yoruba have never dared to attack the Edo of the kingdom of Benin, and the tradition remains of the great war in which the Bini conquered the east Yoruba tribes, which have since remained their vassals. Although historical records are lacking, there is little doubt that the Yoruba state was built up by a process of military expansion, and that many of the Yoruba-speaking peoples of to-day are the descendants of subject groups who have adopted the speech and customs of their conquerors. Throughout the eighteenth and nineteenth centuries the various Yoruba rulers fought continually both among themselves and with the neighbouring states.

For a century or more the Yoruba and other west coast tribes have had flintlock guns supplied by traders, and before this more primitive touch-hole muskets, probably introduced from the north, were known. These may even have been manufactured at Benin. The native weapons, both of warfare and the chase, were long bows with poisoned palm rib arrows, swords and clubs. To these were added in medieval times or during the Age of Discovery the cross bow and a short heavy sword or matchet.

There was no standing army, but every man could be called on by the chief of his village, town quarter or district. Most chiefs did, however, keep a bodyguard of trained slaves. The hunters were the scouts and skirmishers. The foot soldiers were supported by cavalry, and all officers and chiefs were mounted. This was the only important use to which the horse was put, and the details of its employment in war point very clearly to the fact that the horse was introduced in comparatively late times as part of a military technique, derived from the Mediterranean and the Near East. Prisoners of war and large numbers of women and children from the raided towns and villages were carried off as slaves.

The more important crafts are practised by specialists, who offer their services in return for payments in food and currency, or barter their products in the great markets.

The Yoruba smith works in iron, copper and brass. He can smelt, forge, temper and weld. The iron working is the same in general technique as that of nearly all central African cultivating peoples. Hand-forged iron hoes are generally superior to cheap trade goods, and the finely tempered swords of earlier days were remarkable pieces of craftsmanship.

Most of the iron is obtained from a ferruginous shale which is widespread in Yoruba territory. The ore is smelted on a relatively large scale in districts where it is abundant, while the forging and casting of tools is done in the towns and villages with metal obtained from these centres. In one village about a day's march from Oyo more than a hundred craftsmen devote themselves entirely to iron production.[1] The iron-bearing shale of this district has to be extracted from beneath six feet of clay. It is removed in lumps of several pounds and first roasted overnight in a special oven fired with green timber. The roasted ore is pulverized by the women and children in large wooden mortars, passed through a coarse basketry sieve and washed in a shallow pit; it is then placed in the kiln while still damp. In this particular village there are eleven smelters each set under an open shed with conical thatched roof. The kiln is a large cupola of baked clay seven feet in diameter and five feet high from its sunken floor. It is filled with successive layers of ore, charcoal, selected clinker to serve as flux, hardwood and palm nut shells. A large clay pipe leads the draught from the bellows into the base of the furnace. The twin bellows are large bowls of hollowed wood loosely covered with goat skins, which are alternately raised and lowered by wooden rods attached to their centres. The furnace is raked and refilled with flux and ore ten times before the fire is drawn for the product of a smelting to be removed. About sixty pounds of ore are obtained at each smelting. In this and other smelting villages very little finishing work is done. The pigs of iron are broken up with large stones and sent straight off to the markets for the village smiths who repuddle the metal to cast and hammer it for tools and ornaments, of which hoes, knives, razors, bangles and door-fasteners are the most important.

[1] As described by C. W. Bellamy in the *Journal of the Iron and Steel Institution*, 1904, 99 ff. The native iron industry has now declined almost to extinction wherever trade goods can readily be obtained.

The more restricted manufacture and mainly ornamental use of copper, bronze and brass suggests that it is of more recent adoption than iron, but there is little doubt that they were already being produced before the arrival in the fifteenth century of the Portuguese, to whom the introduction of brass and bronze into Central Africa has frequently been ascribed.[1] It is nevertheless probable that bronze and brass working did not begin in West Africa until the Arab expansion across the Sudan, which began in the tenth century. The Hausa, to the north, still refer to bronze as 'red iron'. With bronze and brass the *cire perdue* process of casting also appears to have arrived. Beeswax models of the required objects are made. These are coated in clay, which is then heated so that the wax flows out through a small hole. The clay casing is baked, molten metal is poured in and the clay is later broken away to obtain the cast. Ife, the holy city of Yoruba territory near which there are large, accessible sources of copper and tin, is famous for the finest bronze working in West Africa. As elsewhere in the Congo-Guinea area the smith and his craft receive great respect.

Cotton is grown in northern Yoruba territory and is traded throughout the area. It is a prolific and fairly long-stapled variety which is planted in summer for collecting at the end of the following winter. Men were formerly the only weavers. They make long, narrow strips of cloth only five to six inches wide on a horizontal loom in which two heddles are operated by treadles. These narrow strips are sewn together to make garments and coverings. This type of loom is found throughout the grasslands to the north of the Niger. But a vertical hand loom on which cloth four or five feet wide can be produced has been introduced in more recent times. Yoruba women have adopted this loom and weave this wider cloth. On both types of looms patterns are made by using threads of different colours. Weaving, which is, after all, uncharacteristic of the forest area, has not entirely ousted the production of bark cloth.

Pottery is made by the women in almost every Yoruba village, although settlements with access to superior clays and large markets often specialize in pot making. No wheel is used, the pots are built up by coiling and are fired in the open. Although there is a considerable variety of forms, some of them very large, the ware is not of high quality. It is very porous and cooking-pots are boiled in oil before they can be used.

[1] The evidence on this important question is set out at length in Talbot, P. A., *The Peoples of Southern Nigeria*, Vol. 1, p. 18 seq.

Wood and ivory carving are both fine, but they have never reached the standards of the most elaborate work among the Bini peoples to the east. Doors and door-frames, one-piece three-legged stools and images are characteristic objects of the wood-carver's art.

The Yoruba have only recently reached the coast and their boats are only simple river craft. To ferry passengers and goods across rivers large pottery bowls and calabashes are often used. The ferryman swims and pushes. For river travel and coast fishing dugouts are excavated with fire, iron hatchets and chisels. They vary in size from one-man canoes to large war canoes which carry crews of twenty to forty men. Small triangular matting sails are often erected, but no outriggers are fitted to ensure greater stability.

Land travel is, however, of greater consequence, and it is clear that the degree of specialization that exists among the Yoruba, not only within a single village but between different parts of the country, calls for an extensive system of markets and trading. Markets are characteristic of the whole Congo-Guinea area, but among the Yoruba the range of trading activities is unusually extensive. Although a few goods and manufactures are dealt in exclusively by men, the greater part of the petty trading in the local markets is in the hands of women, but long distance trading between remote centres is undertaken by men, who organize trains of porters which cross the country with loads of dried fish, salt and metal work. A good porter will carry a load of fifty to one hundred pounds on his head.

Much of the trading is conducted by barter, but lengths of cloth and cowrie shells are used as currency in the larger markets and in the payment of tribute. To the native African cowrie of the coasts the smaller Indian cowrie, formerly traded right across Africa from the East coast, was added at some unknown date and has a much higher value. Iron, copper and other metal bars were probably introduced as instruments of trading by the European traders of the sixteenth century.

The Yoruba are at once town dwellers and farmers. They combine great skill in hoe cultivation, with enterprise in trade and industries. Allegiance to the sacred kings who perform the great ceremonials essential for the welfare of people, land and crops, and a hierarchy of executive and legal authority, has overcome the separatism of village communities so characteristic of the semi-Bantu peoples to the south-east and has welded this people into one of the most remarkable native states in Africa.

Political organization is far less elaborate among the Boloki, who occupy a number of villages and townships on or near the Congo main stream over a distance of about a hundred and fifty miles within a few degrees of the Equator. Like nearly all the Congo peoples they are Bantu in speech and show considerable racial variations. The negro stock appears to have been slightly modified by the intrusion of Brown race elements from the north-east.

Their territory lies near the centre of the elevated Congo basin at about twelve hundred feet above sea-level. Temperatures never fall as low as in south-western Nigeria, but there is a definite rise of a few degrees during the months from November to June. Rain falls throughout the year and totals sixty-five to seventy inches. The heavy rains with torrential downpours and thunderstorms are, however, concentrated in the period following the later equinox from August to December, while from January to March during the warmer season the rains are light, and occasionally there is actual drought. Towards the end of the rainy season the humidity is very high, the sky almost continuously overcast and the atmosphere steamy and oppressive.

The Congo river is here a huge braided system studded with islands, and its channels extend over a belt of seven or eight miles. The river rises twice a year, in May and November, after the equinoctial rains of this equatorial basin, and it then inundates wide stretches of riverine land which emerge later as swamp and marsh. The vegetation is not continuous equatorial jungle as in Malaya, the Amazon valley and the coastal parts of Yoruba territory; belts of lower lying forest and jungle swamp are separated by stretches of parkland of tall grass and scattered trees. The oil palm is again native, and the riverine marshes are fringed with dense groves of the raffia palm, from which wine is made.

The population is concentrated in a number of closely settled villages of variable size, ranging from hamlets of two or three households to townships of several thousand. Each village has its own territory, with established boundaries. The rectangular gabled huts with palm thatch and walls of bamboo and matting are set on low foundations of raised earth in rows parallel to the river. Between the rows are wide roadways and often a grove of bananas. Only the poor are monogamous, and the head of every family builds his houses in a row, his own in the middle and those of his wives to each side.

The vegetable food-supply is provided by the women from their own plots and cultivation is almost entirely in their hands.

Men clear the heavy trees with a wedge-shaped iron axe and gather together the dried vegetation towards the end of the drier season so that it may be burned to provide fertilizing ashes. They may also help with the major planting undertaken when the heavy rains are expected. But the women do the cultivating and harvesting of all the crops. Wet and dry periods are very uncertain and planting and harvesting go on throughout the year. Yams and millet are the native staples, but the New World plants, cassava and maize, have to a large extent supplanted them. Cassava is highly valued, because it can be preserved for several weeks after cooking, and large supplies are dried and stored. Plots are exhausted after about four years and new clearings have to be made. A large variety of wild products, including kola nuts, oil palm and other fruits, are gathered in the forests. Land can be cleared freely by all villagers within the tribal territory and effective occupation is the only valid title to land. Land itself is not sold, but a cultivated plot, together with the produce growing on it, can be transferred for payments.

The men provide the meat and fish for their households. Poor breeds of domestic dogs, goats and sheep afford only a small amount. A large range of game is hunted, from the elephant and wild buffalo to the bush pig, but the annual floodings of the river are apparently very destructive of game, and it is not abundant in relation to the density of population. Hunting is restricted to the village territories, and under the local hunt-leaders large parties of spearmen are formed to round up game and to erect large pit traps and snares for hippopotamus, elephant and antelope.

Fishing is probably more productive, and the stretches of river within a village territory are carefully preserved against intrusion. During the flood periods wicker fences and traps are set up in the swollen tributaries, and the fish trapped when the water recedes are often kept in small pools and fed on snails and cassava for several weeks until required. A considerable variety of basketry traps and nets are used on the main streams, and parties are formed to spear fish at night, when they can be lured to the surface with torches. Euphorbia juice and other poisons are thrown into pools.

Smiths, carpenters and canoe builders are specialists who usually learn their craft from their fathers and are often wealthy. But other utensils are made by individuals for their own use; pottery, basketry and matting are contrived by the women, and the barkcloth, nets, spears and traps by the men, who also do the leatherwork. There are no fixed market-places and any surplus of food or goods is hawked round the villages. The smith is honoured as a skilled craftsman and is accredited with the knowledge of a special magic for his work. He therefore enjoys a high social position and his fire has sacred qualities. The furnace is a small open fire pit fired with charcoal. The double bellows consist of two cylindrical cavities cut in a single block of wood with loose leather covers worked up and down to produce the blast. Both iron and brass are worked into tools and ornaments. Iron is imported from considerable distances and the pigs are beaten out on wooden anvils into hoes, axes, knives and spearheads. Brass rods form a kind of currency which is continually being debased by the smiths, who cut pieces from the rods and so obtain part of their material for nothing. Brass rings are made by the *cire perdue* process, and brass wire, poured in bamboo moulds, is made up into leg rings and other ornaments. Copper is not worked pure and the brass itself is obtained by trade from the coast.

There are no paramount or even district chiefs among the Boloki. The head of a family, usually the eldest son of the senior male line of a group of kinsmen exerts an informal control over that group and is responsible for its misdeeds. The heads of families act in concert as a village council, in which the head of the largest and most powerful family has the most influence. Groups of villages do, however, co-operate and usually agree to recognize, on inter-village matters, the decisions of a district judge selected by agreement.

Slavery and the pawning of debtors generally resembles the practices of the Yoruba. Nearly a quarter of the population were formerly slaves. In general they were well treated for they could fairly easily run away. Although slaves could acquire and own property only with the permission of their masters, the slave owner who was responsible for their actions and debts usually found it more expedient and profitable to encourage them to acquire land and goods of their own. Women slaves were cultivators and child bearers, and were both more numerous and more valuable than men. Weak families often attached themselves to more powerful ones in order to avoid the formal enslavement that almost always befell the unprotected individual.

Only the headmen of strong families were socially and economically free, for all others were bound by ties of kinship or slavery to them. While slaves could be sold and killed, pawns, usually children handed over as sureties by debtors although they worked as slaves, could not be disposed of and were redeemable at any time.

External relations, including trade between the villages, were on a far smaller scale and were more sporadic than among the Yoruba. Travel in strange country formerly involved the risk of molestation and enslavement. No large bodies of traders were formed and the small parties moved cautiously, mostly by night.

Although fighting between villages and between families within villages occasionally broke out, there was little organized warfare or slave raiding, far less any idea of conquest. In the larger and more decisive conflicts the defeated settlement was pillaged and razed to the ground while the captives, including women and children, were enslaved.

Among both the Yoruba and the Boloki hoe cultivation is the basic economy, but the effectiveness of exploitation and the political organization associated with it are very different. The distinction between a lower and less efficient female hoe culture and male cultivation has long been recognized and a variety of causes has been invoked. It has been suggested that the one is more generally associated with root cultivation in the forests and the other with millet growing in the savanas. In this connexion differences of habitat have been put forward in explanation. In the dense jungle the harder work is that of clearing the ground, and this the men do. The damp, loose soil is easily cultivated with little hoeing, and the vegetable growth is so great that a considerable yield is obtained with very shallow cultivation. Frequent and laborious weeding is more important than the turning of the soil. In the savana lands, on the other hand, the burning of the grasses is a relatively easy matter, but the hard surface soil must be loosened with powerful hoes and the actual cultivation is more arduous. In general this scheme appears to have some basis. The female cultivation of root crops appears to be earlier and more widespread in the forest regions, while for the cultivation of millet, a far more appropriate crop on the drier tropical grasslands, men usually share equally in the work. The contrast between the intensive male cultivation of the western Sudan and the poor female cultivation of yams in the Congo forest is indeed striking. But while men are the cultivators among the Sudanese millet-growing peoples along the northern and eastern margins of the forest, male cultivation also penetrates the forest in parts of West Africa, and is there, as among the Yoruba, mainly devoted to root growing. Since the division of labour between the sexes often becomes rigid, subsequent movement of peoples would produce such exceptions. On the other hand, the adoption of cattle raising as a male pursuit in eastern Africa leaves agriculture nearly everywhere in the hands of women. There are in fact many examples of forest peoples in which men do nearly all the cultivation, and of grassland peoples among whom the men only clear the ground.

There appear to be two phases of hoe cultivation in Africa: an earlier, associated with root crops and dominantly female; and a later, probably developed primarily in the savana lands in connexion with millet growing in which men share in or take over nearly all agricultural pursuits. The Yoruba and other peoples in West Africa, among whom yams are intensively cultivated by men as the main crop, would appear to exemplify an adaptation of the grassland patterns to the forest zone with transference from millet to the more suitable and prolific root crops of the tropical forest.

CHAPTER XI

OCEANIANS: PEOPLES OF THE EASTERN SOLOMONS AND THE SOCIETY ISLANDS

I. Oceania

To the west of the Asiatic mainland, of the archipelago of Indonesia and of the continent of Australia there extends the vast ocean of the Pacific, with a span of over eight thousand miles from Southern China to Mexico. But the Pacific is not an empty ocean; in its western and central parts island groups are more closely studded than in any other great ocean of the world. These islands are not scattered aimlessly, but are the pinnacles and crowns of submerged mountain arcs, the great majority of which, both exposed and submarine, have been formed by volcanic action. Thus the islands often stand out boldly from the sea, rising steeply beyond a narrow foreshore to heights of several thousand feet. Elsewhere thick deposits of sea muds have been raised above the surface to form lower and smoother islands of stratified rocks. On the tops of the submerged mountain peaks, however, another process of land building has been slowly going on—the formation of limestone rock by the building of corals. Coral polyps are marine insects which construct, each for itself, a hard casing of lime which endures long after it is dead. Building continually out and over their dead ancestors, the polyps produce great thicknesses of coral which are in time worn down by current and wave into a consolidated limestone. But these little animals can only live and build within a narrow range of physical conditions. For coral growth the water must be warm, shallow, salt and clear. Thus the coral reefs of the world are restricted to tropical seas in which the mean surface temperature of the water is about 70° F. The polyps cannot live at depths below about thirty fathoms and are killed off where the entry of a river freshens the sea water and clouds it with mud. The multitude of small islands and shallow submarine ridges in clear warm water afford ideal conditions for coral building in the 'South Seas' of the Pacific. The formations are of three main kinds: *fringing reefs*, which lie close along the shore; *barrier reefs*, which stand out perhaps a half to several miles from the coast-line on the far side of a lagoon of calm deep water; and *atolls*, reefs which surround a central lagoon in which there is no island. The coral of the barrier reefs and atolls extends to far greater depths than the polyps are now able to build, and it is clear that they have been built up by progressive sinking, relative to the level of the sea, of the coasts and islands which they fringe. Finally, considerable thicknesses of coral have on some islands been lifted above the sea-level, forming low plateaux and coastal plains. With the problems of the nature and causes of these movements we are not here concerned, but it is essential to understand the general character of the coral formations, for they are the background of so much of Oceanian life.

The volcanic peaks and the coral formations are the basis of the usual division into High and Low islands. High islands may be flanked by fringing and barrier reefs, but their core consists of mountainous country ruggedly carved out of volcanic rocks. The last phase in the geological history of most of the islands has been a relative rise in sea-level which has drowned the estuaries of the rivers and much of the fore-shore, so that the coastal flats are very narrow and the streams and rivers enter the lagoons in small steep-sided bays. Of level land there is therefore very little, and the bush-covered ridges and plateaux of the interior often come right down to the coast. The low islands, however, are but the reefs of former island peaks that have disappeared beneath the sea, or coralline masses built up to sea-level on shallow submarine platforms and then carried by wave action a few feet above the surface.

The greater part of this island zone lies in the tropical belts of the trade winds and of the equatorial calms into which these blow. As the wind belts migrate seasonally there is nearly everywhere a long season of trade winds, followed by a shorter season of variable westerly winds and heavy rains. Traversing wide stretches of ocean even the trade winds cannot be dry, and the mountainous relief of many of the islands induces very heavy precipitation. The high islands, sending ranges and peaks of several thousand feet into the stream of the trade winds, are well watered; their interiors are clothed in dense tropical forest of fern bush, and the weathering of the mountain sides has provided tracts of deep rich soil in coastal valleys. In the western Pacific, where the proximity of great continents complicates the climate and a strong monsoon from the north-west follows the trade wind season, over two hundred inches of rain fall on many of the high interiors and over one hundred inches at sea-level on many of the islands. Farther east rainfall is abundant but less heavy. In the Society Islands sixty to seventy inches fall at sea-level, while the island groups farther north, especially in Micronesia, suffer occasional but severe droughts.

The low islands, whose only soil is powdered coral mixed with seaborne sand, receive much less rain, have no rivers and are far more barren. On them many of the plants of the high islands will not grow, and drinking water is often found only in a few brackish pools. Although most of the low islands are atolls or narrow sections of reef, greater width has been attained on some by shifts in the zones of coral building and by the throwing up of shingle. These are wooded and the sheltered coasts are colonized by mangrove swamps.

The land areas are so small and the maintenance of warmth by wind and sea current so continuous that temperatures are everywhere very equable and vary only a degree or so from 80° F. from one season to another. The important contrasts are not in temperature but in humidity, between the more bracing trade wind season and the damp, enervating heat of the monsoon and equatorial rain season.

Into this island world only a very limited number of plants and animals have been able to penetrate. Although certain Asiatic plants have reached the more westerly island arcs of Melanesia, only plants whose seeds can float without damage in sea water or can be carried by birds have been able to penetrate far into Oceania. So far as animal life is concerned Oceania lies east of the famous divide running between Bali and Lombok and Borneo and Celebes. This is known as Wallace's Line, along which there has, throughout later geological history, been a sea barrier which prevented the advance of the higher mammals into Australasia and the Pacific. Moreover, many of the animals which did reach New Guinea and Australia have been unable to cross the farther sea barriers into Oceania, so that apart from birds, bats and, in parts of Melanesia, a few tree-dwelling opossums, there is a striking lack of game in the Pacific, and the other animals found there have all been introduced by man. Of these the only early introductions were the dog, the pig, the chicken and, probably without intention, the rat.

Oceania has long been divided into three main regions— Melanesia, Polynesia and Micronesia. Melanesia in the western Pacific consists essentially of the arc of island chains which swings round from New Guinea roughly parallel to the Australian coast, but a thousand miles farther east. It received its name from the appearance of its native inhabitants, who are darker and more negroid in appearance than the peoples of south-east Asia or of Polynesia. They are a short people, with very dark brown skins and crinkly hair, but their noses are in general less broad and their lips less averted than those of most African negroes, and it is generally agreed that racially they are a mixed stock. In physical characters they merge gradually with the more negroid Papuans of central and western New Guinea, and Melanesians—that is, people related in race, speech and culture to those of the outer islands—occupy the coast lands in south-eastern and several parts of northern New Guinea. Melanesia contains a large number of high islands, some of which are of considerable area; but surrounding and linking the larger ones are many smaller volcanic islands and atolls.

Polynesia lies to the east, from Fiji to Easter Island, and includes the outlying territories of Hawaii and New Zealand. It, too, in the race, languages and culture of its inhabitants, forms a unit area; but it is difficult to draw any sharp line between the two regions. Not only are there several outlying settlements of Polynesians within Melanesia itself, but the Fijians are hybrid in both race and culture. There are, moreover, indications of a widespread occupation of Polynesia by Melanesian peoples before the arrival of the Polynesians themselves.

The Polynesians, although there is undoubtedly a varying substratum of negroid race in their composition, are both in physical type and in language related to peoples of south-eastern Asia, and an important element in their racial composition is derived from the same stock as the Mediterranean or Brown Race type of south-western Asia and southern Europe. They are rather tall, often quite pale in complexion, although their wavy hair is always black and their eyes dark. But their appearance varies in different islands. While the Samoans and Tahitians, for example, were recognized by the voyagers of the eighteenth century as being almost 'European' in appearance, the Fijians, although culturally closely related to the Tongans, are in appearance more like Melanesians.

Micronesia, so named from the multitude of small and mostly low islands, lies to the north and north-east of Melanesia, but its inhabitants are more closely related to the Polynesians, on whom they have exerted considerable influence. The close proximity of Micronesia to the east Asiatic mainland has afforded opportunity for more frequent cultural and racial influences from Indo-China and China than is characteristic of Melanesia, or even Polynesia. In some island groups there is a marked mongoloid strain in the racial composition of the population.

II. THE EASTERN SOLOMONS

Although the major features of physical environment, economy, crafts and social grouping are fundamentally similar throughout Melanesia, there is considerable variation in detail. Moreover, these differences are often sharply localized, so that between one group of islands and another only twenty or fifty miles away the relative importance of certain food plants and the salient features of social organization may show important contrasts. While it is necessary to grasp the general character

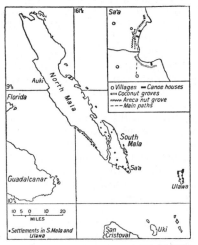

FIG. 64. SKETCH MAP OF PART OF THE
EASTERN SOLOMONS
(*After Ivens*)

of Melanesian life a generalized account can be very misleading. Settlements in the islands of Little Mala and Ulawa in the Eastern Solomons will therefore be considered in greater detail, leaving significant comparisons with other areas to be made as occasion arises.

The people of the Eastern Solomons, like most other Melanesians, are rather short in stature. The men are about five foot two or three inches tall and the women usually under five feet. Their skin is dark brown. Their hair grows in sharp crinkly waves, but is longer than that of the African negro and by constant combing is often made to stand up in a thick bush. The Melanesian also differs from the African negro in the heaviness of his eyebrows, in his more prominent and sometimes aquiline nose and in his thinner, less everted lips.

Decorations rather than clothing are prominent in Melanesian attire. Nose and ear ornaments are characteristic. The ear plugs are spool-shaped pieces of wood which are increased in size as the slit in the lobe is distended, until a plug three or more inches in diameter can be worn or a ring suspended from the hanging lobe. Forehead and chest ornaments, sometimes elaborately carved, are made of highly valued pearl shell. The peoples of Mala and Ulawa obtain their supplies of pearl shell by trade with Florida and elsewhere. Large arm rings are worn by the men. Most of these are laboriously shaped by punching, scraping and polishing with flint and coral from the thick hinge of the giant clam shell. The manufacture of an arm ring takes many weeks of desultory labour, and when bartered or offered as gifts the rings represent considerable value. They are white and stone-like in appearance, circular, cylindrical or disc shaped and the heaviest may weigh as much as a pound.

No cloth is woven in the Solomons, and indeed weaving is absent throughout Melanesia, save in Santa Cruz and the Reef Islands. Some features of the small Santa Cruz loom suggest that it was introduced there from the more advanced peoples of Micronesia to the north. Bark cloth is made for men's loin-cloths by beating out strips of the inner bark of the 'paper mulberry' tree or of the inferior banyan fig. It is prepared by the women, who beat out the bark with a large, smooth stone or rolled flint. Melanesian bark cloth, like that of Malaya, is much inferior to the fine tapa cloth of Polynesia on which coloured designs are stamped. The only woman's garment is a light, short skirt of loose fibres attached to a cord waist belt.

Most of the larger islands of the Eastern Solomons, such as Mala and San Cristoval, rise steeply from the sea to a sharp ridge four or five thousand feet high, from which equally steep spurs run out into coastal promontories. The interiors are heavily timbered. The coastal cliffs, weathered from volcanic rock or uplifted masses of coral, are deeply cut by a multitude of ravines through which the heavy rains of the interior reach the sea in little estuaries fringed by mangrove swamp. Mala consists of two islands of this type, Big and Little Mala, separated by a narrow channel. In places only a few hundred yards wide and nearly thirty miles long this channel is walled by steep cliffs probably due to recent faulting. Ulawa, twenty miles to the east, is a smaller island whose igneous core is largely covered by deposits of marine muds and limestone.

There are two well-marked seasons in the Eastern Solomons: the long period of the south-east trade winds and the shorter one of north-westerlies with calm spells and clear weather. The trade winds blow strongly on to the east coasts for the seven months from June to December. The currents set against the wind at this season and the tides are strong, so that the sea is nearly always choppy and navigation is difficult, unpleasant and often dangerous. Towards the end of December the trades abate and there is a short period of calm weather, when a smooth sea offers ideal conditions for overseas voyages. But the wind soon rises again and, veering round to the north, brings rough weather and a long swell until March, when the light westerly winds of the second and longer calm period herald the six or eight weeks of intensive activity during the main fishing season.

On the windward, eastern coasts of the islands, save where protection is afforded by other islets and points, the surf breaks continually on the fringing reef—the latest phase of coral building—and there is little or no beach. But on the western side, wide sandy beaches are better developed, while fringing islands and outer reefs shelter quiet lagoons from the open ocean.

Settlement in the Solomons extends inland up to at least three thousand feet, and the interior villages lie in clearings in the bush on the rare stretches of smooth ground from which trackways, flanked by steep cliffs and deep ravines, run out along the sharp ridges. These interior settlements are often separated from the sea and all it means in Oceania. Their few planted coconuts bear poorly and their range of other food plants is more limited. But some of them own landings on the coasts which they visit in the fishing seasons.

The coastal settlements are built on the upper margins of the shore. They are small and scattered in plan, and there is little tendency to concentrate in large villages. Sa'a, on the eastern coast of Little Mala, a rich and prosperous district, consists of four main villages and several smaller hamlets. No one of the villages is very much larger or more important than another. Each has about twenty houses and only a hundred or so inhabitants. (See fig. 64.)

The islands of Mala, with an area of about two thousand square miles, had until recently a population of about fifty to sixty thousand, of whom only four or five thousand lived on Little Mala, but these figures are probably much smaller than in the days before the disturbances and the depopulation which have followed European penetration. The interior of Ulawa reaches only two thousand feet, and its relief is less sharp than that of Mala, but all the settlements are coastal and extend right round the island. To-day there are nine, each consisting of three or four hamlets, but there are many other deserted districts, and the population must formerly have been considerably larger than the present total of about a thousand.

These small villages or hamlets, the characteristic units of settlement in Melanesia, are occupied by small groups of real or nominal relatives holding their land in common. In favourable districts, as at Sa'a, the hamlets may lie within less than a mile of one another and form a district united by common interests and activities. The total population of Sa'a a few years ago was about two hundred and fifty, but it was probably considerably greater a century ago. The very small scale of Melanesian society has many inevitable consequences for the life of the people, and must be borne constantly in mind. In Little Mala alone there are three separate languages, and the speech of the Sa'a people is confined to the coast and interior of the southern quarter. Sa'a lies behind the first opening in the shore reef three miles north of the south cape of Little Mala. The villages and hamlets are scattered to north and south of the stream, whose fresh water breaches the reef at this point and so provides the main harbour. The larger settlements are built on the lower hill-slopes above the shore, but others, especially to the south, occupy the sandy ground immediately above the beach, where the coconut groves run continuously along the coast for more than two miles. They are all unfenced and are approached by narrow paths through the bush. The houses are set up without plan and the site itself is not permanent. When buildings become dilapidated, or the cultivated land too remote, or, again, if death and other misfortunes seem to dog the place, a move is made to clear a nearby tract of bush and build anew. (See inset sketch in fig. 64.)

The extended family or kindred is the essential unit in many of the economic and social affairs of the peoples of Sa'a and Ulawa. Each kindred, for example, has its own accustomed land, which its members cultivate. A kindred here is said to include persons between whom genealogical relationship can be traced, whether through the father or the mother. Since such relationships are remembered over about four generations and but little more, a man may include among his kindred those whom we should call his first, second and third cousins but the actual composition of these groups is far from clear. This type of kindred is found throughout Mala and Ulawa and in other parts of the Eastern Solomons.

At Sa'a there are larger groupings known as 'sections of men', each of which undertakes various public duties, and goes on expeditions as a unit. The senior and cadet branches of the chiefly families form two sections, and there are seven or eight sections of commoners. Each section has a large canoe which bears its name; each has allotted tasks in the preparation of feasts and in the building of the canoe house and lodge. The names, e.g. 'Cut Down in Fight', 'Emerge in Daylight', 'Talk of Fight', suggest that in some cases they were formerly fighting groups.   The sections are believed to derive from the extended family groups or kindreds. A man can, apparently, join any section, but would usually choose one in which his father's or his mother's relatives are numerous. They are not exogamous; members of a section are free to marry women related to their fellow-members, provided no close blood relationship between the parties themselves is known to exist.

In many other parts of Melanesia kin grouping follows the mother's side and relatives (in our sense) on the father's side are not considered members of the group which is thus unilateral and matrilineal. Within the divisions of society controlled by this matrilineal reckoning marriage is prohibited. These exogamous divisions or clans are often two-fold and are then usually known as moieties. In parts of the Northern Solomons, however, there are six. These clans are in no sense political, nor are they territorial units like the patrilineal settlement groups of the Boro. They are wider than village, district or even language group and frequently hold for peoples of different islands. The matrilineal system of these parts of Melanesia does not confer any more formal authority on the women than is found in the islands of the Southern Solomons, but it does have the important social consequence that a man's sons are not considered to be of his own kin group, and his proper heirs are his sister's sons for whose training and well-being he has special care.

Polygyny is usual in Melanesia, but only prosperous men take more than two wives and many have only one. The chiefly families are more markedly polygynous and the chiefs at Sa'a often have many wives.

Children at Sa'a and in most parts of Melanesia are betrothed at a very early age. All members of the boy's kindred contribute to the marriage gifts to be handed over to the girl's father, but they in return receive a share of the pigs provided by the girl's kindred for the feast. Instalments of the marriage gifts of dog and porpoise teeth are handed over from time to time long before the actual mating.

Children are often adopted, sometimes by the childless, but most frequently by the chiefs who desire numerous heirs. An adopted boy acquires the full status of a son. Such children are paid for, and in former times child stealing for sale to chiefs in a distant village was frequent. Children were, however, also stolen to provide immediate or future victims for human sacrifices.

A warlike family, said to have come to the Sa'a district from the hills of the interior during a period of unrest twelve generations ago, has established itself there as a chiefly group with claim to considerable spiritual and temporal power. Families from the same district, according to local tradition, established themselves as chiefs in A'ulu, north of Sa'a, and elsewhere. This chiefly family or kindred, like others in Mala, counts descent and membership in the patrilineal line alone, and a long pedigree is recounted. But as children are adopted and sold into the chiefly house, descent is in fact strict only in name.

The many local chiefs of Little Mala and Ulawa are not rulers. Village disputes at Sa'a are settled within the families concerned or by the pressure of public opinion. The chiefs take no part and indeed are expressly excluded. They really have little root in the communities in which they dwell. They are regarded, and regard themselves, as feast givers and controllers of certain ceremonies. By the splendour of their feasts they enhance the prestige of their district and win the approval of the commoners who make gifts of food for yet more feasts. The chiefs gather round them bands of retainers, many of them refugees from other villages, who act as priests, messengers and bodyguards. The Sa'a chiefs appear to have established and maintained their position by arrogance and determination. They convinced those they settled among and who gathered round them afterwards that they could ensure prosperity by the rituals they controlled. In Ulawa every hamlet in a district has its own chiefly line, but at Sa'a and in Little Mala generally a single line controls a district of several villages.

Every member of the chiefly families is in a sense a chief, but the eldest son of the main line succeeds to the position of his father as principal chief unless he is incompetent or vicious, when he will stand aside, or be effectively replaced, under the influence of public opinion, by another chief.

The keeping of chiefly genealogies found at Sa'a and elsewhere in Mala is very unusual in Melanesia, where there is in general a conspicuous absence of tradition and fame endures only so long as a living man has personal remembrance. Ceremonial chieftainship itself, however, is not absent in all other parts of Melanesia. Chiefs are found in Santa Cruz, in the Trobriands and elsewhere, but their rights and powers are often less strictly hereditary. Their authority depends rather on ability to communicate with powerful ghosts. Such magical power is generally passed on to lineal descendants, but since it is greatly enhanced by personal qualities it is the more easily lost by weakness and failure.

The rights of the chief nearly everywhere consist essentially in the imposition of fines for offences against himself and against the community as a whole, and also in the imposition of prohibitions or taboos on actions, places and things for the infringement of which fines are equally payable. The band of retainers who share much of his wealth, do his bidding in the collection of fines or the destruction of the property of rare recalcitrants.

The origin and development of chieftainship in Melanesia is by no means clear, but everywhere the chiefs claim the same essential rights and powers. They are nearly always real or alleged immigrants, who make similar claims to sanctity, superiority and to the control of valuable ritual.

A village in the Eastern Solomons is a cluster of houses which usually lie irregularly round an open space. Among them stands the chiefly lodge, larger and more elaborately decorated, and often a pile house in which the young unmarried boys live. Down on the beach is the canoe house round which much of the social and ceremonial life centres. On Ulawa the lodge though nominally owned by the chief is not occupied by him, but is used as a meeting place for men during the day. In it visitors are welcomed and entertained, while at night it serves as a dormitory for boys and young men.

The houses of the Solomons are probably the best built and most commodious of Melanesia, but those of Mala are less fine than the large pile dwellings of Florida and Ysabel. At Sa'a they are rectangular structures with gabled roofs about twenty feet long and ten to twelve feet wide. The three horizontal roof poles of the side walls and the gable, made of long, straight aerial roots of the banyan tree, each rest on three hardwood pillars whose upper parts are often carved with human and animal figures. Three lighter beams run along each roof slope, and these are closely covered with bamboo rafters which project as low eaves. A heavy thatching of the long leaves of the sago palm is tied to strips of split bamboo, and these in turn are tied to the rafters in rows, six inches apart, working up from the bottom to provide a smooth and thick waterproof covering which drains freely. For the slow and laborious work of thatching all available relatives and friends are called in.

FIG. 65. SCENE IN A SA'A VILLAGE, E. SOLOMONS
(*After photographs by Ivens*)

The walls are generally built of three thicknesses of bamboo, the inner and outer faces being first set up vertically and shorter lengths are placed horizontally between these uprights. Cords are laced to and fro through the bamboo layers in a horizontal or lozenge pattern to hold them together and, finally, three horizontal stays of wood strengthen the walling on the outside. The entrance, which may be under one of the eaves or in one of the short sides at the gable ends, is placed two feet or more above the ground and is covered at night with a sliding door of bamboo poles secured from inside by a wooden crossbar. This small entrance admits little light and, although some comes in through the interstices of the bamboo walls, the house interior is always dark.

For sleeping places low wooden frames covered with split palm laths are built against the walls. The fire pit is set within a ring of stones close in front of the centre post. For more important meals hot stones are carried to an oven set on the inner side of the centre post. The rear of the house is often screened off as an inner apartment for the women, high shelves are set up along the walls for storing yams and a stage is built near the fireplace for smoking foods and storing utensils.

Young boys leave their families and live together in dormitories. The boys' houses in the Sa'a villages are raised on piles and walled with interwoven bamboo. Food is brought there by the mothers, but no woman may enter the house.

The chiefly lodge is larger, higher and more elaborately decorated. Five rows of carved pillars support the roof. The thatch ridge is ornamented, and carved projections or finials are attached to the ends of the ridge pole. At Sa'a the chief occupies this lodge and the front is often closed in with painted laths, but it is also a place of public assembly. On Ulawa and in many other islands it is in fact a club house, and the front is open, with only a low fence or platform. The pillars are everywhere carved and frequently represent a shark from whose gaping jaws protrudes a man who appears to support the roof. Flat tie beams connecting the two gables are carved with representations of fish, birds and canoes. Large logs hollowed out through a narrow slit, used for drumming at feasts and ceremonies, are kept in the lodge. These gongs, closely similar in principle, design and use to those of the Boro and other Amazon peoples, are made in sets of three in Little Mala and each has a different note. They belong to the chief, who alone commands their use to announce a feast and decides the rhythm to be played to lighten the work of preparing food for the feast and to accompany the ceremonies.

The houses at the landing places in which the large canoes are kept are the largest of all structures; one at Sa'a, now in ruins, was sixty feet long. These are the great meeting places for men and they are forbidden to women. The long gabled roof is supported by carved central pillars, but the walls at Sa'a are built up of rough coral blocks which project beyond the roof in front to enclose a stone platform on which sacred coconuts and catches of bonito fish are placed. Shrines are set inside in the front corners of the house. Canoe houses are built at the instance of the chiefs and their dependants; in front of them are held the ceremonies which open the bonito fishing season and in them are secluded the boys who are to be initiated as bonito fishers.

There are thus two official houses of the chief, the lodge and the canoe house, but both serve public needs, and their construction is the concern of the village as a whole. Every household contributes food for the workers, and the various 'sections' undertake different parts of the work. On these houses is lavished the greatest skill in construction and carving.

Coconuts, yams and taro are the staple foods of the Melanesians, while breadfruit and sago are important in certain areas. The cultivated plots of the coastal villages are scattered widely in the surrounding bush, extending from the shore to considerable heights on the rising ground behind. Inwards and upwards from the shore at Sa'a four zones or levels of land are generally recognized:

(1) The raised sandy belt of the old beach where the coconut groves are found and wild arrowroot grows;

(2) The low-lying, often flooded land of rich black soil, where *hana*, the soft-skinned yams with prickly vines, are planted and where the fruit trees—especially breadfruit trees, canarium and areca palms—grow;

(3) The first slopes, up to about four hundred feet, on which are grown the best and most prolific yams, including those prepared by roasting in the embers of a fire; and

(4) The higher levels where hard yams, suitable for grating and cooking as puddings, and the best taro are raised.

The coconut groves lie along the sandy belts immediately above the beach. They flourish on the light saline soil formed by the distintegration of old reefs. The coconut, dispersed by the rolling and floating of the ripe nuts fallen from trees, will propagate itself naturally on these beaches, and the nuts may be carried hundreds of miles by the currents from island to island. But the village groves of palms have been extended by planting at various times and continue to reproduce themselves. They are cleared of weeds and undergrowth from time to time as required. The trees bear throughout the year, and, save for a slight midwinter pause in June and July, flowers and nuts, both green and ripe, are found on a single palm at one and the same time. Six different varieties are known at Sa'a, and every stage in the growth of the fruit is accurately judged and named. The nut is used in all its later stages. Taken green from the tree it provides about a pint of clear, refreshing fluid and a soft flesh; when ripe and picked off the ground the milk is thrown away, but the harder flesh is grated in large quantities for mixing in dishes of cooked yam and taro. When other food is scarce, especially before the beginning of the yam harvests, the coconut is often the staple food for several weeks. The cover and fibre enclosing the ripe nut are husked off and the nut split in two by impaling it on a sharp stake set upright in the ground. The meat is removed with the naturally serrated edge of a piece of cockle shell. When preparing large quantities this work is done sitting astride a sloping wooden frame to which the scraper is attached. Moving rhythmically to and fro the worker scrapes the meat from the core of split nuts, letting it fall into a large wooden bowl below. The scrapings are soaked in water and squeezed to obtain a thick, creamy liquid, which is heated in half shells on the embers of a fire until it curdles to form a paste which is used to fill large sandwiches of yam and taro baked in leaves.

To the inland villagers coconuts are far more precious. The palms grow far less well and are slow to bear fruit. Nuts are not wasted by picking them green when the meat is thin; and the inland peoples will drink the harsh milk of the ripe nuts like schoolboys at a fair, and even eat the dry meat left after the creamy juice has been squeezed out.

When a feast is planned the coconut trees are ceremonially washed with water and struck with a leaf of the prolific cycas tree to make them bear well. Coconuts are offered to the spirits of the bonito fish when a new canoe is launched. On setting out for a journey overseas two nuts are placed at both the bow and stern. When the destination is safely reached, the nuts are tapped and thrown back into the sea after calling on the ghost who protected the voyagers.

The yam and taro plots of the coastal villagers are scattered over a considerable area. Between these two tuberous foods there are important contrasts. The yam is a large tuber with a dark brown skin and a white potato-like interior. It has a definite season for planting and harvest but will keep for many months. Taro grows throughout the year but is a smaller growth forming at the base of a lily-like plant. It is perishable and must be eaten when dug. The yellow, soft-skinned yam with a prickly vine, known as *hana*, grows well in the damp but rich black soil behind the coastal sands and also in the damp plots of the higher villages of the interior, but the yam proper requires well-drained soil and the plots are found on patches of natural terrace on the coastal slopes. Taro, which also requires much moisture, grows well in the interior where it far outweighs the yam as an article of diet. In Polynesia taro is nearly everywhere irrigated from streams, but this is rare and sporadic in Melanesia. Some sixty varieties of yam, twenty of hana, and over a hundred of taro are recognized by the villagers of Sa'a. All are cultivated and are recognized as having peculiar demands and qualities. Within the tracts of ground habitually used by a kindred fresh yam plots are cleared every year, for there is no manuring and the roots soon exhaust the soil, while the growth of weeds and of the plants themselves rapidly chokes the ground. When the yams have been dug up the plot is used for planting banana cuttings,

which form groves in which pawpaws, betel pepper and an
edible reed (*awalosi*) are also raised.

Clearing for the new yam plots at Sa'a is done in July and
August. The bigger trees are ringed and barked and left
standing so that the yam vines may climb up the dead trunk
and branches. To keep out the pigs a stout fence of logs must
be built round the plot. A kindred which includes a number
of households co-operates to make the clearing in its common
land, and within the clearing each household or small family
cultivates a particular plot. The whole garden often measures
well over a hundred yards in each direction. Each plot has a
'head' and 'foot' and sticks are laid both along and across at
intervals of a few yards, marking out small areas to be worked
by given persons. In the centre a small rectangular shrine of
logs is built, and round this the garden magic centres. After
the drier weather of September and October the cut undergrowth of the intended garden is burnt, and its ashes provide
the only fertilizer applied to the soil. Each plot is then raked
clear to await the planting in November and early December.
For this large parties are formed, and all the families having
holding combine to plant the plot of each in turn. Thus, the
work on any one plot rarely takes more than one day, while
the household concerned feeds the entire group at the end of
that day.

The ground as a whole is not dug over and the yam holes
set about two feet apart and made with sharp stakes, are only
a few inches deep; they are usually made by the men. Into
these the women drop the sets or 'seed' yams, which may be
an entire yam or slices of larger ones each containing a sprouting
'eye'. Stakes have next to be set up to supplement the trunks
of dead trees. Wild creepers cut in the bush are tied from
stake to stake for the yam vines to climb along. Up and along
these stakes and creepers the climbing vines may run twenty
or thirty feet. Without this staking no light could reach the
ground, no weeding could be done and the harvesting would
be far more difficult. Under the shade of the vines the garden
is weeded a few weeks later, when quick-growing wattles which
have sprung up are prised out with sharp stakes. The crop
ripens after four or five months and the large tubers are dug
and pulled out of the ground. For this again the related
families working in a garden co-operate as a body. The community of ownership of gardens and their produce does not
seem to be so complete at Sa'a and elsewhere in the Southern
Solomons as on Eddystone Island farther north and on Ambrym
in the New Hebrides, where any member of a kindred is free

to take produce from any part of the common garden and fellow villagers are never refused supplies if they ask. This freedom does not, however, breed slackness or refusal to share in the garden work, for, unless they are legitimately engaged elsewhere, the social disapprobation and scorn which slackers encounter quickly compels their participation.

The yams of Little Mala are small when compared with the giants of over a hundred pounds raised in some parts of Melanesia. They average three or four pounds, while large ones may go up to ten. As they are dug up, generally by the men, they are stored in temporary shelters on the plots, to be taken to the village by the women in large burden baskets carried on their backs. Here they are sorted, stored in the house and inspected at intervals lest any begin to rot.

On Ulawa, where little taro has been grown in recent times, yams play a correspondingly greater part in the food-supply. The work on the preparation of yam gardens is more protracted, and in certain villages the planting and harvesting fall a month or two later despite the difficulty of keeping the seed yams from sprouting in the house before they are planted. A small quantity of yams is planted earlier than the main crop either in the taro plots, as at Sa'a, or in last season's yam gardens. These are dug as soon as ready and provide an early supply but are not considered part of the harvest proper.

The garden ground at the disposal of a group of relatives is considerably larger than that which is laid out in plots at any one time. After one or sometimes two crops of yams a garden is allowed to revert to bush, although bananas and fruit trees may be planted in it. But the vegetation does not grow up as densely as on virgin ground and after eight or ten years it will usually come into cultivation again.

The cultivation of the yam gardens is the most important labour of the Melanesian, and round it centres a great deal of his magic. The village magician is called in to secure the safety and fertility of a garden when it has been first cleared and fenced. Putting charms of lime and leaves on the fence, the magician or priest calls with secret incantations on ancestral ghosts to ensure fertility and ward off evil influence. The digging sticks for planting are sharpened by the priest himself and to them charms are often attached. The owners of individual plots utter incantations like the following as they begin their work:

> A dracaena takes root, a yam takes root.
> It takes root in my garden like
> A pair of big fish of the deep which can't turn round.
> It takes root like what?

Like a pair of big fish of the deep
Who are sunning themselves in my garden.
Like a pair of whales of the deep . .
Yam cuttings upwards,
Yam cuttings downwards,
Yam cuttings sideways. . . .

This is thy spell, Lord Black Fly
And Lord One Sole,
And Lord Maato'u ni walo,
And Lord Travel-along-the-Ridge,
And Lady Fold-the-cooking-leaves;
May my yam cuttings fill the bag.
May they be poured over my garden.
May they spread like water over the garden . .
May they spread like convolvulus in my garden.
Climb like a creeper in my garden. . . .

This is thy incantation, One Sole,
Whatever man breaks the tabu of my garden,
Do thou tie him up on the branches of a live *hata* tree
At Pwela ni kana.
Take all thy enclosures of gongs,
In every compartment of thy chiefly lodge,
And beat the gongs to stop them
That he spoil thee not this day,
Oh! One Sole.[1]

An offering is placed on the central shrine of logs and the planters fast until the end of their day's work.

When the main yam crop is ripe the first fruits are offered to the ghosts before the general digging may begin. On Ulawa this is done by a priest for each village as a whole. The people remain indoors fasting, while the priest carries two yams through the village down to an altar on the beach. The head of each household will probably hang a few yams as offerings from the centre pillar and rafters of his own house.

The taro plots in the Eastern Solomons receive less regular attention than the yam gardens, although the same plot can be used for several years before it is exhausted. The taro gardens at Sa'a lie farther inland at higher levels and may be four miles from the village. They are worked like the yam gardens, but as the crop cannot be stored and the plant will grow throughout the year, there are no definite seasons. When a part of the crop of rhizomes is dug up the tops are set back in the ground, or suckers cut from them are planted out in fresh clearings. Most time is spent in the taro gardens in the off season for yams. Taro receives much less attention in Little Mala than in some other parts of Melanesia. In the

[1] Ivens, W. G.: *Melanesians of the S.E. Solomon Islands*, p. 335.

New Hebrides water is diverted from streams to irrigate the taro beds which provide the major food supply, but in Mala irrigation is unknown.

Besides the coconut and the root crops a large number of trees afford supplementary food. These are found in old garden ground and on the flats behind the beach; some, like the areca palms which propagate themselves, form large groves. Others like the *su'e* tree, whose nuts, leaves and catkins are all edible, the breadfruit and the 'Malay apple' (*Eugenia*) grow sporadically. They are sometimes planted but often seed themselves. Groves of coconut and areca palms are owned by kindreds whose members weed the land, thin out the young trees and share the produce. But most of the other trees are owned by individuals who pass on their rights to their children.

The breadfruit (*Artocarpus incisa*), which provides a large and heavy starchy fruit, a staple food in many places from southern India to eastern Polynesia, is relatively unimportant in the Eastern Solomons. The fruits are eaten when abundant in August and February, but the trees receive no attention and new ones are rarely planted. Any surplus breadfruit is dried over a fire and stored in a wrapping of leaves, but the large chests of dried breadfruit characteristic in the houses of the Banks Islands are not found.

The sago palm, which stores up within its main stem large quantities of starchy food for its single flowering when it is eight or ten years old, is lacking at Sa'a. In the north-western Solomons, as in New Guinea, the tree is felled before it flowers and the trunk is split open. The sago washed from the fibres of the interior is stored in bags.

The lofty areca palm supplies the small yellow nut which is chewed together with lime, made from burnt coral, and the leaves of the betel pepper creeper, which is planted to climb up the breadfruit and other fruit trees. This is the well-known but misnamed 'betel-nut chewing' of Melanesia. The mixture is both a food and a stimulant. It is taken after nearly every meal, at intervals throughout the day, and especially on all ceremonial occasions. The nut itself is also used extensively as a charm in magic. 'Betel chewing' is found throughout southern India, Indonesia and all but the more southerly parts of Melanesia. The distribution of this practice and of the plants used in it is but one of the many instances of the close relations between Melanesian customs and those of south-eastern Asia.

The canarium almond tree provides a store of dried nuts. These first ripen towards the end of July; they are cracked out from the hard shell and are packed in long, bamboo baskets which are set for smoking on a platform in the house. Each family has its own shrine in the bush where the first fruits of the nut are offered to the ghosts. The smoked nuts are pounded for mixing in nearly all dishes of yam and taro which alone are insipid in taste.

As with the yams, first fruits must be offered to the ghosts before the canarium harvest is gathered. The harvest of these two important crops, one the main food and the other the chief flavouring of that staple, are landmarks in the year from which dates are reckoned.

Within the territory of a village, the land on which houses are built and gardens made belongs to the kindreds which occupy it. Land has no value unless there is need to build a new house or to lay out a garden. The bush surrounding the village is considered to be at the disposal of the village, and its members would resent outside interference, but the uncleared lands have no individual owners until a family or individual establishes a claim by actually setting to work on a house or garden in some part of it. Such clearing gives no rights to any fruit trees already growing on a plot which are already claimed by another.

In the bush no precise limits are marked out or agreed upon as the boundaries between the territories of adjacent villages. Hunters and collectors of wild fruits are free to come and go so long as relations are peaceful and no attempt is made to disturb the immediate vicinity of another village. Since the small Melanesian community can cause no serious pressure on the land, which is, moreover, useless unless it is sufficiently close at hand to be worked and is actually maintained in cultivation, there is no inducement to acquisitiveness in land. So that, although a particularly bountiful or well-situated stretch of ground may occasionally be transferred to another family on payment of an agreed length of shell beads or other property, such transactions are rare.

The sentiment that land belongs in perpetuity to the kindreds installed on it, and is protected by their ancestors is very strongly felt. The chiefly families at Sa'a have made no attempt to expropriate the commoners, and have been content with tracts offered to them and with the rights of those wives who are commoners in lands of their own kindreds.

Fishing at Sa'a is most active in the calm season of March and April. For nearly all the rest of the year the trade wind blows strongly onshore and prevents deep-sea fishing, and this period of light north-west winds is the season for catching the bonito and flying fish with lines from canoes. The lines, which are made of a dried forest creeper, are often as much as a hundred fathoms long. They are weighted with stones, each set in a slip-knot which is released when the fish bites. Hooks are carved from the shells of turtles, pearl oysters and clams, and the shapes vary with the fish sought. Turtle shell is rare and at Sa'a must be obtained by trade from considerable distances. V-shaped gorges of sago palm midrib are used for taking flying fish, while special baits are prepared for many others.

A large garfish is caught with a ball of spider's web attached to a kite of sago palm leaves. The fisherman paddles against the wind holding the string of the kite, whose tail trails along the surface. The teeth of the biting fish are quickly held fast in the web and the kite is pulled in. This use of kites in fishing and even for towing light craft is widespread in Oceania and very common on the coasts of China.

The bonito is a silver-blue scaleless fish, weighing as much as eight to ten pounds, which arrives along the coast in small shoals in March and disappears six to eight weeks later. The appearance of these shoals is the signal for a period of great activity, for these fish are the prize catch of the Solomons and of many other parts of Oceania. Around this short season focus many of the most important interests in life. The bonito are caught with rod and line from the prow and stern of canoes. The beautifully carved shell hooks are of different pattern and material for stern and prow fishing. The bonito have a sacred character. At Sa'a a company of maiden spirits is believed to live with the bonito in the sea pools and to send them forth at the proper season. The first catch every year is sacred and may be eaten only by the priests of the chiefly families who are in communication with the spirits. With the bonito there arrive large numbers of sharks (see p. 207), which prey on the shoals and are a constant danger to the fishermen. Some of these sharks are regarded as embodiments of spirits which protect the bonito

Thus the catching of the bonito requires more than mere skill, and the boys of Sa'a and Ulawa undergo a period of seclusion in the canoe houses on the beaches in preparation for their first catch. These ceremonies are under the control of the chiefs at Sa'a, but elsewhere they may be undertaken by any man of prestige who can gather together the materials for holding the necessary feasts and rites.

The boys who are to be prepared for their first catch of bonito are taken down to the local canoe house at twelve or fourteen years and remain there for two or more years in charge of the men. Meanwhile their relatives with extra planting and redoubled industry prepare to supply the food and materials for the feast which will accompany their initiation. No women may approach or see the boys during their seclusion; their food is taken from their mothers and carried into the canoe house by men who have already been initiated. The boys must be kept ritually clean and avoid all association with the village, but otherwise they are free to play, to fish from the shore and to mix with the men who congregate on the beach. On the arrival of the bonito in the selected season the boys

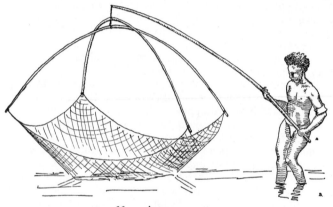

FIG. 66. LA'A NET, SOUTH MALA
(*After photograph by Ivens*)

are elaborately decorated with strings and mats of shell beads, cowries and other ornaments, usually provided by the chief, and are taken out one or two in each bonito canoe. As the first bonito is hooked and lifted from the sea the boy grasps the bamboo rod, shares in the catch and is thus initiated. He becomes *malaohu*. On the return to the village a feast is given in honour of the initiated boys. They stand in public view during the proceedings on a platform which is elaborately decorated with carvings and shells to represent figures of fish and seabirds. After this they may marry, and may take part in bonito fishing and in other adult activities of the village.

In the villages of Ulawa and Sa'a a ceremony is usually held before the bonito fishing opens. A priest, usually the chiefly owner of the particular landing place and canoe house concerned, invokes the sacred sharks, places some bonito on the beach altar, cooks a fish in an oven in the canoe house and eats it there.

For ordinary fishing along the shore nets are used. Shoals of fish are caught in quiet water by using the large, suspended *la'a* net which lies in the water attached by cords to a long pole (fig. 66). When the fish cross the spread net the pole is quickly raised. A still larger net, used for shoals in shallow water, is handled by four men, each of whom sits atop an upright pole set in the water holding a rope attached to the net which lies on the bottom. When the shoal crosses all four haul quickly on their ropes and lift their catch out of the water. This type of net is also used to catch birds and flying foxes in narrow gorges. Long nets hanging vertically in the water from elaborately carved floats are used to surround shoals in deeper water. The crews of the canoes then dive for the fish which are trapped in the meshes.

A small net and a live decoy are necessary for taking the wary parrot fish. The decoy fish are kept in closed pools or submerged baskets until required and are then attached to a rod. A net similar to the *la'a* is held submerged below the decoy. The parrot fish, enticed from the rock crannies to attack the decoy, are dexterously caught and hauled out.

Mackerel and sardine shoals which appear on the west coast from August onwards and on the weather coast during the December calms are caught by rod and line or with hand nets from stages built up on piles in the harbours. River fish are taken by poisoning the water with a compound of stupefying vegetables juices.

Regularly every year a sea worm—*Palolo viridis*—swarms in great numbers at the surface of the coastal waters of Oceania. Although the rising of the palolo takes place at different seasons in various parts of the Pacific it recurs at the same time each year with amazing regularity in any one district. At Sa'a this happens on the second night after the November full moon. They also swarm after the full moons of October and December but are not then edible. These annelids are from six to eight inches long and live in the submarine crevices in the coral rocks. Once a year the rear half of every annelid breaks away and rises to the surface, where it bursts to scatter the eggs it contains. Millions are simultaneously propagated in this way and the surface waters along the reefs are choked with them. Closely woven hand nets and coconut leaf torches are prepared beforehand and the worms are scooped up in great quantities from the reef and from canoes. The greater part are dried and smoked over the fire, where they hang in strings like sausages to be eaten as relishes with the monotonous yam diet.

Women are not allowed to fish and some fish are forbidden them as food; but they collect shell-fish, crabs and frogs on the reefs and in the swamps.

The only cooked meal of the day is prepared at sundown when the women return from the gardens. For the rest, the leavings of the evening meal, pieces of coconut, areca nut, or a yam roasted in the embers, are eaten by individuals at irregular intervals.

Water containers are made of five or six foot lengths of thick bamboos whose knots are broken through with a hardwood rod. The women, when they fetch water from the river, carry five or six of these containers bound up with rope.

Yams, *hana* and taro, the main foods, are all very similar in character, but from them a great variety of dishes is prepared by adding other ingredients. Vegetables for the daily meal are often cooked by roasting on the hot coals of the fire, but for large meals and feasts the stone-oven is prepared. A fire is built on a flat bed of stones and on it another layer of stones is set; when the fire has burnt out the top stones are removed with wooden tongs and the oven swept clean. The food to be cooked is wrapped in leaves, placed on the hot oven floor and covered with the other hot stones and still more leaves. The two chief dishes, yam puddings (a sandwich of grated yam and curdled coconut milk) and pounded taro as well as fish and meat, are all cooked in this way. Bowls and receptacles are all of wood, mostly of the light *tapa'a* wood, and cannot therefore be placed on the fire. For cooking mashed yams and taro in large quantities at festivals, large and beautiful wooden bowls and troughs are used. The food is boiled by dropping in red-hot stones that are lifted with bamboo tongs. Oil is extracted from coconut meat in the same way. Men are skilled cooks, and for feasts, from which women are excluded, prepare all the food themselves.

While no pottery is made in the Southern Solomons it is manufactured in the islands of Bougainville Straits in the north and also by some of the Melanesians of south-eastern New Guinea, who trade it by sea over great distances in exchange for food and other goods. The general absence of pottery in Melanesia is by no means always due to the lack of suitable clays, and in several islands pot-sherds left by former communities have been found.

The wooden bowls used for preparing and displaying food at the great feasts are sometimes of enormous size. Long, narrow troughs into which taro is scraped for feasts on Ulawa may be over fourteen feet long while large circular bowls with flat, projecting handles are made for serving foods. These feast bowls, which are kept in the lodge, are often inlaid with cone shell and their handles are carved with geometric ornament.

Apart from the dog, the only domestic animal of the Melanesians is the pig, which has certainly been introduced by man in the islands of the Pacific. The Melanesian pigs are related in breed to those of New Guinea and Indonesia. They roam freely in and around the village and are a considerable nuisance, since they will break into food-stores and root up plants and trees. Against their depredations all gardens have to be strongly fenced and the bark around the base of fruit trees must be protected. When a feast is planned a village is often fenced round to shut out these untiring scavengers. Pigs are fed by the women with the unused milk of ripe coconuts and the dry scrapings of crushed nut. But the feeding is irregular, and for much of the time they must fend for themselves, scavenging round the houses and rooting in the surrounding bush.

They are, however, by no means numerous; an ordinary household may have two or three and a chief a few dozen. They are of great value, for they provide the only sure and readily available supply of fresh meat, but they are sacred animals to be used only on ceremonial occasions and may in modern times have increasingly replaced human victims in making sacrifices to ghosts and spirits. Since they are slaughtered in considerable numbers and at such frequent intervals for the many feasts and ceremonies their numbers do not increase. Indeed, important ceremonies have often to be delayed until there are sufficient pigs for the purpose.

Pigs are not therefore to be regarded as the source of the everyday meat supply; for that wild animals provide the scanty supply. Bush pigs, descendants of animals that have run wild, wild rats, flying foxes and the more abundant opossums are hunted. The opossum is surprised in tree branches, where it sleeps through the day, and if not caught at once can be driven to the ground, where its movements are clumsy, so that it can easily be dispatched.

Large numbers of birds, especially seabirds and fruit-eating pigeons, are found on the islands, but they play little part in the food-supply. The fruit pigeons are, however, of great indirect service to man, for they swallow, transport and then disgorge the seeds of many edible plants.

Individuals possess small canoes, but the larger ones are the property of chiefs, or are held in common by a group such as the 'sections' at Sa'a.

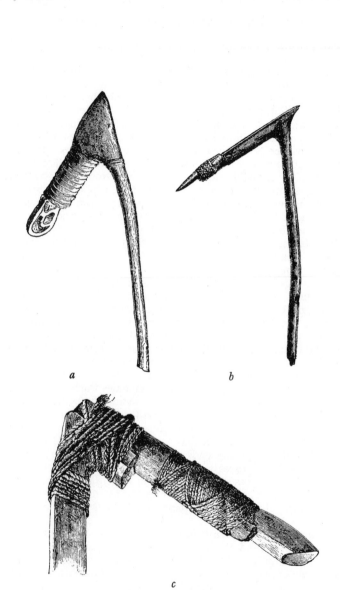

a   *b*

c

FIG. 67. MELANESIAN ADZES

a, SHELL, LEPER'S ISLAND; *b*, STONE, SAN CRISTOVAL; *c*, SHELL, SANTA CRUZ,
SHOWING LASHINGS OF COCONUT FIBRE

(After Codrington)

Canoe building is a specialised craft. The prospective owners with their relatives and friends collect and prepare the materials, but the actual work of building and decoration must be done by one who by descent and training has the necessary skill and magical power. The larger canoes in Mala, Ulawa, San Cristoval and in most of the Solomon Islands, are plank built. Such a canoe at Sa'a is built up with seven main planks —three on each side of the keel, which is cut out of a heavier and harder wood. The *iola* (canoe) trees are needed for the side planks; each log of this fairly hard yellow timber is first split lengthwise, and each half is laboriously adzed down to a plank about an inch thick. The native adzes are of clam shell or volcanic rock ground to a cutting edge and bound with coconut fibre to a naturally crooked wooden handle (fig. 67). On each plank projections or cleats are left near the margins of what is to be the inner face. To these struts and seats are attached. The rough adzing of the planks is done on the spot where the trees are felled by the prospective owner. He seeks the aid of his kinsmen during slack times when neither yams nor fishing demand their attention. Every kindred maintains a supply of these trees near its gardens, planting new ones if there is not a natural growth. The builder is called in when the planks have dried out. He sets them out roughly in position, adzes down the keel and planks more finely and levels their edges to fit. Holes are bored every few inches along the fitting edges and the hull is built up by temporary lashings of strong bark fibre. The native method of boring these planks with flint or shell punches is extremely slow and laborious and requires considerable skill. The second plank on each side is shorter and narrower than the others and tapers at each end so that the bottom and top planks come together beyond it where the hull rises at each end. The ends of these are cut off in an oblique curve and lashed together to form the sharp curved prow and stern. Cross struts of strong, hard wood are also fixed with temporary lashings through bore holes to the cleats. When the planks have set to their proper shape the temporarily assembled hull is dismantled and the work may be held up until a later season when the owner can again secure the labour of his relatives and friends. The planks have to be adzed down again, trimmed where necessary and finally rubbed down and smoothed to a thickness of about a quarter of an inch with coral rubbing stones. Every one available is summoned to assist in this lengthy and laborious process. The planks are now lashed permanently together by the builder with a tough and durable creeper. In the meantime large supplies of wild 'putty' nuts have been collected by women and children, and these are scraped into a paste with coral and the 'putty' is hurriedly smeared along over the joints before it hardens. All holes that are bored and any flaws in the wood are similarly plugged with the putty, which hardens quickly and becomes black in colour. The prow and stern have still to be built, for in all but the smallest boats these are built up higher with further planks to prevent the shipping of water in choppy seas and give tall and graceful lines to the vessel. On additional short lengths of side planking at each end a solid carved top piece or *haku* is erected. The prow haku is the taller at Sa'a and is more elaborately decorated with carvings of birds, fish and geometrical ornament. The large overseas canoes which are built for the chiefs have a carving of a porpoise

FIG. 68. AN OVERSEAS CANOE FROM ULAWA
(Based on a native drawing published by Ivens)

at the back of the prow haku, facing the bow, while on bonito canoes a dog should be carved on the upper part of the stern haku.

The overseas canoes are usually rather more than thirty-five feet long and about three feet wide. They are fitted with seats to carry a dozen or so paddlers, and are often fitted for long journeys with an extra wash strake on each side. The finest of these and of the bonito fishing canoes are elaborately decorated with painted and inlaid shell designs. Each piece of shell must be ground to the required shape and set in putty. Two or three thousand laboriously shaped pieces of hard cone shell may be used for the decoration of one of the finest canoes.

The canoes of Sa'a and Ulawa are smaller than the great canoes formerly built in some parts of Florida, which ordinarily held twenty or so men while the very largest carried a crew of more than fifty.

The bonito fishing canoes are rather smaller, but those

holding four men may be twenty-four feet long and over two feet wide. Still smaller canoes for one or two men are made for use in calm water along the beach, and some of these are dugouts hollowed out with adzes from the solid trunk of breadfruit trees. On these small craft the high prow and stern are not usually built.

The canoes are propelled by paddles about five and a half feet with narrow, tapering blades. On the large overseas canoes a large steering paddle over six feet long is used by the helmsman, who sits on the gunwale in the stern haku.

The building of the larger canoes involves a very great deal of patient labour and takes a long time. The rough work is done by a relatively large group of a dozen or so, but the building, finishing and decorating fall to the canoe builder, who may take several years over his task. Certain families are renowned for canoe building, and their men, when too old for gardening and active fishing, devote themselves to the craft. A canoe builder must be fed while he works and is paid with shell money according to the size of his task—three or four strings for a small canoe, as much as ten for a good bonito canoe and even a hundred for one of the large decorated overseas craft. The canoes of the Ulawa villages have a high reputation and many are taken for sale to Little Mala and San Cristoval.

The Solomon Islands are exceptional in the general absence of outriggers on the canoes. Throughout the greater part of Oceania these are attached to nearly all canoes and give increased stability. The outrigger consists of a number of spars or yokes, generally three, lashed across the canoe and projecting well out on the starboard side. To them, either directly or by intermediate struts, is lashed a trimmed log of light wood rather shorter than the canoe itself. Outriggers are particularly necessary on the heavy dugouts of eastern Melanesia. Those of the New Hebrides and Banks Islands, for example, are much narrower than the plank boats of the Solomons and far more easily upset (fig. 69). An outrigger is fitted to the small dugout canoes for use close in shore in some parts of the Solomons, but on the larger plank vessels confined to this group they are not used.

The larger dugout canoes of Melanesia are, however, deepened by top-straking, that is, by attaching one or more planks to the dugout hull in the same way that the Solomon Islands canoe is built up on the keel, which may itself be regarded as the vestige of a dugout hull. The outrigger canoes have the great advantage that sails may be used and in eastern Melanesia, as in Polynesia, a small triangular mat sail is set up on a short mast and boom stepped on the centre spar of the outrigger. The large Santa Cruz outrigger canoes of former days also carried a large stage built up on the narrow hull on which a small house or shelter was provided for the crew. (Fig. 69.)

The peoples of Mala, Ulawa and the other Solomon Islands

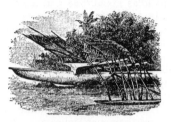

FIG. 69. A LARGE SANTA CRUZ
OUTRIGGER CANOE WITH SHELTER
(*After Codrington*)

have not of course remained in ignorance of the outrigger. The plank-built vessels are rather to be regarded as a later addition to their equipment. Their pride in the form of their own craft and the greater ease with which the single canoe can be manipulated by an expert crew has probably been responsible for their refusal to use outriggers on their larger vessels. Guppy has suggested that the protection afforded against the Pacific swell by the double line of islands in the Solomons has favoured the use or retention of the lighter, faster plank-built vessels.

Payments and exchanges in many parts of Melanesia are made with shell rings and strings of shell disc beads, the famous Melanesian 'shell money'. For canoes, pigs and food, for fees in the men's club, fines to the chiefs and offerings to the ghosts, strings of shell beads are handed over. To the wife's father on marriage and to the relatives of a man who has been killed or injured shell money is also transferred. In the Solomons small bright-red discs of spondylus shell have usually the highest value. These shells are found in the narrow channel which divides Mala into two islands, and the villages of the Langalanga lagoon at one end have a local monopoly of shell disc manufacture, but perhaps the greatest centre is the island of Auki off the north-west coast of Mala. Almost the whole of this small artificial island is settled and practically all the vegetable food supply must be obtained from the mainland. It is with shell money that this is purchased. But the mainlanders are enemies and fighting constantly occurred between the two in former times. There have always been truce days, however, on which the Auki people could land at customary neutral places on the mainland to carry on their trade, exchanging shell discs and fish for agricultural products and utensils. Armed men of both sides would stand by, but the truce was rarely broken.

Beads of different shades and sizes are recognized and graduated in value. The pieces of shell are pierced with a flint-tipped pump drill, ground down to the required size and strung on coconut fibre cords or creeper. Discs of white and grey shell and sections of black creeper are added to the red strings to improve their appearance. The longest strings are a fathom long measured between the finger tips of the outstretched arms, while other standard lengths measured along the arms and body are recognized. Ten strings, each a fathom long, is the highest 'denomination', but four strings bound together is the more frequent unit of payment. Shell money is not all stored away when acquired. Some of it is made up into necklaces for women and children and into belts for men. Necklaces of human teeth taken from the skulls of dead relatives are also worn but are not used for payments.

Porpoise teeth obtained from North Mala and the canine teeth of dogs are also strung and used for payments at Sa'a. They have fairly definite values in terms of the more abundant shell money.

In the northern New Hebrides the place of shell money is taken by long narrow strips of matting made for this especial purpose, while in Santa Cruz the red feathers from the breast of the honey-eater bird, bound into lengths on cords, are used in the same way.

In some parts of Melanesia especially in the Banks Islands, large club houses are built in the bush by secret societies and membership is obtained by payments of pigs and shell money (see p. 207). Advance in rank within the club is obtainable only through the acceptance of further payment by the members of the various grades above who have already made such payments and will devote what they receive to obtaining admission to a yet higher rank. This system gives a far more mercenary cast to society in such areas and money acquires a greater importance than in the rest of Melanesia.

From Little Mala trading voyages are made in all directions. Overseas trading is in the hands of the chiefs whose big canoes lead the expeditions. Every village has a number of places with which it maintains friendly contact for many generations, while others, perhaps only a few miles away, are ignored. The Sa'a canoes visit many villages on San Cristoval and on the smaller islands to the south and they occasionally travel as far as the northern end of Mala. Stores of food that are locally abundant, such as taro, pigs and canarium almonds are carried on these expeditions and exchanged for other products or for shell money. It is also incumbent on the guests to give a feast for the visitors and to make them handsome presents of shell money. These help to pay for the building of the canoe but are reciprocated when the guests become hosts in their turn. Trading voyages thus serve both economic and social ends. They are not thought of as a means of livelihood but as occasions for display of wealth and generosity.

In parts of northern Melanesia overseas trading is stimulated and regulated by the *kula*, a ceremonial interchange of gifts between individuals of different districts and islands. The objects formally exchanged in this way are restricted to necklaces of red shell discs and armlets of white shell. They are passed on in opposite directions from individual to individual in the many villages of the Trobriand Islands, the Amphletts and the neighbouring mainland of New Guinea. The red shell disc necklaces always move clockwise and the armlets counter-clockwise, so that an individual participating in this exchange receives a necklace from the one side and repays it with an arm ring received from the other. The objects themselves are valued ornaments only shown at festivals. To ensure friendly relations and to obtain a moral lien on the best articles that come into the hands of his nearer colleagues, a member of the kula 'ring' makes gifts of other objects to his fellow traders. Each journey of a kula trader is also the occasion for extensive transactions of a more commercial character in food products and utensils. But even here the barter has the form of an exchange of presents. The prodecure in the kula exchange involves considerable magic and ceremonial. The bigger journeys are great events prepared for long in advance and enjoyed by the whole community. The kula maintains friendly intercourse between distant areas and gives a stability to economic relations which is lacking in most parts of Melanesia.

In the low-lying Trobriand Islands there is also extensive exchange of products between the coast and the interior and between the villages rich in food supplies and those which specialize in handicrafts or overseas trading. In the yam-growing villages of the interior the strong spirit of emulation in cultivation produces a considerable surplus of yams. These are proudly displayed, kept in large storehouses and are even left to rot. But individuals in these villages generally have partners in the coastal fishing villages with whom in a series of gifts they exchange the surplus of their respective products.

Quarrels between districts resulting in serious fighting have been rare in the Eastern Solomons, but rivalry between groups of villages, or more particularly their chiefs, have led to feuds which were formerly precipitated by open insult, accusations of sorcery and the stealing of sacrificial victims, canoes or pigs by marauding parties. A man who has blood on his head for the murder of another is always in danger of attack by one who is anxious to earn the blood money. The native weapons are spears, bows and clubs. The bow has long gone out of use in Ulawa, but was used both on land and in sea fighting on Mala until recent times. It is the weapon of the coastal peoples in Melanesia, but where, as at Sa'a, the influence of the interior becomes strong the spear, which is more useful in the bush, often ousts the bow. The Mala bow is of palm wood. The reed arrow shafts are unfeathered but the foreshaft of hard palm wood is barbed with sharp slivers of sago palm rib or, what is magically far more dangerous, slivers of bone taken from human victims. But palm wood spears, often barbed with palm or pig bone splinters, are the favourite weapons both in fighting and hunting. The flying spears are parried with heavy wooden clubs which are tied to the wrist for use at close quarters. A warrior formerly protected his left side against glancing spears and arrows by many layers of bark cloth which hung from the shoulder while shields of hardwood and larger ones of bark, which could be planted in the ground, were also used.

Although every man always carries weapons even when going to his own garden, fighting has rarely been protracted or widespread. Traditional battle-grounds were often used in the past for the settlement of serious disputes between neighbouring villages. The trouble was usually settled quickly by the retirement of the weaker party, and the exchange of presents which followed had little regard to the merits of the dispute, to the losses of the two sides or to the outcome of the battle.

The immunity of neutral villages is respected and women of mutually hostile settlements are often free to come and go in safety. In war time, concealed pits holding well-sharpened bamboo stakes are dug across the approaching trackways, and inland villages are often able to protect themselves more completely by digging trenches across the pathways along the narrow ridges by which travel is alone possible. In a short time these are often weathered into deep chasms by the rains and are crossed by a log which can be removed in time of danger.

It is impossible and unnecessary here to embark on the complex subject of Melanesian religion, but since belief in supernatural power and great awe of the powers of spirits and especially of the ghosts of the dead are salient characteristics of Melanesian life it is essential that the important effects of these beliefs on economic and social activities should be considered.

A host of supernatural forces in the unseen world are believed to influence daily happenings in all kinds of ways for both good and evil. Supernatural power is not conceived as fixed in any one thing although anything may convey it and it is of the greatest advantage to control this power which is widely known through the Pacific as 'mana'. In the Solomons this spiritual force is associated primarily with persons and especially with the ghosts of the dead. An object acquires spiritual power only by the action of a ghost, by its contact with an ancestral relic or by the use of an incantation directed to a ghost. Ghosts remain in the neighbourhood of the village in which they have lived and are potent for good and evil, for aid and frustration according to their former qualities as living men. Thus the invocation of spiritual aid and the placating of the wrath of the ghosts and spirits are matters of supreme importance. The precise character of the supplication and worship of spirits varies considerably, however, in different parts of Melanesia. The people of the Solomons, unlike those of eastern Melanesia, pay little attention to non-ancestral spirits and devote themselves almost exclusively to ghosts. Everywhere it is usual to throw aside a small portion of food, when eating, as an offering to the dead and this is often accompanied by a short prayer for help.

In the Solomons, unlike the New Hebrides and the Banks Islands to the east, there are also elaborate sacrificial rites in which offerings to the ghosts are burnt and eaten at their shrines. For these purposes human sacrifices were made in former times in many parts of the Solomons. They were believed to be necessary to secure the favour of ghosts in any great undertaking, such as the building of a canoe house or the launching of a canoe. Portions of the victims were eaten to acquire physical strength and the bones were hung prominently in the lodge. To obtain victims, marauding expeditions were made or an alleged offender against public morals or the chief's property was slain. In certain areas children were captured and brought up unaware that they would in time serve as sacrifices. Pigs have been substituted for human victims in recent times. When an important project is in view a pig is strangled and a bit of its flesh is burned in a fire at the shrine containing relics of the ghost whose help is required. The rest is eaten by the supplicants.

The ghost to whom offerings are made may not have been dead more than a few years but, on the other hand, he may be a personality quite unremembered as an actual human being. When a powerful personality dies he often replaces some one to whom offerings had previously been made.

At Sa'a a man keeps the relics of his dead father in a special case and calls on his ancestors for aid in difficulties. Pigs are offered to them when sickness falls upon a house, or the crops fail. These pigs appear to be regarded as substitutes for the individual himself whom the ghosts are plaguing. First fruits of the bonito and flying fish, of the canarium nuts and the yams must be offered to the appropriate ghosts before the harvest can safely be taken. For all these tasks specialists are required, men who know the proper incantations and methods of approach. Some ghosts are, as it were, public and others, generally the immediate ancestors, concern only a particular family.

Although many of the sharks which accompany the bonito shoals are regarded as wild and dangerous beasts to be killed if they attack, others are believed to be incarnations of guardian spirits, some of them former human beings, who belong to and protect certain families, landing places and even whole islands from the attacks of wild sharks and human enemies. To these tutelary sharks, who are known by name, prayers must be offered to maintain their guardianship. They are appealed to if the bonito fishing is not successful. Two of great importance which live in the waters between Sa'a and Ulawa are known as the 'Two Fierce Marauders'. When a canoe is attacked by sharks the evil is set down to the sharks of some other district which may have been sent by enemies.

Secret Societies, like the famous Duk-duk of New Britain, the Matambala of Florida, and the Tamate of the Banks Islands which have club houses in the bush and claim to associate with ghosts in secret rites and, after suitable payment of pigs or shell money, initiate young men into their ranks, are not found in the south-eastern Solomons, nor in Santa Cruz, although Mala is only thirty miles from Florida and the peoples of the islands are in frequent contact.

The agriculture and craftsmanship of Melanesia are far in advance of that found among the Boro and other Amazon peoples. Men take a full share in cultivation. Care and skill are lavished on the production of food and the embellishment of houses, canoes and other equipment. The social unit is no larger but it has a far wider range of contacts and experience. The wide stretches of sea that separate Melanesia from Asia and one island group from another have proved less serious barriers than the equatorial forests of South America.

But the achievement of man in the equatorial islands of Oceania cannot be estimated in terms of Melanesia alone. In Polynesia both technical skill and social elaboration outstripped those of the more western peoples. Some consideration of the extent of this greater achievement, of its conditions and development must be made.

III. POLYNESIA—THE SOCIETY ISLANDS

Although generally quite distinct from the Melanesians in type the Polynesians are by no means homogeneous in race. They appear to be a variable blend of a negroid element with a light-skinned, wavy-haired strain fundamentally Mediterranean in type and akin to some of the peoples of Malaya. There are also traces of a paler skinned, bearded and round-headed element which may be the latest of all and approximates to the Alpine type of Europe and western Asia. In some groups there is also a mongoloid strain, but this is more marked in Micronesia to the north-west. These racial mixtures were probably effected to a large degree in Polynesia itself, for the negroid element is variable and is distributed in such a manner as to suggest an early Melanesian occupation of the greater part of Polynesia. In Tonga, New Zealand and especially in Easter Island in the far west, skin colour is darker, noses are broader and the hair more curly than elsewhere. In Fiji, which lies on the borderland between Polynesia and Melanesia and is culturally hybrid, the population is still closer to the Melanesian type. Moreover, certain crafts and customs characteristic of Melanesia are widespread in Polynesia, including the more remote areas. They appear rather as survivals of an early phase than as late infiltrations from Melanesia. The negroid element has however been so extensively modified by mixture with the later arrivals that the Polynesians as a whole are light brown in skin colour, fairly tall in stature and were truly described by the early explorers as 'European' in countenance.

Taken as a whole the island groups of Polynesia differ from those of Melanesia in several characteristic features. There are in the first place fewer large islands. Tahiti, the largest island in central Polynesia, is only about thirty miles long and about fifteen miles across at its widest point. On the other hand coral atolls are more numerous and are inhabited by groups whose economic life had to be adapted to the restricted conditions. Furthermore, the islands of the Central Pacific were not, like parts of Melanesia, connected with Australia in

recent geological times, thus much of the characteristic vegetation and fauna of Melanesia is absent. The natural flora was
restricted to plants whose seeds could be carried long distances
by water, wind and birds; the coconut and pandanus palms
had reached the shores by water, but the interiors of the larger
islands were largely clothed in tree ferns whose minute spores
could be carried hundreds of miles by wind action. These
meagre resources discouraged inland settlement, and the
mountainous interiors of the high islands were generally
uninhabited.

But the cultivated plants found in the western Pacific were
also introduced into Polynesia and in many groups agriculture
is more elaborate than in Melanesia. Far more attention is
paid to taro and breadfruit than to yams. Since the rainfall
is in general considerably lower, irrigation is more necessary.
Taro, nearly everywhere associated with irrigation in Asia,
is in Polynesia cultivated in terraced plots, watered by diverting
streams before they descend to the narrow shores so that the
water can be led down from one level to another. Breadfruit
trees, propagated from roots or cuttings, are planted round
the houses and established on the hillsides which are too
steep for taro beds. The globular fruit of this large, shady
tree is second only to taro as a food. Coming into bearing
after five years the breadfruit continues to yield for nearly
fifty years, and since different varieties ripen at different
times of the year, ripe breadfruit is always available. Taro,
unlike the yam, will not keep; surplus breadfruit is prepared
in large quantities for storing by roasting whole or baking in
the stone ovens, and it is one of the most valuable foods for
carrying on sea-journeys. Large quantities are baked whole
in large, stone-lined pits in which fires have previously been
lit, and the cooked fruits are cut up, dried and packed away.

The areca-betel chewing mixture is unknown in Polynesia,
but *kava*, a mildly intoxicating drink, is prepared from the root
of a variety of pepper similar to that whose leaves are chewed
in Melanesia. It is generally planted in damp places along
streams and prepared by chewing the fresh root, adding
water and straining off the fluid. *Kava* drinking is nearly
always a ceremonial procedure, and the cup is handed round
in order of rank.

Pigs are highly valued as the main source of meat and are
more carefully reared than in Melanesia; they are regularly
fed and usually tethered near the houses. Chickens, little
different from the wild jungle fowl of southern Asia, had
been introduced in early times, but except in remote Easter

Island, where they are the only domestic animal, they are little cared for and the eggs are not eaten. Apart from pigeons and seabirds the only wild animals are lizards and rats, though in some of the larger islands pigs that have escaped from domestication live wild in the bush. Rats are trapped for food and pig hunting is a favourite sport, but the return in food is meagre.

Fishing plays a far greater part in the economy. In general the equipment of hooks, lines and nets is similar to the Melanesian, though larger fish are taken and the resources are more intensively exploited. On many of the low islands where taro and breadfruit can only be grown with difficulty fish are the staple diet. They are speared, shot with bow and arrow, and stupefied with plant juices in tidal pools. Divers descend a hundred feet to gather oysters. which provide the magical

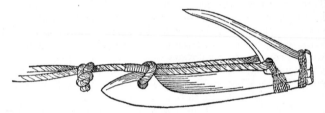

FIG. 70. SHELL-FISH HOOK FROM THE SOCIETY ISLANDS
(*After Linton*)

pearl shell as well as food. The giant ray, fourteen teet long, is caught with detachable harpoon heads, and elaborate stone weirs and fish-traps are built in Samoa, the Society Islands and elsewhere. Large fishing expeditions visit distant banks at the appropriate seasons.

In Polynesia long wraps and elaborate ceremonial costumes are made from bark cloth or *tapa*. The inner bark of paper mulberry saplings, which are cultivated for the purpose, provides the finest material. The strips of bark are beaten with short, bat-like clubs and overlapped at their edges during the process so that a sheet of any size can be produced. Nearly everywhere in Polynesia tapa is decorated; it is painted and stamped with vegetable pigments. Tapa is surprisingly durable so long as it remains dry, and it can also be made resistant to water by oiling it or smearing on varnishes obtained from tree saps.

Although the physical conditions and cultural resources are fundamentally so similar, the social organization of Polynesia contrasts profoundly with that of Melanesia. The differences which have considerable effect on the economic life centre round the sacred ruling families which dominate aboriginal Polynesian society. These features may be briefly illustrated from the Society Islands (Tahiti and the Leeward Islands), a group of prime importance in the development of Polynesian culture.

The majority of the people were formerly landless commoners or serfs who supplied all heavy manual labour.[1] They cultivated for a landowning class of sub-chiefs who were themselves in feudal dependence on the *arii*, an interrelated group of sacred chiefly families. Inheritance of rank, office and property passed to the eldest child. The head of an *arii* family controlled a large autonomous district in Tahiti, or often the whole of one of the smaller islands. In theory he was both its absolute master and at the same time the sacred embodiment of the prosperity of both land and people. The ruling families had little direct contact with the commoners but acted through the landowning sub-chiefs, who provided supplies of food and materials and led their own detachments in time of war.

Skilled craftsmen were virtually a class of hereditary priests, for every craft had an elaborate ritual and was handed on from father to son. A special society known as the *Areoi*, whose members might bear no children and were regarded as divinely inspired, wandered from district to district. Enjoying hospitality of the chiefs they gave dramatic performances and dances, which were vaguely believed to promote prosperity and abundance. Attached to a chief were his high priest, war leader, orator and a number of minor officials. All the more important of these were themselves *arii*, relatives of the chief and selected by him. The priesthood was largely the prerogative of the hereditary heads of the cadet branches of the sacred *arii* families, and was divided into a number of orders devoted to various gods and rites. The chief priest of a major god ranked close to the chief himself. The men of these cadet branches were also trained in fighting and provided a bodyguard for the chief.

The machinery of government was, however, informal. Important affairs were decided by councils in which the chief met the landowners, whose support was vital for any large enterprise or military expedition. The authority of the *arii* depended fundamentally on their sanctity. Numerous

---

[1] This account is given in the past tense because here, as nearly everywhere in Polynesia, the native organization has largely disintegrated as a result of European influence.

prohibitions or taboos protected their persons, clothing and possessions. Everything in the least degree connected with the chief became sacred. Any place he walked on, any house he entered, any object he touched or commanded could no longer be used for secular purposes by any inferior. When travelling he was carried on the shoulders of sacred bearers. His orders were sacred. An edict he pronounced suspending any activity had a magical and religious validity. It was possible in this way to accumulate stores of food and materials by suspending for a time the gathering or eating of certain foods or the cutting of trees.

Every chiefly family had its sacred enclosure, which was both a temple and burial ground. These were usually stone-walled enclosures with a stone platform or pyramid at one end. All important rites concerning the family were performed within the enclosures, and in them were placed stone images into which the gods entered on ceremonial occasions. The similar shrines of the lesser chiefs were consecrated by the *arii*.

Since the title to land, to authority and to sacred office depended on descent, genealogies were carefully studied and every well-born individual knew his own pedigree for many generations. Certain priests memorized the pedigrees of related groups of families and tested all claims. Instances are recorded in which individuals have come to a district claiming descent from chiefs or landowners who had left several generations before, and, having proved their titles, have had their lands restored to them. When need and opportunity arose, however, the priests were also expert in faking a high-sounding pedigree to confirm *de facto* authority.

The relative rank of individuals within the chiefly and land-owning families was strictly based on descent. The rank and claims of an individual depended on the rank of both parents and on his own order of birth. The eldest child of whatever sex by the first wife ranked first within a family and inherited the rights and social prestige of the father. Although a first-born daughter might not exercise certain privileges, she received the respect of any brother who might do so, while her children, unless she married a man of much lower rank, stood before those of her younger brothers. The sacred chiefs carefully controlled their marriages to maintain the high rank of their families. But although the marriage alliances of *arii* of different tribal districts effected temporary political unions, there was no stable federation of large areas or groups of islands.

The Polynesians had little superiority over the Melanesians

in actual tools and constructional materials. They made no pottery, did not weave and had no metal. Their shell and ground stone adzes were intrinsically no more efficient than the Melanesian counterparts. But their superior organization and the desire of the ruling families to enhance their prestige resulted in a far higher technical achievement.

Although the mass of the people in the Society Islands lived in small, rectangular huts no more imposing than the houses of a Sa'a hamlet, the assembly houses and the dwellings of chiefs and landowners were capacious buildings often fifty to a hundred yards long and nearly half as wide. These were erected on stone-faced platforms or had their plank floors

FIG. 71. TYPES OF CHIEFS' HOUSES AND ASSEMBLY
HOUSES IN THE SOCIETY ISLANDS
(*Based on photographs by Handy*)

raised two or three feet from the ground. They were long in plan, with parallel sides and rounded ends, and were built by professional carpenters. The frame of breadfruit timbers consisted of massive king posts supporting a ridge pole from which rafters descended to the wall plate. All the timbers were carefully shaped and smoothed and fitted together with mortised joints. The roofs were covered with a finely made pandanus thatch. The light walling of split bamboo or palm leaf matting, and the more usual lattice of bamboo rods or hibiscus withes permitted free ventilation, and they were sometimes made in removable sections. The coconut fibre lashings which secured the framework and thatching were skilfully arranged in order to produce elaborate ornamental patterns of varied colours.

Boats of several types and many sizes were built in the Society Islands. Small rafts of flat bamboo bundles were used to carry goods across the lagoons. These were generally poled or pushed by waders, but kites were also used to tow them. The best canoes were made of the durable and hard *ate* wood, but breadfruit, coconut, mango and other timbers were used. For fishing and travel within and near the reefs small round-bottomed dugouts with upcurving ends, hewn from a single log, were used, while for longer journeys and bigger crews there were larger vessels, which, although similar in shape to the dugouts, were as much as seventy feet long. Since a single trunk of that size was unobtainable these vessels were made in two parts in Tahiti. The fore and aft were hewn and adzed from separate trunks, and by cutting back the lower part of the front half and fitting it into a reciprocal projection of the rear they could be lashed securely together. The fitting edges were then lashed together with coconut fibre cords passing through numerous bore holes. A flat bow piece of five or six feet was fitted to project horizontally over the water, while the stern curved up as in the smaller dugouts.

Large vessels of different shape and construction were built in the Leeward Islands. These were keeled craft built up in several sections and of many short lengths of wood. The lack of large timber in these islands might account for their composite build but not for their remarkable heart-shaped cross section. The V-shaped keel piece was carved from one or more long trunks. The bulging sides were built up by lashing together two tiers of short planks each only about four feet long and a foot wide. These planks were split with wedges and carefully shaped one by one so that they fitted together, giving the required curves. Above them longer moulded top strakes were set vertically to form the gunwales, and tall up-curving pieces were attached at the prow and stern. All these separate planks were lashed together with sinnet cords passing through bore holes in the planks and through projecting lugs or cleats left on their inner sides. No grooving or overlapping was used in securing them one to the other. The joints were caulked with coconut fibre and a pitch of burnt breadfruit gum. The hull was strengthened with struts and cross-pieces, and when complete was both stronger and more seaworthy than the dugout hulls.

The hollowing of trunks and the shaping of planks was all done with basalt adzes of various weights which were constantly sharpened on a grindstone as the worker proceeded. Chisels and gouges were usually made of tough human bone.

The sides of a canoe were smoothed and polished with abrasive sands and coral rubbing stones, while the bow and stern were elaborately carved with human and animal figures.

Canoe building was in the hands of a guild of professionals with its own special regulations and rites. The building of larger vessels at the command of the chief was an elaborate and ceremonial affair which involved the whole community. Apprentices and labourers assisted the expert builders and the landowners levied food-supplies to feed the workers. The building shed, the workers and the tools were all consecrated

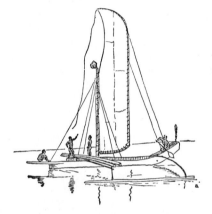

FIG. 72. TAHITIAN OUTRIGGER
SAILING CANOE
(*From an eighteenth century drawing by
Tobin*)

and kept apart throughout the work lest any evil influence should contaminate the boat.

Boats were usually stabilized by building an outrigger, but for long voyages and larger parties two of the large two-piece dugouts or of the plank-built vessels were lashed together about four feet apart and on the cross bars a large deck was constructed on which a hut or awning was erected. These double canoes were also used in war when the opposing forces grappled with one another so that club bearers who crowded the decks could fight hand to hand.

Sails were in regular use on all canoes. The removable mast was held in place by stays running fore and aft to the forward outrigger spar and to a cross plank which projected on the opposite side. This plank tilted up so that the vessel could be balanced and the wind taken on either quarter by shifting the position of a man who stood out on it. The tall and narrow sail of pandanus matting was lashed between the mast and a short upcurving boom from which a vertical spar ran up. It was stretched by an oblique sprit running up from the mast, and was controlled by a series of ropes belayed to the stern and to the outrigger spars. In western Polynesia from Fiji to Samoa larger triangular lateen sails were also used. On sailing voyages extra wash strakes were added and lashed on to canoes to increase the free-board. Canoes were also propelled with simple paddles with long and rather narrow blades rounded at the end. In the upraised stern sat the captain, who steered with a larger paddle six to eight feet long.

Small double canoes were used in deep-sea fishing and for voyages between islands. The largest were built for long voyages, such as to the Tuamotus, for war and as floating temples. Powerful chiefs had large fleets of more than a hundred double canoes, and held reviews and regattas in which all vessels specially decorated took part. Voyages to distant groups were made for purposes of trade in special objects, often of little intrinsic value. Adventure, prestige and ceremonial played a great part in promoting these long voyages. Vessels from the Society Islands had according to tradition made voyages to the very limits of Polynesia, to Hawaii in the north and to New Zealand in the south. The Tuamotu and Cook Islands, and probably Samoa, Tonga and Fiji, were well known to the Tahitians at the time of European discovery. Lacking all mechanical aids to navigation, the conditions of winds, seas, sky and stars were minutely known to the experienced navigators, and they were amazingly skilled in holding to a course.

The larger ocean-going vessels were more than a hundred feet long and five feet deep, and could if necessary carry several hundred people with provisions and water. In this way whole communities often set out in search of other land making temporary halts for re-victualling at atolls until the encountered desirable land whose inhabitants they could over come or placate, and taking with them pigs, poultry and young food plants that they could raise in their new home. When seeking land the large fleets often spread out along a wide front, each vessel several miles from its neighbours, so that small islands, mere specks in the great ocean, could be picked up.

Equipped with these boats the Polynesians covered millions of square miles of sea in the space of a few centuries. The

Society Islands were one of the great centres of expansion. From them repeated journeys were made to Hawaii and New Zealand during the centuries following the arrival of the *arii*. In the great voyages from Tahiti to New Zealand the navigators ran down to Raratonga in the Cook group, and from there launched out on a ten to twenty day voyage of about sixteen hundred miles, which was made in December when the wind was favourable. The return could best be undertaken in June.

The Polynesian colonization of the central Pacific probably began in the early centuries of the Christian era, and there were several periods of extensive voyaging. It has been estimated, from the comparative study of genealogical records and of cultural distributions, that the sacred *arii* families of central Polynesia arrived from the West little more than a thousand years ago. That they introduced many new customs and modified much existing practice is claimed from the cultural distinction between *arii* and commoners that existed in Tonga, Samoa and particularly in Tahiti in recent times. The migrations of peoples from central Polynesia to such outlying areas as the Marquesas, Hawaii and New Zealand, both before and even since the coming of the *arii*, have carried but few of the new customs, so that the economic and social life of older Polynesia has survived relatively unchanged in many of these marginal areas. The Polynesian migrations are not to be thought of as a deliberately planned movement maintained over long centuries with a single ultimate purpose. It was rather a sporadic process in which social, religious and economic factors slowly became insistent enough to stimulate a further movement. Some of them were undoubtedly accidental. Within recent times many vessels sailing between islands fairly near to one another have been forced from their course by wind or current and have drifted in search of land. Captain Cook found castaways from Tahiti on an island in the Cook group, and in the early eighteenth century a hundred canoes reached Guam in Micronesia after drifting for twenty days. These involuntary voyages must have had far-reaching effects, and the first Polynesian inhabitants of New Zealand may have arrived in canoes that had drifted off their course.

But it is also quite certain that deliberate voyages of many hundreds of miles were undertaken. Many have ascribed this enterprise to the adventurous nature of the Polynesians, and point to the fact that Melanesians have been consistently averse to long sea voyages and have undertaken them only in the company of Polynesians. Even the Fijians, who constructed fine vessels and may even have been the inventors of the double canoe, made no independent voyages outside their own group, although Tongan canoes visited them frequently. But so little is known of racial differences in these matters, and apparently similar ethnic groups have displayed such different qualities at different periods and places, that one must be reluctant to adopt them as a complete solution. It is probably safer to allow great importance to social and cultural factors as well in accounting for the persistence of these voyages. The sacred chieftainship, which appears to have existed in a somewhat different form even before the appearance of the *arii*, has certainly been associated in more recent times with the hiving off of junior branches of the ruling families, often in consequence of disputes over rank. The great desire for high-sounding achievement and the search for economically and magically valuable resources from fishing banks to pearl beds also played a prominent part. The green jade from New Zealand was carried back to central Polynesia and was accorded great magical value.

The Polynesian expansions involved areas very different in their physical condition from the equatorial islands of the central Pacific. In Hawaii the Polynesians reached a land in which many of their staple foods were difficult to grow and the sweet potato, of second importance elsewhere, became the food staple. In New Zealand the contrasts in the habitat were even greater and led to extensive cultural modifications. The large area and wide plains of New Zealand, the dense forests of large trees and the cool temperate climate which excluded many of the important Polynesian foods were met by extensive modifications in social organization and crafts. Dense populations in large tribal territories permitted the chiefly rivalry of Polynesia to express itself in more elaborate warfare. Although Polynesian food plants were brought by the voyagers, taro and yams could only be raised on the northern tip of North Island, while even the sweet potato could not be grown over the greater part of South Island. The more southern Maori were compelled to revert to a food-gathering economy, and the edible root of a native tree fern became the staple food. No pigs or chickens were brought into New Zealand and the native fauna was poor. The moa—a large ostrich-like bird—was hunted until it became extinct. No tree was suitable for making tapa cloth, but a suitable clothing material of very different type was found in the fibres of the New Zealand 'flax' (*Phormia tenax*), which was made into matting and skirts and capes of loose hanging fibres. The light-walled Polynesian houses were not suitable to the cold winters in these southern islands. Heavily thatched pit dwellings were constructed for use at this season, while planks split from the great Kauri pines were used to wall the larger structures, and especially the assembly houses. The Kauri pine, abundant in North Island, also made it possible to hew large and capacious canoes out of a single trunk. The extensive use of soft timber gave an opportunity for a unique development of wood-carving, the patterns of which were also laboriously executed in hard stones with the aid of sand and a simple tubular drill. The Maori of New Zealand developed a substantially new economy in these large southern islands, but their social life remained essentially Polynesian.

CHAPTER XII

THE HOPI AND YUMA: FLOOD FARMERS IN
THE NORTH AMERICAN DESERT

IN western North America, to the south-east of the Great
Basin which was briefly characterized in an earlier chapter
lies another arid upland region extending from the southern
Rockies to the Lower Colorado river. This great area, usually
known as the 'Southwest', resembles the Great Basin in many
of its physical and climatic features, but the high plateaux are
often more extensive and flank wider river basins. Although
the highest peaks rise above eleven thousand feet, most of the
country to the west is lower-lying than the Great Basin. In
the north the high plateau, which has an average elevation of
over six thousand feet, has been dissected into flat-topped
eminences or *mesas* and cliff-faced canyons. The Grand
Canyon, although unique in scale and grandeur, has many
minor counterparts. But to the south-west the country slopes
down to the low-lying Gila basin and to the Colorado delta
Winters are less cold in this lower and more southern region
but except at high altitudes the rainfall is even lower than in
the Great Basin.

In the higher mountains there are forests of firs, below
which dwarf pine and juniper woods are found. Although there
are some considerable tracts of poor grassland, the scanty
vegetation of the lower-lying lands consists mostly of low
shrubs, of leathery fibrous-leaved plants like the agave and
yucca and of many kinds of cactus.

The greater part of this desert area was occupied in pre-
Columbian times by food-gathering peoples, similar in their
general economy to the peoples of the southern Great Basin
But there were also 'islands' of sedentary cultivating peoples
some of whom have retained their native life until the present
day. In the east the cultivators live in compact villages called
pueblos by the early Spanish explorers. These pueblos, each
usually several miles from its neighbour and the main cluster
separated from others by wide tracts of more than a hundred
miles which are occupied only by alien hunters and collectors
are scattered unevenly along the tributaries of the Rio Grande

and the Little Colorado rivers. They are most numerous in the Rio Grande drainage to the east, but the westernmost group, the Hopi villages, have preserved their native economy the most completely.

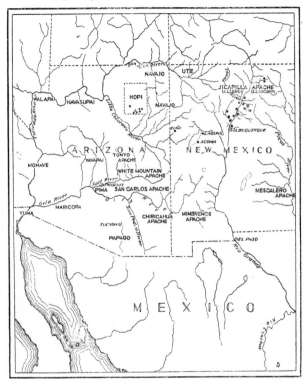

FIG. 73. SKETCH MAP OF THE NATIVE PEOPLES OF THE SOUTHWEST. PUEBLOS ARE SHOWN BY BLACK SQUARES
(*After Goddard*)

Although they are a typical Pueblo people the Hopi are Shoshonean speaking, and therefore linguistically related to the Great Basin peoples to the north-west. In contrast to most of the non-agricultural peoples who surround them, they are a rather short, thickset people, the men being rarely more than five feet three or four inches in height. They have, however, the warm brown colour, straight black hair and rather broad face common to all.

The Hopi, like all the Pueblo dwellers, are maize cultivators in a desert region. The precipitation is however quite inadequate for their staple crop, and agriculture is therefore

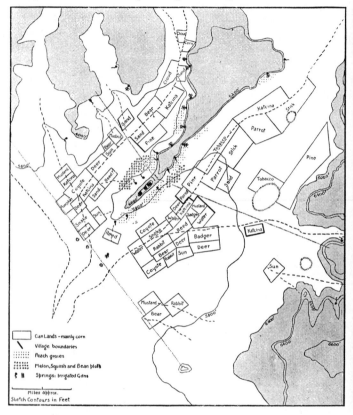

FIG. 74. SKETCH MAP OF THE TERRITORY OF THE HOPI PUEBLOS ON FIRST MESA. THE VILLAGES SHOWN BY BLACK SQUARES ARE WALPI, SICHOMOVI AND HANO; THE LANDS ON THE SOUTHWEST BELONG JOINTLY TO THE FIRST TWO

dependent on the availability of water from streams and springs. The nature of these resources must first be considered.

The villages are grouped on the southern spurs of a large culminating plateau, to the south of which extends a high basin sloping down to the Little Colorado river. This basin has been filled to considerable depth with finely divided rock waste eroded from the plateaux and carried out by floods on the intermittent streams. On the plateau there is a general slope to the south-west from the northern heights of eight thousand feet. While steep and lofty cliffs from one to two thousand feet border the mesa on the north and north-west, the southern side has been cut into a number of tongues of lower plateau projecting into the sand-filled basin a few hundred feet below and separated by the widening valleys of the streams which drain the plateau. On account of the tilt of the general surface the larger streams rise close to the northern edge and receive practically the entire surface drainage.

No records of the precipitation on the higher plateau are available, but the relatively dense vegetation of juniper and pine indicates a considerably greater fall than in the lower country to the south, which receives an average fall of barely ten inches. Precipitation is not only low, but very uncertain, varying for any one year from half to twice the mean, and this uncertainty is even greater for any single month. Late summer is the period of greatest rainfall when local but extremely violent thunderstorms develop; these are accompanied by sudden and often heavy downpours; but lighter showers and a more even distribution of rain over the days of July and August may also occur. Light snowfalls occur in the relatively severe winter season. In January the mean temperature is around freezing point, while over forty degrees of frost have been recorded on exceptional days. Late killing frosts in May and even June are a real danger to the Hopi in their dependence on so slow-growing a staple as maize, which requires three to five months to mature. Between the winter snowfalls, equal to three to four inches of rain, and the later summer storms, there is a dry period. The spring rainfall averages less than two inches, and June is the driest month of the year; this is particularly unfortunate, since the crops require water urgently during the early growing period.

The precipitation at the southern mesa edge and over the alluvial basin to the south is alone quite inadequate for agriculture, and supports but the scantiest sage-brush vegetation, with occasional cotton-wood trees and yucca. The absolute necessity for more water than that provided by the direct fall is obvious. The existence of streams draining from the high plateau to the flat valley floors between the southern tongues of the mesa affords such a supply. In addition to the surface drainage from the plateau there is also an important southward seepage of underground water, for the surface rock on the plateau top is a fairly permeable sandstone which dips southward. This is underlaid by impermeable shales, so that the imprisoned water seeps southward along the plane of contact. The junction of the sandstone and the shales in the neighbourhood of the pueblos lies some twenty to fifty feet above the base of the cliffs, and along this line many small springs and seeps emerge.

These two circumstances—the southward drainage of the relatively well-watered high plateau and the development of a spring line along the edges of the southern spurs—are of the greatest importance in Hopi economy.

Furthermore, the utilization of this water supply is closely related to the peculiar character of the run-off. Since so much of the rainfall occurs during heavy thunderstorms of short duration, the ground surface is rapidly saturated and a high proportion of the fall reaches the streams. On the plateau the intermittent streams flow in narrow canyons which they have cut in the floor of the valleys, but they emerge from these miniature gorges at the mesa edge, and, with reduction of slope, their velocity is considerably reduced, so that they cease to flow in well-defined channels but fan out over alluvial flats where the valleys open out into the southern basin. The accumulation of alluvial material and the imperfect gradation which follows from the alternation of flooding and drying up of the streams leads to the formation of shallow but short-lived lakes. The water, which may lie nearly a foot deep after a heavy rain, is dispersed in a few days by evaporation and underground seepage. During the later part of the summer season there is generally a continuous supply of water in the plateau streams which drain considerable catchment areas, and these emerge as shallow gullies or 'washes' in the flats. Thus the lower-lying parts of the flats receive a number of inundations during late June, July and August. The land is temporarily drenched or even flooded to a depth of six inches or more, and there is also a considerable underground percolation of water. Similar flooding and underground percolation is produced on a smaller scale along the sides of the valleys, the water in this case being derived from direct run-off from the scarps, and from the seeps and springs, whose flow responds rapidly to rainfall on the plateau above. There are, therefore, two zones which offer the most favourable conditions for cultivation: first, that in the middle of the valley down which the greater part of the flood waters pass; and second, a strip along the foot of the mesas which receives a lateral supply. Where the valley is relatively narrow the two zones coalesce to form a single belt of cultivable land.

Hopi cultivation depends essentially on the utilization of these naturally flooded areas; it is flood-water farming, and not an organized system of basin and channel irrigation. These fortunate circumstances are not unique; they are found widely on the southern margin of the Colorado plateau, and similar flood water farming is practised by other Pueblo peoples, notably the Zuñi, by groups of sedentary Navajo, and in Spanish Mexican settlements of southern New Mexico and Arizona.

The precise site of the planted area depends on local and variable conditions. An excess of water at considerable velocity will wash out the crops, while a heavy silt load may bury them. Neither of these dangers can be entirely averted, and destructive floods are the second hazard of Hopi cultivation. Severe storms, bringing heavy rains on the plateau may, even though there is little or no fall in the vicinity of the villages, destroy whole fields. The run-off is so rapid that even the deeper channels cut in the flats during recent years are unable to contain the flood which rushes down after these storms. The waters may sweep violently over the fields, temporarily reducing them to a spongy marsh and uprooting almost every plant.

The conditions of run-off have, moreover, been considerably modified in recent years by the trenching of the washes. This cutting of steep-sided channels or *arroyos*, often twenty to thirty feet deep, has reduced the cultivable value of much land that was formerly subject to natural irrigation.[1] The arroyos have cut across old field sites, and by the erosion of the concave banks they continue to encroach on fields in their vicinity. The concentration of the surface flow in miniature canyons well below the field-level has often seriously reduced the amount of water received by the fields themselves, and mere scraps of land on the floors of the arroyos are valued on account of their superior water supply. If a man finds that an erosion channel is beginning to develop in his field, he endeavours to arrest it while it is still small by erecting barriers of logs and brushwood; against these alluvium and wind-blown sand often collect to fill the incipient channel. Level stretches favourable to water conservation are also constructed artificially on a

[1] It is possibly due in part to the increased sheep grazing of the catchment areas in the plateau and of the valleys themselves which, by reducing the vegetation cover, have increased both the volume and the rapidity of run-off, giving it greater erosive power. But there is evidence of recently accelerated erosion and of deepening of arroyos throughout the Southwest and a new cycle of erosion may have been established quite apart from human interference. *See* Kirk Bryan, 'Flood Water Farming in Southern New Mexico', *Geog. Review*, Vol. 19, 1929.

small scale in narrow gullies cut back into the side of main valleys. These are dammed across at frequent intervals with low walls of stone and brush, against which fine, sandy detritus rapidly accumulates to form a small flat in which is consumed a considerable part of the water supply from freshets which flow down after rains. These sheltered gully flats, with their more assured and less violent water supply, are particularly suited for growing early corn. The introduction of American methods and appliances, which have modified Hopi practice in recent times, has to some extent compensated for the evils of arroyo cutting. Increase in the number of horses, donkeys and wagons has enabled them to farm land on a larger scale and at greater distances from the villages.

The villages of the Hopi consist of three groups—two perched a few miles apart on the tops of the mesa tongues about two hundred feet above the fields, and one fifteen miles to the west on lower ground. The retreat to the summits is relatively recent. Disturbance by the Spaniards and the raids of the hunting peoples, particularly the Ute after they had acquired horses, induced the Hopi to resort to these defensive positions. The lowland predecessors of the mesa villages are well known to the Hopi, and they are aware of the recency of their desertion, but they now resist all attempts to induce them to return to the valleys. All water and crops must be carried up the steep and narrow mesa trails.

On the easternmost tongue of plateau known as First Mesa there are three villages. Two of them are separated only by a hundred yards, where the mesa narrows to a neck a few yards wide, and one, Sichomovi, is an extension of the other, Walpi, rather than a separate village. The clan and ceremonial organizations of the two villages form one system, and lands are jointly owned. The third village, Hano, is occupied by an alien group, the descendants of recent Tewa immigrants of quite a different speech from the Rio Grande. The Tewa people are now bilingual. These First Mesa villages farm land on the flats to either side of the mesa peninsula on which they stand. The group of villages four miles to the west on the plateau known as Second Mesa, farm land on the lowlands adjacent to their villages and out on the valley to the south and west where they march with those of the westernmost village of Oraibi. There are definite boundaries between the lands of the individual villages; their main direction is often defined by sight lines across the flats between two eminences on the plateaux, while minor hillocks in the valleys, formerly marked with boundary stones, indicate them on the ground (see fig. 74).

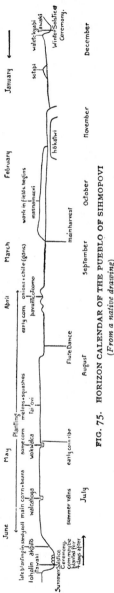

FIG. 75. HORIZON CALENDAR OF THE PUEBLO OF SHMOPOVI
(*From a native drawing*)

The agricultural season opens in February with the clearing of the fields and ends with the last days of September when the last corn and beans are gathered in. Although the condition of the weather and the season determine the precise time of various agricultural operations, each stage is also anticipated and regulated according to a precise calendar. This calendar, which serves also to determine the dates of the many ceremonies, is provided by the daily shift in the position of sunrise on the horizon. The smallest irregularities on the southern sky-line are well known, and the more significant within the sun's path, probably some twenty or more, are named with reference either to their form, to ceremonial events or to agricultural operations which fall due when the sun rises immediately behind them. For a well-educated Hopi such terms as *neverktcomo* and *lohalin* have as precise a significance as have for us May 3rd and June 21st with which they correspond. The daily observation of these positions of sunrise is the duty of a religious official, the Sun Watcher, who forewarns the people of important dates and announces them in due course; he also keeps tally on a notched stick.

Maize or Indian corn is by far the most important crop. The first corn is planted towards the end of April. This early planting is of great importance, for it provides green corn for the ceremony of the Departure of the Ancestor Spirits at the end of July; but the bulk of the corn planting takes place considerably later. It is probably postponed as long as possible in order to escape late frosts and to obtain the greatest advantages of the summer rains. Sandstorms are also particularly severe in the late spring; these, while very destructive to young plants, appear to serve one useful purpose in filling cracks on the field surfaces and thus reducing evaporation.

Water-melon and pumpkin (or 'squash') planting follows the early corn in the first week of May. The main planting of corn and beans, with further squashes and water-melons, begins a fortnight later and may continue until midsummer. The whole

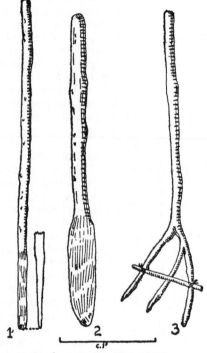

FIG. 76. AGRICULTURAL TOOLS
I, PLANTING DIBBLE; 2, WEED-CUTTER; 3. RAKE

period of planting, from the end of April until the solstice, is divided into a number of smaller periods of rather less than a week in duration, named from successive horizon points. All these points are announced by the Sun Watcher, and individuals generally follow the same programme each year, waiting for the announcement of the day or period in which they intend to plant. Field parties of relatives and friends are formed, for only a few fields are planted at any given time; these parties are arranged beforehand, and the helpers, if they are not members of the owner's household, are paid with presents, reciprocal services or the promise of a certain share in the crop.

When the clearing of the fields is begun, branches of gnarled shrubs are gathered to repair low brush fences which are set up to protect exposed plots against blown sand. Weeds and sage brush are dug out with a paddle-shaped tool and are dragged off with rough wooden rakes made from juniper branches. The surface soil is then loosened between the still standing stumps of last year's harvest which have been left as

FIG. 77. A HOPI CORNFIELD

guides for planting. Later in the season weeds must be kept down by frequent chopping and uprooting during the growing season, for they consume moisture needed by the crops. For these tasks the same bladed tool is still often used, although imported iron hoes of the square-bladed Spanish type and wooden copies of them, as well as American spades, have now frequently superseded it.

A typical Hopi corn-field is usually about an acre in area, but the plants are very widely spaced. The field is divided into strips about twelve paces wide, each of which is planted in turn by means of transverse rows of seed holes. The rows are three or four paces from each other and the seed holes in a row two or three paces apart. The rows of adjacent strips are planted so that they alternate with each other, and the seed holes of one year are placed between the rows of the previous one. The seed is planted nearly a foot deep and from ten to twenty seeds are dropped into the hole scooped out with the dibble. Women occasionally help the men, especially if planting is behindhand: they hold the corn bags, drop in the seeds and fill up the holes. This deep planting assists in the development of the rooting system, reduces the risk of the seedlings being parched out in a dry year and protects them from being washed out by heavy rains or flood. The large numbers of seeds are required not only to insure against the ravages of field-mice and cutworms, but on account of the destructive powers of the violent sand-laden winds, usually blowing from the south-west. The numerous seeds sprout to form a young bush with a dozen or more stalks, but the wind-blown sand cuts away nearly half the stems before they are able to develop enough foliage to protect themselves; by harvest time the leaves of the corn clumps on the windward side of an exposed field have been torn into withering shreds. The ground is not hilled up around the plants as in the east, but low banks about a yard or so in diameter are often scooped up to encircle each corn clump and so retain water after rain and flooding.

The heavier land in the middle of the valleys is considered best for corn, but beans and melons like sandy ground close to the mesa. Beans, of which there are four or five native varieties, are occasionally planted between the rows of corn, but are more often set half a pace apart in another and smaller plot. Squashes and melons are likewise planted in alternating strips, while a few gourds for making dippers, bottles, rattles and other implements are usually planted in the melon plots. The plants receive considerable care during their growth. Parts of the plot which fail to receive flood water are levelled off or roughly trenched to promote a readier flow. Where plants, especially squashes and melons, are growing in an exposed position, a miniature wind-break is constructed with twigs to protect each young plant from being tattered or smothered by blown sand.

The Hopi fields are not abandoned after a few years. Fertility is maintained by the annual accumulation of alluvium and blown soil, as well as by the wide spacing of the plants. The crop on a particular plot is rarely changed, and that most suited to its quality is, as a rule, continuously grown.

Work in the fields began at sunrise in the old days, and except at harvest-time was abandoned before the heat of the day. Where fields are at any considerable distance from the village small temporary huts are erected and serve as shelters from heat and storm; these are often occupied by the whole family during the period of roasting green corn and during the main harvest.

The native corn is of many colours. Blue and white corn are said to ripen more quickly and to yield larger cobs than the other varieties; red or pink corn is little grown because it yields poorly. It is, however, prized for a dish known as *pikani*, which is made to-day by roasting a mixture of ground corn and sugar in an earth oven.

The first corn is cut green in July and is roasted in pit ovens in the fields. A good deal of this is however obtained from the irrigated plots at the springs. The main corn harvest begins late in September and continues during the first weeks of October. As for the planting, working parties are formed and they may stay in the fields from dawn to sunset. The ears are broken off, husked and carried into the villages. Larger wicker baskets supported from a head band were formerly used, but sacks, panniers and donkeys, if not carts, are now available. The rest of the plant was formerly left standing; it was recognized as 'good for the field because the juice goes into the ground when the snow comes'. Nowadays, however, the greater part of the leaves and stalks are broken off and carried in for animal fodder. On the mesa the corn is dried on the flat roofs and then stacked, according to colour and harvest, in the small window-less rooms at the back of the houses. Seed corn is separated from the rest of the harvest, and a thrifty household endeavours to maintain the greater part of a whole year's crop in reserve until the eve of harvest, since drought, flood, wind or pests may destroy an entire crop. This is, however, an ideal by no means always attained.

The squashes when ripe are cut spirally into long strips about two inches thick which are dried in the sun and then folded and wrapped for storing. Beans and squashes and melons are usually harvested before the corn at the beginning of September. Sunflowers are grown for their edible seeds which also afford a black dye. They are planted both in the irrigated gardens and in the squash patches.

In addition to providing an assured supply of drinking water for the villages, and in modern times for livestock, chiefly sheep and donkeys, the larger and more accessible springs are used to maintain irrigated gardens. The water is in the first place stored in tanks formed by building up retaining walls round a rock or clay bottom; crevices are stopped with a mixture of mud and dried vegetation. The gardens themselves are disposed in terraces. Some lie below the spring and its storage tank. The tank is then provided with an outlet, stopped with a bung of cloth or hide, and grasses; by removing this bung water is allowed to run from a main discharge channel a foot or so deep and about two feet wide, to the various distributing channels. Sometimes, however, the springs lie lower in hollows which have been deepened artificially. Water is then carried up in jars from the well to the garden plots which surround it. Some of these gardens are very extensive and more than a dozen families have three or four plots each.

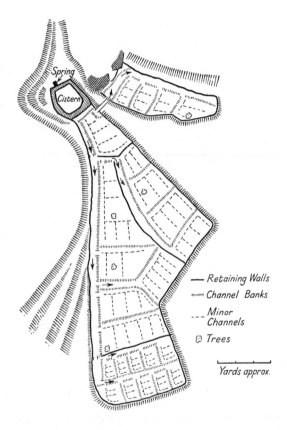

FIG. 78. SKETCH-PLAN OF AN IRRIGATED GARDEN AT SIKYATKI

The maintenance of the irrigated gardens is not laborious apart from the occasional repair of walls and the clearing of channels. When the small plots of chile, onions, *cita* (a kind of cress), sweet corn and various plants grown to provide vegetable dyes used mainly for colouring corn bread have been sown, they are visited about twice a week in the early morning for watering and weeding. The trees which are encouraged to grow extensively round these irrigated plots assist in reducing the loss of water by evaporation.

The seepage of several of the springs which are not used for irrigated gardens is of great importance for peach groves which lie clustered on the slopes below them. These peach trees are raised from seeds planted in October or from cuttings taken in spring. Young plants must be carefully watched and are watered when necessary; they are protected by a circle of piled stones, and are now wrapped against sheep and donkeys which will eat the shoots and strip off the bark. They are grown on common land and in contrast with the field crops, the trees, not the land, are the objects of ownership. The planting and tending of trees is done by the men but the peach harvest is gathered by the women and the trees are usually inherited by daughters. The sons of the family should plant trees for themselves. The harvest continues for about a month from the end of September, during which the family may move out to a hut in the peach groves. Each picking is laid out for a week to dry out in the hot sun on large stone slabs. A small waterproof shelter of stones is provided nearby and into this the drying fruit is carried at the first sign of rain.

The Hopi formerly grew cotton, but it has now gone out of cultivation because trade goods and yarn are cheap and wool has largely replaced it for weaving. The plant, which was grown without artificial irrigation and depended on natural floodings like other Hopi field crops, reflects the severity of its environment. Small and low and branching very near the ground, it is unique in its precocity. It flowers ten weeks after planting, yielding ripe bolls after three months, that is nearly a month earlier than American commercial cotton; but the bolls are small and their lint content scanty.

Tobacco is not cultivated. The leaves are gathered from wild plants which are fairly abundant in the upper parts of the flats.

Within the village territories the greater part of the arable area is divided into a number of large sections from a few hundred yards square to a square mile or more, apportioned among the matrilineal clans of each village. These clan lands are delimited by numerous boundary stones placed at the corners and junction points and, although few are left to-day, many of the more significant of these small upright slabs or domed boulders were formerly engraved with symbols of the clans concerned.

The lands vary considerably in size and the area available does not correspond at all closely with the present number of individuals in the clans. In some the population has dwindled to a dozen or more persons, but extensive lands are available. At the present time there is generally no shortage of land, and the cultivated fields rarely occupy more than one-half of the total clan lands. But the whole area is never available for cultivation, since flood and blown sand are continually spoiling land. Severe flood may wash out the soil, sand may accumulate and render it sterile, and the value of a given patch may be completely changed by the events of a single season. Freedom to shift the boundaries of plots is essential under a system of cultivation which is dependent on the distribution of natural flood water, and hence on minute changes of surface slopes.

Each clan usually has several of these stretches of land in different parts of the village territory. This dispersal is of very great practical importance since it reduces the risk of crop failure; where the crop on one group of fields may wither from drought or be washed out by floods there remains the chance that the others may be spared. In particular, disastrous floods rarely occur in all the flats in the same season. The lands closer in to the mesas and those out in the middle are still more definitely reciprocal. In an abnormally wet year, when many of the latter are liable to be destroyed by the high floods, the scarp plots are well watered, while, on the other hand, in a dry season when they in their turn are liable to be parched out, enough water is usually brought down by the streams to afford a harvest for the mid-valley fields. (See fig. 74.)

The main clan lands are devoted principally to corn: the smaller patches on the sloping grounds at the foot of the scarps, planted with beans, squashes and melons, are not always regarded as clan land, and some are disposed of by individuals as personal property.

The springs and irrigated gardens are all associated with particular clans. The garden plots are nearly all in the hands of the clan concerned; they are cared for by women chiefly and are passed on from mother to daughter. But the water of springs is available for drinking and stock watering to members of clans other than those which own them, keep them in repair and are ritually associated with them.

The families composing each clan cultivate fields within the clan lands. These fields again are, where possible, not confined to a single stretch of clan land, but are scattered over the various sections held by the clan. They are not usually marked by boundary stones, but their extent is well known to those concerned. A stone or small post may be put at the corners, and the boundaries are considered to run along sight lines between them. Fences are erected only to protect plants from the severe winds, to keep off blown sand or to exclude live stock. Where cultivated land is partly concealed in a depression or gully the cultivator generally erects small piles of stones on the high ground to either side, to warn others against driving their sheep over the field.

Although they take but little part in cultivation, women are considered rightful landowners, just as they are the house-holders. The ownership and disposal of fields is closely associated with the matrilineal system. In any general account of their agriculture the Hopi will explain that their fields belong to the women and that they receive them from the clan. The mother of each family has several fields at her disposal, and when her daughters marry she hands them one or more, or parts of several; on her death her female relatives take over any land she has retained, the direct descendants having prior claim. The question of disposal of lands to married daughters has often little practical importance, since the daughters continue to live in the household of the mother. Except at harvest-time, however, nearly all the actual cultivation is done by men, that is, by the husbands and unmarried sons of the women who control the fields.

Since many clan members live in close proximity as an extended family group, the precise title to land is often not clearly defined. The idea of responsibility for work in the fields on the part of a woman's husband is often more clearly conceived than that of ownership of field or produce. In practice, individuals rarely refuse demands for a share in the crop from kinswomen should occasion arise. The clan mother, the senior woman of a clan who keeps the clan fetish and ceremonial paraphernalia, intervenes in any dispute as to land or houses and settles the matter after discussion. Land ownership is thus vested in the clan; the individual women have the use of plots, which their men clear and cultivate, and also the right of disposal of the lands so used, subject to the veto of the clan, expressed either by mass opinion or as a decision of the clan mother.

The clans of the Hopi are matrilineal. Each contains one or more maternal lineages or groups of persons actually related in the female line. When there are several lineages within a clan the right to direct the social and ceremonial activities of the clan, including the use of land, is normally handed on in one particular lineage, in whose house the ceremonial objects are kept.

The composition of the clans, at least in recent times, has changed on account of the merging of remnants of some clans with others. But the fact that individuals do, in general, refer habitually to their fields as belonging to the clan as a whole, and exhibit considerable solidarity in the sharing of field labour and of the food thereby produced, suggests that the lineage or extended maternal family, which has been claimed as the normal and original content of a Hopi clan, continues to exert its influence even where in actual fact the clan contains a number of apparently unrelated families. After the merging of two clans the old names may cling to the once separate lands for some time, but eventually, and apparently within a generation, the distinction is forgotten and they are all known by the same clan name, the ceremonially more important being carefully retained and more usually employed. In this way with the reduction of strength of one clan its lands are eventually taken over by another. The merging of clans and the virtual transference of land from one to another is, however, not haphazard, nor apparently does a dwindling clan necessarily merge with the one most in need of land. The clans are linked somewhat irregularly together to form a higher group of units, sometimes referred to as phratries, which have ceremonial associations. These linkages may reflect a former unity of the phratry as a single clan which later subdivided. In any case the unit as a whole is exogamous and there is usually a mythological account of the reason for linkage. The merging of clans and their lands appears to follow these pre-existing linkages.

Most of the names and many of the groupings of the Hopi clans are found throughout the Pueblos despite the fact that they are so widely scattered and are divided in language into four distinct groups belonging to fundamentally different linguistic stocks. In the Rio Grande Pueblos, the clans are grouped into two moieties, the 'winter' and the 'summer' people, which play a prominent part in both ritual and political organization.

Although agricultural land is normally held by the women for the benefit of their households and is passed on by them to their daughters, the rule is by no means rigid, and where land is abundant or daughters are few, sons are given the direct use of plots. It is, however, rare that a man's children, who are of course members not of his but of his wife's clan, would acquire the use of such fields and they would have to obtain permission of their father's clansmen to do so.

Ceremonial and dancing societies are also involved in the distribution of land. These societies are open under varying conditions to all the people of a village, men or women as the case may be, but the leadership of the society is usually retained in one clan, generally within one family of that clan, by descent in the female line. The leaders of such societies have fields set aside and cultivated for their benefit. In some villages they are in the lands of the controlling clan; in others they are distinct. These fields are cultivated on behalf of the holders of the offices and pass on to the next incumbent, but since, however, he or she is generally a close relative on the mother's side the use of the land normally remains within one lineage. Until recent times the chief, it is said, was expected to devote himself to the rituals of his society, and no clan or society chief cultivated for his family or engaged directly in any economic activity. His fields were cultivated by working parties, who supplied all the needs of his household. The chief himself did not himself demand and organize these services. They were voluntary and the initiative had apparently to come from individuals of another clan in recognition of the value of the ritual performed by the chief and his clan.

Hunting has never figured very prominently in Hopi economy. The people of the more eastern Pueblos formerly journeyed regularly to the western Plains to hunt buffalo, but the Hopi knew little of these risky invasions, and their game was confined to small herds of 'antelope', occasional deer and elk, and, above all, rabbits. Although game was always relatively scarce and provided only a small part of the food-supply, a considerable part of the winter was devoted to hunting trips on the neighbouring plateaux. Communal hunts for rabbits (in which large parties of men and boys surround a considerable area, driving the rabbits to the centre where they can be killed with arrows and throwing sticks) are still undertaken. Deer and antelope were formerly hunted in a similar manner and brushwood pounds were built. When skins were more plentiful, shirts and leggings of tanned deerskin were frequently worn by the men. Moccasins are still worn by them and high boots by the women. Skins and meat were also obtained from the food-gathering peoples in exchange for corn, and this trade survives to-day in the visits of the Navajo to the Hopi Pueblos. The Navajo bring the produce of the flocks of sheep that they first acquired in Spanish days, and after the harvest there is a lively trade for their wool and meat in return for corn, squashes, peaches and other produce. Skins were also obtained in the old days from the Havasupai, an agricultural and hunting people nearly a hundred miles to the west, who made the long journey along the southern rim of the Grand Canyon to visit the Hopi villages and carried back Hopi blankets in exchange.

The fruits of yucca and cacti, wild berries and pine nuts were also gathered by the women, and yucca leaves afforded a fibre which supplemented the cultivated cotton. Wool has to-day largely replaced both except for ceremonial use.

Although the Hopi now raise sheep and donkeys they had no domestic animals of economic value in pre-Columbian times. They had domesticated turkeys like the other Pueblo peoples, and these are an important cultural link with southern Mexico. But these birds were not looked to for meat or eggs; they were pets which also provided feathers for ceremonial purposes.

The large squares of cloth used as wraps by the women and made into men's shirts and kilts are woven by the men in a simple vertical loom lashed to two straight horizontal beams. The heddles must be pulled by hand and as the shuttle is passed through the shed is kept open with a wide batten, for foot treadles were unknown in the New World and cannot easily be applied to a vertical loom. Belts woven on narrower looms of the same type have elaborate patterns, achieved by the primitive method of picking up the required warp threads by hand, one at a time.

Pottery is made by the women. The modern wares are elaborately painted in a style which had become extinct until revived by recent archaeological discoveries! Round-bottomed vessels, dishes, jars, cups, dippers and water-bottles of simple but very various shapes are made. Clays of very fine quality found in pockets in the sandstone of the plateau are mixed together. Any coarse material is removed before the levigated clay is softened in water and kneaded. Apparently no tempering material is usually added, and the pot is built up in spiral coils which are pressed together and smoothed as the work proceeds. After it has been dried in the sun a wash of a special finely divided clay is applied and burnished to give a smooth polished surface. For the painting, yellow ochre and dark ironstone are ground down and mixed with water or plant juices and are applied with simple brushes of yucca fibre. Baking takes place in the open with a fire of dried brushwood or, more usually to-day, of sheep's dung. The pots are first placed round an open fire to heat slowly; they are then set on the embers in a pile separated by broken sherds or stone.

Round and over them a domed pile of fuel is built which burns for several hours at a very high temperature.

Baskets are of far less importance among the Hopi than among the surrounding food-gathering peoples who make no pottery. The shallow wicker-work and coiled trays are, however, remarkable for the very elaborate multicoloured patterns representing animals and mythological characters which are worked on them. Bright red, green, yellow and other dyes prepared from various minerals are used to colour the stems of the rabbit brush and yucca strips with which they are made. Other basketry similar to that of the Basin Shoshoneans is obtained by trade from the collecting peoples.

The stone axes, mauls and knives which were formerly used in working wood and the barbed stone arrow-points used in hunting are no longer made. The simple pump drill with a stone or metal point with which wood and turquoise, the favourite bead material, can be bored is, however, still used by the Hopi and other Pueblo peoples.

FIG. 79. PASSAGE-WAY BETWEEN TWO HOUSE GROUPS IN WALPI
(*After Mindeleff*)

The clans form a number of wards or house groups in the compact stone-built villages of two or three hundred inhabitants. The houses are variously arranged, but a tenement-like grouping, several stories high, is characteristic. Sometimes, as at Walpi, there are one or more large buildings of three or more stories, terraced back on all sides to form a somewhat irregular pyramid. In others the houses are grouped, again in several stories, to enclose a courtyard, or are set in long rows on either side of wide streets. Although sun-dried brick is often used in new building to-day, the walls of the older houses are of roughly dressed local sandstone, laid in courses without mortar and one or two feet thick. The flat roofs of laths, brushwood and stamped clay are laid on heavy pine beams. The low, narrow entrances now often have hinged wooden doors and

FIG. 80. A HOPI INTERIOR SHOWING THE CORN-GRINDING SLABS
(*After Mindeleff*)

the windows are glazed, but in former times the entrance to the rooms, especially on the ground floor, was often by a notched ladder pole running down from a hole in the roof. The room themselves are often very small, rarely more than twelve feet square, and much of the day's work takes place on the flat roofs and at the clay baking ovens set up outside the houses. The walls are whitewashed with gypsum and the floors paved with stone slabs. In one corner a number of boxed-in grinding slabs are set at an angle, and before these the women kneel at the slow task of grinding the corn. Only small fires could be made in old times, but now hooded fireplaces and chimneys are often built. The inner rooms of the lower stories are without light or ventilation and are used only for storing corn and utensils (see Frontispiece and figs. 79 and 80).

FIG. 81. THE CHIEF KIVA OF SHIPAULOVI
(*After Mindeleff*)

Nearly all ceremonies are held in separate chambers belonging to the societies responsible for particular rituals. These are large, rectangular underground rooms, some twenty-five

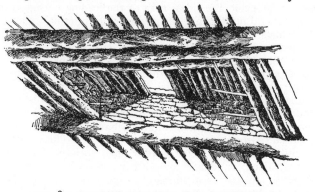

FIG. 82. INTERIOR VIEW OF A KIVA HATCHWAY
(*After Mindeleff*)

feet long, known as *kivas*; they are often built in gaps and ledges on the sides of the cliff and are roofed with crossed layers of close-fitting poles. A low masonry wall, straddled by a second layer of poles, runs round the *kiva* above ground.

They are entered by a double hatchway and ladder pole which projects ten or twelve feet into the air. At one end a small hole in the floor is covered with a wooden plank in which a hole has been bored. This is the entrance to the lower world, by which the people and animals originally entered this world and through which the spirits now come during ceremonies. Along the wall are fitments of quite a different character— long timbers with slots to hold the posts of looms; for weaving, the men's task among the Hopi, is usually done in the *kivas*, which are also used as club-rooms by the society members and as places of retreat for priests and officials who must at certain times retire from everyday activities.

Although there is much co-operation and intermarriage between the villages, each is an independent unit, and in the past serious quarrels and fighting occasionally occurred. The government and organization of a village is shared among the ceremonial officials of the various societies and clans, for religious and political offices are not distinguished. During the periods of preparation and performance of each of the many rituals the performing society controls the village and prevents unpropitious acts. A number of offices and duties, from that of the Sun Watcher and the Town Crier to that of the Leader of the Rabbit Hunt, are all hereditary in particular clans. Arrangements are made and difficulties are settled within a clan by its chief, the oldest man of the leading lineage, while more general matters are dealt with by an informal council of clan chiefs. The leaders of clans and societies make no bid for personal prestige. They occupy positions of trust and carry out well-defined duties. There is in Pueblo culture an almost complete rejection of that preoccupation with personal prestige and prerogative which is so noticeable in the western Plains and is carried to such extremes on the North-West Coast. Moderation is characteristic both of individuals and institutions; there are established rules of behaviour for nearly every situation. Group action by clan, society and village for the general good is the keynote of Pueblo society. Fields and harvests like ritual dances are not narrowly defined as personal property, and the usual forms of distribution and inheritance are generally adapted to meet the emergency needs of particular families.

The rituals of the Hopi societies are extremely complex. They centre round the magical achievement of many desires which range from the general well-being of the village to the promotion of rain at particular times. Many of them are dramas in which ancestral and other spirits appear, and the more significant parts are often performed in the secrecy of the *kivas*. The society members, wearing elaborate masks, impersonate the ancestors and animal spirits. But there are also many minor ritual acts to be performed by individuals.

In the more elaborate ceremonies several motives are inextricably interwoven, but the needs of agriculture and the hazards of the environment feature prominently in many of them. There are rites for every stage in cultivation; ceremonial activities throughout the year have nearly always some reference to agricultural prosperity, while corn is used symbolically at every turn. Pursuing cultivation with primitive tools under semi-arid conditions where the rainfall is very unreliable, it is to be expected that rain-making, so widespread in the Southwest, should play an important part in agricultural ritual; but rain-making does not exhaust the magical resources, and rites are also performed for the direct promotion of crop growth.

When a plot is first cleared a slab of stone about one foot square is set up on edge somewhere near the middle. Every year when the land is being prepared in the spring 'prayer sticks' are stuck in the ground against a smooth boulder before the eastern face of this shrine. They are small bundles of two-coloured rods and feathers to which are tied small packets of ground corn wrapped in a strip of corn husk; others are slender twigs with small tufts of eagle and other feathers tied to the tip. Essential to the maintenance of fertility of the fields, they are also placed at the springs to ensure the water supply and on fences to keep out sand or to prevent the development of destructive channels (shown in fig. 77).

During the winter 'hockey' matches are played between the young men of the societies occupying the various *kivas*. A buckskin ball filled with seeds is used and the spilling of the seeds ensures a good harvest, but should the ball not burst the crops are likely to fail in the coming season.

Ritual is also prominent in the activities of the working parties which are formed during the planting and harvesting seasons. Members customarily run a race during the first day of planting in a particular field; the speed of the running men promotes the rapid growth of the planted seed. These plantings are recognized as expressions of clan or village solidarity. To promote such a party benefits not only the owner of the fields worked and the workers who receive gifts, but also the whole community.

The promotion of plant growth is also more elaborately effected by forcing beans and corn in the *kivas*. At Walpi from the end of January until late in February the Ancestor Spirits Society, which is particularly concerned with growth and fertility, conducts a ceremony one of whose objects is to ensure the success of the approaching season and to protect the fields. The chief retires to the *kiva* about a month after the winter solstice. There he plants beans in small box-like receptacles. On the success of this planting depends to a large extent the character of the coming season. A warm temperature is maintained by a constantly tended fire and the sprouting plants are frequently watered.

About a fortnight later the society as a whole assembles at night, and after a long ritual the chief and another member of the society, who wears a mask and impersonates the sun, representing in ritual during the night its slow awakening, emerge at dawn to make a circuit of the mesa, visiting *kivas* and clan houses. At each halt the 'Sun' bows deeply and slowly to each of the cardinal points, symbolically retarding the motion of the sun, thus to prolong the growing period of the coming season. He then plasters corn meal on the door or hatchway of the building, receives prayer sticks from the occupants and gives them some of the bean sprouts which have been forced in the *kiva*. These the people put away with their seed corn to induce it in its turn to rapid growth when planted. Beans and corn can now be planted by the members of the various societies in all the *kivas*. About a fortnight later the sprouts are used in an elaborate bean dance and are finally distributed among the men who take them out to their fields and bury them.

At the summer solstice another effort is made to prolong the summer. The clansfolk of the Sun Watcher prepare prayer sticks, which are given to a boy who sets out before dawn to the upper mesa. He arranges the sticks in the ground in a line, running north to south, and awaits the sunrise. The boy must then dawdle home, picking flowers, thereby inducing the sun to advance slowly. Later in the season the time of the celebrated Snake Dance, which is intimately connected with rain-making, may even be retarded if the crops are backward, apparently on the assumption that the season may be prolonged or curtailed by delaying or advancing the ceremony beyond its proper time.

The increase of the harvests by the indirect method of rain-making is an element in many rites which are only less frequent than the ceremonial use of corn. Ceremonial smoking for rain occurs during many public ceremonies and *kiva* rites. Meeting of societies for that particular purpose are called whenever the season threatens to be poor; prayer sticks are deposited in the direction of the four cardinal points and even the custom that brides of the previous year should wear their white wedding blankets to witness the last dance, is said 'to show the clouds they want rain'. It is also a common practice to douse a man with water before he sets out on his first day's planting to ensure an abundance of water in the fields. This is done by his womenfolk and he may retaliate.

By careful adaptation to local conditions and by the use of ingenious but unelaborate devices all the characteristic plants of the American maize-squash-beans complex are successfully cultivated by the Hopi in an arid environment. At the same time the agricultural practice is deeply interwoven with the elaborate ritual and social organization of Pueblo society. Shrines, with their prayer feathers, are set up in the fields and skilful husbandry must be supported by individual and collective rites. Agricultural needs and anxieties are, on the other hand, dominant elements in the ceremonial cycle. The agricultural practice, while exhibiting the characteristic western pattern of male cultivation, has been also deeply influenced by the matrilineal bias of Hopi society. The transfer of lands is adjusted according to the rights deriving from the maternal clan, and the desire of the individual, male or female, to provide for children and relatives of whatever clan or sex.

The agricultural peoples to the west of the Pueblos are far less advanced in both their economic life and in their organization of society and ritual. Among some of them maize-growing has been grafted on to a food-gathering life similar to that of the Plateau Shoshoneans. The Havasupai, for example, to whom reference has been made, occupy a narrow ravine and the surrounding plateaux on the south side of the Grand Canyon and pursue a hunting and gathering life during the winter; but in spring they move down into the ravine, to cultivate maize on its narrow floor, and enjoy a period of plenty. After the harvest a considerable part of the crop is stored for the next spring in cliff granaries and a limited quantity is carried up the canyon trail. Burden baskets, seed beaters, parching trays and other basketry are prominent in their equipment. Their older houses resemble the conical earth and brush shelters of the southern Paiute across the Colorado, whom they closely resemble during the wandering life of winter. Family groups scatter at this season wherever seeds and pine nuts are abundant. The men hunt in small parties or go on trading trips to the Hopi and westwards to the Mojave on the Lower Colorado. Large quantities of skins were formerly tanned by the Havasupai for the Hopi trade and many of them were obtained by barter from their neighbours in exchange for corn. Woven blankets, pottery and beads were obtained from the Hopi (see fig. 73).

With the return to the watered gorge bottom in spring the life of the Havasupai is transformed. Forsaking the scattered migratory existence of the past season they apply themselves with Pueblo-like devotion to agricultural pursuits. Fields are cleared and fenced, dams across streams are repaired to fill irrigation ditches running through the plots. The family groups cultivate their own fields, men and women sharing the labour. This is the socially active period of the year. But here again the Basin-like character is fundamental. Political and ceremonial organization is of the slightest; there are no clans or societies and their contacts with the Hopi Pueblos, although so frequent, have resulted only in the performance of a masked dance which in its vague ritual purpose has the air of an ill-learnt Pueblo rite.

Still further west, on the southward flowing sections of the Colorado river as well as on the Lower Gila, more favourable physical conditions and considerably larger groups of cultivators are found. The Colorado, emerging from its narrower gorges about sixty miles south of the great bend which forms the Arizona-Nevada boundary, flows in its lower course through a longitudinal oasis created by the annually flooding river and flanked on either side by barren ranges and mesa edges whose curves segment the valley into a series of plains, ten to twenty-five miles across, separated by stretches of gorge. A few miles below the final constriction at Yuma, where the river has cut a narrow ravine across a low spur, the muddy waters forsake a single channel and splay out over the great alluvial fan of the delta which extends sixty miles south from Yuma to the present gulf head (fig. 73).

In both its valley and delta courses the river flows over deep alluvium and is nowhere at bed rock. Low bluffs, some fifty to a hundred feet in height and varying in distance from a few hundred yards to several miles from the river, border the valley and mark the limit of the flood plain.

The river rises every summer after the melting snow and the rains in the Rocky Mountains head waters, and, under aboriginal conditions before the construction of modern American dams, a great part of the river plain and upper delta was normally inundated every year. Apart from occasional floods on the Gila in February and March, the river does not rise appreciably until May or reach a maximum before the end of June. This is a true hot desert region and since precipitation is almost negligible the flooded lands present the strongest contrast to the sandy and stony desert above the bluffs which limit the flood waters. On the one hand creosote brush, cacti and occasional shrivelled trees are scattered sparsely over the waste of sand, gravel and boulders; on the other, the vegetation often approaches jungle. Dense groves of cotton-wood and willow flank the river, while impenetrable thickets of tall arrow weed, cane and rushes through which trails had to be cleared anew every year, formerly occupied the greater part of the flats that were inundated for a few weeks of the year. Mesquite trees, intolerant of moist conditions and able to derive water from considerable depths grow abundantly along the upper margins of the plain.

The aboriginal population of this region was considerable. It depended on no great elaboration of material civilization such as characterises the comparable riverine lands of the Old World, but on fortunate circumstances which crude cultivation and further reliance on the gathering of wild fruits could exploit with relatively little effort.

The life of the Yuma at the head of the delta was less arduous than that of the Great Basin collectors, while their economic security was probably greater than that of the Pueblo peoples. Their native cultivation, of which little is left to-day, depended entirely on the natural irrigation of the Colorado flood. The main crops of maize, beans, squashes and melons were planted in clearings of low-lying land near the river into which the flood waters spilled to form sloughs. This planting was done chiefly when the water began to retreat towards the end of June. The corn, although a poorer, smaller eared variety than that of the Pueblos, ripened in little over two months, so that, in damp hollows with the aid of the slight spring showers an earlier spring crop could also be raised before the flood. For the summer planting a patch of ground likely to be flooded was cleared in the spring by hacking out the arrow weed and canes with wooden blades. When the drying mud began to crack seeds were planted a few inches deep and a pace or two apart. Several crops were grown together in the plots which were irregular in shape, varying according to the configuration of the sloughs. Only two simple tools, similar to those of the Hopi, were used—a paddle-like blade for cutting weeds and a wedge-ended planting dibble. Although animals attacked the crops no traps were set to catch them, and the scanty game of the region was almost entirely neglected. Scares were made of poles wrapped with reeds hung with pot-sherds, but the racoons and coyotes which devoured the melons went un-molested unless the cultivator camped by the plot.

Seeds were collected from uncultivated grasses, and the seeds of some grasses were sown like maize, generally on less fertile patches of land, but often in considerable quantities. So far as is known these had not been improved by selection, and were identical with their uncultivated counterparts. This practice has not been reported elsewhere in North America, and the unique régime of the Colorado may help to explain its occurrence. It illustrates a very primitive stage in food pro-duction and, had corn growing been unknown, might have been regarded as a concrete illustration of transition from the gathering of wild seeds to true plant cultivation. But both the main crops and cultivation methods of the Lower Colorado are as a whole directly related to the American maize-beans-squash agricultural complex, and may be considered as im-poverished versions of the Pueblo type of agriculture. While it is impossible to define with certainty the historical relation of wild seed planting to agriculture proper, it would appear probable that the practice was the consequence of agricultural knowledge rather than its precursor, a happy adaptation of local products previously collected where they happened to grow. Had the practice been known among the western Basin peoples, especially the northern Paiute of Owen's Valley, who irrigated some of their root and seed lands (see p. 35), its historically transitional character in this region might have been more plausibly argued, although it could not affect the question of the introduction of the truly cultivated plants which are common to a vast area in North America.

The relative importance of cultivated and gathered food is difficult to estimate. The Spanish accounts of the abundance of agricultural food, especially corn, melons and squashes, found by them in the villages in the late eighteenth century, indicate that agriculture in the Colorado region was no mere accessory to the collecting of wild plants. Yet it is also clear that the sweet, nutritious pods of the mesquite trees were important items in the food-supply and assured against hunger in years of irregular flood. Mesquite trees were not owned by individuals except where they happened to grow near a habita-tion, but families were in the habit of collecting the 'beans' from the same districts every year and erected permanent storage bins secure from animals, both in the groves along the margins of the valleys and near the houses. On platforms often six feet square and raised four or five feet from the ground, large cylindrical bins were made of roughly interlaced bundles of arrow weed plastered with mud. The pods were pounded into a meal with rough stone pestles in wooden mortars hollowed in cotton-wood boles. A considerable quantity would be prepared at one time, damped and kneaded into lumps, which, after drying, could be stored indefinitely in the house.

Corn, according to the western pattern for grass seeds, was parched with live coals in a shallow basket before being ground on a flat square stone. Melons and squashes could be stored for winter use by placing them whole in a dry earth pit, lined with dried leaves, which was then earthed over with a low mound. The pumpkins which kept less well in this way were often sliced and dried in the sun.

Both hunting and fishing were very perfunctory and provided but little food. The game was poor: a few deer could be taken in the cotton-wood groves of the valley, while antelope and mountain sheep were stalked by individuals and small parties in the surrounding mountains, but there was no communal hunt even for rabbits. Rabbit skin blankets were a luxury, and most of them were obtained by barter with hunting peoples to the east. The fish of the Colorado were few, bony and poor as food. Cactus spine gorges were used as a lure for small fish, and the largest were occasionally shot with unfeathered arrows; but most were caught with nets and traps. Long nets of willow bark and smaller scoops were used to drag the sloughs. Semicircular walled traps of withes stuck into the bottom were built on shelving banks, and crushed melon seeds were scattered to entice the fish to enter the small gap that could be closed at need.

The Lower Colorado peoples, all closely related in speech, and formerly numbering several thousand, were divided into a number of tribes occupying sections of the river and delta. Although they fought among themselves there was a surprising degree of unity and coherence within such tribes as the Yuma, Mojave and Cocopa, even although they might be divided into a number of villages. The more permanent settlements were often situated on eminences in the valley which escaped inundation by the flood, or where projecting spurs of the mesas approached close to the river. According to the condition of the river sporadic seasonal movements took place. They were straggly settlements, sometimes of considerable size, but consisting of a few solid houses and more numerous shelters apparently scattered without plan.

The Yuma, who occupied four or five main villages in a

stretch of fifty or more miles along the Colorado in the neighbourhood of its confluence with the Gila river, probably numbered more than three thousand in the late eighteenth century. For the greater part of the year they lived in open flat-topped shelters—rectangular brushwood shades supported by poles. Sand-covered houses of timber and brush were also built, but they were occupied only in winter when a number of related families crowded into the few in each settlement. The house was square in plan, from twenty to thirty feet each way, built in a sandy depression and the floor was excavated two or three feet. Four centreposts set in a square and about eight feet high, and a number of wall posts were first erected; a roof of brush was carried on rafters from the centreposts to the walls. The front wall was of leafy brush lightly packed between horizontal slats and a central section was left open for the entrance. The walls of the sides and rear were built by tying horizontal slats closely together between the poles. Against these a thick layer of brush was placed and held in position by a bank of sand which reached to and extended over the roof. Finally, the roof itself was covered with loose stones and sand. The excavated floors, low doorways and sand covering gave early travellers the impression that they were excavated in sand hills. There was apparently no smoke hole, and storage granaries were frequently built on the roofs. Rectangular shades were sometimes attached in front.

The houses were built by general labour, one man or family rarely undertaking the labour alone. The leader of a village was expected to see to it that there were sufficient and large enough houses to shelter all. Cooking and other daily tasks with which wind and blown sand might interfere were done in semicircular roofless enclosures like the summer wind-breaks of the Paiute.

The Yuma and other tribes made coiled pottery and painted rough patterns on it, but it was much less elaborate than Pueblo wares, both in form and ornament. They grew no cotton and used willow bark to make small loosely-woven blankets and breech clouts on a horizontal loom. The warp was a continuous length of twine and the weft thin untwined ribbons of bark that were inserted with the aid of a thin rod. As weaving it was enormously inferior to that of the Hopi

The crafts of the river tribes were crude and even slovenly and the same indifference extended to much of their social life. Marriage was regulated by a number of patrilineal exogamous clans, but they did not apparently form local groups and quite often families transferred from village to village.

The clans had no corporate unity and appear to have played little part in the social life. Yet despite the apparent lack of systematic cohesion there was a real sense of tribal unity which centred mainly round two distinct things: the tribal chief and the conduct of war.

The tribal chief of the Yuma was less a ruler than a visionary who was magically able to promote the welfare of the people. The validity of every plan of action among the Yuma was believed to depend on auspicious dream visions of spirits, received and publicly declared by those who had spiritual power to conduct important enterprises such as the curing of the sick or the leading of war parties. The tribal chief was a specialist in none of these but displayed his spiritual inspiration and practical wisdom in his accounts of dream experiences and in his general bearing which should be happy, generous and thoughtful. He was expected to get together a considerable store of food and to this every one contributed. This was not, however, in any strict sense his own, for he was expected to provide supplies for public feasts and to feed the needy. The chief was looked up to for advice in all general matters and was the centre of most tribal activities even though he might not personally play a leading part. He had, however, a few specific duties. He was the rain-maker—a somewhat unnecessary function in this environment, where it so rarely rained and cultivation depended not on rain but on the river flood. He had also the care of the enemy scalps and of any captives taken in fighting. Scalps, although of considerable magical power in war, were considered very dangerous to all but the chief. He did not, however, control or direct military operations; indeed, his duty was to remain apart from the battle, preserving the strength and integrity of the tribe in the security of his own person. The chieftainship was in fact a title rather than an office and although there were duties and functions associated with it the title was acquired by voluntary undertaking of the duties rather than by any elective procedure. Recognition depended on the general acceptance by the leaders of the villages of claims expressed in dreams and visions. There might, indeed, be temporary divisions of the tribe and more than one such chief at a time.

Unlike the Pueblos to the east or the Californians to the west, the Lower Colorado peoples engaged in continuous if desultory warfare. With a food-supply that was relatively secure and no elaborate ceremonial cycle to maintain, they were free to devote a great part of their energies to the incessant fighting that was remarked by Alarcon, the earliest explorer of this region in the sixteenth century. Most of the fighting was among the river tribes themselves and more or less stable alliances were formed. Warfare was not justified by the Yuma as a virile pursuit, nor did economic needs play any significant part. Fighting was believed to be the essential condition for spiritual well-being. It possessed a strong mystical value; through it the spiritual power of a tribe was enhanced and at the same time demonstrated. A mimic ritual battle remains one of the most prominent features of the annual ceremony in which the dead are mourned and the well-being of the living is increased.

But in warfare, as throughout their culture, they showed no desire or ability to develop or maintain any elaborate organization. There was usually a single tribal war leader who attained his position by the display of bravery and resourcefulness. The warriors were divided into clubbers, bowmen and spearmen, and the fighting itself was often of a somewhat formal character in which the contestants drew up in opposing ranks and the battle was preceded by one or more duels between leading warriors. Yet, although some of the conventions and insignia of battle show resemblances to those of the Plains and may indicate a common origin for both, there were no warrior societies and no system of counting 'coups'. The campaigns themselves were mostly short-lived sallies and although the pitched battles which were fought between enemies of long standing were often arranged by challenge, they involved relatively few men and could often be successfully broken off by the defeated. Moreover, their military equipment—poor bows, light arrows, hand clubs and wooden staves—was not of the most lethal character.

The Lower Colorado, in the fertility of its plain and delta and in the cycle of its flood, reproduces on a small scale the physical conditions of the riverine lands of the Ancient East, the seats of early civilization in the Old World. Here no such development occurred and the wide deserts of north-western Mexico appear to have acted as an effective barrier to prolonged cultural stimulus from both the remarkable civilization of southern Mexico and from the Pueblos to the east. Having acquired maize cultivation the Lower Colorado peoples stagnated technically, living an easy if rude life in what thus became an easy region.

Cultivation was practised nearly everywhere in eastern North America from the Gulf of Mexico to the St. Lawrence river and extended several hundred miles west of the Missouri and

Mississippi rivers. The essential plants—maize, squashes and beans—were the same as those of the Southwest and Mexico, and it was from these eastern peoples that the early colonists learned methods of growing and preparing maize which have become permanent features of American life. Native agriculture was, however, of a strikingly different pattern in this wooded eastern country. Throughout this region hunting was of considerable importance in the economy and men took little or no part in cultivation. Unfortunately no detailed studies of the economy of the more eastern peoples were made in early times and the disruption of their culture by the advance of the white man and of western civilization has long since greatly modified the economy of the few surviving native communities. On the western margins of the woodland, cultivation by aboriginal methods did, however, survive into modern times among peoples who cultivated at one season and hunted the buffalo on the Plains during the remainder of the year, and for one such group, the Hidatsa on the Missouri river, a most valuable study of cultivation methods has been made. (Fig. 15.)

The Hidatsa territory lay in the wooded tall grass country where forest was fading into steppe. Their permanent settlements were considerable stockaded villages of large circular houses built of timber and turf, often thirty to forty feet in diameter, and from ten to fifteen feet high in the centre. The floor was usually excavated a foot or more. The wall frame was of stout posts about five feet high and set in a ring; on these, horizontal beams were laid. Four stouter posts about ten feet high, erected round the centre, supported similar beams. Long rafters sloped down from these to the outer ring and shorter poles covered the square between the posts, leaving only a small smoke hole; this framework was then covered with willow saplings and finally with grass, earth and turf. A well-built earth lodge could be occupied with minor renovation for several generations and was a comfortable and commodious dwelling. The Hidatsa deserted their villages at the beginning of winter when they moved west to hunt the bison and lived in hide tipis, but in March they returned in good time for the planting season.

Near the villages, in the wooded bottom lands by the river where the soil was richer, softer and easier to work, corn, beans, squashes, sunflowers and tobacco were planted in a number of fields. Men may have helped to burn down the trees and to set fences to keep horses out of the plots, but all cultivation, including the breaking of the ground with digging sticks, was done by women. Corn was planted in small low mounds or 'hills' one or two paces apart, which were made in rows along a plot. The seed was planted in a number of small holes, dibbled in the centre of these hills. As the plant matured the weeds were cut out and more soil hilled up to cover the

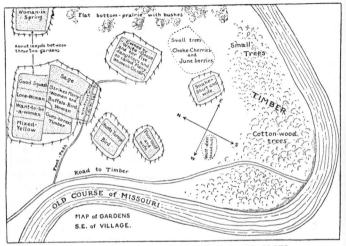

FIG. 83. SKETCH MAP OF HIDATSA FIELD PLOTS
(*After Wilson*)

roots; for this a light hoe made from the blade bone of a deer, bison or later a horse, was used. Beans were planted in rows of smaller hills between the corn, and squashes bordered small

FIG. 84. HIDATSA BLADE-BONE HOE, ABOUT ONE YARD LONG
(*After Wilson*)

unit plots of corn and beans into which the fields were divided. Sunflowers were usually planted round the border of the fields. Cultivated land was entirely in the hands of the women and was passed on to their daughters. The plots were cleared, owned and tended by individual families, although kinsmen were invited to help at harvest time. A large household in which a woman had the help of her old mother and daughters often maintained a plot more than a hundred yards long and nearly a hundred yards wide (see fig. 83).

After three or four years the crop became so meagre that the field was left fallow for two or three years. But new ground was not continually being cleared; most households had several fields of which only about a half were being cultivated at one time. New land was cleared only when plots proved disappointing or failed to recover after fallowing. Manuring was, however, unknown. Burnt grass and corn stalks were not dug into the ground and dung was removed from the plots if the horses were let in to eat the stubble. The Hidatsa thought it merely harmful because it caused more weeds to grow.

Young and able-bodied men took no part in cultivation, but old men who no longer joined in the buffalo hunt or war parties would help in clearing the fields and in hilling and harvesting the crops. Tobacco, which was of considerable ceremonial importance was, however, cultivated by the old men alone and in separate plots. The seeds were sown thickly in shallow furrows on a carefully prepared plot, but after the weaklings had been weeded out, the soil was hilled up round the remaining plants as for corn.

This practice of male cultivation of tobacco was characteristic of a great part of the Eastern Woodland area. Still more remarkable is the fact that tobacco was cultivated in this way among peoples farther to the west and north-west who knew nothing of agriculture for food-supply. The ceremonial uses of tobacco were retained by western peoples who abandoned cultivation in favour of buffalo hunting, and they were also transmitted to hunting peoples who, like the Blackfoot described in an earlier chapter, had never been agriculturists. Tobacco planting in the north-western Plains had in this manner been extended beyond the range of cultivation proper.

The Hidatsa planted their corn in May before the summer period of heavier and more frequent rains. The women would wait until they saw that the wild gooseberry bushes in the woods were in almost full leaf before they began planting. During the growing season stages were erected in the fields, from which young girls watched and endeavoured to keep off birds and rodents; scarecrows were also set up. Green corn for boiling could be harvested at the beginning of August and a small surplus was preserved for the winter by half boiling and drying in the sun. But the main harvest came when the corn was fully ripe, nearly a month later. Families co-operated to husk the corn cobs in the fields, and the harvest was carried back in baskets to the large drying stages, often nearly thirty feet long and six feet high, permanently erected before each lodge. Here the corn cobs were spread out for a week or two on the raised flooring of split logs to dry in the air and sun. The finest ears were braided into strings and kept mainly for seed. The rest were threshed with wooden sticks. For this, small closed booths walled with an old tipi cover were erected under the drying stage, so that the loose corn might not be scattered and lost. By removing planks from the stage above, corn for threshing could be dropped into the booth as required. The shelled corn cobs were burnt and the ashes, rich in salts, were used as seasoning.

For squash planting, which followed the corn, the seeds were usually made to sprout by placing them in a bed of damp leaves rolled up in a hide and placed near the fire in the lodge. Hills like those for maize were prepared for these seedlings. The first squashes, which began to ripen even before the green corn was ready, were eaten fresh, but a great part of the later pickings were sliced, spitted on long rods and dried on the stage for winter use. Beans were threshed from their pods by trampling and were also dried for storing.

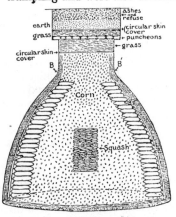

FIG. 85. HIDATSA CACHE PIT
ABOUT 7 FEET DEEP
(*After Wilson*)

A number of bell-shaped pits with a narrow opening were excavated, some of them within the lodges, for storing the food of each household. These pits were made and filled by the women and were often six or seven feet deep; they were lined with dried grass held in position by willow rods, pegged into place. The corn, both loose and in the ear, and dried squashes were carefully packed in and finally covered with a layer of grass, a circle of hide, small split logs and lastly earth and ashes. The greater part of this food was required on the return in March from the winter hunting season, during which the lodges had been abandoned and the Hidatsa lived much like the Blackfoot. The positions of these store pits were concealed as much as possible to guard against plundering of the deserted villages. (See fig. 85.)

In eastern North America the cultivation of the three great staples of New World agriculture extended to the climatic limits of these crops. The Iroquois and other tribes who occupied the country south-east of Lake Ontario, the peninsula between Lakes Huron and Erie and the lowlands of the St. Lawrence river, were nearly all cultivators. The early explorers among the Iroquois encountered permanent villages, some with a population of over four hundred and surrounded by fields of corn which extended for several miles.

In the villages large granaries and store pits were built and in the houses great bark chests were filled with corn. Cultivation was again in the hands of women, who also gathered a wide range of wild products. Men fished in summer, and hunted deer, moose and other game in winter. Hunting was of great importance not only for the supply of animal food, but also for providing the hides and skins necessary to comfort during the cold winters.

On the damp flats flanking rivers and lakes from New England to Nova Scotia to the Great Lakes and beyond, there grew a wild grain, the so-called 'wild rice' (*Zizania sp.*), which was collected in large quantities by the hunting peoples, especially the Ojibwa to the west of Lake Superior. This food was, however, neglected by the corn-growing peoples, who never attempted to transfer their knowledge of corn growing to the cultivation of this plant. Some of the hunting peoples such as the Ojibwa of Georgian Bay dropped wild rice seeds wrapped in little mud balls into the swamps to increase the crop for the next season, but regular cultivation was never adopted. The prestige of corn among the true cultivators and the wealth of wild game, seeds and roots among the hunters, seems to have inhibited this development.

In the south-eastern parts of the present United States larger settlements, sometimes true towns of nearly a thousand inhabitants, were built and large and more stable political confederacies were built up. The economy was more elaborate. Weaving and the hammering of copper ornaments from nuggets of pure copper were widespread. The stockaded villages of timber and mud-plastered houses were often laid out round a central square and the resources of agriculture were increased by the addition of another crop—the sweet potato—restricted climatically to sub-tropical and tropical areas. Among some of these peoples men took a share in the agricultural work, which was more prominent in the hunting and cultivating

economy of the south than in the North-East Woodlands
Cultivation remained, however, primarily a woman's task.

The fact that North American agriculture, despite the
fundamental unity of the crops grown, falls into two great
provinces of male and female cultivation, offers a problem of
great importance. It cannot be resolved by any simple appeal
to differences in type of social organization and in the status
of women. Matrilineal institutions and considerable authority
of women can be found associated with both male and female
cultivation, to say nothing of non-agricultural peoples. Women
have great authority and are even the landholders in the Pueblos
where men cultivate. The Iroquois, among whom men hunt,
fish and fight but never till, are also remarkable for the
importance of their matrilineal institutions.

The solution more probably lies in the dual history of the
northward expansion of the higher crafts, including agriculture,
and in the differences of the resources of east and west. The
cultural relations of the Pueblos with the south Mexican area
are undoubted, and everywhere among the higher civilizations
of Middle America, agriculture appears to have been practised
and largely directed by men. The Southwest is, moreover, an
area poor in game in which collecting rather than hunting may
be expected to have predominated in pre-agricultural times,
so that maize growing did not encounter an economy in which
men were fully occupied and thus attach itself solely, as it often
did in secondary areas, to the gathering activities of women.
This northward expansion of agriculture which, as the early
prehistoric sites in the Southwest show, had its beginnings at
a very remote period, did not, however, extend thence into
eastern North America. It was arrested by the arid western
plains which largely if not completely cut off the Eastern Woodland peoples from western and south-western stimuli.

There is on the other hand much evidence to suggest that
cultivated plants and agricultural practices together with other
crafts and equipment including, for instance, the blowpipe,
reached eastern North America by way of the Antilles, from
the forest lands of Central America and the northern South
American coast. Although again ultimately dependent on one
or more of the great centres of civilization that straddled the
waist of the two continents from South Mexico to Peru, agriculture ceased to be, or failed ever to become, a male activity.
That there were good environmental reasons for this can hardly
be doubted. Agriculture had to establish itself among food-
gathering peoples, among whom hunting, particularly in eastern
North America, offered a considerable reward. Unlike the

west, beyond the Plains, the native game in the east was both abundant and varied; it included deer, woodland bison, opossum, racoon, otter and other animals. These resources would inhibit complete dependence on cultivation and might cause male cultivation, if introduced, to relapse in favour of a female pattern. Only where the size of communities and the closeness of settlement reach high proportions, do the game resources progressively dwindle and reliance on cultivation becomes more exclusive. The participation of men might, in such circumstances, be expected to increase. This point was probably reached in parts of the South-east in North America and joint male and female cultivation is claimed for such a people as the Yuchi, but male participation was, in general, progressively less important towards the north, as the scale of political organization, the development of crafts and the density of population declined.

CHAPTER XIII

COCHIN: AN INDIAN STATE ON THE MALABAR COAST

THE native state of Cochin exemplifies the economy of the richer, well-watered lowlands of India where an ancient system of plough cultivation and the complex sanctions of the caste system dominate the activities and organization of society. Less than fifteen hundred square miles in area but with a population of about one million, it lies on the Malabar coast land of south-western India only ten degrees north of the equator.[1] Malayalam, the native speech of the Malabar coast, is a Dravidian language akin to Tamil but including in its vocabulary a very large number of Sanscrit words.

The peoples of India are very mixed in race. An earlier australoid strain of which pure representatives survive in the jungle tribes of the hills of Cochin, has been modified by admixtures of Mediterranean, Alpine and other elements. The marriage restrictions of the caste system have not tended to perpetuate physical differences between various strata of society on the Malabar coast as much as in many parts of southern India, and the people of Cochin by no means fall into sharply distinct racial groups so far as the high and middle castes are concerned, but grade insensibly into one another. This is due to the prevalence of 'hypergamy', the mating of women with men of the next higher caste. The members of highest castes of southern India, who claim to be descendants of immigrants from the north, do, however, show closer resemblances to the fairer, tall and bearded peoples of north-western India, and to the dark-haired, brown-eyed people of

[1] Down to 1881 the population was only about 600,000, but it has been doubled in the last half century (exceeding 1,200,000 at the 1931 census) in consequence of improved conditions and, in particular, of the growth of the export trade in copra. The description of social and economic conditions to be given here does not take into consideration the rapid changes that have been taking place in Cochin and elsewhere on the Malabar coast in the present century. Many caste regulations relating to marriage, untouchability and occupation have been greatly relaxed. For an account of these changes and their consequences see *Census of India*, 1931, Vol. 21; Cochin (by T. Sankara Menon). Chapters 11 and 12. Ernakulam, 1933.

southern Europe. The peoples of Cochin, or of the Malabar coast as a whole, do not therefore constitute a distinct and homogeneous racial group. The presence of an old aboriginal strain found pure among the few remaining Veddahs and other australoid jungle tribes is often indicated in the lower castes by very dark skin colour and a very broad nose. As a whole the Malayalis are of rather short stature; few individuals are taller than five feet six inches and most of the poorer classes are shorter and very slight in build. Skin colour varies from very light brown to black. The nose is frequently prominent with rather flaring nostrils and while among the lower castes it is often very broad and approaches the great width characteristic of the hill tribes, in the higher castes it is little wider than among European peoples. Many of the Nayars, the largest high caste group, could be mistaken for southern Italians. Although their black wavy hair grows fairly long on the head, beards are generally scanty or absent. Many members of some of the higher castes, however, and particularly the Brahmans, have considerable beards and fairly abundant body hair. Such people are often of fairer complexion.

The life of Cochin depends on the intensive cultivation of rice on the thousands of acres of laboriously prepared plots which cover the coastal plain. Less than forty miles from the sea the Cardomom Hills, southern extensions of the Western Ghats, rise in steep terraced escarpments to heights of over five thousand feet. Along the coast the strong parallel current has built up great bars of sand and gravels so that the short, swift rivers from the mountains, continually blocked and diverted at their exits, flow into a zone of inter-connected lagoons or backwaters. A few breaches in the sandy coast belt made by the larger rivers are kept open by the scour of the tides. They admit the sea at high water and afford entrances for small craft. Behind the backwaters the undulating plain, seamed by a multitude of streams, rises slowly to the mountain foothills. (See fig. 86.)

Since Cochin lies so far to the south of India the rain-bearing monsoon winds from the Arabian Sea arrive early and continue late. They blow strongly from June to November. They back to the north after September but still bring rain. After a dry period of light breezes from December to March the approach of the monsoon is again indicated by showers in April and May, and June and July are months of torrential rain, when some fifty inches fall on the coast land and over seventy-five inches on the mountains. After slackening somewhat in September the rainfall frequently rises to a second maximum of ten to twenty inches in October, during the retreat of the monsoon and before the short dry season sets in again. In an average year, about a hundred inches of rain fall on the coast and more than a hundred and fifty inches on the higher slopes of the Western Ghats. The climate is always relatively

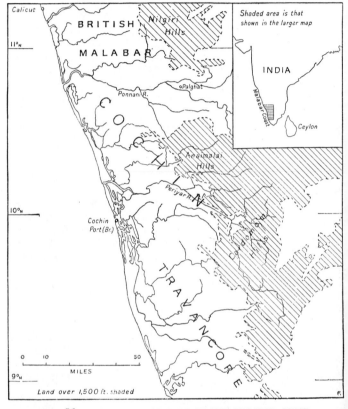

FIG. 86. SKETCH MAP OF PART OF THE MALABAR COAST

warm in these low latitudes. The mean annual temperature is around 80° F., and the range is small, but the nights are chilly at the beginning of the dry season, while the greatest heat of the year precedes the heavy rains in April and May. The wet season, although actual temperatures are not high, is very oppressive on account of the high humidity.

The whole country was once clothed in dense forest, mostly

deciduous in the lowlands and foothills, but evergreen on the higher mountains. The centuries of agricultural occupation have, however, left only scattered remnants of the virgin forest on barren hillocks in the lowlands. But the forest jungles of the Cardomom and Nilgiri hills, although valuable timber, especially teak and ebony, has been obtained from them for many centuries, are still uncleared and are occupied by backward hunting tribes. Terrace cultivation of the hillsides so characteristic of southeast Asia is not found in southern India. The coastal plain has for many centuries been densely settled by a population of rice growers; more than half the population is engaged directly in field cultivation and over one third in various native crafts and industries, which include fishing and tending groves of coconut palms and other cultivated trees and bushes from which fruits and nuts are gathered. Over the greater part of the plain there are to-day more than a thousand inhabitants to every square mile, while along the seaboard the density of population rises to over two thousand. But despite the dense population, and unlike the greater part of India, the people of Cochin and of the Malabar coast as a whole have never been concentrated in compact villages. The settlements are loose and straggling clusters of houses round temples and bathing tanks on patches of higher ground unsuitable for rice cultivation. The house of every landowner or wealthier tenant stands within its own garden and grove of fruit trees. The hovels of the agricultural labourers and poorer artisans are scattered among the fields and on the outskirts of settlements. Even the larger centres or towns, which are of recent growth and hold only about a tenth of the total population, are broken up by stretches of cultivation and groves of trees.

Almost all the low-lying ground which can be flooded by impounding rainfall or river water is devoted to paddy or lowland rice cultivation. Rice takes from sixty to a hundred and twenty days to ripen, according to the variety sown, and the yield also varies from eight to more than twenty fold. On about a third of these rice lands or *nilams*, in the most favourable tracts where the soil is rich and there is neither drought nor destructive flood, two and even three crops of paddy may be obtained in a single year. But most lands yield only a single rice crop and the growing season varies according to the particular conditions. Some bottom lands are inundated at the height of the early rains. The paddy cannot then be planted until the later part of the rainy season when the flood has begun to subside. On other low-lying tracts with heavy soils that are easily waterlogged and cannot be drained a single slow-growing crop is sown before the rains and matures only at the beginning of the dry season ten months later. But the greater part of the rice lands are liable to a spell of drought between the early and the late monsoon rains. Paddy is

FIG. 87. PLOUGHING A RICE PLOT ; A CULTIVATOR'S HUT ON THE RIGHT
(*Based on photographs in Slater: 'Some South Indian Villages'*)

therefore sown early with the beginning of the monsoon rains, and is harvested during the drier spell in September.

Before rains or irrigation the rice plots are tilled with a simple wooden plough shod with an iron point. This plough is without wheel, coulter or mold-board; it merely furrows the ground and does not turn it over. Water buffaloes, stronger and more enduring than the indigenous oxen and more frequently used for all purposes, are yoked in pairs for ploughing. The plough is attached directly to the yoke by a long pole, and the ground must be gone over many times to bring it into condition. Women follow the plough breaking up the sods with sticks. Cattle dung and green manure gathered in the patches of forest and waste land are scattered over the plots and after

FIG. 88. A MALABAR PLOUGH
(*After Leser*)

they have been thoroughly drenched they are furrowed again. Clods of earth are again crushed with a heavy wooden plank on which a man stands as it is dragged lengthwise and the ground is finally levelled by dragging a log over it. A second dressing of manure should be applied before sowing the rice. The banks, a yard or more high, which surround every rice field to impound or exclude water at different stages of the growth, must be repaired before the rains. When the plot has been thoroughly soaked the rice is sown broadcast. As the seedlings spring up the banks of the plot are raised, or breached, at appropriate places, should excessive rains or river floods threaten a destructive inundation. If more water is required it is brought into the plots from adjoining water channels by Persian wheels or simple water hoists. The harvest is gathered by hand with serrated iron sickles and the grain is trodden out by bullocks on the threshing ground.

Where a second crop is to be grown seedlings are raised in specially prepared and irrigated plots during September and are planted out in the field, usually by women, as soon as the first crop has been reaped and more manure has been ploughed into the field. The planting out of seedlings four or five weeks old always gives a higher yield than broadcast sowing and reduces the risk that the crop may be choked with weeds; but it demands far more labour and, for first crops and single crop lands, it is not usually undertaken. After two successive rice crops land usually lies fallow from January until the next paddy sowing in June. But a third crop can be raised by irrigation from wells or rivers during the dry season, from January to May. This, however, demands very high fertility and considerable manuring, while the yield is relatively low and a long fallow must be allowed at a later period. Save in exceptional circumstances, therefore, triple cropping of paddy land is rare.

Particularly fertile paddy lands, which require neither ploughing nor manuring, are afforded by the bottoms of shallow fresh water lakes in parts of the western coast lands, and by the swamps lying between the sandy shores and the backwaters. The fresh water lakes, separated by natural and artificial banks from the brackish backwaters, are flooded by the swollen rivers during the monsoon rains. For their cultivation suitable areas are divided into small plots during the dry season when the water is but a few inches deep. These are surrounded by barriers of wattle and mud four or five feet high, and between them channels a few yards wide are left to carry the floodwater and to serve as canals during the wet season. After the first monsoon rains each plot is drained into the adjacent channels by lifting out the water with Persian wheels, or sometimes at the present day with portable steam-engine pumps, and rice seedlings that have been reared in raised beds are planted out. The banks require constant attention and the water lifts are kept at work throughout the growing season so that the crop may not be drowned. These rice plots can generally be reached at this season only by small boats moving along the narrow channels which fill with the flood waters and with the drainage from the plots themselves. Although some part of the crop is lost every year through the failure of particular banks the yield on the greater part of these lands is very high. When the harvest has been gathered the banks are breached and the inflow of water carries sufficient silt to restore the fertility of the plots for the next crop.

The swamps on the seaward side of the backwaters are similarly banked off during the dry season. When the heavy rains and river floods of the wet monsoon season freshen and raise the level of the brackish backwaters, water is admitted through gaps in the banks to irrigate the seedlings that have been planted out. On this land a special variety of rice immune to the relatively high salinity of the soil is grown. It affords a very high yield and the grain is very large, but it is slow growing and cannot be harvested until October.

On most lands where a single paddy crop is grown a second crop of millet, pulses or oil seeds, especially gingelly (sesame) is raised. These crops require less moisture and the pulses are particularly valuable in restoring nitrogen to depleted rice lands. They may be planted either before or after the rice crop. Millets which require least moisture are often sown towards the end of the dry season in May and ripen with the first monsoon rains in June. They thus provide food for the poorer cultivator while his new paddy crop is being grown. Pulses and oil seeds can be grown at this time or during the last rains after the rice has been harvested. During the dry season from December to May most of the paddy land lies fallow.

The cultivation of the higher land on the slopes of valleys and on the low hillocks so characteristic of the Malabar plain, contrasts strongly with that of the wet paddy fields. In some areas, where the land suitable for *nilams* is very restricted, a kind of paddy is grown in rotation with millet and after long fallow periods on upland fields without irrigation. But on most of the higher ground root crops, vegetables and fruit trees alone are raised. These include the castor plant whose seeds are crushed to provide the native lighting oil burnt in pottery and brass lamps. The gardens and orchards are scattered among and around the houses. The house of every landowner and prosperous tenant is surrounded by a compound of several acres in which breadfruit, mango, areca nut, banana, pomegranate and other trees are planted. In gardens near the house pumpkins, melons, yams, taro, sweet potatoes and other roots and vegetables are raised.

The most important single orchard crop, however, is the coconut. It is claimed that the coconut was introduced into Malabar from Ceylon more than fifteen hundred years ago, and its cultivation for the modern export trade has increased enormously in recent times. The groves are most extensive on the salt and sandy belt immediately above the shore, but they are also found in the interior along the banks of streams, round the bottoms of hillocks and surrounding the paddy fields. For planting, ripe nuts are dried in the sun for a week, soaked in water for a fortnight and set in beds of rich soil where they sprout in three months and are ready for planting out in manured pits at the end of a year. In their early years at least, the coconut palms must be watered during the dry season. The soil of a coconut grove should be stirred up twice a year and each tree is generally manured during the monsoon. After seven or eight years the palms begin to bear, each yielding some forty nuts a year for thirty years or more. The nut shells and leaf stems are used for fuel and the trunks past bearing provide an abundant if inferior building timber. The leaves are used for thatching and the fibres which surround the nut inside the husk afford material for rope and matting. A fermented liquor, toddy, a distilled spirit, arrack, and sugar are made from the sap which flows from the cut ends of palm fronds and flower stems into earthenware pots which are attached to them. The sun-dried nut kernels (copra) are crushed in mills to supply oil for food and cosmetics and the crushed oilcake for cattle food and manure. A great part of the copra is to-day sold for export to Europe.

Betel pepper vines are trained on the coconut palms and their leaves compounded with areca nut and slaked lime provide the material for the narcotic used throughout south-eastern Asia from India to Melanesia. Pepper groves supply both red and black pepper according to the treatment of the fruit.

Water buffaloes, and a few cattle, sheep and goats, are, except for the pigs reared in considerable numbers in the Syrian Christian communities, practically the only live stock found in the villages. The native cattle are of a poor type, feeble at the plough and poor milkers. Milk and *ghee* (clarified butter) are obtained in greater quantities from sheep and goats than from the cows. Beef is eaten by none since the cow is sacred, but mutton and goat flesh are eaten by those that can afford it among the lower Hindu castes. While bullocks are often used for draught in the fields the more powerful water buffalo is the better animal for working the heavy wet soils of the *nilams*. The livestock is allowed to graze on the field banks and in waste lands under the charge of herdsmen. The natural herbage is supplemented by rice straw and small amounts of oilcake in the dry season. Breeding is badly neglected for there is practically no selection of bulls and rams and few cows calve more than once in two or three years.

Although wells are here less needed for irrigation than in almost any other part of India water must be raised from them or from river channels at critical periods. Well irrigation is practically restricted to the cultivation of gardens and to raising a third crop of paddy in the dry season. But wells are very necessary for the supply of drinking water in the dry season, for despite the heavy rains during the rest of the year many of the smaller streams dry up during the great heat of the early months of the year. They are built in the gardens and compounds surrounding the houses of the landowners. The poor tenants and labourers are usually permitted to take water from them when there is abundance, but at times of drought they are often compelled to carry it from streams and stagnant pools over long distances. The *picotah* affords a means of raising water from deep wells or low-lying streams and ditches. A leathern bucket is suspended at the end of a long rope or thin pole which is attached to a wooden counter-weighted beam. This is pivoted on a timber support ten to twenty feet high. For a large *picotah* a scaffold is often erected alongside so that one or two men standing on the beam can supplement the counter-weight by moving away from the fulcrum when the full bucket is to be raised.

For raising water more quickly and in greater volume a bullock-lift (*mhote*) is used. The special leathern bucket (*kabalai*) here hangs on a rope which runs over a pulley. This is set on a frame which juts out over the well or stream. The *kabalai* is raised by a pair of oxen which pull on ropes while descending a slope running down and away from the edge. It has an open leather tube hanging down below its belly. In addition to the rope which is attached to the rim another is tied to the end of the tube. This rope is somewhat shorter and runs over a roller well below the pulley so that, when both ropes are being hauled by the oxen, the opening in the tube is raised above the rim of the bucket and no water escapes. When, however, the bucket has risen to the level of the pulley the water empties through the tube, which has been pulled over the roller, and passes along a trough into the irrigating channel. The only labour required is that of the driver of the oxen. Both these devices were known in the Ancient East and are still in use from Egypt to Further India at the present day. The *kabalai* is, however, not used in northern India, where a second man has to be employed at the bullock-lift to empty a bucket of the ordinary type. More elaborate are the Persian wheels and the pivoted troughs which raise water more rapidly but through less height. In Cochin they are used for the important task of draining plots which have received an excess of water as on the low-lying ground along the backwaters and on reclaimed lake bottoms. The vertical wheels equipped with buckets like a dredger are driven with cog wheels by means of oxen.

FIG. 89. A SOUTH INDIAN MHOTE WITH KABALAI
(*Based on photographs in Slater, op. cit.*)

Fishing is carried on by various methods in the rivers, the backwaters and the sea. In the rivers, fish are caught with cast nets and lines from dugout canoes and are shot with blowguns and cross-bows from the banks. These last methods are of considerable interest for, while the blowgun of the river fisherman is almost certainly a survival for a special use in the cultivated lowlands of the hunting weapon still used by the food-gathering peoples of the mountain jungles, the cross-bow, as details of its construction show, is modelled on the weapons introduced by the Portuguese in the sixteenth century. Although the cross-bow is made entirely of wood the arrow is an iron shaft which for fishing is attached by a line to the bow so that it may be recovered.

In the backwaters large labyrinths leading to baited chambers are made by setting up in the muddy bottoms close fences of split bamboos which project above the surface. Basketry and large funnel-shaped nets are also attached to stakes. Into all these contrivances the fish enter at high tide and can be collected at the ebb. On the backwaters in the rich fishing district round the mouth of the Periyar river great four-cornered nets, five or more yards square, each attached to a tilting bamboo scaffolding, are set up at the end of short wooden jetties. By means of ropes and counter-weights these nets can be lowered and raised at will.

The sea fishers for the most part use long vertical nets with floats and sinkers with which they surround the shoals of mackerel and sardines. Their nets, which vary from a hundred yards to nearly half a mile in length, are manipulated by a number of men in dugout canoes, each of whom owns a particular section of net from which he takes the catch. The catches, especially the large mackerel hauls, are salted in brine, while fish oil for curing leather and preserving timber is prepared from the immense shoals of sardines which are boiled in great cauldrons and troughs. In the coastal zone fish are used extensively for manuring the coconut groves and the paddy lands.

The dense populations dependent on the intensive agricultural exploitation of the humid coastal lowlands of Malabar have long been divided into a number of sovereign states of which modern Cochin is a surviving remnant.

As a separate state Cochin probably emerged from the break up of the ancient kingdom of Kerala in the first century A.D. But until native rule was modified and reorganized under British influence towards the end of the eighteenth century, the political and social organization of Cochin was effectively dominated not by the King or Sirkar but by the hereditary rights of landowning chiefs and by the caste system.

When first visited by the Portuguese in the sixteenth century, the state of Cochin was more than twice its present size. The royal family consisted of five branches each with its hereditary lands, slaves and militia. The succession to the kingship fell to the eldest male no matter to which branch he belonged, and it involved frequent dissensions and civil wars in which neighbouring rulers and particularly the Zamorin of Calicut were able to interfere and to acquire considerable power.

The native warfare of Malabar was, however, a very formal affair in which opposing forces of swordsmen supported by archers advanced against each other in pitched battle. Night attacks and ambushes were disgraceful, and violation of any of the complicated rules of fighting brought great dishonour. The killing of a warrior, save in a formal battle or duel, involved the offender in a blood feud with the victim's relatives—a feud that would continue after formal hostilities had ceased. Before the European penetration in the sixteenth century there appears to have been little desire to acquire territory by means of war. Fighting settled disputes of prestige and reduced the conquered to ceremonial vassalage, but the victor did not normally acquire any property rights over new territory. Cochin itself was a vassal state to Mysore, Travancore and other stronger powers at various periods in medieval times.

The royal house of Cochin was, and remains the greatest landowner in the State, but other considerable tracts of territory were controlled by hereditary chiefs of districts. These district chiefs personally owned some of the village territories within their districts but many other villages were held and controlled by local chiefs with similar hereditary titles. The chiefs had practically sovereign rights over the land and people of the territory directly owned by them, and levied a tax on all the rice lands. The obligations of a village chief to a district chief and of the district chiefs to the king were limited to support in war and participation in ceremonial. The king had rights of disposal and taxation in kind only on the land he owned directly; he obtained no revenue from the territories of the chiefs and, like the chiefs of the districts and villages, leased his lands to retainers who paid a rental in kind and were under obligation of military service. Some of the land was sub-let to cultivating tenant farmers, but much of it was worked by agricultural serfs who were paid in kind.

Cochin remains to-day a land of large estates held by relatively few wealthy families and temples. Landed property must, according to the rules of the higher castes to which former chiefs and present landowners belong, be handed on undivided.[1] Hindu temples also own large estates which they have acquired piecemeal by gifts. Peasant proprietors occupy only an insignificant fraction of the land. The estates of wealthy families, like the lands of former chiefs and retainers in the past, are in part cultivated directly with the aid of labourers, the nominally free descendants of the former agricultural serfs. But a considerable part of the land is held by small tenant farmers whose households cultivate the few acres that they rent either directly from the great landowners or as sub-tenants from leaseholders.

The various native forms of land tenure have changed but little. The simple lease by which most land is held must be renewed every year; to-day, however, the tenant may not be disturbed unless he fails to cultivate the land effectively. Under favourable conditions he hands over to the landowner

[1] Recent legislation in Cochin and Travancore has, however, permitted and even encouraged the division of estates during the past decade.

two-thirds of the estimated rice crop after deducting the cost of seed and cultivation. According to another practice the tenant advances a sum of money to the landlord. He thereby obtains secure occupation for a period of twelve years, receives interest at a low rate on his loan, which is to be repaid at the end of the period together with the value of any improvement he has made. He pays an annual rent on the same scale as for a simple lease and has to pay a substantial renewal fee at the end of twelve years if he wishes to continue in occupation. The origin of this form of tenancy is very obscure and it has been suggested that it was instituted as a means of raising funds by the king and the chiefs for the prosecution of wars. It obtains to-day among the well-to-do Nayar tenants of Nambudiri landlords, who thus control considerable areas, most of which they again sub-let annually or at will. For very frequently the tenant holds his land only at the will of the landlord or leaseholder, and is required to hand over all the produce, or its estimated value, after deducting the bare cost of seed and cultivation. He is virtually a labourer bound by a contract. Since in all cases the landlord calculates his share of the produce on the basis of the amount of seed sown, according to the general fertility of the land, but irrespective of the conditions during a particular season, it may frequently happen that the rent payable is more than the land yields so that a burden of debt accumulates on the tenant, who must nevertheless maintain his favour with the landlord lest he be evicted for arrears and lose all means of livelihood. Every tenant has, in addition to the rent, to make certain customary payments on the occasions of festivals and ceremonials in the landlord's household.

There was no written code of native law, for the use of writing was almost entirely restricted to religious texts. The laws of property and social conduct, based mainly on the Hindu Sastras, were formerly administered by the local and district chiefs with appeal in certain cases to the king. Disputes over conduct which infringed caste rules were, and remain, the concern of the particular caste to be dealt with by its local council.

Punishment depended considerably on the caste of the offender. On men of free castes fines were usually inflicted. The offences of serfs were punished by their masters, who were responsible for their misdeeds.

Into this political and economic hierarchy there dovetails the caste system which is perhaps more highly developed and socially rigid in Malabar than anywhere else in India. An Indian caste is a collection of families, or groups of families, bearing a common name and claiming a common descent from a human or divine ancestor. It usually professes to follow the same hereditary occupation. This occupation is, however, by no means the livelihood of all members and it is sometimes only a ritual activity. A caste is in some ways similar to a clan with the great contrast that it is not exogamous. A man may and sometimes must marry within his own caste and indeed, within the particular division or sub-caste to which he belongs. There are, however, frequently exogamous divisions within the caste or sub-caste. In the higher castes the position is complicated by hypergamy, whereby a woman mates by preference with a man of the next higher caste. The children are, however, considered members of the mother's caste and have no social relations with the father's relatives or caste fellows.

Within a particular district, each caste has an internal organization, with a council and a court for settling its own disputes. Each has its special ceremonies and festivals, its particular usages concerning marriage, food and ceremonial pollution. The castes of India are bewilderingly numerous and have been formed, modified and subdivided by a variety of social processes. Some are to be found in nearly every part of India, others are restricted to particular districts. A systematic account of the castes of Cochin is obviously impossible here but, since caste membership everywhere cuts across local groupings and plays so great a part in the social and economic life, some of the major divisions and salient characteristics will be considered.

The castes of Cochin may be regarded as falling into a number of groups or strata of decreasing prestige, wealth and power:[1]

(1) The royal house, which controls enormous estates as its private property, is acknowledged to belong to the Khshatriya group of castes but has special rank as a sacred ruling family. It probably derives actually from the Nayars.

(2) The Nambudiri Brahmans, an aristocracy dependent on its religious prestige, whose higher ranks have also acquired extensive landed property.

(3) The Nayars—the native freemen of Cochin who formerly bore arms. The landowning chiefs of former times were nearly all Nayars and the rest of the Nayar caste was in quasi-feudal dependence on them. They correspond to the Khshatriyas of northern India but are classed as 'Sudras' in Hindu society.

---

[1] Foreign castes such as the Tamil Brahmans and immigrant or non-Hindu communities of Moslems, Christians and Jews are not considered.

(4) A group of relatively high castes who perform personal services to the Brahmans and Nayars. The weavers rank in this group so far as caste is concerned although, unlike the barbers, washermen and schoolmasters, they are craftsmen who have no close contact with the higher castes.

The remaining castes are 'untouchable' to those above them. They include:

(5) The low castes of artisans. Since manual labour is despised by the high castes all the skilled crafts are undertaken by members of this group.

(6) The fishermen, boatmen and toddy drawers, who are the lowest of the free castes.

(7) The serf castes who provide the greater part of the agricultural labour for the owners of land and were until recently bought, sold and hired out as chattels.

(8) The small jungle groups of the hills which hardly form part of Cochin society but are slowly being drawn from their independent food-gathering economy by inducements to work as forest labourers.

The Brahmans form the highest caste in the Hindu religious and social system. To them the greatest respect and reverence is due for their sacred qualities and priestly powers. The Nambudiri, the native Brahmans of Cochin, probably arrived as an immigrant people with the introduction of Hindu religion in south-western India, and obtained great prestige as possessors of great magical power with control of valuable rituals. While they did not disrupt the existing political organization or become a directly ruling people they acquired, as a result of their great prestige and sanctity, extensive grants of land; although they have remained numerically small, Nambudiri Brahmans are among the largest landowners in Cochin and other parts of Malabar. In former days the Brahman elders were the trusted advisers of the chiefs and of the royal house. To-day they constitute a social and religious aristocracy and the higher grades devote ascetic and secluded lives to the study of the Vedic literature of Hinduism. The life of a devout Nambudiri is governed at almost every point by the sacred texts. Apart from the many ritual sacrifices that have to be performed, a considerable part of each day is spent in prayers, sacred recitations and purificatory bathing; he eats no meat and lives mainly on rice and vegetable curries. By no means all the Nambudiris are wealthy landowners; but they never lack food, for the feeding of Brahmans is a pious act which the wealthy of other castes, including the royal family, are anxious to perform. Large establishments provided and endowed at various times for the housing and feeding of Brahmans are scattered over the country.

The relation of Brahmans with other castes continually affirms their superiority. A Nayar speaking with a Brahman refers to his own house as a dung heap, to his clothes as spiders' webs, to his food as raw rice, but the Brahman's house is his noble residence, his food is ambrosia, his teeth are pearls, his sleep the reclining of a raja.

The Nambudiri family is patrilineal but only the eldest son may contract legal marriages with Brahman women and so produce an heir to the family property. Although the eldest son may and generally does have several wives, eligible husbands for Brahman girls must necessarily be few and large dowries are paid. Younger sons take unofficial wives among the Nayars, but the children of such unions are unrecognized by their fathers; they are considered members of the household of the mother with whom they remain and they have no claim on the Brahman family of their father.

The Nambudiri Brahmans are themselves divided into ten endogamous sub-castes with diminishing prestige and privileges of which the lowest have only the privilege of being able to eat with higher ranks. Only the higher groups are allowed to study the Vedas while the highest grade alone may perform sacrifices in the Brahman temples. The Nambudiri are also grouped into a number of divisions or *gotras* which may correspond with former family groups, established as colonies in different parts of Malabar in early times.

Although there have been Jewish colonies in Cochin from a very early, but unknown, date, Christian communities (known now as 'Syrian Christians') from very early in the Christian era, and Mohammedans of mixed Arab and native blood since medieval times, the mass of the population is Hindu in religion. The Hinduism of the Malabar coast is a complicated compromise between the worship of the Vedic pantheon of the Brahmans and that of earlier divinities, among which the cobra is the most conspicuous, with whom these later gods have been identified, and associated. Between the Brahman temples or *ambalams* devoted to the worship of Vishna and Siva and the *kavus* of the lower caste Hindus there is a sharp cleavage. From the former all low castes are excluded, while none of the higher Brahmans officiate in the *kavus*. Nambudiri Brahmans do, however, visit the cobra shrines in the compounds of Nayar houses to make the sacrifices to the sacred snakes. The gods and goddesses of the *kavus* are often local tutelary spirits who are believed to keep off the many demons which must, however, be coaxed, propitiated and exorcized from the sick.

Brahman children after the ceremony of investiture of the holy thread, a cotton cord worn over one shoulder by all Brahmans, enter one of the *matts*, Brahman schools at which they are taught to recite the Vedas and are instructed in Sanscrit literature. These institutions which have endowments of land and are conducted by learned Brahmans are free to all Nambudiri children but no other castes are admitted. School-masters teaching reading and writing, rhetoric and the recitation of Sanscrit hymns are found in most villages, while well-to-do families of Nayer and other castes often engage special tutors for their own children and permit the children of poorer families to receive instruction for a nominal fee.

The practice and teaching of medicine is largely restricted to certain Nambudiri families who still have a great reputation for curing diseases with their herbal medicines. Visiting their patients' houses they prescribe and supply vegetable drugs and give advice. Although prescriptions and diagnoses are memorized in verses their practice is not a magical one nor a quackery and the Brahman physician charges very little.

Members of the second high caste group of Hinduism, the Khshatriyas, the rulers and warriors, are not numerous in Malabar and are probably all Nayar in origin. In dress and food and religious observances the Khshatriyas follow the practices of the Brahmans, but their regulation of marriage and property approximates closely to that of the Nayars.

Of the Sudras, the third group of castes, the Nayars rank first and are by far the most numerous. They claim to have been the ruling class in pre-Hindu times before the arrival of the Brahmans and Khshatriyas. The landowning hereditary chiefs of districts and villages and their retainers were once exclusively Nayars, although for a long period land ownership has been passing gradually to the Brahmans. The Nayar alone had in former times the right to bear arms and every Nayar youth left his family to join a local military and gymnastic school where he was for several years instructed in the use of sword, bow and lance before being enrolled in the militia of the local chief. The Nayars are matrilineal in descent inheritance and residence. A household or *taravad* is a matrilineal joint family, a group of related women with their brothers and children. Each taravad has its own name which is given to the house and to its individual occupants. The eldest woman is the titular head, but the house, land and other property of the family is administered by the eldest male for the benefit of the family as a whole, and all members of the taravad are entitled to maintenance and support from this property. The mates of the women do not live in the house nor do they support them. Likewise the men of a taravad have wives in other households but these and their children are supported not by their husbands but by the taravad to which they belong and in which they live. Until recent times the women frequently had several 'husbands', often a number of 'brothers', i.e. members of a single but different taravad, and the men several 'wives'. These people were thus at the same time both polygynous and polyandrous. At present Nayar women, although they may and do change their mates at will and as opportunity offers, very rarely have more than one at a given time. The men, however, still quite often have several mates simultaneously.

The Nayar households, as former military retainers of the chiefs, have many of them acquired grants of territory which they cultivate with the aid of serfs and labourers. The property of a household may only be divided if all are agreed on partition, and even when it is so divided and separate taravads are formed, these remain closely linked and marriage between them is forbidden so long as the former unity is remembered.

Among the Nayars and lower castes every girl must be given marriageable status at puberty by the *tali* tying ceremony. This is a ritual marriage in which a man of the same or higher caste ties a gold ornament round the neck of the girl. For the purpose of the ceremony the *tali* tyer is the husband but his relations and obligations begin and end with it. Actual mating does not occur until later and then takes place not with the ceremonial husband but with the Nambudiri or Nayar lover whom the woman invites to her taravad. It is entered upon with no ceremony and although sometimes permanent is dissoluble at the will of either party.

There are many sub-castes of Nayars. Many of the members of the higher ranks are considerable landowners, but the majority to-day are petty farmers and the poorest are landless agricultural labourers.

Below the Nayars in social status are low caste Sudras who follow a number of professions. These include the barber and washerman castes, who are able to serve the higher castes without polluting them and a caste of schoolmasters and tutors employed by the Nayars. The weavers also rank as a low Sudra caste. Although much cotton cloth has long been imported from other parts of India and from abroad the poor continue to wear cloth woven in the local hand looms. Small communities of weavers are to be found scattered throughout the Malabar coast. The cotton yarn is provided by a merchant, often a member of the weaving caste, who either pays a small wage to each weaver or buys the cloth when the work is done. The merchant then distributes the cloth among peddlers who visit the weekly fairs in the surrounding country.

Clothing among all castes on the Malabar coast is scanty and extremely simple. The wealthiest and most distinguished Brahmans and Nayars in Cochin wear only plain white cloths —a cotton loin cloth, a waist cloth wrapped round like a short skirt and a shoulder cloth worn on occasion. The women may wear a white breast cloth but most are naked above the waist. Silks and coloured cloths are not admired and the quality of the white cloths varies only in the fineness of the weaving.

Most of the low caste Sudras have a matrilineal organization similar to that of the Nayars but they are excluded from Brahman temples and, except under certain conditions, their touch pollutes their Brahman and Nayar superiors.

The polluting castes proper rank still lower. Their mere proximity compels a person of higher caste to undergo ritual purification. To prevent 'atmospheric pollution' they are forbidden to approach within specified distances. In former times a man of high caste, as he proceeded along a highway, called out frequently that low caste people might avoid approaching him. A Nayar was at liberty to strike down with his sword any person of low caste who had polluted him by close approach and the polluting castes almost always kept well away from the main pathways. These castes may not worship in the temples of the higher castes and have their own sub-castes of priests. They are thus cut off from the social activities of the higher ranks.

The highest of these and the most numerous caste in Cochin is that of the Iluvan, whose traditional occupation is the growing and tending of coconut palms. They claim to be the descendants of immigrants from Ceylon who introduced coconut cultivation and are found all over Cochin and nearly everywhere on the Malabar coast, where many of them are engaged in all kinds of agricultural work as sub-tenants of Nayars and as labourers who are paid in kind. They usually live in separate hamlets and are not allowed to take water from the wells used by higher castes.

Manual labour of any kind is despised by the high castes, and the skilled artisans are all 'untouchable'. They are divided into castes according to their hereditary vocations, of which the most important are the carpenters, masons, iron and brass workers, jewellers, potters, leather workers and others. Close to every settlement there are separate hamlets of these crafts-men who supply local needs. Until recent times they were paid for their work in kind, usually in rice, for there was no native coinage in Cochin. The carpenters and masons are employed to do elaborate work on the large and sub-stantial houses and temples of wealthy Brahmans and Nayars. When their services are required in a temple they must be ceremonially purified, and considerable ritual accompanies

FIG. 90. A SOUTH INDIAN POTTER'S
WHEEL

the building of a house. The equipment of a Cochin village iron worker is no more elaborate than that to be found in an African negro's smithy. His work is done over an open charcoal furnace, and two pairs of leather bag bellows are worked by his assistants. The brass workers, however, who make metal dishes and utensils of various alloys, do more elaborate work, employing the *cire perdue* process. In this same group, but despised by the other members, are the leather workers, who deal with a raw material which to the Hindu is unclean.

One caste of artisans, however, ranks far lower than the others in the social scale. Although their wares are in constant demand, and they are also employed to set fractured and dislocated bones, the potters are a most impoverished class despised by the metal and wood workers. Their very name is used as a term of reproach to suggest anything that is vile. Their pots are made on a simple heavy horizontal wheel about three feet in diameter. The rim of the wheel is made of pliant bamboo covered with a thick layer of sun-dried clay which has been mixed with hair or fibre; four spokes hold the hard-wood or iron pivot on which the wheel rotates, and above the pivot is a small throwing table on which the pots are moulded. No treadle is used, and the throwing of the pots must be done in short spells of one or two minutes, during which the wheel will rotate when it is spun with the aid of a long bamboo pole. Despite the crudeness of this wheel some of the wares produced are delicate and elaborate. The pots are baked in large batches piled up several feet on a platform of dried wood and dung which is fired when the pots have been covered with a layer of clay-plastered straw.

The fishermen are the lowest of the free castes. They live in small, isolated settlements of flimsy bamboo huts scattered through the palm groves of the sandy shores of the coast and backwaters. The main sea-fishing caste forms a virtually independent community; the head of the caste, appointed by the king, but usually selected from a single family, was formerly virtually the ruler of this closed community and controlled its civil and ceremonial life. He supplied crews for the royal retinue and accompanied the king as an escort whenever he travelled on the backwaters.

Finally there are the slave castes, such as the Cheruma and Parayan, whose legal serfdom was abolished only in the middle of last century. The majority still remain virtual serfs of the land-holders for whom they work, and the wages, now paid in food and clothing, are the same as the rations given to their forebears as slaves. The Parayans, who perform black magic for other castes, have as their hereditary occupation the making of bamboo mats and baskets; they also work in the fields. But although they are the lowest of the serfs they will undertake only two agricultural tasks, ploughing with bullocks, but not with water buffaloes, and the transplantation of paddy seedlings, at which they are very skilled. The Cherumas, who are more numerous, are a paddy cultivating caste by tradition as well as in fact.

The low and slave castes are nearly all patrilineal in their reckoning of descent, but many of them were polyandrous in recent times.

The small groups of hill peoples, such as the Nayadis, many of whom contrast strongly in their very dark skin colour and australoid race characters from the rest of the population of Cochin, collect forest produce and have an economy similar to the Sakai of Malaya. They number only a few thousands in all, and now live to some extent on rice supplied by the forest contractors for whom they work as collectors and tree climbers. But wild game trapped or shot with the blowgun and wild fruits gathered in the forest make up a large part of their food. By the Hindus they are regarded as the lowest of all castes, causing atmospheric pollution even to members of the slave castes.

Kinship and caste and not locality are the unifying bonds of Cochin society. A village has even less unity than elsewhere in India, and the relations between individuals are rigidly governed by the traditional social gradings and occupational divisions of the various castes. In a typical settlement the houses of the well-to-do Nayars and Brahmans stand apart, each in its own compound, loosely grouped around the temples and ceremonial bathing-tanks. The huts of the low caste artisans who supply the local requirements form one or more separate hamlets, while those of the agricultural labourers are scattered among the paddy lands. For each settlement there was formerly a military school, in which the young men of the higher castes, and especially the Nayars, were trained in gymnastics and fighting.

Fairs, arranged to fall on successive days of the week, are held in the various settlements of a district. These bring travelling merchants, pedlars and craftsmen to each in turn. But for the most part each small district is independent in its economy; the hierarchy of landowners, tenants and labourers is fed from the surrounding paddy land and orchards, and the artisans supplying special needs are paid in kind.

The residence of a wealthy Brahman or Nayar should be planned and built according to a number of rules which have a religious sanction. The compound should be rectangular and divided into four sections by north-south and east-west lines. The house should occupy the north-eastern or, less propitiously, the south-western quarter; the burial ground and cow-sheds should lie in the south-east and the bathing-tank and shrines in the north-west.

The house itself should consist of four blocks built round an open rectangular courtyard, and equipped with verandahs on all sides. In the western block lie the sleeping-quarters and stores and in the northern block the kitchens and dining-rooms. The eastern and southern blocks should be open to the court-yard, and in these alone are guests and visitors received and entertained. Save as recent innovations no chairs or tables are found; mats and cushions are used in the living-rooms and the dishes are of pottery, brass and silver. The plastered walls are built of cut blocks of laterite, a soft reddish stone which hardens on exposure. Hard-woods, especially teak and ebony, are used for construction and decoration. The roofs are of palm thatch or of tiles, although until recent times the

latter were reserved for sacred buildings, and royal sanction
was necessary for their use in house construction. (See fig. 91.)

A lesser landlord or a tenant farmer may have but a single
house block built of mud bricks, but his is still a large and
comfortable dwelling when compared with the huts of the
artisans, fishermen and agricultural labourers, who form the
great majority of the population. Theirs are small, low dwellings of one or two rooms, built sometimes of mud but more

FIG. 91. A NAMBUDIRI HOUSE
(After photographs in Slater, op. cit.)

often of bamboo poles, palm matting and paddy straw. The
field labourers often live in the roughest of beehive huts, covered
with paddy straw, which are erected close to the land on which
they are working at any time.

Although carts and chariots have been known and used for
four thousand years in northern India, there were in Cochin
until modern times no roads or wheeled vehicles. Horses were
ridden only by the king and greater chiefs. The king also
rode in ceremonial processions on an elephant; individuals of
consequence and wealth were carried in litters, or palanquins,
by bearers. Even pack bullocks are a recent innovation, and
all goods were transported on land by trains of human porters.
Far more merchandise travelled on the many waterways
afforded by the rivers, canals and backwaters. The native
boats of Cochin consist essentially of canoes hewn with iron
adzes and chisels from the trunks of the hard-wood forest
trees; cheap inferior canoes are also made from breadfruit
and mango trees. Catamarans, built with small poles and so
common on the east coast, are apparently entirely absent in

Malabar. For small fishing boats ten or twenty feet long a simple dugout canoe is made, but the larger craft are heightened by the addition of further planks or wash strakes. The larger cargo boats, known as *wallams*, may be sixty feet long, seven feet broad and eight feet deep. The greater part of the boat is then covered by an arched roof of bamboos and matting to protect the cargo. These capacious vessels are restricted to the calm backwaters since they are too heavy and too difficult to beach on the open coast. They are sometimes equipped with a small square sail on a mast stepped near the prow of the vessel, but as a rule they are punted along with bamboo poles and are paddled in very deep water. Cabin boats of similar form, but rather smaller and elaborately decorated, are propelled by a dozen or more paddlers. On ceremonial state occasions very long, narrow dugouts, known as 'snake boats', each paddled by as many as fifty men, precede the cabin boat of the king, or chief. Plank-built canoes are constructed of teak and bentek wood, but they are less common. Most of them copy the shape of the dugouts, but some are clumsy flat-bottomed craft like deep punts, which are used both for fishing and as beach lighters. In both the planks are sewn together and bolted to ribs. The only large boat which regularly carries sails is the recently introduced copy of the Bombay *machwa*, or harbour boat, which is itself essentially an Arab type of craft. These sailing vessels are only used in the vicinity of ports, where they serve as lighters taking cargo to and from sea-going vessels.

There are no native sea-going craft in Cochin, or elsewhere on the Malabar coast. Although the region has since early times been in active trading contact with distant areas, and, in particular, with southern Arabia and has, moreover, long been an important source of shipwrights' materials, notably teak wood and coconut fibre, all the traffic has been done by foreign vessels. The Malabar coast was a great source of spices for the Roman world, and throughout medieval times and down to the present day Arab vessels have visited the ports of Cochin every year during the later more moderate period of the south-west monsoon. Bringing dates from the Persian Gulf and a mixed cargo from the north-west Indian ports they have taken up timber, especially teak, coir yarn, fish oil and other products for the Arab ship-building yards at Koweit and Bahrein. In more recent times a few ocean craft have been built on the coast itself, but they are the closest copies of Arab and north Indian vessels. Despite its magnificent teak forests whose resources were so widely used in north

Indian and Arab yards, and despite a considerable skill in boat-building, there was in Malabar a lack of sea trading tradition and maritime enterprise that would have shamed a Melanesian village.

In its climate and physical resources the Malabar coast bears many resemblances to areas that have been already considered. The climatic conditions are broadly similar to those of the Solomon Islands in Melanesia and, more closely, to those of the coast lands of southern Nigeria. But in economy and social life it differs profoundly from these areas. The cultivation of a prolific cereal by methods which, however crude and inefficient they may appear to a Western agronomist, are far in advance of root cultivation with digging stick or hoe, makes possible a density of population far greater than can be maintained by any people dependent on tropical root crops and migratory hand tillage. The far more elaborate preparation and manuring of the soil permits the long and continuous use of the fields and gardens.

But the social system of Cochin is no inevitable consequence of the economic advance. Although they are inextricably interwoven in the living society the two have indeed little genetic relationship. The economy and its productivity are but the foundation on which the social superstructure has been erected. The complicated history of social evolution in India has resulted in the sharp caste divisions of society which have reduced the corporate spirit of the state and even of the village far below that which can be found in a West African kingdom. These are, however, not native growths in Cochin which have developed spontaneously from the economy, but the local applications and adaptations of a complex of religious and social values which took shape far to the north. These have here been grafted on to a still older culture, of which many traces survive, and this in its turn derived many of its salient characteristics from still earlier transmissions. The overwhelming importance of religious sanctions, exceeding those of Polynesia, and the contempt for manual labour and craftsmanship among the leaders of society are alien to any of the peoples that have so far been considered. The superiority in food production has not been accompanied by a corresponding advance in other crafts. Substantial houses are the privilege of the gods and of the land-holders. The labourers and artisans, lacking personal or group property, and with no internal cohesion, have probably enjoyed less physical and social well-being than the occupants of a Congo village.

PART III

PASTORAL NOMADS

CHAPTER XIV

THE MASAI: CATTLE HERDERS ON THE EAST AFRICAN PLATEAU

THE tropical grasslands that border the southern margin of the Sahara Desert and curve southwards round the Congo Basin in East Africa are the great border zone of racial and cultural intermixture between the negro peoples to the south and 'European' types to the north. Over the greater part of the Sahara, the hinterland of the Red Sea and the Abyssinian highlands, the rather small, lightly built, long-headed and finely featured type, often referred to as the Mediterranean race, is dominant. Elements of this Mediterranean stock have in the course of history been incorporated in the racial composition of the negroid peoples to the south, and while the degree of racial mixture is sometimes slight and becomes progressively weaker towards the south and west, there is probably not a single Bantu tribe in Africa that has not some trace of Mediterranean or other northern stock in its racial character.

The Masai are a people from the northern tropical grasslands among whom, probably as a result of many contacts and periods of interbreeding, a blend of Mediterranean and negroid racial characters is found. They are the best known of a number of cattle pastoralists who occupy the interior plateaux of the more northern parts of East Africa in Kenya, northern Tanganyika and eastern Uganda. Although dark in skin colour they are clearly distinct from the more negroid people who surround them on the south and east, and since their language is related to the Hamitic speech of the still more markedly Mediterranean peoples of Abyssinia and the eastern Sudan they are often referred to as Half-Hamites. This term is intended to indicate that they are peoples among whom the Hamitic speech of north-east Africa and the Mediterranean racial characters generally associated with that tongue have been mixed with the negro blood and different speech of pre-existing peoples.

This blending is probably not, however, of the recency and simple character that the term Half-Hamite might suggest;

the modifications have more probably passed through a number of stages over a long period of time. Since there live in the swampy grasslands of the Upper Nile a number of peoples related in way of life and racial type to the Masai and their immediate neighbours, but rather more negroid in physique and showing little or no trace of Hamitic language in their speech, it has been suggested that the Half-Hamites represent the effect of a further racial and cultural mixture of such a Nilotic people (already pastoralists and partly Mediterranean in blood) with a further advance of Hamitic Mediterraneans from the north. To suggest this development the Masai and some of their neighbours are often referred to as Nilo-Hamites.

These points are raised at the outset because in considering the life of the Masai and other East African pastoralists it is important not to over-simplify their racial and cultural development nor to conceive of them as having existed in their present territory unchanged in race and speech or custom for an indefinite period. Such an assumption of stagnation is generally false and is a potential source of error in treating of the life of any human group, but there is often so serious a lack of knowledge or reasoned inference of earlier conditions and influences that only the most general deductions can usefully be made. While the analysis of the movements of peoples and cultures in East Africa is very far from complete and may never be achieved save in the broadest outline, sufficient indications of complex movements have been brought to light to make it necessary to consider them in relation to the present economy and organization of any one people.

The Masai proper are probably the last comers of three groups related in speech and in many customs. They have driven their immediate forerunners, the Wandorobo (or Asi) and Lumbwa (Kipsigi and Kwafi) westwards and southwards out of the richer areas. The Wandorobo have interbred with negro and negrito elements, have lost their live stock and forsaken herding for the hunting of wild game and small scale trading between negro and Hamitic groups. Many of them are virtual serfs among the Masai. The Lumbwa have interbred with more negroid groups in recent times and are largely agricultural in economy. Between the Masai and the Lumbwa severe fighting occurred in the latter part of the last century. In this struggle the Masai were generally, although not always, successful and drove many Lumbwa groups out of their lands in the north.

In appearance the Masai are tall and slender, with long, small limb bones, narrow feet and hands and long fingers.

The skin colour varies from light chocolate to very dark brown. The head is high and narrow. The rather thin face usually has fine-cut features and more particularly a long straight and rather large but often thin nose, while the lips, though often full, are less thick and everted than among more negroid peoples. The men have little hair on the face but on the head it grows longer and with a less crinkly curl than among negroes. Warriors twist it into long, thin rolls, which they plait at the back into a thick pigtail; but the girls, women and older men shave off their hair closely to the head.

The Masai may have numbered forty to fifty thousand at the period of their greatest power and prosperity in the middle of last century. To-day, after the epidemics among themselves and their stock, and with the restrictions on their life, there are few more than ten thousand in the Kenya and Tanganyika reserves.

The Masai occupy the central part of the great dome of equatorial highland about three hundred miles broad which lies east of Lake Victoria. This elongated highland zone is traversed from north to south by one of the great rifts which dislocated the earth's surface in eastern Africa and let down wide, deep valleys from the Jordan and the Dead Sea in Palestine through the Red Sea to Lake Nyasa in Rhodesia. Great volcanic eruptions were associated with the disturbances which produced the rift valleys. Lavas were poured out over the plateaux and many craters and soda lakes formed in the rift itself, and the volcanic mountains such as Kenya (seventeen thousand feet) and Kilimanjaro (over nineteen thousand feet) were thrown up. Much of the highland in southern Kenya and northern Tanganyika lies above six thousand feet and rises in its central dome to eight and nine thousand feet. The floor of the rift valley rises and falls in a number of separate and closed lake basins as it crosses the highland, but almost everywhere it lies one to two thousand feet below the adjacent plateaux, whose escarpments bound it on either side. In a few places, especially to the east, the walls rise in great precipitous cliffs nearly two thousand feet high and are quite unscalable. But much of the eastern wall is terraced into a number of smaller cliffs, with intervening platforms cut by gorges, while there are also many sections of fairly even slope, and easy gradient, especially on the west. Thus while the rift is some seventy miles across from rim to rim the valley floor is usually only forty miles wide and narrows to twenty miles in places. (See fig. 92.)

The territory of the Masai, including all the lands occupied at the period of their greatest strength in the latter part of last century, extends from about the latitude of Mount Elgon 1° north of the Equator to about 5° south. It covers all the rift valley in this section save the far south, and spreads irregularly across wide tracts of the high plateaux which flank

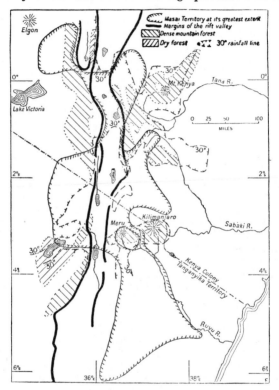

FIG. 92. SKETCH MAP OF THE MASAI COUNTRY
(*Distributions after Hollis (Masai territory), L. R. Jones (rainfall) and Shantz (forest)*)

it, reaching to the lower slopes of Mount Elgon, Kenya Mountain and Kilimanjaro. Within this area, however, considerable tracts, both in the north and south, were formerly occupied by the agricultural Lumbwa. From most of the northern districts the Masai drove them out, but Kipsigi groups remain in occupation of much of the southern part in Tanganyika.

On account of their considerable altitude the climates of the rift valley, together with the plateaux, and the ranges which rise from them are much cooler than those of the lowlands on the East African coast lands or of the floor of the Congo Basin to the west. Temperature, as is characteristic in equatorial latitudes, varies but little from month to month, and the mean values range only from about 60° to 65° F. Greater and more important are the changes from warm, sunny days to cool nights.

In consequence of their cooler temperature, and probably still more because of the interference of the great Asiatic land mass away to the north-east, the rainfall also differs considerably from that characteristic of equatorial areas. The rains are equinoctial indeed, but they are of relatively short duration, leaving long dry periods between, and the total amount nowhere rises much above forty inches until great heights are reached, as on the summits of the loftier escarpments and the slopes of the great volcanic mountains to the east. On the lower plateaux below four thousand feet at the northern and southern ends of the highland, and on the floor of the rift valley itself, the rainfall is reduced in places to well under thirty and even twenty inches. The major rains of the year fall in April and May, when a strong monsoon blows inland from the Indian Ocean. A shorter and lighter season of rain occurs on the higher lands in November, but between June and September the drought is severe everywhere below four thousand feet.

The greater part of this territory, therefore, is a tropical grassland. In the areas of lower rainfall (c. twenty inches) on the rift floor and the lower plateaux, the grass reaches only a foot or so in height. In the more favoured areas it forms a complete cover; elsewhere it grows in tufts separated by patches of bare soil. Most of this country is studded like an orchard with flat-topped thorny acacia trees, occasional euphorbias and many thorny bushes. During the long drought the grass dries up, turns deep yellow and the trees lose their leaves. The land looks barren but the sere grass, where available, remains good pasture, and with the January rains a new growth springs up. Where the ground is more impervious, or if subsoil water is available, the thorny trees and bushes close up, especially on the lower heights above the margins of the rift. Here they form tracts of a dense and often impenetrable low thorn forest, with trees and bushes ten to twenty feet high, that is useless to men and herds.

But most of the higher plateau country receives more rain and is covered by a savana of taller grass studded with loftier acacias. The grasses stand three or more feet high and the flat-topped acacias reach thirty to fifty feet. The grass shrivels and turns brown in the dry season, but can still be grazed. Local patches and some extensive tracts of dry forest are found in this tall grass savana. The grass-burning fires, which are started during the long drought to improve the pastures of the next season, at the same time burn out most of the bushes, while the thin-trunked acacias, the euphorbias and baobabs are well spaced and do not prevent light reaching the carpet of grass on the forest floor.

At still higher elevations, where the rainfall approaches fifty inches or more, the drought is much shorter and mountain grass pastures are found; these have in many places followed the former destruction of the high mountain forests for cultivation. Growing to a height of two or three feet, green throughout the year and interspersed with many flowering plants, they have rather the appearance of temperate grassland and offer very rich grazing. The country beyond the scarps of the rift valley rises in many districts, especially in the north, to well over six thousand feet, as in the Aberdare range east of Lake Naivasha rising to over eleven thousand feet and the Mau Plateau on the west with a general elevation of eight to nine thousand feet. In these high ranges there is no drought, and rainfall is often more than sixty inches. They are covered by the mountain rain forest, which also girdles the high volcanic mountains between about six and nine thousand feet. These forests of juniper, cedar and white-trunked fig trees are choked with undergrowth and are often denser than the tropical rain-forest of the lowlands. (See fig. 92.)

From the drier short grass savanas of the rift valley which they occupy in the wet season many of the Masai migrate during the long drought to the richer pastures of the tall grass and to the perennial meadows of the higher plateaus and ranges.

Masai marriage and the inheritance of livestock and other property are governed by clan membership. The clans are patrilineal exogamous groups, and some of them are divided into smaller divisions or sub-clans which are themselves exogamous. The clans in Kenya are grouped into two major divisions—the people of the Black Ox and the people of the Red Bullocks—but since clans within one of these groups may intermarry they cannot be considered moieties in the ordinary sense. The clans are of domestic rather than political importance and coincide only to a limited extent with territorial divisions. The members of one clan within a district do, however, often occupy neighbouring encampments and migrate more or less as a body, while the organization of other pastoral Nilo-Hamites farther north suggests that there may in former times have been definite clan territories.

Although a girl may be betrothed to a man when she is an infant or even unborn and he is still an immature youth, marriage does not take place until he has passed through his warriorhood and becomes an elder, i.e. when he is twenty-five or thirty years of age. The marriage settlement of a few cattle and sheep and large quantities of honey beer is not usually handed over to the girl's father until a first child is born. When a man marries his first wife he hands over to her care a large portion of the stock which he has received or inherited from his parents. Polygyny is general and most elders marry other wives at intervals and in time acquire three, four or even more, of whom the last is a young woman but recently initiated. The second wife gets a rather smaller herd than the first, who may also contribute to it. Later wives are given animals from the herds of senior wives. The wives are considered to hold the cattle in trust for their husbands and sons, and on the death of the head of the family the live stock not already given to sons by the father is divided among the sons of those wives who have had charge of them.

A single household of an elderly father, his wives and his married sons may form a considerable group, and often has its own separate encampment or kraal of some twenty to fifty huts which migrates at intervals as a unit.

When setting up an encampment in new pastures a well-drained site is selected. Access to a good salt lick for the stock and the shelter of a grove of trees are also sought. The construction and maintenance of the kraal is the work of the women. The oval huts are built close together in a circle round an open space forty to a hundred yards in diameter. Encircling the huts a stout fence of thorn brush is erected to keep out both wild beasts and enemies. Two, or sometimes four, gaps each three

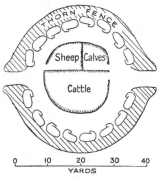

FIG. 93. DIAGRAMMATIC PLAN OF A MASAI KRAAL

or four yards wide, by which men and cattle may leave and enter are left on opposite sides of the circle. The centre of the encampment is occupied by paddocks, again fenced with thorn brush, into which the live stock is herded at night (fig. 93).

Each wife has her own hut, which she builds and keeps in repair. The ground plan, which is rectangular with rounded corners about four or five yards long and three or four feet wide, is scratched on the ground (fig. 94). Long, pliant stakes are set up a foot or so apart all round and strengthened by horizontal pieces or ropes of withes a foot or so apart for about a yard from the ground. Stouter uprights are set in the ground along the long axis of the hut, and a roof pole is lashed

FIG. 94. PART OF A MASAI KRAAL

to their tops about five feet from the ground. The wall stakes are then bent over to meet the roof pole, and when lashed to it form a low vault which is strengthened with fairly close interlacing of thinner sticks. The spiral plan leaves place for a doorway, which projects sideways from the main body of the hut. When cattle were more abundant, before the severe plagues at the end of last century, the hut frame was covered with a number of ox hides lashed into position. Small huts of this type are still built in the temporary kraals set up during seasonal migrations. But in the more permanent settlements the huts are walled and roofed with layers of long grass a foot or more thick bound over the frame and finally covered with a layer of fresh cow-dung and mud which dries into a hard cake and is renewed as required. Hides are used only to cover the doorways at night and to protect the perishable surface against heavy rains. These huts are of course extremely dark, and are ventilated only by a small smoke hole, and they are used only at night and in bad weather. Their contents are meagre. Large sleeping-places for the man and for his wife and small children are found at the ends on the side far from the door; these are raised couches of close-set poles or pads of dried grass on which ox hides are laid. The milking gourds, wooden food bowls and weapons lie on the ground with a three-legged stool roughly carved from a solid piece of soft wood. Young calves and sometimes lambs and kids are housed in the hut at night, and for them corners are fenced off at the upper end near the door.

Cattle are by far the most important live stock of the Masai, and nearly every family formerly had a considerable herd. They are very mixed in type, for as a result of predatory raids on all neighbouring peoples every variety of cattle in East Africa has found its way into the Masai kraals. But all are humped cattle, and two main types are found, a rather small, lightly built strain with long and splendidly curving lyre-shaped horns, and a thickset short-horned strain which yields nearly twice as much milk but is nevertheless less valued. The hump is a layer of fatty tissue which forms between the shoulder-blades. A calf or a calf skin must be smelt by the cow before it will give milk, and the yield is poor even from the best; three pints at a milking is a large amount. The milking is done by the women before daybreak, before the cattle are taken out to pasture by the men and boys, and again in the evening when they return after the sun has set. For the collection and storage of milk and other foods wild gourds are collected, cleaned out and cut to the required shape. Milk vessels are washed out with cow urine and fumigated before use.

Most of the male calves are gelded soon after birth and kept to swell the size of the herd and to provide hides and meat for payments, gifts and feasts. Wandorobo are employed to do the slaughtering, for no Masai should kill a domestic animal. Cows are never slaughtered although they may be eaten when they die. They are indeed treated with the greatest care and much affection. Each has its personal name and the herdsman has his favourites among them. They are branded with cuts or burns on the ears and flank, but with the clan mark, not the individual mark of a particular owner.

Milk is drunk either fresh or sour; it is boiled only for the sick. Butter is made from cream by laboriously shaking it in a large gourd, but cheese-making is unknown. Blood is a favourite and important element in the diet, obtained from cows, and especially bullocks, by tightly strapping the neck with a leather cord so that a large vein swells up; this is then

pierced with a special arrow with a wide, transverse blade
which is released from a light bow. A considerable quantity
of blood is then collected and drunk fresh, clotted, or mixed
with milk. (See fig. 95).

Sheep are almost as numerous as cattle, and their milk,
blood and meat are eaten, but they play a far less important
part in the social life of the Masai. Most of them are of a
white fat-rumped breed with a coarse curly fleece, although

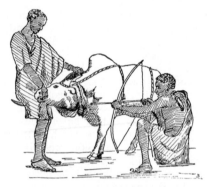

FIG. 95. MASAI CUTTING THE NECK VEIN
OF A BULLOCK WITH AN ARROW TO
OBTAIN BLOOD
(*After photograph by Hollis*)

they are mixed with fat-tailed and black-faced strains. The
ewes are regularly milked after lambing. The wethers are bled
from veins over the eyes and slaughtered for food. Goats are
less numerous and are herded with the sheep. To prevent
mating at the wrong season or between different herds leather
flaps are often tied to the bellies of bulls and rams.

Most households have a few donkeys which are used as
beasts of burden, while some of the eastern groups have
acquired camels from the Somali for this purpose; cattle are
never made to carry loads when these animals are available.
No animals are ridden and all herding and travel is done on
foot. The live stock of a kraal is herded as a unit by the
young men under the directions of the married men. The
Masai dogs are of little use in herding, and only give warning of
the presence of strangers and beasts of prey around the kraal.

For a number of public ceremonies and family feasts animals
are slaughtered, but meat must not be eaten in the camp. It
is cooked and served in secluded spots, and rock shelters are

often chosen for this purpose. Meat and milk may never be eaten on the same day, nor may they be allowed to come into any contact with one another. The infringement of this rule would, it is believed, cause serious disease among the cattle.

A considerable amount of millet and maize is eaten by all except the warriors, while root crops and bananas, although scorned by the men, are eaten by women and children. These cereals and vegetable foods are obtained in exchange for hides and live stock from wandering groups of negro and Wandorobo traders. They are boiled and mixed with milk or butter, for the restrictions on the use of meat do not apply to these. Some wild game and birds are hunted or obtained by barter for their skins, horns and feathers, but their flesh is almost never eaten. Wild honey eaten fresh or diluted and fermented into a beer is, however, a favourite food.

The herding of the live stock does not absorb the energies of the entire population, and the young men from the ages of about sixteen to thirty live apart from their families and clans as warriors. The young men of a district, according to a system to be considered later, form separate kraals of fifty to a hundred men. These are similar in plan to the ordinary encampment, but no thorn hedge is built to encircle and protect the huts. When the young men leave their family groups to join the warriors' kraal they are accompanied by their mothers and several of their sisters. The mothers build the huts. They and girls milk the cattle that are taken to the kraal or are captured in forays, although warriors do not keep permanently the cattle that they take in their raids but pass them on to their families. The girls are the companions and mistresses of the warriors. The important duties and main desires of the warriors are to defend the herds of their district and to add to them by raids on the live stock of neighbouring people. At frequent intervals, in former times, they planned an attack, and the leader of the kraal sought the sanction of the elders of the district and of the Masai priest-chief for the expedition. The priest-chief might give advice on strategy and forbid unwise attack. He prescribed the ceremonies of the preliminary feast, the amulets to be worn and the magic to be used on the expedition. The leader of the warriors' kraal and his lieutenants often directed a most efficient system of spying; individuals were sent out in all directions to locate vulnerable enemy settlements and caravans. The spies might pose as Wandorobo pedlars, might even stay weeks in an enemy village affecting all innocence and even seeking blood brotherhood to acquire familiarity with the position of pastures and movements of the cattle. Having conveyed messages back to the kraal they often stayed with their unsuspecting hosts until the moment of the attack.

When finally an expedition set out, each warrior carried a long-bladed spear, a leaf-shaped sword of forged iron, a wooden club and a circular shield of ox or wild buffalo hide. Bows and arrows were sometimes used, but were more generally kept as defensive weapons by the married men in the family camps. Although many neighbouring negro groups have long since acquired muskets the Masai scorned to adopt them. Cattle, not slaughter, were the object of these attacks, but since the Masai had long been a scourge to the settled people of neighbouring areas and to the Arab and Swahili caravans that used important routes through their territory, the fighting was often severe and no mercy was shown on either side.

Iron weapons and ornaments are made by families of smiths. Although they are members of the tribe similar in race and speech, and there are smith families in every clan, they constitute a distinct caste, for the craft is handed on from father to son and a man is counted a smith whether he works at his trade or not. The smiths marry among themselves and even extra-marital relations with their women are considered dangerous by others. They are both despised and feared by the rest of the Masai—a magical atmosphere surrounds their work and they are said to be unclean because the weapons they make lead to the spilling of blood! The weapons themselves must be purified by rubbing with cow fat or butter when they are taken over. The smiths move their kraals less frequently than others, for they obtain their food in return for their manufactures and maintain few cattle of their own. Their young men do not become warriors, but settle down to the business of smithing after their initiation at puberty. The smiths make and collect supplies of charcoal, snail shells for flux and iron ore. The ore is obtained from ferruginous sands found in certain streams. It is packed in leather bags after washing and must often be transported a considerable distance on donkeys. The smelting takes place at an open fire on which a few handfuls of ore and charcoal are thrown every few minutes. After two or three hours a few egg-shaped pieces of impure iron have formed at the base of the slaggy pile; these are removed, mixed with a flux of powdered shells, and reheated with bellows, to be welded into a larger mass. The greater part of the iron supply has, however, been obtained in recent times by barter from the Arab and Swahili traders who supply it in lengths of coarse iron wire which are melted down and hammered into a mass.

The smithies are built close to the kraal, and the open fire pit is set under a grass-roofed shade. Double goat skin bellows of a conical shape or a single wooden bowl bellows with a loose skin top are made to produce the draught. The smith makes his own tools, heavy iron hammers, hinged tongs and chisels, while a smooth river boulder serves as anvil. The metal is not cast, and the shaping of both blades and sockets is done by hammering which produces a finely wrought metal. The socketed spear-heads which may be as much as a yard long, are the most difficult pieces to make. The tanged swords with blades from eight inches to two feet long are fitted with a wooden grip and a finely worked hide scabbard. The longer swords are not usually made by Masai smiths, but are obtained by trade from the Bantu Kikuyu, who are more skilled metal workers. The size of Masai spear blades has increased considerably in recent generations as traded iron has become more abundant. Before that, when nearly all iron was hardly won by local smelting, spearheads and the points set on the butt of the shaft were rarely more than a foot long. The old native sword was only a long dirk. The smith also makes cow bells, hatchets for wood-working and iron wire, which is made up by his wives into the heavy coiled leg, arm and neck ornaments which are worn by women. He is paid in live stock and milk. For a spearhead he might receive an ox or two goats, for a sword, an axe or ten barbed arrow-heads a single goat, and for smaller articles a skin of milk.

The Masai wear only scanty and simple clothing of skins, but the young women and warriors wear elaborate ornaments, especially on ceremonial occasions. The preparation of skins is done by women. The hair is usually removed with an iron scraper For clothing they are soft dressed in the sun by repeatedly rubbing in butter and fat. After each application they are trampled under foot for a long time to work the fat well into the skin, which when finished is soft but greasy. Other hides are tanned with the juice of a common wild plant. The warrior's only garment is a calf's skin wrap a little over a yard long and two feet wide with the hair left on; the strip is folded over lengthwise and sewn at the corners so that it can be slipped over the head and left shoulder. A triangular flap of skin is sometimes worn over the buttocks, hanging behind from the sword girdle, to give protection from thorns when sitting down. Apart from thick bull hide sandals, which are worn by all, the rest of the body is naked. Young boys wear a still smaller wrap, but the married men have a larger ox hide wrap, and when old often wear an apron. Women wear goat skin aprons, a short one hanging from the waist and a larger one crossing over the right shoulder. (See fig. 94).

For ceremonies, dances and war parties the warriors wear elaborate feather head-dresses set on a frame of leather or wood and held by a chin strap. At other times are worn high pointed caps of lion, baboon and other skins of wild game, or close-fitting caps cut from a cow's paunch, which cover the ears and are decorated with shells. A thick cape-like frill of hawk's feathers is often worn round the neck. Bracelets and neck bands of iron and sheep skin and girdles closely covered with beads are further items of a warrior's attire.

The daughter of a well-to-do family prides herself on the size and massiveness of the long, close coils of iron wire that are fitted on her lower arms, legs and neck.

The wide dispersal of encampments over the country is made necessary by the economy of the Masai. The larger territorial divisions unite only occasionally, and for a short time, at the great ceremonies of the induction and promotion of warrior grades. The people of a small district quite often maintain complete independence of action for long periods, and in addition to their many wars with other peoples severe internecine conflicts have sometimes developed between Masai groups.

Yet the Masai have recognized a paramount religious leader, the Laibon, who has for considerable periods been able to effect a real unity of action, despite the wide scattering of the kraals and the strong individualism of the local warrior bands. The Laibon has been compared with the chief priest of the Israelites, and his clan with the Levites. Although he can have little direct executive power, the prestige of the Masai priest-chief is nevertheless very great. He, the head of the chiefly clan of the Aiser, is not only the recognized religious leader of all the Masai but is respected and held in awe by the Wandorobo and Lumbwa or Wakuafi. The Laibon is a religious rather than an executive authority, and his influence is based on the firm belief in the success of his prophecies, the great power of his magic and the efficacy of his intercession with the god of the Masai. For the Masai contrast sharply with the adjacent Bantu negro tribes in the monotheistic character of their religion, and the Laibon organizes and ensures the success of the great prayer festivals of the god En-Gai. The office is hereditary and descends from father to son in one family. The obligation to ensure the welfare of the people is impressed on the heir to the office from his earliest years, and, although in recent times, under the stress of increasing European pressure, the succession has been disputed and the Masai have been divided in their allegiance, the great Laibons of former generations were leaders of great devotion and public spirit.

Whenever the Laibon has political and strategic ability he can use his influence to control and unify the action of all divisions of the people. He can direct and concentrate the attacks of the various warrior groups and can maintain a policy calculated to safeguard the tribes against external attack. Neither he nor his clansmen take any part in actual warfare, but he alone can prepare and give power to the war magic necessary for success in raids and victory in more serious fighting. Defeat must come, on the other hand, if he foretells it and withholds the magic. He also controls the most effective magical remedies against diseases among both men and cattle, and he can perform miracles of healing. His diet is carefully restricted to goat liver, milk and honey, for other food would deprive him of his power. Round the Laibon cluster a large number of kraals, especially those of elderly men of ability and wisdom who serve as his advisers.

The magicians or medicine men who deal with sicknesses of men and stock and live scattered over the various districts are also recruited exclusively from the clan of the Laibon. Their power and knowledge passes from father to the chosen son, generally the first-born by the principal wife. By divination, prophecy and oracle they serve spiritual needs as well as curing physical sickness.

Another clan is also particularly concerned with religion and magical rites and from it all the rain-makers are drawn. When the droughts are severe and prolonged they are called upon to invoke rain and mutter incantations as they lie concealed beneath a large hide. Regarded as guardians of religious traditions and as less warlike than most Masai, the protection of their stock is the duty of all other clans.

One of the most remarkable features of Masai society is the system of periodic drafting of the youths of a district into warrior groups to take the place of retiring warriors who then become elders and marry. This is effected by what is generally known as a system of Age groups. When the boys of a district have attained puberty they form small bands which visit all the encampments, demanding presents, which they hand on to influential elders while asking them to arrange for their initiation. Initiations cover a period of four years or more during which the candidates are circumcised one by one in their own kraals by a limited number of skilled Wandorobo, not Masai, who travel from camp to camp and district to district. When all those eligible have at last been circumcised and the elders are prepared to admit a new group into the warrior class they are assembled for a hair-shaving ceremony, which is the signal for their entry into the warrior stage. All youths that are shaved at the same time form a single Age group. They receive weapons from their fathers and take a common name such as the 'Raiders', the 'White Swords' and so forth, and form local groups, each of which goes off to a special warrior kraal or *manyatta*, prepared by their mothers.

The promotion and retirement of the warrior groups is, however, regulated by somewhat complicated rules. Successive periods of circumcision which end with hair-shaving ceremonies are named alternatively, circumcisions of the Left and circumcisions of the Right. While the Age groups enter the warrior class singly they may only retire in pairs consisting of one of the Right and one of the Left hand which together form a Generation. Moreover, there may never be more than three Age groups in the warrior class at the same time, and the senior group must always be an Age of Right hand circumcision. Thus two Age groups, a Right and a Left, retire together and a third group, the Right hand Age group of the next generation who were the last to enter the warrior class, become senior warriors and for a short time the only Age group in the warrior class. In due course two more Age groups, a Left hand and a Right hand, are successively initiated. One result of this procedure is that no Age group of Left hand circumcision ever stays in the warrior class as long as an Age group of the Right hand. A Right hand Age may remain for about fifteen years, a Left hand only for about ten years. The actual length of the periods and the time of retirement depend largely on the number of circumcised youths available for entry into the warrior class.

From three to five years after its first initiation into the warrior class an Age group holds a festival attended by all members of that Age group in the district. Their hair, which has grown and been worn in a long plait, is again shaved and the group takes another name which supersedes the first. When two such ceremonies have been held, one for an Age of the Right hand and one for an Age of the Left hand, the Generation as a whole may retire as soon as there is a new Age group waiting to move in as junior warriors.

All the warriors of a single Age group in a district form one or more companies each with its own encampment and leader. The camps of each Age are distinct and independent. Age membership survives the period of warriorhood and plays a considerable part in the life of the married elders. When visiting another kraal an elder receives hospitality from men of his own Age group; all members of an Age group are expected to give mutual help in any difficulty, and the mourning of a dead man is conducted by his Age mates.

Thus there are among the Masai three stages through which every male passes—the boy, the warrior and the elder, and these are further subdivided. At any given time there is a large fighting force divided into a number of separate encampments each wholly devoted to the defence of its district and to the raiding of neighbouring peoples.

The district leaders, who have nominal supervision over the discipline and expeditions of the warriors of their territory, are selected by the elders from among the senior warriors themselves. On assuming office, however, they are considered as elders. They retire from their warriors' camp and no longer join the war parties. Their authority often carries less weight, however, than that of the medicine men, who can divine the future from the inspection of animal entrails, interpret the dreams of the warriors and proclaim oracles and prophecies when intoxicated with honey wine.

The system of Age groups with a warrior class is found among several other peoples of East Africa. Most of them are pastoralists, but some elements of the system have been adopted by neighbouring agricultural peoples, like the Kikuyu. Although the grades of the Masai were among the most elaborate and were functioning the most efficiently at the time of modern European penetration they cannot be regarded as having originated among the Masai themselves in their present habitat. Comparative study has suggested that the system developed farther north among the Hamitic Galla of Abyssinia and has been carried south by the advances of the Nilo-Hamitic pastoralists of whom the Masai are the largest and most powerful group.

When the warriors of a number of districts combined, armies of two and three thousand spearmen were often formed; and although such forces could not be maintained in combination for long periods, the bravery and ruthlessness of their mass attacks gave them practical invincibility against the more settled tribes. As an instrument for maintaining and expanding the strength of an advancing pastoral people intent above all on increasing the size of their almost sacred herds and extending the range of their pastures, the system of Age groups, with a standing military force, has been of immense importance to the Masai. It also enabled them to maintain themselves in relative security against the reprisals of the enemies they made on every hand. Over a wide tract of country, much of it suitable for hoe cultivation, they maintained their scattered kraals for many generations against all the attempts of culti vating peoples to dislodge and replace them.

On the other hand, although the religious and magical authority of the Laibon compensated the military power of the warriors and mitigated their influence on Masai society the maintenance of large warrior bands and the enormous prestige of raiding and warfare reinforced the tendency of pastoralism to restrict the development of social organization and to limit arts and crafts to simple practices required for herding. Weapons are made by segregated groups of smiths and even the buffalo hide shields and feather head-dresses of the warriors are obtained from Wandorobo, who indeed have in many areas become virtual serfs of the Masai, making and supplying ornaments and utensils, hunting the wild game from which these are made and acting as intermediaries in the trading of live stock for millet and other crops.

The Masai provide an instance of a people who deliberately limit their exploitation of their physical environment. Despite their many contacts with peoples of other economies they have rejected hunting as well as cultivation. They have dis possessed cultivating peoples of land which they themselves use only for grazing, and have driven their agricultural rela tives, the Lumbwa, into the more arid parts of the region Their life shows in an unusually clear way how completely a cultural bias and traditional mode of life may determine and restrict the use of territory which offers other possibilities.

The exclusive pastoralism of the Masai is, however, by no means characteristic of the greater number of the cattle rearing peoples of Africa. Cattle rearing extends throughout eastern Africa to the far south of the continent, but it is nearly everywhere combined with agriculture. Among some peoples like the Bakitara and Banyankole on the grassland plateau to the north and east of Lake Victoria, the pastoralists consti tute a superior caste who dominate agricultural serfs. The herdsmen, descendants of peoples very like the Masai in physique and way of life, have invaded and conquered an earlier Bantu population of millet cultivators. The powerful and semi-divine kings and the district chiefs own large herds of cattle which are cared for in the kraals of the pastoral freemen whose diet consists almost entirely of milk. The cultivators, although they can move freely about the country and raise their crops of millet and bananas very much as they please, are dependent on the good will of the herders, to whose chiefs they supply millet for brewing beer in return for their freedom to occupy the land. The chiefs live in fenced villages and towns; the herders, whose lives are entirely devoted to the interests of the cattle, are scattered over the country in temporary cattle kraals; and the peasants live in beehive grass huts among their plots.

Among these peoples the two economies—hoe cultivation and pastoralism—co-exist without fusion. The two classes or strata of society live under entirely different conditions. Many ceremonial observances emphasize the exclusiveness and superiority of the pastoral aristocracy, while the arts and crafts of the cultivators have withered under the dominance of the herders who give them no part in social and political life. But in the great kingdom of Baganda, still farther east, extending down to the shores of Lake Victoria, fusion of the two peoples and economies has occurred. The pastoralists appear to have entered later and in fewer numbers into this lower-lying and wooded region which is less suited to a pastoral life. The fusion has here produced a remarkable cultural development which transcends the achievement of both invader and invaded. Large towns and villages of substantial houses are occupied by a free peasantry, cultivating the land and raising live stock; while the land-holding chiefs are dependent on the good will of their tenants for their prestige and power.

South of the Lakes Plateau cattle retain their position as an index of wealth and prestige throughout eastern Africa, and ceremonial observances in connexion with them are more developed than among the purely pastoral peoples of the north, like the Masai. But there is, again, no division into pastoral and agricultural classes, and the products of both economies are eaten by herder and cultivator alike. The supply of agricultural produce is, however, nearly everywhere the work of women, who are largely excluded from any association with the cattle.

This cattle-raising area is limited in the north-west by the growth of dense tropical forest and by the tsetse fly, which renders the rearing of cattle impossible in most of the areas where the rainfall exceeds sixty-five or seventy inches. Between Lakes Tanganyika and Nyasa, where the coastal and interior forest zones converge, it is almost impossible to raise cattle successfully, but several peoples in this area, notably the

Wakanda at the northern end of Lake Nyasa, contrive to rear a few, despite the unfavourable character of the habitat, by protecting them in barns.

Throughout eastern Africa the religious and ceremonial value of cattle overrides their purely economic value. Mere numbers are valued above the quality of the stock, and the restrictions on the killing and eating of cattle render them far less important than they might be in contributing to the food-supply.

A related series of economies is found in the western Sudan. The Moslem Fula, whose cattle-herding economy is adapted to the semi-arid margins of the southern Sahara have invaded the more humid savanas occupied by negroid hoe cultivators. There has been relatively little extermination or crippling of agriculture here, and the Fula do not despise agricultural food, but, on the contrary, obtain it in large quantities from the cultivating villagers among whom they live. The herding economy has, nevertheless, been kept largely distinct from that of cultivation by social and racial barriers. Although there has been considerable mixing of race, the majority of the Fula herders who never cultivate are in race of fairly pure 'Hamitic' type. Such fusion of cultivating and herding as exists has resulted not from the conversion of the Fula to agriculture on entering a moister region, but from the acceptance by the cultivating tribes along the Niger of the herdsmen's standards of prestige. They purchase cattle from the Fula not for economic but for social reasons. Their live stock is not used to facilitate agricultural tasks, nor is it kept in good condition as a provider of meat and milk. Cattle as in eastern Africa have a prestige value and herds are judged by their mere size.

An outlier of the eastern African cattle economy is found on the west among the Herero of Angola, whose women also raise millet crops. But when the far south-west of the continent is reached pure pastoralism appears again among the Hottentot of western Cape Colony. These people, who are racially and linguistically akin to the Bushmen, have acquired cattle from the north-east, but have not at the same time adopted the ceremonial observances so important there. The women milk the herds, the milk is drunk fresh, not soured in special vessels as among the eastern Bantu, and the cattle are used as beasts of burden. Gifts of live stock are made to furnish wedding feasts, but the elaborate system of cattle gifts or bride price, the *lobolo* of the Bantu, is not found. The manner in which live stock was introduced among these peoples, and the period at which they first became economically differentiated from their Bushmen cousins, remains obscure; but their practices are in many ways closer to those of the pastoral Nilo-Hamites many hundreds of miles away to the north-east, than to those of their Bantu neighbours in the east. Their economy may indeed indicate the terminus of an early wave of pastoral advance which has been overlaid by later movements and the development of more complicated social and economic relationships in eastern Africa.

CHAPTER XV

THE RUWALA BADAWIN: CAMEL BREEDERS OF
NORTHERN ARABIA

OUR interest in the most famous of all pastoral peoples, the Badawîn Arabs of Arabia, has been heightened by the slowness of modern exploration. Religious and political factors have reinforced the natural difficulties of a country which remains an island of primitive economy in the heart of the lands of early civilization. So foreign to more sedentary peoples are the ways and customs of these wandering peoples, and so impressive their response to a severe environment, that the Badawîn have, in fact, falsely coloured our picture of Arabia. It is not one vast desert strewn with the bones of camels slain for the fetid water in their paunches, but a land of grass, often poor and short-lived grass, indeed, but adequate for the feed of a large number of beasts, domestic and wild, over the greater part of its area for most of the year.

The pastoral nomads of the more desert areas constitute but a small proportion of the population of this vast peninsula. The lofty scarps and ranges of Yemen—'Happy Arabia'—at the southern end of the uplifted western edge of the great plateau block, receive good rains both in spring and in late summer. These permit the growth of considerable harvests of cereals, dates and wine, as well as the famous coffee exported from Mocha and Hodeida. Like much of Asir and the Hedjaz to the north, Yemen is a land of villages and fortified towns, and its people number at least a million. In south-eastern Arabia the 'Green Mountains' of Oman, whose ridges reach nine thousand feet in height, give rise to perennial streams which water the coastal plain—el Bätina—where cereals, dates and fruits are grown on wide tracts of land, and again support a peasant population of perhaps half a million. In the heart of Arabia, in the Nejd plateau, at the foot of the Shammar Mountains and elsewhere, oasis towns and villages are strung along wide valleys whose surface or subsoil water again makes possible a settled life for more than another quarter of a million people. Finally, on the northern borders of Arabia, balancing as it were the Yemen and Oman to the south, are the richer borders of Syria and Palestine on the west and of the Euphrates flood lands on the east.

Compared with the settled peoples in and on the margins of Arabia, the nomads are numerically weak. There are probably less than a million of them, or about a fifth of the total population, all told. Occupying fairly well-defined tracts of coarse grassland (*hamad*) which affords permanent vegetation and water-holes in the hollows, they only penetrate the true sandy desert (*nefûd*) or the rocky country (*hana*) for short-season pastures in good years, or in passing through to other steppes beyond. These steppes are best developed in the north and west, where, from Syria, Palestine and the Hedjaz, they extend in a great curve round the Great Nefûd to the Nejd in the south and to the foothill country between the Euphrates and Tigris in the north. The Nefûd itself has pastures to offer in good years, while the famous Rub' al Khâli ('The Empty Quarter') between Oman and Nejd, in southern Arabia, where rains may completely fail and subsoil water is very hard to find, is nevertheless inhabited by a few small tribes who gather round its precarious water-holes.

The close juxtaposition of desert, steppe and fertile oasis in a land long within the orbit of great civilizations has inevitably resulted in varying adaptations of human life to these divergent resources, and this variety is reflected in the number of Arabic terms for different economies. The sharp distinctions we are apt to make between settled peasant and nomad herder require amplification; there is rather a gradation from one social and economic pattern to another. Besides the major division between *'arab*, the dweller in a movable tent, and *hadhar*, 'the dweller in brick', i.e. the peasant living permanently on tilled land, there are *qarauna* (villagers), owners of tilled land and permanent dwellings, who, nevertheless, move away at the end of summer after sowing their crops and live in tents during the rainier winter season on the neighbouring steppes, where they herd their flocks of sheep and goats. Such groups grade into *šâwaqa* (drovers), herders on the settled margins who rely mainly on flocks of sheep and goats and never penetrate the poorer steppe-desert of the interior.

But the *Badawîn*, the occupants of *el Bâdia* (the desert), are set apart from other *'arab* by a real difference in economy. For nine or ten months of the year they remain in the interior on arid pastures that rank as desert to the marginal folk, who could indeed scarcely survive a month in them. Camels, few among the sheep herders, are the essential beasts of the Badawîn. Sheep and goats are kept only occasionally and in small

numbers, and the horse is the only other animal of importance
At the height of the summer drought alone do the Badawîn
converge on the settled country in order to save their beasts
from starvation, and to replenish their stores for the next
sojourn in the interior by trading their surplus live stock for
grain, clothing and weapons. Some of the poorer Badawîn
rarely, if ever, leave the semi-desert pastures, but congregate
during the summer drought round the few surviving water holes.
Such groups are entirely dependent on others for a scanty supply
of traded goods, and their herds are reduced by the limited
resources of grass and water available in the summer.

The extent of these various economies and of their interrelations at any one time depends to a considerable degree on
the wider political conditions. If a central authority over a
wide region can guarantee security to villagers and townsmen
the herdsmen of goat and sheep re-occupy deserted oases, build
houses and hamlets and are transformed into settled farmers
They in their turn entrust their live stock to groups of Badawîn
who, ceasing to enter the inner desert, are often themselves
transformed into drovers of the margins. But if there is no
strong government in the settled country, the cultivators of
the territories exposed to the attacks of raiders often abandon
their villages for movable tents and come to depend partly on
entirely on their flocks.

The desert Badawîn are not men of commanding appearance,
but a small lean people who often appear stunted by the severity
of their life. While they are not racially pure and show a
mixture of all the stocks found in south-western Asia and the
margins of the Mediterranean, the typical individual belongs
to the Mediterranean race and is not readily to be distinguished
from an Egyptian or Syrian peasant. Generally no more than
five feet three inches in height, and lightly built, he has a long,
narrow face with prominent nose, dark eyes and hair, but a
rather pale complexion.

The group of tribes known collectively as the northern
'Anaza, who control the steppelands between Aleppo, Damascus
and the Hauran plateau on the west, the Middle Euphrates on
the east, and the Shammar Mountains in the south, are the
most powerful Badawîn of Arabia. They comprise nearly
twenty thousand tents and own in all over half a million
camels. These tribes by no means form a close-knit group.
Among them rivalry and enmity are almost as common as
alliance, while a faction within a single tribe may break away
to form an autonomous unit. The largest and most important
of the 'Anaza tribes is the Ruwala, of about three thousand

five hundred tents. They occupy the eastern part of the 'Anaza territory and extend from the tributary villages east and south of Damascus at the north-western end of the Sirhân depression, which they visit in summer, to the borders of the Nefûd and the northernmost oases of central Arabia. In 1909

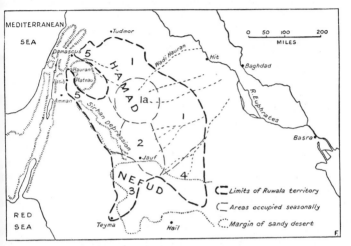

FIG. 96. SKETCH MAP OF RUWALA TERRITORY

THE NUMBERS REFER TO PASTURES OCCUPIED SEASONALLY AS FOLLOWS:
1, WINTER; 1a, RICHEST IN WINTER; 2, SPRING; 3, OCCUPIED IN WINTER WHEN RAINS ARE GOOD OR PASTURES FAIL IN THE HAMAD; 4, OCCUPIED WHEN PASTURES FAIL TO THE NORTH AND WEST; 5, SUMMER (OASIS SETTLEMENTS)

(*Based on data from Musil, Doughty, Raswan, etc.*)

the Ruwala captured and obtained firm control of the oasis city of Jauf after a long period of dissension among the central Arabian Badawîn. When their 'Anaza rivals and foes to the east, the Fad'ân and 'Amarât, are weak or divided, some Ruwala bands wander farther east in the summer drought to the Euphrates villages. (See fig. 96.)

Their annual migration is roughly circular. In September they leave the villages in the west to pass the winter moving slowly in scattered groups over the pastures of the Hamad. In spring there is a general migration southward to the fringes of the sandy desert of the Nefûd. The herds pass to the west and south along this interior belt of scattered pastures towards the oases of Teyma, striking north and west again in early summer to travel along the string of water-holes in the Sirhân depression and on to the tributary villages before the height of the drought. If the year is bad they may break up into small groups and scatter still more widely, and larger numbers will then work their way along the eastern borders of the Nefûd.

The seasonal movements and the number of tents and camels in any one part of the country depend on the period and duration of the rains, which are never precisely the same in any two years. The climax of the hot season in August and September, when the Ruwala are forced out of the steppes to the villages, is one of parching heat. The power of the sun is terrific, gusty winds whip up dangerous sand-storms during the heat of the day, and rain never falls. But in the autumn, as the heat dies away, some slight moisture is borne eastwards from the Mediterranean, and from October to the middle of winter light rains are expected. These autumn rains are critical, for on them depends the revival of perennial plants which have so far withstood the parching summer. Without them the steppe grasses lack the moisture needed for their first growth and the herbage will remain poor even though the later rains are normal. If the rains are poor and there is a danger of failing pastures, the women of a camp form a procession which goes, singing a rain prayer, from tent to tent, headed by 'the mother of rain', an effigy consisting of a woman's robe stretched over two crossed poles borne aloft by a maiden. The winter season, especially in January and December, is severely cold; hoar frosts are common and snow may fall. The less reliable rains of early spring maintain the growth of grass and carry it over the drier period, which precedes the early summer showers of May and June. But if the summer rains follow on a long period of drought, they fall on hard, dry ground and are rapidly evaporated in the hot sun. The scanty blades of grass are parched out before they have really grown. These rains do not usually continue into July, but valuable dews collect during the cool nights that follow on torrid days. As this month wears on, however, all vegetation withers, the land becomes desert, and the annual return to the settled lands must be made.

These northern Badawîn control richer pastures and have more frequent access to large towns than many of those farther south who have smaller herds and are dependent on small interior oases. The unfortunate Sherarat, described in the opening chapters of Palgrave's account of his famous journey, who occupy parts of the south-eastern end of the Wadi Sirhân in the direction of the Shammar Mountains and the oasis of Jauf, are far more impoverished than the 'Anaza tribes to the north. The small groups of Suleib, a gipsy-like people with no cohesion, widely scattered over the northern desert, although generally considered as Badawîn, breed asses and goats rather than camels, and are subject to the more powerful tribes in whose territories they live.

The requirements of the camels control both the movements and the organization of a Badawîn group. Although a large number of tents may congregate round the tribal *sheikh*, the Ruwala do not wander in large bands and the tribe is but rarely united. The more widely they are scattered over the scanty pastures the more secure are their resources. Thus they migrate from pasture to pasture in a number of small bands of fifty to a hundred, each independently seeking grass for its own beasts. When the grasses in one place fail, scouts are sent out in the most likely directions to find the nearest water-holes and fresh pastures available.

The essential virtues of the camel are the infrequency with which it must be watered, and its ability to store in its hump a reserve of fat on which it can live for many days if pastures give out. If the vegetation is green and fresh a water-hole need be visited but once a month; even if parched grass and salt bushes alone are to be had it can go nearly a week between waterings. A strong fat camel can be coaxed into drinking as much as sixty or seventy quarts of water before setting out along a route on which wells are few. These living water bags then, in the last resort, reduce the risk to the travellers of death from thirst. At the height of the hot season alone must the camel drink daily, and this, above all, compels the annual migration to the oasis villages. The camel is the fundamental source of wealth, for not only does it supply food and valuable materials, but it is the only important marketable thing that the Badawîn have. Sold to itinerant traders, or to peasants in oasis markets, it pays for the weapons, clothing and auxiliary food-supplies that are carried into the desert. However much a man's wealth may be shown by the display of other possessions, be it slaves, horses or tent trappings, all depends ultimately on the size of his herds. While the rich *sheikh* may own a thousand head, even the poorest herdsman endeavours to maintain a few beasts of his own.

A Badawîn camp is usually pitched within a short distance of a water-supply most central for a wide range of pastures. If surface water is not available, wells are cleared out or fresh ones dug, and the water hauled up in camel hide buckets is poured into leather troughs. Wells a hundred and more feet deep are found in the inner desert. These tap the rain-water stored in

the sands above impervious beds, and, after a season of good
rains, they refill as fast as they are drawn upon and may yield
abundant water for a year or more. Prolonged droughts may,
however, cause even the best and deepest to run dry.

When the pastures are close at hand, the herdsmen go out
daily, each riding at the head of his own camels, singing the
song he has taught them to recognize and follow. When
hundreds of camels are converging on the camp at sundown
the herdsman's song is indispensable, for the beasts easily stray
and wander aimlessly when lost. At night they are hobbled
by bending and tying up a fore limb; and the herders sleep
among them. Although usually docile, camels are notoriously
stupid beasts and must be watched carefully if they are not to
get lost, for they wander blindly in search of pasture, and
having strayed have little sense of direction to help them regain
the herd. The breeding camels must be particularly cared for:
not only do they miscarry easily if they eat any noxious herbs,
but they often try to break away to bear their young in
secluded spots, whence they would often fail to find their way
back to the herd. 'Lost camels' is a call that rouses all the
available men in the camp.

But, as the closer pastures are grazed down, the herds must
move farther afield and may remain away from the camp for
days and even weeks at a time. It is then necessary to rein-
force the herdsmen with patrols of armed men who watch the
approaches to the pastures from high ground and are prepared
to drive off would-be raiders. The herdsman's work is no
menial task and his advice is rarely gainsaid. The bravest
youths covet the charge of a large herd.

Breeding is carefully controlled and pedigrees are known for
many generations. Animals are carefully selected for various
purposes, for fast riding, for women's litters, for carrying water
and heavy burdens. The majority are yellowish-brown or
grey, but white camels are the most highly prized for the very
reason that they are always conspicuous and therefore demand
a stronger defence against raiders. A herd of white camels is
usually owned in common by a group of kinsmen, and its care
is a main charge on their vigilance and bravery.

Camel milk is the main and often the only food for months.
It is drunk fresh and sour and is stored, but neither butter
nor cheese can be made from it. The camel alone can travel
long distances and carry burdens in the desert. With its long
legs it covers the ground at four miles an hour when travelling
slowly, and a good riding camel, when pressed, will travel a
hundred miles in a day, while a pack camel, with full burden,

will do at least half as much. The she-camel in milk gives from a quart to over a gallon each day, according to the pastures. Camel hair is the raw material for ropes and weaving, and the hide for bags and bottles. Males are kept only for stud purposes, since they have much less endurance, are less docile, and above all neither yield milk nor bear young to increase the herd.

The camel is saddled with a massive contrivance consisting of two inverted V-shaped pieces whose lower surfaces splay out like shovels and fit the body, one before and the other behind the hump. Connected by cross-pieces on either side, these

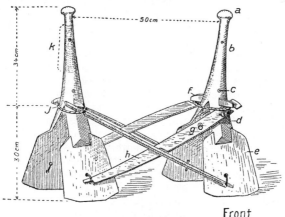

FIG. 97. A CAMEL SADDLE
(*After Musil*)

hold the burden rigid. A rider sits cross-legged on cushions between the grips, controlling his animal with a single rein on a halter, kicking its shoulder-blade to urge it on and patting its neck on the side he wishes it to turn. Although they are galloped only in emergency, riding camels can maintain a steady ten miles per hour on good ground at their normal gait.

Still more highly prized, although of far less direct economic value, is the horse. Save as a means of executing short, swift raids which may yield booty, the horse is of little utility, and its maintenance demands constant care in an environment which is much too severe for it. The dry herbage of the pastures must be supplemented with grain bought in the villages and carried on camels, and even when the grass is freshest the horses must be watered once a day; on journeys when the water supply at the wells is uncertain, sufficient for the horses must be carried on camels. Horses cannot travel long distances, easily go lame, and in hot weather shed their hooves when travelling long over burning sand and gravel. In short, the horse requires more care than a child and usually gets it. In time of stress the barley left in the store bags is fed to the horse and not to the household. The ownership of a horse is regarded as essential to any one with self-respect and any pretension to importance. Yet even the richest can have but few, while the ordinary bedu may own only a third share in a mare or be waiting to realize his claim to the next foal of a kinsman's mare. Stallions are kept only for the stud and geldings are not used, for it is the mare with her promise of fillies that is valued; male colts are thrown away at birth unless another stallion is needed. Thoroughbreds alone are reared in the desert, and values are assessed on a large number of arbitrary points and markings. Since they are so rarely sold or transferred outright, fixed values do not exist, but a yearling mare would be worth at least ten camels, while a young breeding mare might be exchanged for anything from fifteen to thirty thoroughbred riding camels. As with camels, white is the most prized colour, and a white mare is the proper mount for a chief at festivals. The fastest are, however, believed to come from a light yellow strain. A lost or stolen mare is often sought from tribe to tribe for many years, so that the fillies, if not the original mare, may be recovered or compensation may be exacted. The foal is nourished on camel's milk, as well as its dam's, and the owner of a filly may half starve himself and his family in providing for it. The women and slaves of the household are expected to devote themselves to the feeding and grooming of the horse. If the wells are far from the camp they must bring in water, for it is not wise for any but armed parties to risk taking horses far from the camp. During winter they must be protected from severe cold and in summer sheltered from the heat; always they must be guarded against theft, while the part owner must look to his rights when fillies are born. In all, they cause endless trouble and are a constant source of temptation, friction, bickering and bloodshed; but they are, nevertheless, a great pride and joy.

Clothing and weapons are generally bought in the villages or from travelling merchants. A man wears a long white under-shirt reaching to his heels, a long wide-sleeved coat, and over these a striped or coloured cloak—a large square of cloth with holes for the arms. Sheep skin jackets are used in winter when the cold is severe. On his head, over a close-fitting woollen cap, he wears a large square of cotton or silk. Folded in a triangle with the points hanging down at the back and sides, this is held in position with a thick braided head coil wound twice around. He may go barefoot the greater part of the time, wearing camel hide sandals or merely rags bound to the feet when any distances have to be covered or rough country traversed. A woman's clothing is very similar, although the headkerchief is larger, somewhat differently arranged and held by a band of folded cloth.

The Badawîn have now for several generations used firearms, and every tribesman has some sort of gun to-day; but the older weapons, spear, sword and sabre, are still used. Every man of consequence carries a sword, and the spear is often a more reliable weapon than the old musket of the poorer *bedu*. Swords and spearheads of steel are obtained by trade, while rougher ones of iron can be forged in camp.

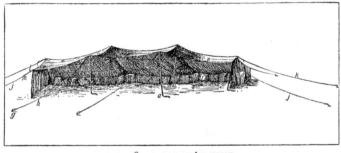

FIG. 98. A BADAWÎN TENT
(*After Musil*)

During the migration well-established camp sites near good wells are usually revisited year after year and occupied each for a month or so in sequence. The camp site is decided on by the chief of the dominant group of kinsmen in the band. The Ruwala scorn to camp in a circle like the weaker Badawîn, who thus endeavour to protect their stock by herding them at night inside this compound of tents. Each tent is made from a number of long strips of goat hair cloth about two feet wide, usually bought from village weavers and sewn together by the women of the household; their length, which may vary from ten to over forty yards, and the number sewn together depends on the size of the tent required. The usual tent cover is rarely more than ten yards long and about four wide, with a separate narrow strip for the low back valance. The cover is supported by three or four pairs of poles, and held by long guy ropes pulled taut when the cover has been spread out and the poles propped into position. Whether it be to catch the breeze or to seek protection from blown sand, the open face of the tent can be quickly reversed by changing over the poles and taking the back strip to the other side. In cold weather the front may be closed in with more strips of the black goat cloth. (See fig. 98.)

The tent of a chief or of the head of a group of kinsmen may be considerably larger. It will then be divided into two unequal parts with a transverse partition of cloth; the smaller third is reserved for the owner and his guests, the larger two-thirds being occupied by his women-folk, children, slaves and stores. The main cooking hearth, set between three flat stones, on which the kettles and cook-pots stand, is in the women's section, but another fire pit which gives warmth and on which the evening coffee is made lies at the front edge of the master's quarters. The furnishings depend on wealth, but are rarely elaborate and would not strike a Plains Indian as at all luxurious. A few carpets to sit and sleep upon, cotton quilts and camel hair pillows for warmth and comfort at night are all that is usually to be found beyond the weapons, cooking utensils and stores. Wheat, barley, rice, dates, salt and coffee are stored in sacks, which are woven by the women who spin on the march and weave the yarn of camel and goat hair on small horizontal looms in camp. A well-to-do man when he leaves the settled country at the end of summer carries a camel load (about three hundred pounds) of grain for each member of his household, and an extra load for the entertainment of guests. The chief of a large group may, however, have to carry fifty or sixty camel loads of grain for his numerous dependants, for the entertainment of guests and for the replacement of stores stolen by enemies from members of his group. On the other hand, poorer groups or needy families in richer bands may not eat grain from one summer to the next. The wheat and barley are ground as needed in wooden mortars or in a rotary quern of basalt, and eaten either boiled to a thick paste, or, more occasionally, baked in wafer-like cakes on sheet iron plates. But bread is a luxury of the rich, and a few roasted grains of wheat or barley, or even a mouthful of raw flour, is the more usual portion. Stores of water and soured camel's milk are kept in camel skin bags.

As occasion permits the women gather small supplies of wild products, such as the small fruits and juices of shrubs, a few tubers and bulbs. In June the sweet red berry, *mesa'a*, which grows on a low gnarled shrub, is collected, and in July the harvest of *samh*, the bread of the poorer Badawîn. The minute hard red seeds of *samh* are contained in the fruit capsule of a small herb, which is itself a favourite camel food. These farinaceous seeds are collected in large quantities, stored in bags, to be ground and perhaps boiled when needed. A richer harvest is provided when a locust swarm appears. They are caught in great quantities and the surplus dried and stored whole or ground to a powder. Meat is as great a luxury as bread, for camels are killed only on special occasions, and cuts from the slaughtered beasts have then to be given to many relatives and friends. Game also, although it is hunted, provides only a very small part of the food-supply. The small herds of antelope and gazelle in the sandy wastes of the Nefûd are able, the Badawîn say, to live on dew. Ibex live in rocky country, while hares and bustards are found far and wide and are hunted with falcons. There are a few specialist hunters attached to most camps, who for a fixed reward, hunt game for the chief. The trained hunting falcons, which are kept by the wealthier, ride on the saddle knob and are released when the dogs put up a hare or bustard.

Little food is eaten until the evening. A lick of salt or a gulp of milk on rising, and a further drink of milk fresh or soured taken about midday, must suffice until the meal at sundown, when a paste of dried dates, some roasted grain or baked flour and more rarely meat, supplement another draught of camel's milk. Meals are prepared by the women and are taken in their company except when guests are present. But coffee drinking is the occasion for great connoisseurship, and the wealthy sheikh has it prepared at his own fire pit. A roasting-pan and an array of four pots are necessary. Here at least there is no economy of utensils.

When camp is to be struck and the march to a new pasture begins, the stores are loaded and the tent is let down; folded lengthwise into a band a yard wide, the two ends are rolled up separately towards the middle on two poles to form a double bundle, so that the rolls can easily be set on either side of a burden camel. The chief and fighting men ride ahead on the soundest riding camels, with saddled mares alongside, either tethered to the camel saddle or ridden by small boys. The main body of pack camels, led by slaves, the litter camels on which ride the women and children and the herds all follow close behind. If an enemy is sighted the warriors mount their horses to attack on their own behalf or to prepare to hold off the enemy while the caravan moves out of danger. Unless forced marches are necessary, when the band moves on from dawn to sunset, the daily camp is made before the heat of the afternoon, and little more than ten to fifteen miles is covered in a single day.

The Badawîn society blood relationship in the male line is fundamental. All the tribesmen of the 'Anaza group consider themselves to be ultimately related in this way, while the divisions of a tribe which habitually camp together will consist almost entirely of a few groups of related kinsmen.

A man's kinsmen (*ahl*) in the restricted sense are defined in relation to himself alone; they are his paternal ancestors to the third generation, other descendants of those ancestors to the third generation from each, and finally his own descendants in the male line to the third generation. Thus a man's kin ranges from his great-grandfather to his great-grandson, and second cousins in the paternal line are the most remote members. Although two men, say a boy and his patrilineal great-uncle, may be kin to each other, yet the list of the kin of each will not be the same. This is the group that in the first place protects him from injustice and suffers for his misdeeds. The kin in the broad sense of clan or 'house' is a group descended from the same paternal ancestor, which usually remains together to form the whole or a close-knit part of a camp. Each may often be distinguished by the colour or pattern of its cloaks and headgear and the decoration of saddles and bags. A collection of such kins or patrilineal clans forms a camp unit and recognizes an immediate chief or sheikh, who is a member of the dominant kin.

The emphasis on male descent appears also in inheritance. A man's property—his tents, camels and horses—are inherited by his sons, the eldest receiving a larger share, while the widow receives but a single camel and the daughters two each. No one may lawfully accept gifts of a substantial part of a man's property, and such gifts could always be reclaimed by his heirs. A woman may inherit, purchase and own camels, but her kin has no claim to them at her death. They pass to her husband and sons.

The effectiveness of the kinship tie is, however, ultimately dependent on physical proximity. The group of relatives between whom the mutual obligations hold is one which normally moves as a unit, whether alone or as part of a larger camp, and the obligations to the leader and to the group as a whole ensure the solidarity of the group as a physical unit; once the members are scattered they can less readily be invoked or carried out. If a kin should break up and its members seek work or asylum in the camps of a number of other tribes, it becomes increasingly difficult for them to reunite, and the individuals become the founders of independent kins. Loyalties and obligations to the new groups replace the older sense of unity. Even if no violent territorial disruption should occur, the increase of prolific families may rapidly exceed the practical size of a single camp group or tribal division. Moreover, the increases of different branches will be uneven; thus, if a man has twelve sons of whom six have large families of male descendants while the others have but few, the descendants of the latter may dwindle to one or two, while their cousins may number hundreds.

Although descent is most carefully reckoned in Badawîn society the group name which indicates the affiliation of individuals is usually the patronymic of a recent ancestor—a father, a grandfather or perhaps a great-grandfather—and ties going back more than three generations are of little weight so far as immediate solidarity is concerned. This is not a result of short memory but of the scattering of descendants of the prolific families, who must, under conditions of desert herding, form separate camp groups. As the territorial separation increases, beginning in distinct households, proceeding to distinct sub-tribe and ending in tribal independence, so the mutual obligations and solidarity dwindle away. The Ruwala consider that all members of the 'Anaza tribes are descended from a single ancestral group, and this is probably in a general way true. But between the Ruwala and the Fed'ân or 'Amarât and the other leading 'Anaza tribes there is not co-operation but constant rivalry and often a state of war. This is the end product of rivalries which grow up between households as they separate in distinct camps, herding their beasts in different areas.

Their way of life, scattered over thin pastures, is constantly tending to break up and subdivide the Badawîn into small groups. The kin and tribal system serves to reduce this tendency, to give strength to the camping groups and unite them into a larger tribe, which depends not only on their actual kinship but on their common ownership and defence of pastures.

The sheikh of a camp group and of a tribal division may extend his patronage to remnants of other groups reduced by war or other misfortune, and even to individuals of other tribes. Such individuals owe a special loyalty to him, and, although they are free to depart at will, it is shameful to do so without good reason. The chieftainship should properly descend in the male line, but the successor is not necessarily the senior claimant, for much depends on the personalities of available successors. Actually there is a constant tendency for successful war leaders to usurp the chieftainship, to raise their kin to dominance and to hand on the chieftainship in their line until it is again usurped. In the same way the chieftainship of the tribe as a whole descends in the main line of a kin, but is similarly liable to usurpation.

By Islamic law a man may take four wives, and can divorce them by simple declaration. The ordinary *bedu* cannot often afford to exercise these rights, but a man of substance provides a tent for each wife and her family and others for concubines and slaves. The paternal cousin (father's brother's son) is considered the proper husband for a woman. This right, again, is by no means always exercised, but should the woman wish to marry another the cousin's consent must be obtained. When her sons are grown a woman often goes to live with one of them, leaving her husband with his younger wives.

But the group of kinsmen and their women-folk do not constitute the entire population of a Badawîn camp. The well-to-do, particularly the elders of kin groups, and, above all, the chiefs, have slaves of mixed negro blood. These slaves, although living with their masters yet form a separate social group, and their intermarriage with Badawîn is absolutely forbidden; the infrequent breaking of this rule is often punished by death and the destruction of any offspring. Slaves may be killed and are rarely sold or transferred against their will, but they can hold property only at their master's pleasure. Their main duties are watering camels, assistance in striking and setting up of tents, and loading and guiding pack animals on the march. A chief alone, as a rule, has many slaves, and they are often his chief support in maintaining his ascendancy and control. The senior slaves in a sheikh's household are frequently his more important advisers and confidants; he can trust them far more than his ambitious kinsmen; on their fidelity his influence and power often depends, while a weak sheikh is frequently dominated by them.

In every camp there are also one or more families of smiths, who again stand outside the Badawîn community. They are generally 'foreigners' from the Euphrates country or Persia. They marry among themselves, or very occasionally with slaves, but are never permitted to take a *bedu* woman as wife. The smith works for the camp as a whole, shoeing the horses with the flat iron plates necessary for desert travel, making swords and spears and repairing muskets and utensils. In the summer he receives a fee, based usually on the number of horses in the camp, with which to buy clothing, grain and other supplies for the ensuing year. The smiths take no part in fighting and are not knowingly attacked by raiders. Anything that they lose in raids they may get back by the intervention of their fellow smiths in the enemy tribe or of their 'brothers' among the Badawîn of their own camp who protect their rights. The smith profits from the raiding for which he equips the warrior, for he receives all the saddles and gets a young female camel for every horse captured.

Finally, there is often to be seen among the black tents of the Badawîn the round white tent of an itinerant merchant. These merchants come out from Damascus and other Syrian cities and from the Euphrates country, and move about with the wandering groups, passing occasionally from one to another to become the guest of each in turn. They are often the agents of great trading firms and sell clothes, coffee, utensils and ornaments, for which they give credit at high interest or receive camels which they brand and take over at the end of the season to drive to the large markets. The Badawîn herds are the great source of supply for the peasant populations of the Near East, who rarely breed camels themselves. Thousands are driven annually from Arabia through Sinai to the Egyptian markets. The Badawîn pays his debts fairly regularly in the summer after the camel sales, for fear that the merchant with his highly valued wares will desert a defaulting camp.

The life of a Badawîn camp is not one of peaceful migration from pasture to pasture. It is punctuated by raiding expeditions small and large against enemy tribes and their herds. Powerful tribes invade the traditional territories of weaker groups, attempting to drive them out and to steal their beasts; weak groups reluctantly accept the protection of the stronger, who vie with each other for the prestige of dominance. In dreaded years of severe drought, raiding and the invasion of pastures is a matter of life and death; and hostility has a real economic foundation. During the better periods, however, raids do not cease. They are undertaken not merely for the lust of possession, although the size of the herd is the mark of wealth and power, still less for the sheer satisfaction of any innate bloodthirstiness. The thrill of success in a well-planned attack, the prestige of victory over long-standing rivals, the fear of disgrace if an attack is not met, repulsed and rewarded with counter-attack: these are powerful motives in the perpetuation of hostilities, which in many ways parallel the spirit of Plains Indian warfare and horse raiding.

Hostilities usually develop from trivial beginnings—an

assertion of superiority, the temporary trespass of coveted pastures or petty thefts of animals. These are met by attacks on the only wealth of the offenders—their herds of camels and mares. Such raids may be initiated by an individual and his immediate kin, or by the camp as a whole under a recognized war leader; tribal expeditions under the paramount sheikh are rare, and are undertaken only after considerable preparation when it is intended to deprive another tribe permanently of its pastures. Minor raids by a handful of adventurous individuals may be made by camel, or even on foot, during moonless nights; but larger expeditions are carefully planned and will involve up to half the fighting strength of the camp under a commander who has acquired a reputation for skill and bravery. Each kin taking part usually has its own leader who co-operates with the commander. The party sets out in small, separate groups to congregate at a secret rendezvous. Each warrior has his mare which runs alongside his camel until needed for the last swift raid. The march on the enemy's territory proceeds in stages, and a party of scouts keeping about a day's journey ahead sends back messengers to report to the main body. The enemy's camel herds are the main objective. If they are grazing away from the camp conditions are particularly favourable. A surprise attack is, however, difficult as warriors are almost certainly patrolling the surrounding country. Leaving a small party in charge of their own camels in the secluded place at which they have waited their opportunity, the raiders mount their horses before dawn and ride swiftly upon the herds as the sun rises. If this raid is successful the captured animals are quickly driven off by a small body, while the rest turn their attention to the camp itself in the hope of capturing horses and stores and terrorizing their victims by cutting down tents and killing where resistance is offered. These raids are but rarely murderous in intent, and indeed the raiders are so frequently outnumbered that they cannot stay to inflict great damage.

When, however, from hunger or the development of fierce enmity one tribe determines to drive another permanently from its pastures, the warriors of the various camps combine to form a great armed force and the tribal emblem is carried into the battle. This is a high litter borne on a camel and, among the Ruwala, elaborately decorated with ostrich plumes. It is said that at one time a young girl, selected from an eminent family and possessed of great courage, was seated in this litter; it was her duty to shame the timid and encourage the brave by satirical and exciting cries and recitations. To-day girls riding on camels join the picked band which defends the emblem. After the first onslaught these battles usually break up into duels and small knots of fighting men. If they succeed in breaking up the defending force the attackers destroy the camp, forcing the defeated and their families to relinquish their rights and sue for peace. Submission is offered only in the face of complete defeat, for the prestige of the tribe is entirely lost and may never be regained. Such a weak tribe will be compelled to pay a regular tribute of camels to its overlords, who can thus maintain their superiority indefinitely, unless intrigue and the development of new combinations offer the underlings an opportunity of throwing off the yoke.

Most tribes have a number of enemies, so that preparations for raids and precautions against attack are almost continually proceeding. Fierce hostility on a tribal scale is not enduring between adjacent peoples, for the issue soon comes to a head; but the more distant the pastures between two hostile tribes, the more intermittent are their contacts, and the smaller are the raiding parties that each can send out. The state of war is in consequence more prolonged. The Ruwala and their allies have for nearly two centuries maintained hostilities with the powerful Shammar tribes to the south of Nefûd.

To the dangers of raiding must be added the expiation of blood feuds, for murder must be avenged by the victim's kin by the killing of the murderer or one of his kin. A murder is regarded primarily as a reduction of the strength of the group of the murdered man, of his household or of his tribe; corresponding reduction of the offending group is therefore the logical requital. The murderer can, however, sometimes obtain protection by taking sanctuary with a powerful chief of another group, and the feud is settled by paying over a blood price in camels. The price is far higher for a kinsman than for a victim of another tribe, but no blood money is expected when a state of war exists between the two groups concerned. The group responsible for the payment and receipt of blood money may vary from the immediate kinsmen to the sub-tribe as a whole, according to the circumstances and to the arrangements and undertakings previously made. Such individual feuds may also give rise to wider conflict by the prolonged reciprocal attacks of members of the two camps concerned.

Where raid and counter-raid are always likely and any trespasser can be attacked on sight, travel, save in large parties would appear to be dangerous in the extreme. But a number of customs and practices accepted by all tribes afford some protection to the individual and serve to make travel across a number of tribal territories possible. In the first place, it must be realized that the traveller is usually very welcome. He affords an unexpected break in the monotony of the many months of herding, and he brings news of events in the outside world to the members of small isolated camps; moreover, the provision of protection and safe conduct of a traveller is felt to be a display of power and authority and a sign of assured control of the territory occupied. Safety is thus assured by obtaining the protection or 'countenance' of a tribesman of the territory concerned, preferably the chief of the tribal group. To attack or plunder a man who has the countenance of one's kinsman or chief is as serious as murder. The giver of countenance must afford protection against any attack by tribesman or raider, must restore any goods stolen unwittingly and avenge any harm as though the victim were his kinsman. The protector sometimes accompanies travellers to the limits of the territory over which he offers protection. To refuse this countenance is a disgrace, it 'blackens the face', that is, it destroys the reputation for courage, independence and generosity. Protection may be even obtained in this way without the fore-knowledge of those concerned. Should a man declare before witnesses his claim on the countenance of the chief whose territory he is about to enter, that chief must, to save his face, avenge and make amends for any harm that befalls the claimant. The return of a salutation of peace is also a pledge of safety, and an individual in enemy territory has often endeavoured to encounter a small child who would innocently return his salute and thus pledge his safety with the group. The giving of countenance must not be lightly asked, for it involves trouble and risk for the protector and will probably have to be reciprocated by one's own kin at a later time.

The arrival of a stranger at the camp is often the occasion for great competition in offering hospitality; for the host acquires prestige in addition to the presence of his guest. The guest is welcome until sunrise of the fourth day after his arrival, that is, until the third daily meal has been eaten and digested; after that time he should not stay, but his safety is guaranteed for an equal period after he has left or up to a distance of about a hundred miles. Beyond that the obligation is ended, and if the welcome has been a sham, the host may attack his late guest, for the giving of hospitality is no guarantee of real friendliness or good intentions.

The importance of these social devices can be readily appreciated in view of the narrow margins of subsistence and the limited lines of travel in country where the camps are always moving, and attack and plunder are the basis of prestige. Without them intercommunication would be almost impossible.

Although they have firearms, and have long been in contact with oasis towns, the true Badawîn remain a savage people with a rudimentary economy. Their Mohammedanism is but a thin veneer. Its beliefs and ritual are often misunderstood, neglected and superimposed on other older and often conflicting religious ideas. In central and southern Arabia the Badawîn have for many centuries been subject to the intermittent control of the rulers of the settled country and large oases of Oman, Yemen, the Hedjaz and the Nejd. Indeed, it was only in the north that really powerful independent Badawîn tribes have survived until recent times.

CHAPTER XVI

THE KAZAK, KIRGHIZ AND KALMUCK: HORSE
AND SHEEP HERDERS OF CENTRAL ASIA

CENTRAL ASIA is the traditional land of pastoral nomads who wander seasonally in search of pasture for their herds of sheep, cattle and horses. From time to time they have become the instrument of an organizing genius who has led them in rapid invasion over wide tracts of settled country and so given rise to the legend of the invincibility of the peoples of this nomad realm. Until the beginning of the nineteenth century this vast pastoral land had remained substantially unchanged since the times when the Scythians of its south-western marches became known to the Greeks or when Marco Polo journeyed among the tribes tributary to Chingiz Khan. It is only in the present century that the autonomy of the nomadic peoples has been seriously affected. And even to-day, although railways have been pushed across the lowlands of southern Siberia and Russian Turkestan and the herding peoples in some districts have been transformed into settled communities, large bodies of virtually independent pastoral nomads live on in the less accessible parts of Russian Asia and in the Chinese territories beyond.

The heart of the great Asiatic continent is cut off by great mountain ranges from the rainy monsoons of the Indian and China seas, while the mountains and plateaux of Europe deplete the lighter store of moisture in the westerly winds from the Atlantic and Mediterranean. So it is that despite the enormous height of its mountain chains and the great elevation of the plateaux there is a vast track of country from the Volga river to the Hwang Ho and the Great Wall of China in which forests are found only as narrow girdles on the slopes of the higher ranges and rivers dwindle yearly after the melting of mountain snows.

But Central Asia is by no means a desert. Bare sands and gravels, although they cover wide tracts of the poorer country, make up only a small proportion of the total of this vast area. Save on the low-lying floors of a few mountain-hemmed basins, as to the east of the Caspian Sea and more strikingly within the great Tarim depression, sufficient rain falls at some season of the year to provide a rapid growth of grasses, the sprouting of many bulbs and the flowering of shrubs like the tamarisk and saxaul. The time and amount of the rainfall depend on the position in relation to the seasonal winds from the distant oceans, and on the elevation and exposure of the particular tract of country. In southern Siberia and in parts of the Turanian Basin of Russian Turkestan the moisture is brought by westerly winds from the Atlantic, the Mediterranean and the Black Sea. In eastern Mongolia and southern Tibet the last tongues of the summer monsoons from the east and south bring summer showers. Although precipitation on the plains and plateaux is light, the masses of the great ranges, the Hindu Kush, Karakorum and, above all, the Tian Shan and Altai receive more considerable amounts and accumulate the falls as snow during the winter season. While the snow-fields and glaciers of Central Asia are to-day remarkably small for mountains of such scale, they are adequate to provide a fringe of torrents which swell to great streams in spring and unite to form large rivers flowing many miles before they end in inland lakes or slowly dwindle away in the porous sands and gravels of the dry lowlands.

Since it is so remote from the moderating influence of the oceans, the climate of western Central Asia is characteristically extreme or continental. In winter a great tongue of cold spreads to the very borders of the tropical lands, while in summer the great expanses of the interior heat rapidly under the high sun, and temperatures unknown in damp tropical lands succeed an arctic cold. Indeed, it is the intensity of the summer heat, with the consequently rapid drying out of the ground, which so decisively restricts the growth of trees and dense vegetation. The seasonal change is greatest on the lower lands towards the north-east.

The Kazak, often miscalled Kirghiz by the Russians to distinguish them from the European Cossacks, are the largest and most numerous division of Turki-speaking pastoral nomads. Their encampments range from the Caspian Sea and the Volga river for nearly two thousand miles eastwards to the Tarbagatai hills, the northern ranges of the great Tian Shan mountain system and the head waters of the Irtish. From the foothills of the Elburz Mountains in south Turkestan they extend over fifteen hundred miles northwards to the borders of the Siberian forests. Although some of the western Kazaks occupy high mountain pastures, and have an economy similar to that of the Kirghiz to be considered later, the great majority occupy the dry plains and foothill pastures of Turkestan and the smaller but richer area of the western Siberian steppe. In these two areas the people, who probably number about four millions, are about equally divided.

The Kazak are in general mongoloid in race. They are rather short in stature, heavily built, with yellow skin, and coarse and generally black hair. But when compared with the peoples farther to the north-east, including the Altai Kalmuck (see p. 347), the mongoloid element in the Kazak is seen to be frequently modified. The face is usually longer and more oval and the Mongolian eye-fold is quite often absent, while in many individuals the nose is large and prominent, the eyes are less narrow and slanting and the hair, brownish rather than black, may grow abundantly on the face. These characteristics suggest interbreeding of the Mongol type with members of the Alpine race, which is widespread in south-west Asia and Central Europe, and still constitutes the dominant stock in the mountain country to the south and south-west of Russian Turkestan.

In origin the Kazak are probably a conglomeration of once-distinct Turkic tribes together with accretions of Mongols and Samoyeds. Since medieval times, when they formed part of the widespread but ephemeral Turkic empires, the main nucleus appears to have spread south and west from the region of the Jüs Steppe and the Abakan river (see fig. 99). Their organization into three major political and territorial divisions, or 'hordes', occurred in the thirteenth century. They have, however, remained unified in language and custom, although the formal organization and territorial separation of the hordes has, especially since the Russian control of the area, to a large extent decayed.

The main body of the 'Great Horde' still occupies its traditional area south of Lake Balkash from the Ala Mountains, Lake Issik Kul and the north-western Tian Shan as far east as Aulie-ata and Tashkent. The 'Small' or 'Young Horde' is found in the western steppe between the Aral Sea and the Caspian, while the greater part of Turkestan and Tashkent is occupied by the 'Middle Horde'. Although until the middle of the nineteenth century these Kazak hordes remained virtually free of all foreign control, they had no longer any knit organization of their own. For urgent defence alone would any considerable combinations be effected, and the Kazak polity is built up from small family units into a series of widening but progressively less coherent divisions.

The paternal kindred of father and sons with their wives

and servants is the social nucleus. The father owns the greater part of live stock and decides the movements of the family. But a number of these families, many of them actually related in male line, form a clan which recognizes the head of the dominant family as its leader and negotiator with other clans. All men are necessarily members of their fathers' clan and must obtain their wives outside that body. Every clan has its crest, such as a bird's rib or a forked stick, which is branded on

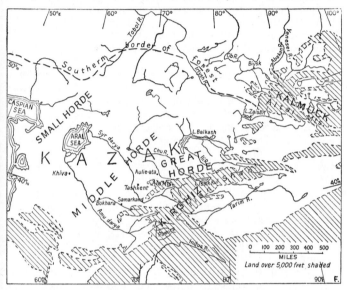

FIG. 99. SKETCH MAP OF WESTERN CENTRAL ASIA

the live stock and marked on the belongings of members. The clan rather than the individual kindred is the unit for social and political relations. Traditional pastures belong to the clan, and contributions to the payment for a bride are often made by all clansmen. For the maintenance and defence of its members the clan is an effective unit. Its poor are fed when destitute by the richer members. Its live stock is branded with a single crest or symbol. But within the clan the leading family of the chief has considerable power and often controls the greater part of the wealth.

Clans (*taypas* or *ak-sakal*) which consider themselves to be ultimately related and may in many cases be the descendants of a once unified group, often migrate together as a group and form a wider unit (*sök*) or phratry. There is no formal leader and the unity of a phratry of clans depends on the concurrence of its separate clans as expressed by their chiefs. The phratries are less stable groups than their constituent clans and appear to have subdivided and reformed in new combinations according to the vicissitudes of migration and warfare and competition for pasture.

The tribal group (*uruk*) of several phratries comprising perhaps twenty or more clans appoints a chief (*bi*), but he has little effective political authority. Selected by the consensus of opinion of the clan chiefs, a man of personality and energy may, however, draw the tribal group into an unaccustomed unity.

The hordes are agglomerations of tribes which by territorial contiguity, and occasional combinations for attack and defence have built up a tradition of solidarity. Leadership of the horde in any emergency falls to the chief of the dominant tribe, but the seasonal scattering of tribes and clans renders such authority ephemeral. In the great rising of the Kazak against the Russians in 1840 the 'Sultan' of the Great Horde achieved this temporary control and endeavoured to reunite the three hordes in an independent and organized nation.

The members of the chiefly families of the tribes, who claim a quite imaginary descent from the Mongol ruler Chingiz Khan and the alleged descendants of the first converts to Mohammedanism in the *hodji*, constitute a superior class, the 'White-bones', whose prerogatives to pastures are recognized by the commoners or 'Black-bones'. The White-bones thus form a wealthy noble class with larger herds and considerable social privilege. They refuse to marry their children to Black-bones, and noble families forming clans within the tribes or hordes cement their prestige and solidarity by the exchange of daughters in marriage.

While most of the commoners possess their own stock there is a poor cattleless group who through the ill success or misfortune of their forbears became dependants of richer men whose herds they tend. Until the middle of the nineteenth century slaves were found among the Kazak, but the majority were purchased to be sold again in the town markets of the settled areas.

Although conditions vary in different parts of lowland Kazak territory, according especially to the time of the more important rains, the two most critical seasons of the year are summer and winter. In summer the grasses, parched out in the heat, afford very poor pasture, so that localities in which moisture has accumulated during the rains are of great importance. Valley hollows and lake depressions and to some extent the windward slopes of the low plateaux yield the better pastures, but none lasts long. Summer must therefore be a period of constant movement. The families and clans do not lay claims to any stretch of country at this season, for the richness of the herbage in any place varies greatly from year to year; small groups with their herds pass from site to site, rarely able to stay more than three or four days in one camp. This period of constant migration and of the greatest scattering of the population begins at the end of May. Among the more northerly tribes movement is generally northward towards the moister forest margins, while the tribes of southern Turkestan and those of the Great Horde in the east move up into the foothills of the mountain ranges to occupy valleys which have received more rain and may also be partly flooded by streams fed by the melting snows and heavier rains on the high ranges above. On the northern steppe rains revive the pastures in July, and autumn is an easier season, but by mid-October it is necessary to migrate rapidly once more to reach winter quarters.

The winter season is again critical, but conduces this time to a concentration of settlement. Protection against the severe cold and high winds of winter, even more dangerous to live stock than to man, is sought in stretches of deep river valley with a fringe of protecting woodland where the winter grass is more abundant. The winter and summer quarters of a group may be two hundred miles and more apart, and during the year a household may cover five hundred miles. The winter quarters alone are thought of as territorial possessions; these are essentially clan settlements, to be claimed and protected by the clan as a whole. For the rest of the year all pastures are free to those with the power to occupy them, and the family or clan which first occupies any tract is rarely interfered with. These winter sites are many of them impossible in summer on account of the plagues of insects which attack both men and beasts. Each kindred of a clan has its accustomed site marked out from those of its neighbours and competitors by natural boundaries—by hills, rocks and streams, or by cairns of stones and lines of stakes. Winter is the period of greatest competition, and if the year is very hard a weak group driven from its accustomed site may lose nearly all its stock and be reduced to dependence on the more successful. Effective control, therefore, depends on the solidarity and strength of the group, but there are obvious limits to the size of the group and of the stock which can occupy a winter site. When the pressure becomes too great the older sons are urged, and if necessary compelled, to move off to find another site.

A camp or *aul* in winter rarely consists of more than three to five huts, but the *auls* of a clan may be strung far along a valley bottom each only a few miles from the next. From November until mid-April the habitation remains fixed, although the pastures may change. Apart from a few riding animals the horses are not usually brought to the winter quarters; they remain with a few herders on the autumn pastures ten to fifteen or more miles away until the first snowfall, and are then taken back to the summer pastures, where, although the weather is inclement, the pastures which were waterlogged and infested with mosquitoes in summer now afford good feed.

In colder and more exposed places many groups replace their felt tents by more solid huts (*kstau*) in winter. The materials may vary from stone in the mountain foothill country to timber branches and bark on the forest border in the north, but the majority are built of turf. The floors of the huts are often sunk deeply in the ground, and walls nearly a yard thick are built up of sods to be roofed with timbers and willow branches and withes, which are again covered with layers of turf. In the more arid areas of southern Turkestan where no mat of turf is found hut frames are often built of reeds and withes and plastered with earth. These winter huts are usually rectangular. One or two small gaps left in the walls are covered with animal membranes to admit a little light. The low, narrow entrance is hung with heavy felts and the walls are lined with felt rugs hanging from pegs driven into the walls. Round a fire pit of beaten clay set towards the front late-born camels and calves huddle among the cooking materials and piles of harness, while at the back are the sleeping quarters of the household. Flanking the main dwelling are other huts for dependants, for young and weakling sheep and stores. Round the whole camp a high wall of turf or reeds is built, against which a light roofing of reeds, supported on poles, is built on the inner side to afford shelter for the other live stock.

Towards the middle of April the spring migration begins. Households pack up and move off unostentatiously, each often concealing from others the plan of movement which has been formed from the reports of its horse herders on the outer pastures. Thus each group may hope to take first advantage of good pastures that are accessible. Since the grass remains short and scanty, for a few weeks migration is constant and as rapid as the reduced strength of the beasts will permit. But the six weeks of late spring and early summer, when the heaviest rains fall in the more northern half of Kazak territory, provide the richest pastures of the year. The stock fattens, milk is abundant. In favoured areas along stream banks that are free of insect plagues many clans may concentrate in a single camp of fifty or a hundred tents. Towards the end of July, however, the intense heat parches the ground, grass and water become scarce and the households must again scatter, migrating every few days to find sufficient feed for their stock. In late September rains fall again, especially in the south, where the season is the most favourable of the year. The pastures improve and for about a month there is another respite and a chance for the animals to fatten against the winter, but by mid-October the cold begins to set in and the households move off rapidly to their winter quarters once more.

There are thus six phases in the yearly cycle. Their duration varies from district to district and from year to year while in exceptional years, both good and bad, the régime may be upset:

(1) The stationary period in winter quarters from November to about mid-April.

(2) The rapid spring migration in the direction of summer pastures until about the middle of May.

(3) A short stationary period on rich early summer pastures which lasts about six weeks until early July.

> This phase is more characteristic of the northern steppes, where the summer rains are the heaviest of the year. In southern Turkestan it is often lacking and continuous migration is necessary throughout the summer.

(4) Frequent migration over parched pastures during the intense heat of late July and August.

(5) More leisurely migrations over the improved autumn pastures until mid-October. In the south where the autumn rains are the heaviest this is the richest season of the year.

(6) Rapid migration back to winter pastures during the later part of October.

The Kazak tent, or *yurt*, so well adapted to a migratory life with beasts of burden, is a circular felt-covered structure with vertical walls and a domed roof (fig. 100). The wall

frame consists of a collapsible trellis set upright in a circle
and standing about four feet high. It is constructed of willow
rods held together with leather thongs passing through holes
drilled where the rods cross, and when opened it has a mesh
of about a foot. Half a dozen lengths of trellis are needed for
the walling of a large yurt of about twenty feet in diameter.
In a narrow small gap left in the circle a door frame of stouter

FIG. 100. A KIRGHIZ ENCAMPMENT
(*Based on photographs by Sir Percy Sykes*)

poles is fitted. To the upper edge of the trellis willow rods
eight to ten feet long are tied, about a foot apart. These
curve upwards and inwards, like the ribs of an umbrella, to
be lashed or socketed to a wooden hoop two or three feet
across which crowns the dome. Lashings of horsehair rope
which pass spirally down from the hoop and round the trellis
strengthen the frame, and over it a number of large sheets of
felt are stretched and lashed in position. The roof ring, which
lies directly above the fire pit, is left uncovered as a smoke
hole. In bad weather and at night when the fire has died down
this too is covered with a sheet of felt. Across the door frame
hangs a felt curtain which can be pushed aside. The floor is
covered with felting, and the inner face of the trellis is often
lined with reed matting decorated with wool, while woollen
rugs are laid face down over the dome before the felt covers are
put on so that their pattern may be seen from within. Similar
rugs are laid on the floor. Over the central fire pit is set an iron
tripod from which cooking-pots are suspended. In large yurts
a space on the right side is screened off with reed partitions to
serve as a kitchen, but the copper cauldrons, wooden platters
and leather vessels often lie around the fire pit. The bedding,
felt and skin covers and pillows of sheep's wool are rolled up
under the walls. Sometimes a large couch, five or six feet

wide, of raised planks covered with layers of felt nearly a foot thick is set at the back of the yurt where the family sleep. Married sons and children who share their parents' yurt sleep on the left, while poor relations, dogs and lambs lie still nearer the door. When honoured guests appear well furnished couches are prepared for them at the rear. Leather and wooden chests containing stores of grain, sugar and tea and great leather bags containing milk products line the side walls of the richer yurts and indicate the wealth of the occupant.

The erection and dismantling of the yurt is the work of the women or poor dependants. Two or three camels or horses are needed to carry a large yurt when packed for migration and as many may be needed to bear its contents. When a party is moving frequently the whole yurt is often not erected; the domed roof alone is set directly on the ground to provide shelter for the night.

The clothing of the Kazak has been considerably influenced by the Moslem Tartars of the west, but the characteristic garment is the kaftan, a long, padded coat with wide sleeves and a narrow upright collar, reaching to the ankles. The coarse cotton and woollen cloth for the kaftan is usually traded from the cities, although the poor weave their own cloth from camel hair. In cold weather three or four of these wool-padded kaftans may be worn one over the other and with a shorter sheep skin jacket on top. Wide, thick woollen trousers are tucked in tall boots of heavy leather. These boots with pointed toes and sharp iron heels are adapted for riding but very difficult to walk in. When expecting to ride on a long journey heavy leather breeches are worn.

The Kazak horse herds graze separately from the other live stock. They will not eat the hard, strong-tasting herbage that is adequate for camels and sheep. A herd varies from fifteen to as many as fifty head led by a stallion which will permit no other stallion to join its herd. About half of the herds is mares, the rest young animals and a few geldings. If a wolf pack threatens the herd it huddles into a compact group, and the stallion will attack the wolves if they approach closely. A stallion is only used for a year or two for breeding and is then gelded to serve as a riding and draught animal. When a young stallion reaches maturity it must be driven out of the herd and grazed alone until a place is found for it in another. The relative poverty of the pastures limits the size of herds, and a rich Kazak who may have several hundred horses divides them into a number of small herds each on separate pastures. The mares foal in March and for the next four months provide a surplus of milk for human use. Foals are tied up round the yurt to ensure the return of their mares for milking, and, since a mare gives little at one milking, they are often milked six or more times a day. A mare yields only about two quarts daily in addition to the considerable amount taken by the foals. If the winter snow is not heavy mares which foal in the autumn are kept near the yurt and milked in the same way, although they give still less at this season. Mare's milk is nearly always a luxury food. The greater part of it is made into *kumiss*, a slightly intoxicating and very nourishing drink, which will keep indefinitely. To make kumiss the fresh milk is poured unboiled into leather bags into which a wooden paddle is thrust. The bag is closed at the neck and the milk beaten to and fro with the paddle for several hours and left to sour for four days. Before festivities kumiss is accumulated in large numbers of these leather pouches which may fill almost the entire available space in a large yurt, and a rich Kazak makes enough to provide a limited supply for the rest of the year. In their second year horses are branded on the haunches with the clan mark, and the unwanted stallions are gelded for use as riding animals. Unlike the Arab, the Kažak and other central Asiatic pastoralists do not ride mares. The pastures are sufficient for larger herds than in the poor Arabian steppe desert and the mares, valued highly for their milk, are spared other exertions. The majority of the riding and pack animals are geldings of four years and more.

At ceremonial races the winning horse is usually set aside as a sacred animal, its mane and tail decorated with ribbons. Such an animal is given the best of pastures but is never saddled or ridden again. At wedding, birth and other ceremonial feasts such races and contests are run, the most characteristic form being the *bagai*. A slaughtered calf or goat is provided by the giver of the feast and is thrown into the midst of a dense group of horsemen which includes all the active men available. Each man attempts to capture the carcass and to break away from the pursuing group in order to skin the animal before he is overtaken and has the carcase snatched from him.

Horse-flesh, especially that of young fat mares, is the most prized meat. The paunch fat is a great delicacy and is salted and packed into lengths of gut and smoked for storage. The toughest leather straps and lines are made from horse-hide, while the hair is braided into stout cords for lassos, halters and yurt ropes.

Geldings are ridden, and although a man may have a favourite among his horses it is used only for short periods and is sent back to the herd to recuperate; for the riding horse is in constant use, and although it is often given a little hay and grain this small extra feed is not enough to maintain it in condition for any considerable time. Horse herds are rounded up by small parties of riders. Until bridled they are difficult to control, and when a particular horse is to be caught a long pole with a running noose of strong hide at the end is used. The pursuer overtakes and rides alongside his quarry until he is in a position to drop the noose and bring it to a standstill.

FIG. 101. ALTAI KALMUCK PACK SADDLE (LEFT) AND RIDING SADDLE
(*After Radloff*)

Poor families who have very few horses let them feed in common with their other stock. They do not milk their mares but reserve their strength for use as riding and baggage animals.

The horse saddle used by men is a light curved wooden frame set on felt blankets (fig. 101). It is held by two girths, and within the frame is set a riding pad covered with a saddle rug. Women's saddles are more massive. They have a pointed pommel and a cradle is attached in front when a young child has to be carried. The horse is ridden with a very short stirrup, the knees raised high and pressed against the front arch of the saddle; the bridle is held in the left hand and a long guiding rein several feet long is attached to the right-hand ring of the snaffle bit. With this trailing rein the horse is caught and tethered.

The superb horsemanship of the Kazak is of course famous, and many travellers in western Asia have remarked on the amazing contrast between the ungainly waddles of the Kazak on foot and the graceful and confident bearing of horse and rider.

Camels are used as supplementary beasts of burden by some Kazak, especially in the more arid southern areas. The

Arabian camel, although it can carry heavier burdens, is rare
for the double-humped dromedary or Bactrian camel, which
is probably native to southern Turkestan, is far better able to
withstand the severe winters. The dromedary is hardly ever
ridden. It is not often milked and its flesh is eaten only when
it is the only meat available. But it will carry heavy burdens
of several hundredweight some fifteen to twenty miles a day,
while the hair of the winter coat which it sheds in spring
provides valuable fibre for the rough cloths woven on a crude
loom by the poorer Kazaks. A rich man may keep as many
as fifty camels if his establishment is large and his stores
considerable, but the ordinary clansman will have but two or
three and the poor often none at all.

Sheep form the largest single element of a Kazak's live
stock and provide the main food-supply. The majority of
Kazak sheep belong to the fat-rumped breed, a large, rather
goat-like variety derived from the wild Urial sheep of Asia.
It is very strong and hardy, and has a thick coat of stiff wool
mixed with coarser hair, and yellow, brown or white in colour.
But the most remarkable characteristic is the large double
cushion of fat which covers and hangs from the buttocks,
obscuring the short tail; in a grown sheep after good feeding
this fat hangs down in two great ropes dragging on the ground,
and may weigh over thirty pounds. An adequate supply of
plants such as wormwood bushes which are rich in soda salts
seems to be essential for this development of fat, and it is
greatest in autumn when little wooden trolleys are often fitted
to prevent the hanging cushions from dragging on the ground.
This fat-rumped breed of sheep is found from the Black Sea
to China, but it is often mixed with other strains. True fat-
tailed sheep are also found in Kazak herds, although these
are more characteristic farther south and west; in this breed
the fat is formed on the long tail itself, but is not usually so
large and heavy.

Sheep are pastured in flocks of a thousand or more in the
charge of boys. A horse is not wasted on sheep herding and
the shepherd usually rides an ox. In the north a ram is kept
for every fifty sheep. Since the winter is so severe that nearly
all autumn-born lambs die felt aprons are strapped on the
bellies of rams after the spring lambing in order to prevent
further breeding that year. Where the winter is less severe in
south Turkestan more rams are placed with the ewes, and late-
born lambs after a few weeks in shelter may be safely left to
themselves. All surplus rams are gelded and generally form
a separate flock. The flocks are driven out from the camp in

the morning and return often without guidance at midday. After milking they are driven out again to return before sundown for the evening milking. Alongside the yurts temporary stalls of stakes and ropes are set up, at which the ewes are tethered for milking. They give milk for three to four months after lambing, and although only half a pint may be obtained from a single ewe at one milking, the gross yield of large flocks is considerable. The milk is at once soured, or laboriously churned into butter in large leather pouches or made into cheeses. Butter is salted and packed into cleaned sheep paunches for storage. Soft cheeses are often kept to mash up in water at a later and less plentiful season as a substitute for milk, but most cheese is made to harden and it largely replaces meat as solid food in the winter and spring. In the autumn, after a spell of dry weather, the flocks are driven through a stream or lake to clean their wool and are then sheared; the fleeces taken off in one piece are packed into bales until required for felting, or sold to traders from the oasis towns.

A large party is needed to make felt and many fleeces are required. The wool is first spread out in a thick layer over hides and beaten loose with pliant wooden laths by a group of young men and girls; it is then plucked out still further by hand, thoroughly damped and spread between two large straw mats between which it is rolled up and tightly bound. The felt-makers then divide into two groups and sit facing one another several yards apart while for an hour or more they push the roll to and fro over the ground between them with their feet. The matting is unrolled and the felted wool is now beaten with the hand for several hours to compress it still further; it is finally bound at the edges with woollen thread, and if required for a special purpose may be coloured with vegetable dyes or decorated with wool stitching.

The older sheep that are not likely to survive the winter are killed off at the end of autumn—a time of abundant if tough meat. Sheep are slaughtered in considerable numbers on many occasions during the rest of the year, but a meal which includes mutton is always, except among the wealthy, something of a feast. Milk products and wool rather than meat are the things for which the sheep is valued.

Goats are also kept in small numbers. They run in the sheep flocks and are milked with them. The goats are believed to protect the flocks from the attacks of wild animals and they afford soft leather for clothing and small bags.

Horned cattle are fewer than sheep and horses among the Kazak. They are less able to stand exposure to the severe winters, but cows give milk in greater quantities than ewes and for a longer season, and soured cows' milk (*airan*) is a favourite food. Moreover, increased markets for cattle in Russian settlements have led to a considerable increase in numbers in the last fifty years. The native breed has long, curving horns.

The cows will give milk only in the presence of a calf, but each yields about two and a half quarts a day for six months, and a small winter supply of milk can be obtained from those which calve in the autumn. Bullocks and cows are ridden by boys and servants on short leisurely journeys, and they are also used at need as auxiliary pack animals. Although the milk of sheep, goats and cattle is frequently mixed in the leather gourds for making butter, cheese and sour milk or *airan*, cows' milk is preferred for making the last. For airan the fresh milk is thinned with water, some airan from a previous making is added and the whole is poured into leather pouches to be stirred almost continuously for twenty hours. Airan will keep for long periods and is regularly mixed with small amounts of millet or wheat to make various broths. But other cattle products are largely neglected, beef is not liked and never eaten by the well-to-do, while the hides are also little used. Horned cattle have not been fully adopted into Kazak economy. They are less hardy and less tolerant of the dry salty pastures that are characteristic of the poorer steppes, and remain half foreign among the herds of sheep and horses.

To supplement the poor winter feed of the riding horses and late-born lambs every household attempts to collect a small amount of hay. Grass is not cut green for this purpose but small tracts in which good grass is found are left ungrazed, to cure naturally under the summer sun. Each aul tries to find a supply near its winter quarters and a small group goes back towards the end of summer to gather and store it for later use.

Extended travel everywhere involves the abandonment of herds, food stores and yurt so that the travelling Kazak is always dependent on the hospitality of other groups he encounters. But on this he can usually rely, for the monotony of the isolated encampments, the avidity for news of other districts and groups and the strong convention of hospitality ensure a welcome for the traveller; indeed he usually provides the occasion for a minor feast. When intending to cover a considerable distance the traveller receives a fresh horse from his host of the previous night in exchange for the one on which he arrived. On the return journey he brings back each horse one after the other to the camp from which it was taken and finally recovers his own at the last stage of the journey. On long journeys in empty country, food in the form of hard cheeses and dried flour or baked cakes can be packed away in surprising quantities in the leather bags which hang from the saddle.

Although the Kazak are essentially pastoralists, agricultural products are produced on a small scale. Whenever physical conditions suitable for the diversion of river water offer opportunities for irrigation, water channels and embanked plots are laid out for millet, wheat and rye and, in the far south, for rice. Much of this cultivation is undertaken by dependent peasants who are not Kazaks, and in former times slaves from the oasis settlements were used. But small groups of true Kazaks are also found engaged in cultivation and remain at work in the fields from spring to autumn. These are mostly poor families with little or no live stock of their own, who depend for their livelihood on service to richer families who provide them with meat and milk products.

Kazak agriculture is technically similar to that of the oases of central and south-western Asia, although the standard of cultivation is often much lower. The stream or river used for irrigation is often embanked to protect the adjacent low-lying land on which the plots are made, and, in addition, must often be dammed back in summer with a strong wall of stones and brush so that the water will flow into the irrigating channels when the walling at the entrance to each is breached for the flooding. Where water cannot be made to flow directly over the plots, wooden water wheels are sometimes used to lift it into the channels; it is often laboriously carried in leather skins. On the retentive soils of the northern steppes, where there is also more summer rain, a plot may need only one watering, but in southern Turkestan the sandy ground must be watered every week during the drought of summer.

The poorest cultivators may till the ground by hand with hoes, but more usually a simple plough, often merely an iron blade attached to a pole, is dragged by horses. The soil is not turned and the furrows are very shallow; the ground is not harrowed but merely smoothed down by dragging long poles across the field with horses, and the harvest, reaped by hand, is threshed by driving horses over the strewn ears. At the larger sites water-wheel grinding mills of central Asiatic type are erected and strong granaries built to hold the harvest.

Hunting has little importance in the economy of the Kazak, but falconry and coursing are favourite pastimes of the richer families, who may also keep specialist hunters to stalk larger game. Falcons and hawks are used to take wild duck, pheasant, hares and other small game, while boars, wolves and foxes are ridden down on horseback. Hunting greyhounds are used only by a few eastern Kazak groups in the Tian Shan. Moreover, the Kazak make almost no use of the dog for herding purposes, probably a result of the influence of Islam, which regards the dog as an unclean animal. Chamoix, mountain sheep and elk are stalked in the higher mountains of the north-west, but the majority of the Kazaks are lowlanders in a territory poor in valuable game.

The mobility of their life and the long-established contacts with oasis towns have limited the development of crafts among the Kazak. Much of their cloth and metal-ware is obtained from the settled peoples, and itinerant craftsmen often do the smithing and even the felt drying; the Kazak tinkers who repair horse bits and kettles are less skilful and self-reliant than the smiths of former days when access to markets and traded goods was less frequent and certain. The copper and silver smiths are still skilled craftsmen, but their products are mainly hammered ornaments for saddlery. Wood-working, the making of yurt trellises, chests, bowls, is done by men, while the women dress hides, do the stitchery and wool embroidery on felt and clothing on which much care is lavished to produce intricate patterns. They use very little pottery and make none themselves.

The Kazak have long been Sunnite Moslems, but they are extremely lax in many observances and many earlier beliefs and rites survive. Boys are circumcised and men usually shave their heads. Ramazan is kept to some extent and itinerant mullahs, usually Kazan Tartars from the west, wander from aul to aul reading the Koran and performing minor ceremonies while the aboriginal horse sacrifice has been adapted to symbolize the offering of Isaac by Abraham. But they have no mosques, and women are neither secluded nor veiled. Sooth-sayers divine the future from the marking on the shoulder-blade of a sheep and magicians cure the sick.

The Kirghiz of the southern Tian Shan and the Pamirs are closely related to the Kazak in race, speech, custom and way of life. Known as the Kara or Black Kirghiz by the Russians, they occupy the high plateau area of the Tian Shan and Pamirs to the east of most of the Kazak and at a greater altitude. But their occupation of this region is relatively recent, for until the sixteenth and seventeenth centuries the main body of the Kirghiz lived in the lower country farther north in the Upper Yenesei Basin. Until they were forced south by internal dissensions among the Turkic peoples and by the Russian advance across Siberia they were a relatively settled people among whom agriculture appears to have been as prominent as stock raising. Although the southern migrations and the greater severity of their new country have modified their life and social organization they retain an esteem for agriculture and traces of more elaborate social regulations which reflect this earlier period.

The Tian Shan, or Heavenly Mountain, is really a vast series of elongated and lofty basins separated by a tangle of rolling ridges which rise in the central core to rugged mountains. The rivers of the smooth-floored basins are from seven to ten thousand feet above sea-level and receive many streams from the higher ranges which rise to fifteen and twenty thousand feet, with a few great summits like Khan Tengri of over twenty-four thousand feet. The Tian Shan, with its western extension in the Ala Mountains, extends for nearly twelve hundred miles from north-east to south-west. The ranges splay out towards the west, so that they obtain maximum benefit from the westerly air currents, which they force to rise and to yield rain and snow. Although the precipitation is far less than would be found on mountain ranges of this scale in more maritime areas, the winter snowfall is considerable in all the higher ranges, and there are also valuable summer rains. From about four to nine thousand feet, conifers and larch trees form a girdle of forest between the drier steppes of the foothills and the richer summer pastures of the high basins and hillsides which extend up to the snow-line. Above nine thousand feet the summer season is too short for the growth of trees, but a thick mat of grasses and bulbous plants covers the ground and springs into luxuriance when the snow melts. The snow-line oscillates with the seasons, descending below ten thousand feet in winter but receding to twelve thousand feet, and even higher, during summer, when it exposes a belt of country offering rich summer pasture. The summer melting of the snows and the snouts of the glaciers on the highest ranges swell the mountain streams and the great rivers like the Ili and Syr which flow westwards to Turkestan.

The Pamirs to the south-west of Tian Shan also form a high plateau area, but one of less strong relief. This rectangular area, about two hundred miles square at the junction of the greatest mountain chains of central Asia, is made up of a number of wide flat valleys over twelve hundred feet above the sea, sloping gently westwards from high ranges and separated by belts of rolling hill and mountain country rising two to four thousand feet above the basins. Lying in drier latitudes and more sheltered from the west, the Pamirs receive less snow and rain than the ranges of the Tian Shan. But the light and patchy snow of the basins lies until May in the higher valleys and is augmented by the flooding of the streams from the deep snows of the higher ranges in summer. The winter is severely cold. Forty-five degrees (Fahr.) of frost is a common average temperature for January, but the atmosphere is dry and violent storms are rare, and both men and herds can withstand it. The summer season is cool and is always characterized by cold nights, so that evaporation of the limited water supply is restricted. Thus the Pamirs, although too dry for forest, have wide expenses of steppe interrupted by tracts of marsh grass, and pasture is available throughout the year, when belts of country at lower levels to the north and west are covered in deep snow-drifts for several months.

The Kirghiz, fewer than the Kazak and probably numbering about a million in all, are more strongly mongoloid in physical type. There are two major divisions known as the Right and Left Wings. The smaller Left wing division occupies the Talas Basin, while the other is scattered widely to the south and west. Each is a grouping of tribes, phratries and clans, as among the Kazak. Tribal chieftainship is hereditary among the Kirghiz and appears to be a more powerful institution than the elective counterpart of the Kazak. There is, moreover, no privileged class of nobles.

The winter quarters of the Kirghiz are strung out along main river valleys below or at the lower margin of the forest zone. Thus they occupy at this season territory adjacent to that penetrated by the lowland Kazak only in summer. The winter camps are often very large and a whole tribe is found concentrated in one spot. Near them are tracts of land which are cultivated by a section of the group which remains behind to raise barley, millet and wheat, both for human food and winter horse fodder; proportionately larger numbers than among the Kazak are involved in agriculture, and less grain is obtained by trade. The rest of the clan or tribe migrates through the wooded belt in spring to scatter over the rich, high pasture which become progressively available as the snow-line retreats across the high basins and their flanking hill country. Clan and families usually keep to traditional areas in their summer migration. This is the prosperous season during which the stock fattens and milk products are accumulated.

During the spring extensive hunting expeditions are made into the wooded country. Maral deer are chiefly sought, for their new-grown horns are then in velvet. This skin is removed and dried for sale in the oasis towns to the south and east, where it is highly valued by the Chinese as a medicine.

The Kirghiz have in general less live stock than the Kazak, for although their summer pastures are very rich the scantiness of winter feed restricts the size of herds. Most of the Kirghiz

FIG. 102. KIRGHIZ HORSE AND YAK RIDERS
(*Based on photographs by Sir Percy Sykes*)

horses are of the smaller and hardier Mongolian breed. The climate and topography of much of the Kirghiz country is too severe for the camel, which is rarely used, but a substitute has been found in the yak (*Poëphagus grunniens*). The yak, protected by a heavy winter coat, flourishes on the extremely poor scrubby pastures of high mountain areas. It is a large and apparently clumsy animal which can be nevertheless safely ridden and used as a pack animal on rocky slopes and narrow defiles. On many of the high passes of central Asia, Kirghiz supply yak trains for the transport of caravan goods. (Fig. 102).

Until restrained in more recent times by the Chinese and Russians, the Kirghiz were more warlike and predatory than the Kazak, many of whom frequently lost herds of live stock to Kirghiz raiders.

The Mountain Kalmuck of the Altai, although essentially similar to the Kazak and Kirghiz in economy and in many of the details of their equipment, present a further variation of central Asiatic pastoralism. The contrasts are related to the special conditions of their habitat and their greater remoteness from the higher civilizations of south-western Asia. The seven tribes in Russian territory were thought to number some forty to fifty thousand in the middle of last century, while the two tribes in Chinese territory, although large, were fewer in total numbers.

The Altai Kalmuck, or Telenget, who occupy the western parts of the high plateaux of the Altai Mountains in both Russian and Chinese territory, are more purely mongoloid than the Kirghiz or Kazak. They are shorter in stature, smaller boned, and with a disproportionately heavy trunk; the face is broad and flat, and below a narrow retreating forehead are narrow, upslanting eyes and a small flat nose. The skin is often a dark yellow and their hard, black, stiff hair is very sparse on the face. The men often shave their heads, leaving only a small patch of long hair which is rolled up into a button. Their speech is of a purer Turki stock than Kazak, into which many loan words from more Western tongues have been adopted.

The Altai or Gold Mountains are a collection of high ranges running from north-west to south-east for over seven hundred miles along the western margin of the high plateau of north-western Mongolia. The ranges rarely rise above ten or twelve thousand feet, and between them are extensive upland plains at five or six thousand feet traversed by the headwaters of the Ob and Irtish rivers. Westerly winds prevail throughout the year and bring a considerable snowfall in winter and good summer rains. Snow lies throughout the winter at considerably lower altitudes than in the Tian Shan, over 500 miles to the south, but most of the higher plains are practically snow free, for the high winds pile the snow into narrow drifts, leaving the rest of the country clear. The climate of the Altai, save on the exposed flanks of the higher ranges, is considerably milder than in the lower lands north-east of the Yenesei in eastern Siberia and although the winter cold is often extremely severe, the summers are warm and sunny weather, occurring at all seasons greatly improves conditions for men and live stock. The great northern forest belt of Siberia tongues southwards over this moister mountain region to clothe the lower slopes of the ranges up to six or seven thousand feet with a dense cover of pine, spruce, larch and birch.

The higher ranges and the leeward sides of the high plains are too cold or too dry for tree growth. They are, however, thickly covered with vegetation, which ranges from rich meadows to tracts of coarser grass a yard or more tall interspersed with marsh where the waters of the mountain streams accumulate in depressions.

Since good pastures are available throughout the year within a relatively small region, seasonal migrations are not forced upon the Altai Kalmuck, and the great majority remain all the year in semi-permanent villages. Tracts of good pasture are left ungrazed during the summer to provide for winter feed, and little hay or grain is fed to the stock.

But the Kalmuck rarely attempt to make dwellings more fixed and permanent than those of the other pastoralists, and where a more solid wooden structure is erected it follows the plan and shape of the felt yurt. Such dwellings are, moreover, considered uncomfortable and cold. The yurts are usually of the same shape and construction as those of the Kazak, although the collapsible trellis is often replaced by more permanent posts. But poorer folk living within or near the forest zone build a simpler but less roomy conical felt tent with pine and spruce poles. This may be regarded both as an adoption of northern forest practice, for Samoyed groups have undoubtedly joined the Kalmuck at various times, and also as an adaptation to new resources and a less mobile life. When such a tent is to be temporarily abandoned the felts alone are removed and the frame is left standing, to be used again when required. The clusters of yurts in the valleys and on the slopes of the ranges are moved from time to time when the herds of beasts brought in for milking have trampled and fouled the site. The better pastures are free from snow throughout the year, and there is no need of shelter for any but autumn-born beasts which are brought into the yurts.

Sheep thrive less well than cattle on the long grass characteristic of much of the pastures and find little suitable grazing in the forests. They are in consequence much fewer than among the Kazak and Kirghiz, although a flock sufficient for the supply of mutton and wool is maintained by every independent household. Considerable numbers of goats are kept and herded with the sheep; rarely eaten and not always milked, they are valued highly for their hair which makes the strongest and most durable felt.

The cattle, a large breed with long lyre-shaped horns, yield an abundant and rich milk-supply, which is available from some part of the herd throughout the year and airan from skimmed and diluted cows' milk is more common among the Kalmuck than kumiss.

The horse is, however, the most highly prized animal. The Altai breed, although much mixed to-day, was formerly distinct from both the Kazak and eastern Mongolian strains. It is a very fine type with well-set ears on a straight head, narrow shoulders, a deep chest and surprisingly small hoofs. It is claimed to be among the fastest and most enduring of Asiatic breeds, and some amazing journeys have been recorded; continuous riding from dawn to sunset, in which over one hundred miles of rough country can be traversed daily, is by no means unusual. Riding horses are kept tied up near the yurts. The saddle used both by men and women is very similar to the Kazak men's saddle, but the harness is often made entirely of leather and wood, including the bit and stirrup, for trade goods have until recent times been rare among the Kalmuck, and the smiths, although skilful in making knives, axes and other tools and in repairing guns, do not attempt to make any complicated implements.

The Kalmuck until recently did not cultivate any of their land, and they eat considerably less cereal food than the Kazak and Kirghiz. The small supplies of barley which are generally eaten roasted or boiled in the grain by the well-to-do are obtained by trading live stock. They do, however, gather considerable stores of wild food plants and particularly edible bulbs, from the harvests of which the months are named.

The summer season is a period of plenty in which airan and a light milk spirit are consumed in great quantities while many cheeses are made and packed away in the large leather chests which line the walls of a rich yurt. Meat is abundant in the autumn, for the weaklings among the flocks and herds are killed off if they are not likely to stand the winter.

The winter season, despite the cold, is a period of far more intense activity than among the Kazak, for the forest belt is very rich in game. Chamois, steinbok, roe deer and the wild Argal sheep are all hunted in the winter season. Both hide and meat are used, for the Kalmuck have not that indifference to wild game which the large flocks and poor fauna of much of their territory appear to have induced among the Kazak. The Kalmuck too hunt the maral deer in spring for the young horns in velvet which are traded eastwards to China.

The winter hunting parties are often compelled to travel on foot with snow-shoes, dragging their equipment and food store on small hand sledges. The old horn and sinew bow of the Kalmuck has long since been replaced by flint-lock and even cartridge muskets traded from the Russians.

The control of the herds and the making of leather and wooden utensils is done by men. but the milking of all but mares, the care of the yurt and the preparation of food is left to the women.

The social organization of the Kalmuck contrasts with that of the Kazak and Kirghiz and seems to show further modifications consequent on a more sedentary life. The eight or nine tribes are each divided into a number of patrilineal and exogamous clans, but these have not, at least in the last hundred years, occupied distinct territories, and a village usually consists of members of several clans. The head of the leading family of a clan is expected to settle disputes and to come to the support of his clansmen, but a family herds its live stock on the grazing lands of its village. Leadership of the tribes and the offices of tribal judges are in the hands of one or two families in each tribe who often claim to have preserved an oral record of their genealogies for several centuries; actual accession to tribal leadership depends, however, on popular support, usually as expressed by the heads of the clans. Since, however, in recent times even the tribes have not been territorially united, the executive authority of the chiefs is slight. Yet they usually receive a tribute of hides and sheep skins, and there is said to be a surprising sense of loyalty and common spirit among fellow-tribesmen, although they may be scattered over villages shared with groups belonging to other divisions.

The more sedentary life of the Kalmuck has not led them to adopt some of the institutions of the Kazak which might have been expected to develop the more readily. Apart from the families of the tribal leaders and judges, there is no noble class nor so large a stockless class of serfs as among the Kazak, while slavery is unknown. Serfdom and slavery would appear to be south Asiatic institutions, which, although they have considerably influenced the Kazak, have not penetrated this more northern area.

CHAPTER XVII

THE NORTHERN TUNGUS AND OTHER REINDEER HERDERS OF SIBERIA

WITHIN and beyond the northern forests of Asia cattle and horses become increasingly difficult to raise and domestic reindeer take their place among herding peoples. The Yakut have, it is true, since their recent northward movement, endeavoured to retain the cattle-breeding economy on the tundra to the west of the middle Lena river. Gathering scanty supplies of hay, constructing winter byres and even inducing their animals to eat meat, they raise a few horses and cattle in these far northern latitudes. The reindeer is, however, native to the taiga and tundra zones and the habits of the wild herds have been discussed in an earlier chapter.

Domesticated reindeer are kept from Lapland to Kamchatka but there are wide variations in their relative importance and in the degree of domestication and use. As for the hunting peoples of this great region, full accounts of the economy, craft and organization of most of the reindeer herders are lacking. For the present purpose a brief sketch of the northern Tungus in Trans-Baikalia will be attempted, and significant contrast with other herders will be noted.

The peoples of Tungusic speech are the most numerous and widespread linguistic group in north-eastern Asia. In language they fall into two broad divisions—the Southern and the Northern Tungus—which also correspond with a very general division in economy. The Southern Tungus of Manchuria and Outer Mongolia, of whom the Manchu are the largest and best known linguistic unit, are mainly agricultural peoples who also raise live stock, although they may often depend considerably on hunting and fishing. The Northern Tungus, who are found from the Yenesei river eastwards to the Lower Amur river and to the sea of Okhotsk, practise agriculture in only a few districts where they have been Russianized in recent centuries. Many of the more southern groups have, however, been strongly influenced by Mongol-speaking tribes, especially the Buriat, and raise cattle and horses. The Tungus of the Amur river basin and the Pacific coast, such as the Goldi and

Gilyak, on the other hand, are fishing peoples with no live stock who use dog sledges for transport. But the greater part of the northern Tungus combine reindeer herding with a hunting and fishing economy. Like the other Tungusic peoples they are mongoloid in racial type but they are generally less broad and flat in the face than are the cattle-breeding Mongols to the south. They are closer to the Yukaghir in appearance although rather taller in stature.

These reindeer-herding Tungus who number perhaps twenty thousand in all are scattered in small groups, each with its accustomed territory, throughout eastern Siberia from the Yenesei to the Kamchatka peninsula and even, as a result of a recent migration, in the northern part of the island of Sakhalin. No sharp division can be drawn between the reindeer-herding and other northern Tungus. On the southern margins of their territory both horses and reindeer are reared while in many areas Tungus groups may, as a result of epidemics, lose their herds and become a purely hunting and fishing people with no live stock. Some groups, like the Kalars to the north-east of Lake Baikal, have large herds which provide a great part of the food-supply while among others there are but a few head of reindeer to a family. Northern Tungus reindeer herding is well developed in northern Trans-Baikalia, on the northern Vitim plateau and on the flanks of the Yablonoi and northern Kinghan ranges north of about lat. 55° N. In this area the Tungus, often referred to as Orochon (Tame Reindeer Men), occupy the forest country for the greater part of the year (fig. 41).

Trans-Baikalia is a plateau country of wide valleys with marshy floors through which braided streams meander. The areas of solid ground are covered with a close growth of trees and shrubs, and on the valley sides spread dense forests of white birch, poplar, stone pine, fir and aspen. At higher altitudes on the Vitim plateau and on the mountain ranges the hardier Siberian birch is the dominant tree, while the summits, too severe for the forest growth, are scantily clad in shrubs and dwarf willow. Mosses and lichens cover the thin soils of the forest floor and the marshes.

At the lower levels there is a short, mild and damp summer from mid-June until the end of August; on the highlands snow lies late in June and freezing begins again at the end of July. Light drizzling rains fall in the later part of the summer. The northward facing slopes are often very marshy at this season, for there is not sufficient time or warmth for the ground to dry out completely after the thaw, and melting water is often blocked by persistent snow-drifts. The winters are long and severe. By October the rivers have frozen over once more, snow-falls accumulate in deep drifts and temperatures fall to as much as −80° F.—more than a 100° of frost—for short periods.

During the short summer the northern Tungus frequently move north with their herds on to the tundra, where the pastures are more abundant. Willow shoots, reed grass and fungi supplement the lichens, and the domestic reindeer will eat fish and meat in small quantities. It is of great importance that the animals should fatten during the short summer that they may be able to resist the hard winter conditions, when they are obliged to live almost exclusively on 'reindeer moss', and during this critical season the animals are spared as much as possible from being ridden or driven. The 'moss' is less abundant in the forest, although there are favoured places where extensive carpets cover natural clearings. Although reindeer can scrape through the snow with the sharp rims of their foretoes and with their antlers this is very exhausting, and they fare best on the more exposed hills of the northern forest borders where the snow is thin and patchy. During winter the herds must move on continually, for their trampling hardens the snow so that it cannot be scraped away; large herds must indeed move forward every few hours, and after a few days of grazing a pasture is generally useless until the next year. One that has been used for three or four years in succession must be rested for several years. This demand for a continuous change of good grazing involves a need for wide territory and the competition between groups has often been severe—indeed, it has been estimated that more than four square miles are necessary for every head of stock.

In summer the herds must be prevented from stampeding under the attacks of the swarms of mosquitoes on the forest border, so if the season is bad they are rapidly moved northward or to the higher altitudes. Smoky fires are also built to keep off the midges, and the herds will huddle round these all day, grazing only at night. The does must be carefully watched during the mating season, for at this time both domestic and wild bucks often attempt to drive them from the herd. Fenced compounds are then built with birch branches and the fawns of the previous spring are separated from their dams; when the does are released to graze, the fawns are kept back in the compound, so that the does will return to suckle them.

The Tungus breed of domestic reindeer is larger than the wild animal. There are white, black and brown varieties in

contrast with the uniform grey-brown of the wild reindeer.
A reindeer lives from twelve to fifteen years. The antlers,
which are shed annually and grow again during the summer,
reach their greatest development at five years, but the Tungus
often saw them off, especially from animals used for riding
and driving, to protect the animal from entanglement in bushes,
from attacking another and, above all, to prevent it from
sweeping off a load or a rider.

While some of the northern Tungus live almost entirely off
their herds, the majority supplement their food-supply extensively by hunting and fishing. The number of animals possessed
by a household varies from a few dozen to several hundred.
When they are large many of the men are engaged in watching
the herds; when small they are cared for almost entirely by
the women while the men are away hunting. The herds move
about rapidly and may wander off for several days, but they
are usually attached to the camp; their need for salt, of which
the herdsmen provide supplies, and their peculiar liking for
human urine also attach them closely to their owners. The
reindeer are also almost defenceless against wolves, and
even wild deer sometimes seek the shelter of a camp when
attacked; wooden clappers are often hung round the neck of
a leader of a herd to disconcert the wolves. Bells are hung
round the necks of does to attract the fawns and to help the
herdsmen to find stray animals. Only a few bucks are kept
for breeding, but geldings are raised for food and draught.

As among the cattle breeders to the south, it is the milk
which is the most highly valued product of herding. Even
when herds are large domestic reindeer are killed for meat only
on festive and ceremonial occasions or when hunting is un-
successful. The female usually yields about a pint of milk a
day in addition to suckling her fawn. The milk is sweet and
thick like cream, but is poorer in butter fat than that of cattle,
and no dairy products are made from it. The women have
charge of all the milking.

The Tungus also use their reindeer to carry packs, and sometimes to drag sledges, but mainly for riding. When the herd is
small its value for pack and riding purposes far outweighs that
of milk and meat. A grown buck or gelding can carry a load of
over a hundred and fifty pounds (as much as a horse can bear
under taiga conditions), and it is much more sure-footed than
a horse in both rocky and marshy country. It will travel fifty
miles in a day, which is considerably more than Russian horses
achieve in this country. The females, however, can carry
barely half this load.

The sledges of the Tungus are usually similar in construction to, but rather larger than the dog sledges of the Yukaghir. In forested and mountainous country, however, they can be little used and are largely limited to the tundra plains, where they can be driven both on the snow and on the smooth mossy ground. The use of reindeer sledges is widespread and extends westward to the Samoyed of the Ob Basin and to the Lapps of northern Finland, both of whom use them more continuously and do not ride their deer. In the forest especially the Tungus ride their reindeer. The rider sits far forward on the shoulder-blades, for the reindeer's back is not strong enough to carry the weight of a grown man; the harness, although somewhat modified, is similar to that of the horse-riding peoples of the south. A riding party or a pack train usually travels in a file led by a trained and docile animal; the animals are often linked together, each tethered by the bridle to the saddle of the one in front. Those Tungus who have too few reindeer to live as pastoralists use their animals for riding and sledging to extend the range of their hunting and fishing activities. (Fig. 103.)

Reindeer hides, as among the hunters, are of the greatest importance for clothing and shelter, and the dressing of skins is one of the main tasks of the women. Fawn skins are preferred for clothing.

The maintenance of the reindeer herds is beset with difficulties. Epidemics in which entire herds sometimes die off over a wide tract of country are very frequent. There are serious losses from the attacks of wolves every winter, and the dogs of the Tungus are used for little else but to give warning of danger to the herds in camp and on the pastures.

The northern Tungus, like all other Siberian reindeer herders, devote a considerable part of their time and energies to hunting and fishing; their methods and equipment are similar to those already described for their northern neighbours, the Yukaghir (see p. 105). Maral deer, elk, bear and several smaller animals are hunted, but the wild reindeer is the most important food animal, and,

FIG. 103. A NORTHERN
TUNGUS REINDEER RIDER

as among the Samoyed to the west, domestic deer are extensively used as decoys for this purpose, especially during the rutting season. One or more does are led out on long ropes to tempt an unwary stag to approach within bow-shot. The hunter may also wear a disguise and crouch down in the middle of a group of does and wait his opportunity to shoot. Another common practice in the rutting season is to lash hide thongs between the antlers of a tame stag, which is then loosed near a wild herd. The wild stag immediately attacks the tame one, catches his antlers in the thongs and is thus held until the hunter can rush up. At other seasons a deer is trained to drag a small, improvised toboggan at the end of a long hide thong; a small screen is fixed in front of the toboggan and behind this the hunter crouches. In this way the hunter can be drawn right up to the wild herd without attracting its attention and he can often shoot down several deer before the herd is frightened away.

The hunting and snaring of fur-bearing animals, especially sable and squirrel, for barter to Russian traders has long been important in eastern Siberia. Most of the Tungus obtain flint-lock guns, iron knives and utensils as well as tea and tobacco in return for their skins. The maral deer is also sought, for hartshorn from the maral is traded south to the Chinese who use it in the preparation of medicine. Among the Soyot or Uriankhai, in the northern Altai to the south of the Tungus, the demand for maral deer has assumed such importance that animals are often captured and imprisoned in large corrals. They are fed, and can be successfully multiplied on a small scale, but they have never been tamed and remain intractable even after several generations of captivity.

The winter camps of the Reindeer Tungus must be shifted frequently, for at this season pastures are poor, while hunting and trapping are very active and long trips are made. Conical reindeer skin tents, like those of the Yukaghir, are used during this period, but for the summer when richer grazing is to be found on the tundra border, larger villages of conical birch-bark tents are set up and these are visited annually.

The Samoyed to the west of the Tungus organize large communal drives. A wild herd is driven between a lane of posts, often more than a mile long. The posts, each of which is topped by bunches of goosewing feathers, converge until they are only a hundred or so yards apart. In winter a heavy net is stretched across this gap, while in summer the lane is generally made to end at the banks of a lake or stream. The reindeer, driven on by beaters and terrified by the feathered posts, stampede down the lane until they become enmeshed in the net or plunge into the water and can be attacked by waiting hunters.

None of the Siberian peoples smelt iron from ore, but among the Tungus smiths forge iron tools from bars and scrap obtained by barter from Chinese and Russians. Spearheads, knives and arrowheads are made. The spearhead, a heavy-pointed blade nearly two feet long and sharpened only on one edge, has a tang with which it can be fixed in a wooden shaft. Although it is primarily a hunting weapon, especially valuable in attacking the forest bear, it is also used for a variety of purposes, such as wood-cutting, when axes and other Russian goods are not obtainable.

The effective social group or tribe among the Tungus is usually larger than among the Yukaghir, and summer camps of more than a thousand people are said to have existed in former times. But the population is very small in relation to the total area, and it has been estimated that in north-eastern Siberia as a whole there has never been more than one person for every hundred square miles of territory.

Close relations with Mongols and Manchus, together with Russian administration of their territory, have considerably modified the social organization of many Tungus groups, but the social structure as found among the more northern peoples is based essentially on the solidarity of the patrilineal clans, of which a tribal group is composed. A Tungus tribe, an aggregation varying from a hundred or so to more than a thousand people, which occupies a continuous and fairly well-defined territory and is made up of two or more of these clans, usually has its own dialect and is an endogamous unit, for individuals rarely marry outside it. But the component clans, which are strictly exogamous and intermarry one with another, are the essential units in the social life. That is not to say that either tribes or clans have been stable over long periods. The subdivision of tribal groups by the combined migration of sections of two clans, and also the division of a growing clan into two or more exogamous units, have frequently occurred. Remnants of dwindling clans are also occasionally accepted as members of stronger ones. The existence of many similar clan names over a very wide area from Lake Baikal to northern Manchuria is probably an indication of the extensive proliferation and migration of clans which has taken place.

The clans alone have names. These are generally derived from natural objects or utensils, such as, for example, 'Woodpecker's Noise', 'Poplarwood Cradle', but sometimes from real or legendary ancestors. Each clan has its own tutelary spirits, while the tribal group as such has none. The tribes, or dialect groups, are therefore aggregations of clans between whom friendly relations and co-operation are maintained and are strengthened by intermarriage. The clans appear to have been territorial units in former times, each having its own seasonal pastures and hunting grounds within the lands occupied by the tribe. While there are definite customs as to the sharing out of hunting rights, pastures and live stock among the families of a clan, arrangements and disputes between clans are settled by less regular procedure. Fights between clans over rights to territory have occurred in relatively recent times and the component clans often show little reluctance to leave one tribal group and to join another.

While a clan may vary in size from a dozen to several hundred households the general relations between the component families are everywhere the same. For the greater part of the year these families are scattered, either singly or in small groups of two or three. It is only during part of the summer when the pastures are richer and river fishing is important that the families of a clan and sometimes of several clans unite in a large community. At this season the heads of the households of a clan meet to settle by consensus of opinion any disputes or problems that have arisen. There is no hereditary clan chief such as is found among the Manchu and authority is collective. It is none the less real: offenders against the rights of other clansmen are thrashed and sometimes put to death; disputes between clan members are settled by the arbitration of the council; in times of danger a war leader is appointed; any changes in the hunting and pasturing grounds of particular families are agreed upon. Although the reindeer herds belong to the individual families which care for them, they may be redistributed after severe losses from disease or the attacks of wolves. No individual family is allowed, or indeed desires, to maintain a large herd at the expense of its clansmen and herding for wages or as a serf is unknown. There are no great distinctions of wealth between families.

The marriages of members of a Tungus clan are nearly always arranged with members of only a few other clans, and quite often with one alone. These marriages are accompanied by exchanges of property, and are often first arranged between the families concerned when the future mates are still children. A considerable gift of reindeer is made by the man's family to the parents of the girl. This gift, known as the 'turi', which corresponds very closely with the so-called 'bride-price' of the central Asiatic and African pastoralists, is often made up in part by donations from clansmen of the man's family. It is promised long in advance, and the settlement of the amount is the occasion for reciprocal feasts between the two families. The amount of the 'turi' varies with the beauty, skill and social prestige of the girl. The greater the amount the more the prestige of both the giving and the receiving clan is enhanced. It is, however, only nominally high. In the first place, about half of it or its equivalent is returned to the man's family as the dowry of the bride, which must consist not only of reindeer but also of all the equipment necessary to establish a new economic unit, a set of skin and birch-bark tent covers, of clothes and utensils. This dowry remains the property of the wife, and the progeny of the reindeer are passed on to her daughters. Moreover, since marriages generally take place between two clans and all clansmen are expected to contribute to the 'turi' or dowry in case of need, these transferences of 'turi' and dowry are exchanges which permanently deplete the resources of neither an individual family nor of a clan as a whole. Where reciprocal marriages are arranged between two families, that is, where a daughter of one is married to a son of the other and a son of the first at the same time marries a daughter of the other, no 'turi' is handed over by either party. Where owing to the poverty of a family or a clan an adequate 'turi' cannot be offered, it is replaced by temporary service of the husband, who for some years after the marriage lives with his wife's family and hunts for it.

It will be realized that where two clans intermarry regularly the families of the two clans are many of them closely related, although the relationships do not infringe the rule of patri-lineal exogamy. Indeed, the marriage considered most suitable among the Tungus is that between a man and his mother's brother's daughter, that is, with his 'cross cousin'. Cross cousin marriages are found in many parts of the world where a dual organization of a tribe into two exogamous units exists. Inter-marriage between two clans is not rigid or universal among the Tungus, but where it exists as a common practice cross-cousin marriages and the exchanges of daughters are often sought.

For the great part of the year the individual households, which usually consist of from four to ten people, are scattered over the country. Two or three such households may camp and migrate in company for many seasons, but no formal tie holds them together. Most of the men go off individually or in small parties with riding deer to hunt and trap. They are often absent for weeks at a time and the women have entire care of the herds. As need arises they strike camp and load the pack animals and move off towards some prearranged site, where the hunters will meet them again. While the women often have the main care of the reindeer for the greater part of the time and almost exclusively during the active hunting seasons the men have definite tasks, such as gelding and the cutting of antlers. Men who are too old for hunting assist the women in all work with the herds, and even dress skins. Although women rarely hunt and are often excluded from fishing, the division of labour between the sexes is not otherwise rigid.

The tent and its belongings, together with the reindeer herds, are usually regarded as the woman's property among the Tungus. Actually there is, and can be, no strictly individual property. The proceeds of hunting and fishing obtained by the men are, like the milk of the reindeer, shared in common by the camp group. Where, as frequently, the men of several households combine for a season or more to co-operate in hunting, the meat and skins are shared among them, although some of them may do little actual hunting and are engaged in cooking or in carrying the skins of fur-bearing animals to Russian and Chinese traders.

The herding and hunting economy of the Tungus necessitates an economic unit of at least two persons: a wife who will herd the reindeer and care for the camp while he is absent is essential to the hunter. Quite frequently the family unit includes three generations, a man, his father and one or more of his sons, together with their wives. Polygyny is rare among the Tungus and is only approved when the first wife bears no children. As has been suggested, the herds are not regarded as the inalienable property of the families. When, as only too frequently happens, attacks by wolves or epidemics wipe out a large part of the herds in the course of a single winter it is the duty of the heads of families to meet as a clan council in order to redistribute the stock so that each household may have enough to raise another herd.

The territory of a group of co-operating or intermarrying clans is felt as its property, and it is defended if necessary by force. Such a territory is sometimes divided among the clans as units, but the customary pastures and hunting grounds of the individual families in all clans are to-day more frequently scattered over the territory irrespective of clan affiliation. The only just claim to a pasture or hunting ground is the ability to use it effectively, and redistribution of such rights is made only to take up vacated lands and to allow for growing families. Families, either as individuals or as camp groups, build storehouses at their customary camp sites. In these miniature log huts, set on elevated platforms, stores of food, clothing, tent covers and utensils are kept. Any Tungus when in need may make use of any stores in a storehouse within the territory of his clan or tribal group. In the same way the tent poles and the fences of the reindeer corrals which are left standing at camp sites may be used by any other group if the owning family is absent. These reciprocal privileges enable any hunter or migrating group which finds itself in the grounds of another to obtain adequate food or shelter if in difficulty. But a tally should be left if anything is taken permanently. This is a piece of wood which indicates by signs what has been taken and by whom, and recompense is expected at a later time.

A hunter should not invade the regular hunting grounds of other families, although wounded game may be followed. The sense of individual, or, more correctly, of family ownership in hunting territories has increased with the trapping of squirrels and sables for the Russian trade and permission must now be sought before traps may be set in the territory of another family. Practically all barter among the Tungus takes place with 'foreigners', with Chinese, Russians or sedentary Russian-ized Tungus. To these furs are sold and from them iron tools and utensils are obtained. Among themselves neither reindeer nor other property are bartered, although the acceptance of a gift carries an obligation to reciprocate at a later time.

When the head of a household dies or becomes too old for active work the eldest or most responsible of the sons who remain in the household takes over the rights and duties of the head. He thus inherits both privileges and responsibilities but there is rarely formal or actual transfer of individual items of property. If a woman dies the herds and tents of which she has had charge pass, if she was young, to her husband's next wife (often her own sister, since it is the duty of her clan to replace her) or to her daughters if she and her surviving husband are old, or if the household is breaking up. But just as these goods, which are in a sense her property, nevertheless remain in the husband's clan, so a woman can, if she wishes and has the ability, retain control when her husband dies, and is then regarded as head of a household in her late husband's clan. On the other hand, if she re-marries into another clan, her herds must remain with her children.

Thus while the hunting and herding of the northern Tungus inhibit the formation of large, permanently concentrated units of population, the families thinly scattered over the forest and tundra are co-ordinated and afford each other mutual support and insurance against privation and loss by the obligations and privileges of clan membership. At the same time the intermarriage and co-operation between two or more such clans provide for the maintenance and strength of the larger tribal unit.

The Samoyed, who occupy the marshy tundra and the northern part of the forest zone in western Siberia from the Yenesei to the Ural Mountains, resemble the Tungus in much of their economy. They are hunters and herders and rear small herds of fully domesticated deer. But apart from the occasional supply of meat and skins the reindeer are used to pull sledges but are neither milked nor ridden. Their herding is of little direct significance in the food-supply. Reindeer are pre-eminently draught animals which supersede the dog team.

The Chuckchi in the far north-eastern peninsula of Asia, and the Koryak on the Pacific side of Kamchatka province, also raise herds of reindeer. They also make far more limited use of them than the Tungus, but the uses are different from those of the Samoyed. The coastal groups among these peoples show some close resemblances to the Eskimo in the seal-hunting activities which they combine with their reindeer keeping. A typical Koryak community in northern Kamchatka is divided between a coastal fishing village and inland herding camps, and individuals pass to and fro from one occupation to another. Nearly every fisherman has a small herd which his family or relatives care for during the fishing seasons.

The Chuckchi and Koryak herds are of a distinct and less completely domesticated breed. They are animals more closely related to the wild reindeer, and are said to fatten more quickly on the tundra pastures, but they are half wild, are caught only with a lasso, and cannot be milked. Riding has not been introduced, and they are not broken for drawing sledges; animals from the herds prove quite intractable in harness, and the dog remains the sledge animal, unless Tungus reindeer can be obtained by barter for this purpose. No watch-dogs are used in herding and the sledge-dogs must be tied up lest they attack the deer. Herds, although often larger among the Chuckchi than among the northern Tungus are therefore only of value in providing meat, and are thus distinct from those of nearly all Old World pastoral peoples. They are left to roam at will, and the herders merely follow them from pasture to pasture, lassooing an animal as it is required for meat. Wild bucks are allowed access to the herds, for the frequent crossing is believed to make the tame animals sturdier. The Tungus, on the contrary, kill all crossbred fawns produced in this way, on the ground that they are of little service and cause the herd to deteriorate if they are used for breeding. In this remote peripheral area reindeer herding is reduced to its most rudimentary form. It is, however, by no means certain that it represents a survival of an early stage. The Chuckchi and Koryak may have been converted from the reindeer hunting phase exemplified among the Yukaghir as a result of contacts with the more southern herders, and the size of the half-tame Chuckchi herds indicates a specialization in one use. When riding, driving and milking animals are not sought, complete domestication is not required, while herds of much larger size can, as on an Argentine ranch, be controlled adequately if the only demand is the availability of animals for slaughter.

These differences in the uses of domestic reindeer in Siberia raise special problems, and at the same time afford an instance of the way in which a reconstruction of the stages in a cultural development may be attempted from a study of the distribution of various elements.

The domestic reindeer is found from the highlands and arctic coast of northern Scandinavia to the Chuckchi Peninsula on the Bering Sea, along the northern margin of the forests and on the treeless tundra beyond. In this belt of severe climate no other domestic animal is found save the dog.[1]

Over most of the 'reindeer belt' the herds are relatively small, and their value lies mainly in providing teams to draw sleds, which on the flat tundra can often be used not only in winter on the snow, but also in summer over the soft, mossy ground. In the rutting season the tame reindeer are also of great value as decoys for the easier capture of wild stags. They are also killed for food, but among the Samoyed this is done only in emergency or when an animal is injured. The Chuckchi and Koryak, however, maintain larger herds and slaughter animals as required.

Farther south, in the forest country of the Sayan Mountains and east of Lake Baikal, the number of domesticated reindeer is still often few, but their use is different. They are less often harnessed to a sledge, but are ridden and used as pack animals on hunting expeditions; they are also milked and the milk occasionally made into butter and cheese. Again, the

[1] Excepting the attempts of the cattle-breeding Yakut already referred to.

tame reindeer is not regarded as a direct meat supply, but is used for decoying wild ones. In addition to the Tungus, riding and dairy uses of the reindeer are found among tribes of the Sayan Mountains, especially the Soyot. These may be an ancient Samoyed group who remained behind in the forest zone, but they have now adopted Mongol or Turkic languages and often keep a few horses and cattle as well as reindeer. The northern Tungus have also introduced these practices in recent times to neighbouring groups of Yakut and Yukaghir. But apart from these few marginal groups riding and driving are mutually exclusive, and the area of riding thrusts a wedge into the sledge-driving area. The Chuckchi and Koryak, as has been seen, do not attempt to ride or place burdens on their reindeer. They carry their packs on their own backs in summer. Finally, the milking, but not the riding, of reindeer is also found in a quite separate area among the Lapps in northern Scandinavia.

There are thus four subdivisions of the reindeer territory: the area of driving and decoy hunting alone, best developed in western Siberia; the east Siberian riding and milking area; the Lapp milking area in the west; and the north-eastern area of semi-domesticated herds whose owners use dog sledges. A comparative study of the practices associated with these various uses makes it possible to establish with reasonable certainty the important steps in the development of reindeer herding.

In the first place, it is important to remember that the reindeer is not the only animal used for pulling sledges in the arctic—dog teams are also used by the hunting peoples. Dog driving is also found outside the tundra among the hunting and fishing peoples of the east Siberian coast lands and on the Amur river, while it extends right across North America to Greenland. Dog-drawn sledges have also been described as formerly in use among some of the more northern Kirghiz tribes, and they still existed in northern Europe in medieval times. The sledge and, in particular, the dog-sledge is far more widely distributed than the domestic reindeer, and it is clearly necessary to consider whether reindeer driving is not an imitation and replacement of the dog team.

The reindeer is a far more useful animal for this purpose. While a dog team must be fed, the reindeer can graze its own food; it can also draw heavier loads, travel over more difficult country and in much rougher weather; finally, in an emergency the driver can slaughter and eat part or all of his team. Apart from the light toboggan-like sledge which appears to derive

from a form hauled by the hunter himself the designs of all
reindeer sledges are very similar both to each other and to the
dog sledges. Furthermore, the harness of sledge reindeer is
fundamentally the same from Lapland to the Bering Sea—
the collar to which the traces are attached passes round the
neck and one forelimb, so that the animal pulls with its shoulder
and chest. This type of harness is the one also used for dogs
in eastern Siberia in contrast to the loin harness of the west,

FIG. 104. EAST SIBERIAN REINDEER SLEDGE SHOWING METHOD OF
HARNESSING

(*Based on photographs and drawings by Jochelson and Bogoras*)

to which there is no parallel for the reindeer. It is therefore
suggested that reindeer driving was modelled on dog driving
and developed in eastern Siberia. (Fig. 104.)

But equally clearly the area of reindeer riding and milking
lies adjacent to the territory of horse and cattle herders who
ride and milk their beasts. This suggests that the pattern has
been introduced from the south and that from its limited
distribution it is a later development.

The reindeer play a very prominent part in the ceremonial
life of the Tungus. Every clan, and often nearly every family,
sets aside a reindeer which is never milked, saddled or driven.
Such reindeer are considered sacred and are thought to carry
the souls of men to the land of the dead, to act as intermediaries
between man and the spirits. Reindeer are also sacrificed at
marriage-feasts and death-ceremonies and many details of
these practices closely parallel the cults and sacrifices of the
horse among the pastoralists of the steppes to the south and
west. In this connexion it should be observed that both in
language and in many details of their crafts there are indications that the northern Tungus occupied more southern territory

ntil relatively recent times. One of the more surprising of
1eir 'southern' traits is their retention of a southern style
f clothing similar to that of the Manchu. Despite its un-
1itability for the rigorous climate, they jealously conserve
1is southern style, of which an open-fronted tailed coat of
1wn skins, very similar in cut to a European morning coat, is
1e chief feature. The Siberian apron which they have adopted
rotects only the lower part of the breast and body.

Among the Yakut the transfer from cattle to reindeer can be
bserved in progress, for they are adopting reindeer from the
ungus as their horses and cattle die out. The Yakut are the
nly reindeer keepers who brand their animals on the rump
1stead of using the otherwise universal practice of marking
1eir ears, and they still call them 'foreign cattle'. Many
etails of the riding and milking practices of the Soyot and
ungus show that it is a transferred pattern. Moreover, the
:indeer is a very poor milker, both in quantity and duration
f the supply, and it is most improbable that it was the subject
f the first—or even of independent—experiments in milking.
he Soyot and Tungus saddles are clearly adaptations of the
orse saddles of the Mongols. It is, however, less clear that the
1sso, which might at first sight be considered a horseman's
evice, was introduced in association with riding, for it is far
1ore widely distributed, the hair rope being used almost
niversally among reindeer breeders to gather in animals, be
for riding, milking, the sledge team or slaughter.

Numerous references in the Chinese annals make it clear
1at reindeer riding was already practised in the thirteenth
:ntury. Dr. Laufer has called attention to references to dairy
ractices among people who raised 'deer' like oxen as early as
1e fifth century A.D., which occur in a garbled and probably
:cond-hand account by the Chinese monk Huei Shen. Both
ses, of course, may have been much older, since domestic
1ttle and horses had probably spread across the Asiatic
eppes at least a thousand years before the beginning of the
hristian era.

There is no need to attempt to bridge the large geographical
1p between the Baikal region of reindeer milking and that of
1e Lapps, for Lapp dairying is clearly derived from Scandi-
avian cattle practices. The methods, terms and even the
1perstitions are largely the same, while dairying has among
1e Lapps no association with riding.

But the recognition that the tamed reindeer has been
1apted first for driving in imitation of the dog team and later
1r riding and milking like the horse and the cow does not

dispose of the problem of its first domestication, for a wil
reindeer presents most unpromising material for these purpos
which could not be achieved out of hand. Moreover, th
animal's need for wide migration in search of food would mal
efforts to tame it by long confinement impossible. There i
however, an economic use of the reindeer, which requires le
complete domestication than driving or riding and which ma
perhaps have preceded the later transferences. This is the u
of tame animals as decoys in hunting their wild fellows,
practice which is almost universal in the reindeer area especiall
during the rutting season.

So long as the herder is willing to remain almost as complia
with the natural movements of the herd as the hunter, th
reindeer has characteristics which facilitate its domesticatio
It can easily be attracted by salt; the Tungus and oth
herders regularly salt a patch of ground for their herd, and t
reindeer hunters often look out for natural salt licks or mal
artificial ones to aid them in finding and approaching the wi
herds. Even more than common salt, they are attracted t
human urine, and wild reindeer often come right up to a qui
camp to paw up and lick on the ground used by men; t
Chuckchi herdsman always carries a bag of urine to assist
attracting his stock. The reindeer is almost defenceless again
the wolf, which takes heavy toll of both wild and domest
herds; when attacked wild reindeer will often rush up to a
encampment, in apparent knowledge that the wolves will n
approach. Wild animals will also creep into the protection
the smoky fires built by men in summer for protection again
midges, and use is often made of this device in summer huntin
The reindeer is a gentle beast whose domestication must u
doubtedly have been favoured by the advantages to be deriv
from close proximity to man.

Reindeer domestication has among some groups an air
incompleteness, but this is to a large extent consequent on t
need for giving the animals freedom to find their scan
pasture. Moreover, they need little supervision and, wh
numerous, cannot in any case be given it. It is no necessa
indication that domestication is imperfect or of very rece
date. It is impossible to apply the standards of horse a
cattle to an animal which must range so widely for its fo
and is raised by peoples whose economic organization
relatively undeveloped.

PART IV

HABITAT AND ECONOMY

CHAPTER XVIII

FOOD-GATHERING ECONOMIES

W E can now proceed to survey the modes of life of peoples falling within the broad categories of the earlier sections, and to consider the significance and consequence of the developments implied. Beginning with the non-agricultural peoples it is necessary in the first place to estimate the extent to which they differ in various parts of the world and the limitations which their economy imposes. In one sense they constitute a genuine category with distinctive activities, and the surviving remnants to-day or in recent times represent a once universal condition of mankind. As we go back in time, the area occupied by cultivating peoples in any continent, or in the world as a whole, shrinks away. It is well known that Europe was occupied by Palaeolithic hunters during and after the later phases of the Ice Age and that the slow spread of cultivation from the east and south began only as late as about 3000 B.C. The evidence for the wide diffusion of the more important cultivated plants and domestic animals will be considered later, but it is important in the meantime to recognize that the surviving hunting peoples are the cultural ancestors of all mankind. They are found in every type of climate and vegetation region from the equatorial forest to the tundra.

But they are by no means in a uniform condition. On the contrary, they display great diversity and in some instances a remarkable specialization. So wide are the varieties and combinations of economies that it is hard to find an inclusive term which will embrace these hunters, fishers, and collectors of wild seeds, roots and fruits. The term 'food-gatherers' is most generally used, although it does not convey the active pursuits of the more specialized hunters and fishers.

The degree of specialization must first be considered. Among many of these peoples there is marked concentration on a single resource of the natural environment—the large wild game of the Bushman territory and, still more narrowly, the bison of the western Plains, the salmon and marine life of the British Columbian coast, the wild reindeer in northern Asia and North

America, and the sea mammals in the Arctic. Vegetable staples like the acorn among the central Californians are also found.

The contrasts in diet between one people and another may be extreme. The Eskimo and the Plains hunters living almost entirely on meat, and the British Columbian coast and river peoples, with their east Siberian counterparts such as the Goldi living so largely on fish, differ fundamentally in their regulation and exploitation of natural resources, in their tools as well as in their food customs from groups which, like the Semang or the Paiute and Californians, only occasionally obtain meat food. Such specialization or limitation is of course never complete. The pure 'gleaner', a type of primitive food-gatherer once postulated, who knows neither hunting nor fishing and lives entirely on gathered fruits, insects and the smallest of animals caught by hand, remains a hypothesis unconfirmed by ethnographical investigation. The Semang who perhaps approach most closely to this condition use simple nets and have a specialized weapon of the chase, the poisoned arrow, even though it is directed mainly against small animals and birds. The Tasmanians whose equipment was still more meagre, nevertheless organized drives against game more considerable than anything known to the Semang. On the other hand the Eskimo, who exhibit the closest approach to a purely hunting and fishing economy, regularly gather berries in such quantities as they can during their summer travels. There is nearly everywhere a wide range of auxiliary foods, and it will be noted that these are often provided by the women, while the specialized production is in the hands of the men. Where, however, no single resource predominates, the food quest is more diversified irrespective of the richness of total resources. The Semang in equatorial forest and the Paiute on a semi-desert plateau gather equally diverse supplies. Among such peoples, although hunting remains a male prerogative, vegetable produce is not gathered by women alone; the durian harvest and the digging of yams in Malaya, and the pine-nut harvests in the Great Basin are achieved by the joint labour of a household, men and women together.

Collecting, hunting and fishing are elements of economy combined in various degrees among different peoples. 'Pure' collectors or hunters or fishers do not exist, but it is among the specialized peoples where hunting and fishing with more elaborate equipment or social arrangements are of greater importance than mere collecting, that the higher levels of food-gathering economy are reached and numerous special appliances make their appearance. The degree to which the Eskimo, the

Northwest Coast and, to a less extent, the Plains peoples excel the more omnivorous but mainly collecting Semang and Paiute will be sufficiently plain. These higher-grade food-gatherers are particularly prominent in North America, although a few fishing peoples in Africa and south-eastern Asia approach them closely. It is also important to note that most of the habitats comparable to theirs in the Old World have long been occupied by agricultural peoples. The Plains Indians enter this higher group, largely on account of the opportunities afforded them by the introduction of an animal already domesticated by a higher civilization. Moreover, the Bushmen, although under favourable conditions they are dominantly a hunting people and also formerly made a crude pottery, did not approach the cultural status of the peoples of the Northwest Coast or the Plains, or even that of the Eskimo in either crafts or size, stability and organization of settlement. Severity of habitat cannot be invoked, save in latter days when they have been pushed into real desert, to account at all fully for the fact that the relatively specialized Bushman economy is associated with so meagre a development of social institutions.

It is not possible to classify the specialized economies of the food-gatherers according to broad climatic and vegetation regions, for it is not the *general* but the *special* character of the particular environment that is important. The territories of the Tasmanians, southern Chileans and Northwest Coast peoples, all maritime, temperate forest areas, show great similarity in their general climate and type of vegetation, but there is marked difference in wealth of resources and still more in the complexity of the economic and social organization designed to exploit it. Moreover, it will also be apparent that areas physiographically analogous to the territories of these food-gatherers are in other parts of the world occupied by the more advanced economies of cultivation and pastoralism.

The food-gatherers are not homeless wanderers. Even among the least organized and the poorest in equipment the unit groups of families each occupy an inherited and adequately delimited territory. In fact, the attachment to a fixed territory seems to be even stronger among such a people as the Semang than among the Eskimo, with a far more specialized economy and elaborate equipment, or among the bison hunters of the Plains who combined a genuine tribal organization with considerable territorial instability. The territories of the small bands of food-gatherers are probably not stable over very many generations: boundaries doubtless ebb and flow with the changes in the numbers of individual groups; but at any one time the lands of a number of adjacent groups are in relative equilibrium. Where abundance of resources within a fairly small area or need and facilities for storage are marked permanent villages or camp sites are generally found. Among the Paiute the hamlets occupied in winter are a response both to the need for storage consequent on the lack of day-to-day supplies of fresh vegetable food in the severe winters and to the need for co-operative hunting. Among the Bushmen a similar but less marked and stable concentration occurs in the dry season, when game and especially water are scarcer. But among the Californians, where large and imperishable food-supplies can be accumulated, and still more on the Northwest Coast, where the wealth of food from river and sea is probably greater than among any other non-agricultural people, permanent villages with enduring habitations are occupied year after year. The Plains, too, offered a rich reward to the hunters, but only on condition that they followed the wandering herds. This instability of habitation and simplicity of dwelling was a condition of Plains hunting life, save where in many cases a cultivating people adopted hunting but retained their corn patches and with them their villages of earth lodges for occupation in the seasons of planting and harvest. The same is true of Eskimo life: their early winter shore settlements are permanent villages of houses far more advanced and elaborate than the *wikiups* of the Paiute, but the food quest compels their desertion for the greater part of the year. The villages are the scene of brief congregations after the scattering during the sealing period and before a second dispersal after caribou. Nevertheless, in conformity with the technical skill that pervades Eskimo culture, their snow igloos and summer tents are neat and efficient though temporary structures, and far removed from a Tasmanian, south Chilean or even Paiute shelter.

But the recognition of a close relation between economy and settlement must not be taken to imply that the permanence and elaboration of habitation will depend inevitably on the resources of the natural environment. It is extremely probable that the Tasmanians had as good natural opportunities for constructing and occupying solid houses in permanent villages as the British Columbians and Californians, but they developed no effective techniques in food storage or wood-working and continued a scattered migrant life more appropriate to the equatorial forest. The resources of Tierra del Fuego again do not naturally condemn its inhabitants to the flimsy, unstable shelters that they occupy, nor to the meagre equipment of tools with which they content themselves.

It is further impossible to regard the economic and material culture of the food-gatherers as arranged in a sequence dependent on general favourableness of environment. Severe or difficult regions may be the scene of technically elaborate cultures like that of the Eskimo; while only the most rudimentary tools and the simplest exploitation of resources are found among the Tasmanians or the natives of well-watered country in south-eastern Australia.

It is of importance to observe that, apart from family and group rights to territory as a whole, ownership and inheritance of particular resources is widespread among the hunting peoples. A rigid classification in abstract terms concerning the tenure of land and other economically valuable property cannot be applied to any large number of peoples, since different methods may operate either one within the other or for different classes of property. Leaders of tribal or camp groups may be described as owning territories when they merely administer them or even have but a symbolical right to them. Among most of the peoples considered, however, and indeed among nearly all food-gathering people about which detailed information is available, the land-holding unit is the group of families which for some period of the year jointly occupies a settlement within a fairly well-defined territory. This does not, however, preclude individual or family claims to specific resources. Even among the lowly Semang durian trees are owned in this way. And they can be matched by the pine trees of some Paiute and by the beehives of the Vedda of Ceylon. Again, the Australian root-gatherer in Queensland transmits to her daughters the root patches she has tended and exploited. Men own and transfer fishing territories and women patches of plants on the Northwest Coast, although these rights are more characteristically associated with larger units, extended families (lineages) or clans.

From the earliest times individual ingenuity and the spread of knowledge have played a fundamental part in the building of cultures. The Tasmanians, as we saw, lacked the bow and even the spear thrower possessed by the Australians; they had not discovered such weapons for themselves and their isolation appears to have prevented the introduction of these and other devices from outside. Among the Eskimo the importance of borrowed elements in their remarkable equipment has been sufficiently emphasized. The problems of discovery and invention and their relation to pre-existing cultural and psychological conditions must, however, be postponed until we have considered the evidence supplied by the crafts of more complex societies.

Although religion and ritual are not within our province, i is necessary to bear in mind that we do not find among the food gatherers any invariable correlation of these elements with th development of the economic life and equipment of weapon and tools. The British Columbian fisher peoples, with thei elaborate exploitation of rich resources, do indeed show a development of social and ceremonial life which is uniqu among non-agricultural peoples, but at the same time th Bushmen and Paiute, with resources and implements superio to those of a people such as the Arunta in the desert and scrublands of central Australia, lack the elaborate regulatio of marriage and ceremonial characteristic of the latter people Furthermore, the ceremonial and social organization of th Arunta is part of a pattern variable but substantially universa in Australia, common to poor and rich territories alike, to th northern forests, the eastern parklands and the desert; thi elaboration is not a function of the local economic wealth Moreover, some of its elements can be shown to have close an almost certainly derivative relations with the more elaborat cultures outside the continent to the north. In brief, the involve problems of diffusion from more advanced peoples.

Nevertheless, the economic patterns of the food-gatherers d appear to set limits to their political institutions. The popula tion that can concentrate in a small area is small even whei the resources are richest, and rarely rises above two or three pe square mile. Although, as will be seen, there is considerabl overlap between the resources, size of community and develop ment of economic and social organization between the mos advanced food-gatherers and the poorest cultivators, yet i general the independent social unit is smaller and less formall organized among the former. Leadership, dependent on genera confidence and approval, tends to be limited to the particula matter in hand, and a strict hereditary principle is more rarel applied. A comparative study of a large number of peoples a all economic stages all over the world has shown that th political institutions of non-agricultural peoples are in genera markedly more rudimentary than among cultivators, and tha there is, as would be expected, a fairly close relationshi between stability of habitat and the accumulation of wealt surplus to mere subsistence.[1] The life of the peoples of th Northwest Coast emphasizes this by its very exceptiona character. With unusual resources and permanence o settlement goes a unique elaboration of social and politica

[1] See Hobhouse, Wheeler and Ginsberg: *Material Culture . . . of the Simpl Peoples*.

institutions. Whether strictly indigenous or ultimately dependent on external influence this could not have been established and maintained without the opportunities for close settlement, surplus wealth and leisure that their rich environment and ingenious techniques made possible.

CHAPTER XIX

DIGGING STICK, HOE AND PLOUGH CULTIVATION

IN Part II a number of cultivating peoples in various types
of country and raising different crops by various methods
were considered. The world distribution of the various
food plants and the problems concerned with the development
of the different methods of cultivation will be considered later;
for the present we shall review the differences of habitat, the
variation in actual methods and the wide variation in the
social and political organizations based on a cultivating
economy. The chapters of Part II cannot pretend to cover all
the variations of agricultural economy in the non-European
world. Nearly a quarter of mankind—the great populations
of China—lacks any exemplification. Our attention is, however, mainly directed to the simpler societies, and, moreover,
the salient characteristics of Chinese agriculture and society
are so well known and have been so well portrayed in a number
of accessible studies that no summary is required here. Nor
has a full account of a people practising a rudimentary agriculture in temperate latitudes been introduced, for in the
Old World Western or Chinese civilizations have long since
invaded the northern areas, establishing plough cultivation,
incorporating earlier peoples in larger political units and
assimilating them to their civilization, while in North America
European occupation also destroyed the native economies of
the north-east before adequate studies and records were made.
Indeed, save in eastern North America and the north island of
New Zealand practically no primitive cultivation survived in
temperate latitudes when European explorers first came to
know the more remote parts of the earth.

The range of economic and social variation among cultivators
is greater than that among food-gatherers, and this variability
is not related in any simple way with the physical conditions.
It extends not only to the nature of the crops grown and the
technical methods of production, but also to the social uses to
which the production is put and the political organization
developed therefrom, while the use of the plough and of
methods of renewing fertility obviously raises into a separate

category the more advanced agriculturists, among whom a far higher density of population is possible.

The cultivation of the simpler peoples is often referred to as migratory hoe tillage, but it is in the first place necessary to realize that some of them, under favourable physical conditions, are *not* migratory. Where annually flooded river plains are available for cultivation the silt borne by the inundations often suffices to maintain fertility for long periods. The Hopi, in whose fields the silt accumulation is slow and rather irregular, supplement it by a very wide spacing and alternation of their plants. Pueblo agriculture is not migratory: irrigation, whether by natural flood waters or by artificially constructed channels, demands a considerable degree of permanence in field sites, and migratory tillage is not characteristic of arid regions. It is, however, almost universally found where cultivation is dependent on direct precipitation alone. Surviving most extensively at the present day in the tropical savanas and forests of Africa, it is also found in the more remote parts of southern Asia and Indonesia as well as in the Pacific.

Further, many of these more primitive cultivators do not employ the hoe. Their tools are no more elaborate than the root-getting equipment of food-gatherers—a digging stick with which to make holes for the seeds and cuttings, and sometimes to break the clods, and occasionally a wooden blade to chop down the tops of weeds. The hoe, with which the surface of the plot can be completely if superficially dug, is practically confined to those areas in which a knowledge of iron working exists, and is limited to Africa and Asia. The stone and shell adzes of Oceania are not agricultural implements, while the so-called hoes of animal blade bone used in eastern North America are of service only in hilling up the loose surface soil round plants. They could not be used to break the ground. It must not be assumed that the hoe was everywhere unknown before the introduction of metals. While maize can be planted in drilled holes, hoeing of some kind is essential for the broadcast sowing of the Old World cereals, wheat and barley, which are of great antiquity. Less efficient stone bladed hoes almost certainly preceded metal ones in the early centres of agriculture in the Old World; they have, however, been nearly everywhere superseded by iron tools. On the outer fringes of cultivation in Oceania—with its exclusive concentration on roots and fruits—the hoe, if introduced, failed to be generally adopted, while in the New World it was apparently unknown.

In the tropical forests, apart from modern and mostly European introductions, the cultivation of roots and the

tending of fruit trees is dominant. The millets in the Ol
World and maize in the New are the only old-establishe
grains in lowland forest country, and can both, on botanic
evidence, be safely regarded as intruders. The millets are eas
crops for the forest cultivators since they are relatively insens
tive to changes in temperature and available moisture. In th
forests they have, however, like maize from the New Worl
been introduced from without, and have everywhere failed to di
place the dominant roots. Some of the relations between mill
and root cultivation in Africa have already been briefly discusse

The cultivation of roots and fruit trees has little technic
relation to the raising of grains, for they are not grown fro
seed but from eyes and cuttings. The produce of tropical ro
and fruit cultivation where there is no prolonged drought is n
concentrated sharply in a short harvest season: yams, ta
and manioc can be dug for the greater part of the year, wh
individual coconuts and breadfruit, pineapples and other frui
are almost continually coming to fruition. The storage
agricultural produce for long periods is therefore unnecessar
save where large accumulations are required for social pu
poses. Grain growing, on the other hand, has a strong
seasonal character. Where cultivation is undertaken in are
in which for reasons of drought, cold or river flood, there
only one planting a year, the harvest of a few weeks has
maintain the community for the entire year. This circun
stance imposed by the character of the habitat finds its parall
among gathering peoples in similar areas; the Hopi store co
as the Paiute grass seeds, and since they are more depende
on the corn and would scorn to eke out the winter and spri
on pine nuts, must accumulate it in relatively large quantitie
Those cultivators in areas with long seasonal droughts or co
winters, who are mostly grain growers, must store food like th
food-gatherers in parallel regions. The root cultivators
equatorial forests need store but little more than the Seman
and in the case of the Boro actually store almost nothing.

It is not possible to regard the root and fruit cultivators
tropical forests as forming an economic category within whi
a fairly uniform level of general civilization, distinct from th
of the grain-growing peoples, is achieved. The contras
between the peoples of the Amazon Basin, of Oceania and
tropical Africa will have been sufficiently apparent. The sk
and attention devoted to crop production in forest Africa a
Polynesia would appear to be generally lacking in equatori
South America and in some parts of Melanesia. This range
cultural achievement can be matched among millet cultivato

Africa and maize-growing peoples in America. The general vel of culture, both economic and political, among the higher vilizations of the New World did not, apart from achievement architecture, excel that of the great negro States of the uinea coast.

Cultivation may replace almost entirely or in part the digging wild roots and the collection of seeds and fruits, but it does t of necessity curtail hunting and fishing. Where the women ltivate the men may be entirely free for these pursuits. In ceania, although cultivation was shared by both men and omen, fishing remains an equally important economic pursuit, hich among the ruling classes of central Polynesia had far gher prestige than agriculture. The noblest chief in Tahiti ould direct and take part in fishing expeditions, but he had) direct connexion with agriculture.

Where, however, cultivation is more intensive and is adopted a male task, hunting and fishing decline in importance or e relegated to specialists. The Yoruba have afforded a good stance of this situation; with increase of population depen- nt on an assiduous root cultivation, the bush has been so tensively cleared that there is little game over the greater irt of their country. The ordinary man is occupied con- nuously with his fields and does not hunt, while fishing, even the riverine villages, is largely a specialized activity. Never- ieless, although the Yoruba and other West Africans are voted farmers, the gathering of wild products has not com- etely disappeared, and one of their most important staples, ilm oil, is gathered entirely from wild trees.

With plough cultivation farming tends to absorb a still eater proportion of the energy of the community and to duce their need and opportunity for gathering and hunting. he coconut and areca palms and the breadfruit trees, so often eated as semi-wild in Melanesia, are in Cochin carefully nded, and more often deliberately planted. Game is prac- cally non-existent on the closely settled plains, and fishing one remains important as an auxiliary source of food.

A limited use of domestic animals as a source of animal od-supply, replacing wild game, is found among the lower ltivators in the Old World. Generally, however, far less tention is devoted to increasing and improving the quality these resources than to the products of cultivation. The mestic animals are indeed often of ritual rather than economic iportance; the pigs of the Melanesians and the goats and wls of the Yoruba are a meagre supplement to a dominantly getarian diet.

Among plough cultivators where an entirely new use f₀
domestic animals is found—that of draught—their value ₐ
food is often not fully exploited. This situation is characte
istic throughout India and China, in the one case associat₀
with a number of definite religious prohibitions and in th
other with an aversion for nearly all meat but that of th
scavenging pigs and fowls. The resistance of the norther
Chinese to the adoption of the pastoral patterns of the nomad
peoples on their northern fringes—especially to the eating ₒ
beef and dairy products—is a remarkable instance in point.

In the New World domestic animals were of no importanc
in the food-supply outside the central Andean region in whic
the llama was reared. This animal, related to the wild guanac₀
had been completely domesticated long before the Spanis
conquest; it afforded meat as well as wool, besides being use
as a pack animal. Large herds were pastured in the area ₒ
Inca civilization, and they were reared in smaller numbers b
marginal peoples to the north and on the central Chilean coas

In the Old World the combination of agricultural an
pastoral activities in a single economy is, outside the highe
civilizations of the Ancient East and the West, largely confine
to the African grasslands. For herding these undoubtedl
offered favourable conditions. But stock raising here, as wi
be seen later, is less a concurrent development than a super
position of cattle rearing on an older hoe cultivation in whic
goats and sheep alone may have been kept in small numbers
The dominance and prestige of pastoral peoples have invest₀
cattle breeding with a religious significance, and herds far i
excess of economic need and with very limited use for food
supply. are maintained. Cultivation over much of easter
Africa south of the Equator is women's work, and stock raisin
has largely replaced hunting as the male pursuit. This dua
economy is, however, restricted to the savanas and, in th
rearing of horned cattle, a consideration of real importance i
the unfavourable character of dense forest country for herbi
vorous live stock. Horned cattle are virtually excluded from
the wetter African tropics by their liability to fly-borne disease
while in monsoon forest the grazing is of very poor quality.
Sheep and goats, although not native to the tropical forests, are
reared in small numbers by most of the African cultivators
and dogs are occasionally bred for food, but the greater pro
portion of the meat is provided by hunting. The pig, which i
a forest animal and lives on roots, fruits and shoots, and the
fowl, originally native to the forests of south-eastern Asia, fall
into a different category, and both have been adopted by the

forest cultivators, although pig rearing is little developed in Africa.

There are great differences in the development of crafts. With their few and poor stone tools wood-working is very inferior among the Boro, despite the fact that they build surprisingly large communal houses, while the finest constructional achievement of any people lacking metals is to be found in Polynesia. Specialized tools of stone, shell and bone are here employed by skilled professional craftsmen in the production of elaborate and beautiful canoes, houses and utensils. The marked difference between Polynesia and Melanesia in this respect exemplifies the great gap that can exist between peoples in similar habitats and with a basically similar economy. The Polynesian standards of craftsmanship, perhaps largely dependent on later cultural introductions from the Asiatic mainland, are generally unknown in Melanesia; where the gap is bridged in Fiji it can be safely ascribed to Polynesian influence. The plank boats of parts of the Solomons are exceptional in Melanesia, and are more reasonably to be regarded as due to an alien influence rather than as a local development.

Weaving is found among the lower cultivators on the fringes of higher civilizations. In grasslands, and even in arid regions, it is favoured by the opportunity for growing textile material itself or for gathering the fibrous parts of wild plants and trees. The relations with the North African and Mediterranean areas of higher civilization implied by cotton growing and weaving in the western Sudan and those of the Pueblos and some other cultivators of the south-west with southern Mexico, illustrate such extensions and the diffusion involved. Weaving is not, however, uniformly distributed among cultivators in accordance with habitat conditions suitable for cultivated or wild plants which would provide suitable fibres. It is absent in the grassland country of eastern Africa, over the greater part of which, had cotton been known or appreciated as a textile material, it could readily have been grown.

Weaving has not generally reached or been adopted by the forest cultivators either in Africa or south-eastern Asia. The Yoruba, who grow cotton in the northern part of their territory, are an exception, and their weaving shows both in technique and in the raw materials used that the craft is an introduction from the north. The general absence of weaving in the forest areas is probably due to a number of interacting factors. Apart from the degree of remoteness and the difficult nature of the country, there is little need for clothing; the inner bark of a number of trees can be beaten out into a fairly durable wrapping. The making of bark cloth appears to be of great antiquity, as it is of very wide extension and once established would tend to inhibit the adoption of weaving. Moreover, there is often a lack of native fibres with which to replace those available to the grassland peoples.

Pottery is more widespread, both in the New World and the Old. Its geographical distribution is nearly everywhere as wide as that of cultivation, and, sporadically, it has extended farther, as among the Yokuts and some Paiute in western America and among some of the southern Bushmen. The potter's wheel is, however, hardly ever found among the lower cultivators. In the New World this instrument for the more rapid and symmetrical production of pottery was entirely unknown. In the Old World, on the other hand, it must be credited with a great antiquity, for wheel-made pottery more than five thousand years old has been recovered from the earliest cities in lower Mesopotamia. Among the settled plough cultivating peoples wheel-made pottery is universal, and the very simple form of the wheel used in Cochin has been described. For the failure of the potter's wheel to reach the lower cultivators of the Old World the relatively small demand for pots at any one time, the general absence of specialization in communities where the majority of women are their own potters, and the sporadic character of trading in such wares, might generally be adduced. It is, however, surprising that it failed to reach the densely populated West African states, in which there was considerable specialization of crafts, while the Melanesians of the Gulf of Papua afford examples of communities which trade hand-made pottery on a considerable scale over a wide area. Such a condition, although it might produce receptivity to the introduction of the potter's wheel, does not of itself lead to the local invention of the device.

The cultivating peoples of Asia and Africa have nearly all of them an advantage over those of Oceania and the New World in the possession of iron tools. The smithing, if not the smelting, of iron is found nearly everywhere in the Old World among both agricultural and pastoral peoples and extends as far as eastern Cape Colony and the western coast lands of New Guinea. Iron knives, sickles, and in most areas hoes, facilitate the work of cultivation, while iron weapons and utensils are of great value in other phases of economic life.

It is well known that the use of iron developed later than that of copper and bronze in the history of civilization, but no people in the Old World has depended on copper or bronze as a primary material for metal working in recent times and most of the lower cultivators and pastoralists are ignorant of their manufacture. The production and working of iron has spread more widely than that of copper and has ousted it as the main material of the metal worker. In Africa, bronze and brass working is undertaken almost entirely for ornamental purposes rather than for the production of tools and utensils. Its manufacture and use here may well be considerably more recent than that of iron. The only copper and bronze users who were, when first known to Europeans, ignorant of iron were the peoples of the higher civilizations of middle America from southern Mexico to Peru.

The use of copper, at first for ornaments and small implements such as needles, appears very early in the oldest agricultural settlements in the Ancient East. Bronze was being manufactured on a large scale in Sumer before 3000 B.C., and the art of core casting was highly developed. But iron does not begin to replace these metals as the material for implements in the Near East until nearly two thousand years later. It is at first sight difficult to understand why this should be so. Iron ores are more abundant and widespread and often more accessible than copper and far more so than the tin also necessary for making the alloy bronze; iron can be reduced at even lower temperatures than copper. Despite its deterioration by rust if exposed and neglected, iron has many and obvious advantages over bronze. It is stronger and yet more elastic. It will take and keep a finer cutting edge. The reason undoubtedly is that the working of iron awaited a series of experiments and discoveries quite distinct from those habitually employed in the smelting of copper and tin. To understand this it is necessary to view the processes of iron smelting from the point of view of a coppersmith. It has already been seen that native copper, although not abundant from a modern point of view, occurs fairly frequently and has in a number of areas been hammered into useful tools. Some copper ores often have a promisingly metallic appearance before smelting but, still more important, when the coppersmith has placed his ore in an open furnace he is rewarded with a flow of molten metal practically ready for use. Throughout two millennia or more the burning of certain kinds of stone in a furnace to produce a reddish metal had become a fixed pattern. Experiments—both deliberate and unintentional—may have been and probably were made with other likely 'stones', but they yielded no flow of metal. To a coppersmith the smelting of iron ore would appear a complete failure—it would result in a spongy mass of fused stone full of air-holes and as unmetallic a product as could be imagined, for the small, pasty globules of iron would be embedded and concealed in the mass of slag and cinders. Fire it as he would no coherent mass of metal would emerge. Hammered cold it merely fractured, while no quickly appreciable result came from hammering it when still hot. The great centres of bronze working in the Ancient East, with their specialized smelting and smithing methods, offered neither good chances for lucky accidents with iron ore, nor rewards to deliberate experiment along traditional lines.

Nevertheless, iron objects were made and used during these times. The number of such objects so far discovered is infinitesimal in comparison with the finds of copper and bronze, but they are quite definite. A few iron beads that must be dated well before 3000 B.C. were found with predynastic objects in Middle Egypt. A few iron objects have been found in the Sumerian city of Ur (c. 3000 B.C.), while very recently a bronze dagger handle, found at Khafaje, a Mesopotamian settlement near Baghdad, occupied probably before 3000 B.C., shows traces of the rust of an iron dagger tang. At Knossus in Crete (c. 1800 B.C.), in the tomb of Tutankhamen (c. 1350 B.C.), and at a few other sites in Egypt, early iron objects have been discovered. In Babylonia in the time of Hammurabi (2000 B.C.) iron was known as a rare and valuable substance, and it had fifteen or twenty times the value of copper. Nearly all of the few early iron objects recovered are ornaments, not tools. Iron was for a long time a rare metal, and both the rarity and the ornamental use indicate fairly clearly that there was not at these times any established technique for smelting the abundant oxides of iron. It is therefore legitimate to conclude that most, if not all, of these objects were made by working iron found in a metallic state. The iron of the Khafaje dagger is, however, of neither meteoric nor telluric origin. Very small nodules of iron might have been occasionally observed and recovered from the slag of copper furnaces in which, as might well happen, had been smelted an ore containing both copper and iron. But natural metallic iron, although rare, is no rarer than the frequency of these finds would suggest, for it can occasionally be picked up on the ground surface in fallen meteorites. The meteoric origin of the iron in these early objects—betrayed by the nickel content—has been proven in several cases where analysis has been possible.

But from the middle of the thirteenth century B.C. iron rapidly becomes far more abundant throughout the Ancient

East. Tools and weapons are made from it, and within three centuries important manufacturing centres have sprung up in many cities between the Levant and the Persian Gulf. The Iron Age was definitely established. The occasion, date and even the place of the first advances are by no means precisely known, but it is clear that at some time shortly before 1300 B.C. the essential discovery was made that metallic iron could, by a new technique, be obtained in large quantities from certain abundant rocks.

The successful smelting of iron ore does not demand a hotter furnace than that required for reducing copper ores, but it does require a larger and more continuous body of heat and a suitable flux with which the impurities of the ore can combine. A larger furnace and a more powerful blast are therefore necessary to maintain the smelting process.[1] Furthermore, the product of a primitive furnace must be subjected to a far more prolonged hammering at red heat than was customary among copper workers, in order to beat out the slag and cinders and to consolidate the metallic mass.

Both the directions in which the new iron objects and later the new process itself spread, and the classical traditions of the beginnings of iron working afford some evidence of the time and place of discovery. In southern Syria iron hoes and sickles came into use before 1200 B.C., and shortly after this the Egyptian Pharaoh was importing iron objects. From 1100 B.C. onwards iron weapons are referred to in Assyrian inscriptions. It is clear from the Egyptian records that in this first period a virtual monopoly of this new manufacture was held by the Hittites of north-eastern Asia Minor, from whom the Pharaoh solicited further consignments of iron goods. Greek tradition coincides with these facts in ascribing the beginnings of iron working to the eastern Chalybes, who lived in the foothills of the Caucasus and continued to be renowned for their iron work in Classical times. By the middle of the thirteenth century B.C. Hittite iron working was already in an advanced state and developed on a fairly large scale, so that the new metal had probably been produced from ores for a century or more in some part of north-eastern Anatolia or the southern Caucasus. By 1200 B.C. local smelting was developing in western Anatolia, Cyprus and Syria, and iron copies of bronze swords appeared in Greece. By the ninth century iron working was probably established in Egypt and Assyria and iron tools

[1] The use of bellows, as distinct from simple tubes blown by the mouth, is not shown in Egyptian wall paintings of metal working until the middle of the second millennium. It may, however, be considerably older in other areas where the technique of metal working was more advanced.

became fairly abundant. Iron had also, by this time, reached southern Italy, whence it spread north by stages into central Europe, where independent centres of iron manufacture were established by about 750 B.C. It is, however, important to realize that for some purposes iron long remained inferior to bronze. Where the furnaces were not hot enough to cause some carbon to combine with the iron and so produce a low carbon steel, weapons and utensils could not be hardened by quenching in water. Although this device was known before classical times in Greece it would be effective only with steely iron. Even in the Dark Ages swords often bent in battle and had to be straightened underfoot. To produce iron objects as tough as bronze demanded an advanced technique or a manganiferous ore.

The archaeological evidence from the Near East is by now sufficiently extensive to refute the once popular hypothesis that iron working was a discovery of negro Africa which spread north into the Ancient World. The earliest evidence of iron working in Nubia is found in the heaps of iron slag in the Egyptian provincial town Meroe which are not older than 700 B.C. The craft of the African smith has undoubtedly spread slowly southwards from people to people in the period that has since elapsed. The use of copper and bronze appears never to have crossed the Sahara in pre-iron days, so that the peoples of Africa first learnt of metals with the introduction of iron working. The production of iron everywhere in the Old World almost certainly derives from a single Near Eastern centre in which the essential discoveries and inventions were made during the latter part of the second millennium B.C.

That the Oceanians, with very few exceptions, lack weaving and pottery as well as any use of metal, although some of these crafts are known to most of the lower cultivators, serves as a reminder that highly developed craftsmanship in certain directions and a considerable degree of social elaboration are neither dependent on nor productive of a wide range of fundamental crafts. It is clear that lack of certain crafts may restrict the scope of material civilization, but it is equally obvious that such a lack does not automatically relegate the culture to a low plane. A mere enumeration of the presence or absence of crafts and comparisons based on this cannot serve to indicate the relative qualities of culture.

In the absence of ores there was no opportunity for the working of metals in Oceania, but reasons for the absence of pottery and weaving crafts in Polynesia are difficult to assess definitely. The limited resources may again be largely responsible, though pottery is made in a few areas, while in parts of Melanesia at least it was made by earlier settlements in places where it is no longer known to-day. Weaving is general in Micronesia, but has spread only to a few Melanesian and west Polynesian islands. The effects of long and sometimes rapid migrations and the great distances between island groups may be in part responsible for the difficulty of introducing new crafts or their rapid loss. But it must not be forgotten that several food plants and domestic animals were brought into Oceania and were successfully carried to nearly every corner of the Polynesian world. It is possible that bark cloth, the skilful use of wood and the stone oven, so well adapted to the climate and food resources, militated against the adoption or survival of pottery in the area just as bark cloth would reduce the receptivity to weaving.

At the one end of the social range the hand cultivating peoples are grouped in communities smaller and less complex than those of the more successful food-gatherers. On the other hand, states with populations of a million and more have been successfully organized. The settlements of the Yuma on the Lower Colorado were probably never as large or stable as the larger villages on the Northwest Coast which indeed, in a very different way, rivalled the Pueblos in size of population and in complexity of social and ritual organization. But under favourable conditions cultivators with their greater and more assured food-supply for a given unit of territory are able to proceed much further in social and political elaboration. In short, the variation is greater by extension at the higher end, and a higher proportion of cultivators is organized in large communities and states with a formal political organization. Most living examples must now be drawn from Africa, but in the sixteenth century native states of great size were to be found in Central America and in the Peruvian Andes.

The regulation of land-holding among cultivators ranges from communal conditions substantially similar to those obtaining among many food-gatherers, to the development of feudal tenures and private property. The local village territory of the Boro or Melanesians, and even of the Yoruba, is in one sense as communal as the lands of a collecting group. With migratory tillage and brush clearing, ownership of the land itself, save in the sense of group control of the territory as a whole, has in general little value. Good land promising a rich reward is undoubtedly appreciated in advance, but there is nearly always an abundance of such land within the territory for all the labour available; it is the actual work of clearing and cultivating that is of great significance. To cleared and productive land there are nearly always individual or family rights. A single plot can be used for several seasons, and a particular area may have special convenience for a household or association with a particular group of kinsmen. In Melanesia it would appear very common for a kin group of several families to have the more or less exclusive cultivation of a definite tract of bush; for others to intrude on it would be unneighbourly. Unfortunately there are no detailed records covering a period of years concerning any of these peoples that would make it clear how far families or kin groups actually do lay claim to tracts of land and retain them for many years during which their cultivation oscillates to and fro allowing periods of recuperation to individual plots. Among the Yoruba magical beliefs and religious sentiments associated with land occupation would, as has been shown, seem to give fairly definite fixity of tenure, including that over land which is recuperating after a period of cultivation. The injunction against occupying land showing evidence of former cultivation in the shape of fences, store huts and so on, embodies customary precept. There is no formal system of renting and leasing land, but the existence of slavery here and elsewhere in Africa does lead to the partial development of estates, and dependants who make regular gifts to the powerful family which guards their rights are in a sense tenants at will. Since, however, trade in agricultural products is limited in its scope, slave cultivators merely relieve their masters of part of the labour of cultivation and provide for the needs of his household. They do not appear, moreover, to be debarred by their slavery from clearing land of their own.

The native land systems of central Polynesia had so largely passed away before detailed investigations were made that their precise character will never perhaps be known, but there does appear to have been a considerable development of manorial estates in the hands of a landed nobility, sometimes paramount, sometimes in both political and economic dependence on a higher chief. The landowners of Tahiti had, it seemed, a lien on the produce of their cultivators, but the detailed manner of their control remains obscure. Since, however, the cultivation, although probably more stable than in Melanesia, involved the frequent clearing of new plots and irrigated beds, the control may have been over a territory as a whole and over the services of the cultivators within it rather than over particular fields.

Under plough cultivation and manuring, however, agricultural land acquires a very different value. With relatively short fallow periods and rotation of crops good land can be maintained in cultivation indefinitely and can feed considerably more people than those required to till it. A large number of specialists in non-agricultural crafts, and others who are agriculturally non-productive, can thus be maintained. Private or family ownership of rigidly delimited fields thus becomes an economic asset of great value in any society which permits the landowner, as distinct from the cultivator, to claim the surplus and thereby enjoy leisure and command the services of craftsmen. The native agriculture and society of Cochin have provided, in an area extremely productive according to the standards of simple plough cultivation, an illustration of the economic specialization and social differentiation that becomes possible. The rich reward in crops from the plough cultivation of ricelands supports a dense population among whom the fruits of cultivation are distributed by a system of feudal tenures, leases and tenancies formerly combined with slavery.

Plough cultivation is nearly everywhere associated with much knowledge and considerable equipment, in addition to the use of the plough itself. These include the use of water-lifting devices such as the *shaduf*, the *picotah* of India and the Persian wheel, the regular use of manures—vegetable, fish, animal and also, in eastern Asia, human excrement. With the plough is found crop rotation and an appreciation of the value of pulses as restorers of the nitrogen content of the soil which is depleted by cultivation of cereals.[1] The ripe grain is trodden out by animals or threshed by driving over it wooden sleds, sometimes studded with chipped stone blades, as was the Roman tribulum. All these and many other details of agricultural practice are unknown to the lower cultivators.

The plough itself is not, however, the *sine qua non* of more advanced agriculture. In some parts of eastern Asia it is of little importance and may even find no use at all. Where rice-fields are built in terraces on steep hillsides, as in some parts of southern China, Java and the Philippine Islands, or where every inch of available land is divided into minute rice plots as in the small plains of southern Japan, cultivation is undertaken almost entirely by hand.

In this connexion the hill-terrace rice cultivators of the mountainous interior of Luzon in the Philippine Archipelago

[1] This frequent planting of beans between the rows of corn in aboriginal North America may indicate an unformulated appreciation of the same fact. No such idea is, however, expressed by the Hopi and I have been unable to find any other consideration of the matter.

should be considered. These people, particularly the Igorot and the Ifugao, are extremely skilled cultivators. The narrow man-made terraces, some of them having boulder-faced retaining walls thirty feet high, are carried up hillsides in tier after tier for many hundreds of feet. Streams and considerable rivers are dammed to divert their waters into canals, which are, in favourable localities, carried for miles along the hillsides, bridging ravines and other rivers in wooden troughs. A typical Igorot village of five hundred to a thousand inhabitants is surrounded by hundreds of acres of riceland. Nevertheless these peoples have no knowledge of the plough, although they possess domestic cattle which could be of service as draught animals and also in the cultivation of the lowland fields which are devoted to root crops and millet, and actually provide a rather higher proportion of the food-supply than do the irrigated rice terraces. In the actual breaking up of the soil they remain low cultivators, for it is merely loosened and turned with long wooden paddles—a slightly elaborated digging stick. Moreover, although their irrigation is very developed, they do not possess any of the water-lifting devices known to the paddy growers of the Asiatic mainland. Where no channel reaches a plot water is laboriously carried in small hand-made pots. Although iron is smelted and forged into knives and spears and small ornaments, no iron tools are used in cultivation.

In social and political organization and general culture they are closer to an African forest people than to the peoples of India or China. The villages are autonomous units, each with its own lands. Slavery existed until recently, but every household cultivates for itself and land is not rented or sold. A large household of related families with many plots of cultivated lands is wealthier than its fellows, while the men of poor villages work for a season at a time for the wealthy owners of numerous rice and sweet potato plots in neighbouring territories. But there is no division into landowners and landless. Even the poorest who have no rice-fields yet possess unirrigated plots in which sweet potatoes and millets can be grown. Both in their technique of cultivation and in their political and social organization these people stand midway between the hand cultivators and the plough cultivators of southern and eastern Asia. Whatever the history of their agricultural and social development, their economy and organization are very significant.

It is legitimate to regard the higher agriculture of the Old World as a complex of activities involving in general a more or less standard equipment (including such elements as the plough, beasts of burden, water lifts and iron sickles), a basic economic pattern of individual land ownership with the leasing or rental of property, and a political organization characterized by a ruling land-owning class at one end and landless serfs at the other. But it must at the same time be recognized that in some areas some elements of this complex have been established where others were never introduced or failed to take root. The rice growers of the interior Philippine Archipelago, remote from the Asiatic mainland, and a few Indonesian peoples afford instances of this partial diffusion.

CHAPTER XX

PASTORALISM

I N Part III a number of pastoral peoples were considered. Ranging in their situations from the Equator to the Arctic Circle and depending primarily on very different animals put to varying uses, they have afforded a view of the wide variety of physical, economic and social conditions implied by the general term 'pastoralism'. Pastoralism as a dominant economy has been developed only in the Old World. It is true that domestic varieties of the native 'camel' (guanaco and vicuña) of South America were reared in large herds in the higher civilization of the Andean plateaux, but live stock was there an auxiliary and integral part of a developed agricultural and sedentary civilization. The flesh of the llama (the domesticated guanaco) was eaten to a certain extent, but this animal served mainly to carry burdens in large trains, while the alpaca (the domesticated vicuña) was kept only for its wool. No autonomous or semi-independent communities of herders were found either within or beyond the orbit of the native Peruvian civilization. The only truly pastoral people in the New World are the Navajo of the North American Southwest, and their present economy has been developed subsequent to and consequent on the Spanish introduction of sheep and horses, already completely domesticated and associated with fixed patterns or uses. The Navajo are indeed of great interest, for they afford an instance of the transformation of a hunting and collecting people into pastoralists within a known period of time and as a result of known factors. The Navajo use their live stock for some of the purposes to which they were put by the Spanish with whom they came in contact. Of new uses (such as, for example, the milking of sheep) they have discovered none. They illustrate within recent times a happening which must have occurred many times in the history of the Old World, and their pastoralism is a transplanted variant of the Old World economy of horsemen herding sheep. It is important to realize in this connexion that the Navajo who graze their stock on the scanty pastures and scrub of the semi-arid mesas and river basins of the Southwest, were not nstructed in their economy by any other dominantly pastoral people, and that from their contacts with the Spanish with heir complex economy, they selected only certain stock-breeding elements. They adopted neither cattle, unsuited to heir arid territory, nor wheeled carts, which were too complex or a stone age community.

In the Old World live stock are and have long been raised n the higher sedentary civilizations of south-western Asia nd Europe, for the same purposes for which they are valued y many purely pastoral peoples: for their meat, their hides, heir milk and the products that can be derived from them. Their further important use in the higher civilizations is also ound among some of the Asiatic pastoralists, namely, their se as beasts of burden or even of draught. But since pastoralists seldom cultivate they are rarely put to the plough.

The distribution of pastoralism in the Old World is clearly elated to a group of natural regions with certain common haracteristics, and it is almost completely absent in other ypes of region. The pastoral regions range from the tundra n the one hand through rich upland and forest margin grasslands on the other, across severely arid deserts into tropical avanas of tall grass on the equatorial margins of these eserts. Equally obvious is the exclusion of pastoralism from orest country, both tropical and temperate, although there s an exception to this in the coniferous forests of northern sia, parts of which are, at least seasonally, occupied by reindeer-herding peoples. These associations have both positive nd negative aspects. In the first place, semi-arid regions, ogether with the high latitude prairies and the high altitude lps', present serious difficulties to cultivators. Crops are ifficult if not impossible to raise on account of the lack and ncertainty of rain or the shortness of the season. The preparation in advance of drought-resistant or short-season varieties f cultivated plants is but a recent achievement of Western ivilization. Such varieties have indeed been developed by ore primitive peoples, as the corn and the cotton of the Hopi lustrate, but only by slow and persistent penetration of nfavourable regions and at the cost of many setbacks. In e arid belts, away from great irrigable river basins, cultiation, where achieved, is restricted to relatively small patches f ground in which the watering of plants, whether natural or rtificial, from rivers, seeps or wells, mitigates the natural ridity. In high latitudes crops will ripen only on sheltered nny slopes. In both types of country the area that can be evoted to cultivation is small in proportion to that over

which domesticated herds can be pastured, albeit that a compac
cultivating settlement may have as dense a population as a
herding community depending on hundreds of square mile
of poor pasture.

Some communities in these regions divide their labour
between cultivation along the margins of streams and spring
and the herding of live stock in the surrounding poor pasture
The Hadendoa and other groups in the desert to the east o
the middle Nile sow millet in the *wadis* before the spring floods
scatter with their sheep and goats over the scanty pasture
during the summer and return in the fall of the year to gathe
in the crop. Many Kazak and Kirghiz communities, as ha
been seen, retain patches of artificially irrigated riverine lan
which are cultivated by some members of the community wh
remain on them throughout the summer.

In Central Persia occupants of the more difficult countr
frequently winter in permanent villages around lowlan
pastures. Here they maintain groves of fruit trees, and i
the spring they also sow crops of millets and barley. Befor
the heat of summer, when the grasses at lower levels shrive
the greater part of the community migrates to the mountair
with its sheep, goats and cattle, and even chickens, to live i
upland camps where grass for the live stock is still abundar
and green.

This seasonal migration from winter to summer quarter
for the benefit of live stock among the more advanced peopl
in semi-arid or mountainous areas, was formerly widesprea
in southern Europe, and is generally referred to as *transhuman*
from the term used in Spain where it was until quite recer
years exceptionally well developed.

The second aspect of this distribution, namely, the gener
exclusion of pastoralism from well-watered and especial
forested areas, follows from two essential conditions. In th
first place, the large herbivorous animals on which pastoralis
mainly depends are not suited to forest country. In tropic
forests they suffer severely from disease, and in Africa th
tsetse fly virtually excludes cattle[1] under aboriginal condition
The temperate forests are, unless extensively cleared, almo
equally devoid of good pasture, and this is particularly tr
of the coniferous forests of the colder areas. Cattle are, it

---

[1] The English language unfortunately lacks an inclusive unambiguous te
for cows, bulls, bullocks and calves. The term oxen is liable to be interpret
as gelded beasts used for draught, while cattle is often used as an equivale
for live stock. The word cattle will, however, be used here to signify 'horn
cattle' alone, i.e. the aforesaid cows, bulls, etc., and live stock will conne
domestic herbivores of all species.

ue, probably descended from woodland ancestors, but they
re not suited to dense forest and damp conditions, and the
striction of the growth of grasses and the difficulties of
ovement consequent on the dense cover of trees and under-
owth render such areas of little value to peoples whose object
is to raise large numbers of animals and to move them as a
dy from place to place. Furthermore, the reward of cultiva-
on in well-watered areas, where suitable crops are available,
far higher than that of stock breeding. To convert the natural
ant growth of an area into animal food before consuming it
always less economic than to modify that growth by cultiva-
on so that it can be consumed directly.

In only a few areas has the knowledge of stock raising existed
yond the limits of the *knowledge* of cultivation. None of the
storal peoples of central and south-western Asia or of
rthern Africa are ignorant of the existence and even of the
neral methods of cultivation. The Hottentot of the south-
stern part of Africa and the reindeer breeders of the more
rthern parts of Siberia are exceptions, but in one case
riculture, save with the resources of modern civilization and
e introduction of foreign plants like the potato, is permanently
cluded by climatic conditions. In other words, any inde-
ndent pastoral economy in the more humid regions of the
d World exists in despite of knowledge on the part of the
ple themselves or of their neighbours that a richer reward
ld be obtained by cultivation. Such a situation has quite
en existed indeed, but only in consequence of the cultural
stige and often, above all, of the military superiority of the
storalists in a particular region and at a certain period. This,
has already been pointed out, is particularly well shown
the tropical grasslands of Africa. In some areas, as in the
sai territory in highland Kenya, the pastoralists, main-
ning the purity of their economy by religious sanctions and
oos, have at the same time by their superior military power
ven out cultivators from lands suitable for hoe tillage. It
however, to be noticed in this connexion that some of the
migrant pastoralists in this particular region have adopted
tivation, earning thereby the scorn of pure pastoralists and
 epithet *lumbwa*.

n other parts of the same general area the pastoralists,
ablishing themselves as an aristocracy (as among the
nyankole and Bakitara), have subjected and limited the
velopment of the cultivators. In the western Sudan a some-
at similar superposition has taken place, while in eastern
ica from the Equator to the eastern half of Cape Province,

pastoralism exists in a hybrid culture as a male economy
juxtaposition with female tillage. The eastern Bantu of th
vast region not only raise their herds wastefully and use the
ineffectively but at the same time limit their agricultural pr
duction by relegating practically all the work of cultivatio
to women. Although remote from any exclusively pastor
peoples in recent times the whole of this area has been dominate
by the rituals and religious concepts associated with catt
which appear to have developed farther north. The detaile
comparative study of this eastern Bantu region has yet to b
made, but there are many indications that the complex patter
of ritual and belief concerning cattle developed among soutl
ward-moving pastoral peoples, by the integration and harde
ing of their customs when they were in contact and were ofte
displacing cultivators. Among the Baganda alone in almos
all Africa has a balanced and effective fusion between agr
cultural and pastoral activities been achieved.

The animals raised by pastoralists and the uses to whic
they are put will obviously not be the same over the who
of this vast area, which extends from the Cape of Good Hop
and Cape Verde to the Chuckchi Peninsula. There is, howeve
no rigid connexion between the nature of the stock and th
uses to which it is put. One can speak in general terms o
camel herders, cattle breeders, sheep herders and reinde
herders, but in fact the live stock rarely consists of but a sing
type even in cases of extreme specialization. The Masai hav
donkeys, the Badawîn horses and the Chuckchi dogs, althoug
with the last the second animal is not related to their pastoralisn
The animals raised change by slow gradation from region t
region. That these gradations show in general an adaptatio
to the physical conditions of the particular area and to th
natural habitat of the animals concerned is obvious, for th
use of valuable animals has tended to expand to the natur
limits of their utility.

The importance of the camel in the Sahara-Arabian regio
is obvious. The economy of the North Arabian Badawî
described in an earlier chapter extends south-west into Afric
Tribes similar in race, speech and social organization are foun
to the south and west over the semi-desert areas of the Sahar
as far as the Moroccan shores of the Atlantic. In the wester
Sahara their economy has also been adopted by Berber peopl
like the Tewarik (Tuareg) of Air and Hoggar. The Arab trib
in the Anglo-Egyptian Sudan have a particularly close relatio
to the Arabian Badawîn, and there is abundant evidenc
literary as well as ethnographic, to show that they reache

their present territory by westward migrations across the Red Sea or through Sinai and the western desert of Egypt. Farther east this camel breeding economy and much of the social pattern has been carried by Semitic-speaking herders almost to the limits of that desert belt for which they have so well fitted themselves.

The use of the camel is not, however, confined to hot deserts. The bactrian, or two-humped camel of Central Asia, finds a place in the economy of pastoralists all the way from the Caspian Sea to the Gulf of Chi-li on the borders of northern China. Among the central Asiatic nomads, however, its use is more restricted. It is rarely milked or kept in large herds, and although occasionally ridden it is almost solely a beast of burden. The settled peoples on the margin of the camel-herding areas use these animals extensively, although they rarely breed them. They are harnessed to the plough in such areas as Syria and the Tarim Basin, and trains of pack camels have for many centuries been used to transport goods from one market and region to another. The function of the herders as suppliers of camels to the sedentary peoples has often brought pastoralists in this great zone into a closer and more stable economic relation with the cultivators than elsewhere; this interdependence is, however, also related to physical conditions, for, as has been seen, the successful maintenance of herds in desert areas is dependent on an annual convergence on oases, while the sterility of the desert in all but animal products creates a great demand for the grain obtainable in the villages, riverine cities and oases.

The camel is, however, as has been said, only the pack animal of the continental deserts and steppelands of Asia. Sheep and horses are the most widespread food providers and the patterns associated with them have been illustrated in the study of the Kazak and the Khirghiz. Towards the forest margins in the north, where richer and more enduring pastures are available, cattle become increasingly important. The economy of the Altai Kalmuck, in which cattle are as important as horses, is reproduced in a more migratory form by Mongol tribes like the Buriat south of Lake Baikal, and the Tougourt of Zungaria. Within the coniferous forest and beyond it all these animals rapidly disappear and the reindeer is the essential live stock of the herdsman. In tropical Africa, south of the hot desert zone, less variety is found. Sheep and goats are minor and often rather neglected sources of food. Donkeys and camels are used as beasts of burden by the Danakil of Somaliland, the Galla of south-west Abyssinia and other peoples of the African Horn. But everywhere from the Upper Nile to the Cape of Good Hope cattle are the essential live stock in woodland, tall grass savana, scrub and mountain pasture.

The correlation of live stock with climatic and vegetational zones is, in detail, by no means precise or universal, and the desert Badawîn economy affords an example of the retention of an animal, the horse, under most unsuitable physical conditions. It may be contended that the horse is a luxury of the Badawîn, a consequence of their long and intimate contact with a higher civilization in which horse riding, especially for war, has long had great prestige. This is, of course, true, and peoples at a farther remove from the higher civilizations do not share the Badawîn esteem of the horse. The Tewarik, but recently elevated from the tending of sheep and goats to the rank of camel herders, have no horses and ride only camels.

But there are peoples who raise live stock in unfavourable habitats essentially for food. The best-known instance is perhaps afforded by the Yakut, a Turkic-speaking people who appear to have been until a few centuries ago cattle and horse herders on the steppes to the south-west of Lake Baikal. They were, however, forced to move north and east during a period of disturbance and expansion among their Mongol neighbours and they took their horses and cattle with them to the taiga-tundra borderland in the middle Lena basin. Many of them have to-day lost all this live stock and have adopted reindeer herding and, in more recent times under Russian influence, agriculture. But a minority still retain a cattle and horse-herding economy in this harsh environment; to keep their beasts alive they have to work feverishly during the short summer gathering in the short-lived grasses for hay; byres of timber covered with sods have to be built in the winter settlements to protect the animals during the long winter. Horses are even persuaded to take meat and fish as a considerable part of their diet, strange counterparts of the vegetarian dogs of Oceania! No horse can be used for riding longer than a month or two at a time, and different animals are used in summer and winter. Cattle have survived better than the horses, of which there are now very few. The Yakut have proceeded to saddle their cattle instead, but they still retain their horse sacrifice and kumiss festival, even though cows' milk must be used. Their reverence for the horse is undiminished.

The mere distribution of particular domestic animals or the enumeration of the stock possessed by a people does not, moreover, serve to indicate the character of pastoralism. The uses to which the same animals are put differ in the various regions, and these differences often hold good irrespective of the animals reared. The known uses to which domestic animals can be put by pastoral peoples are, briefly, first: the consumption of the meat, and occasionally the blood, and the use of the hides; to this extent they are merely tame 'game'; second, the use of hair and wool as a textile or felting material; third, the milking of the females, thus providing a source of food which does not necessitate the slaughter of the beasts and is unknown to food-gatherers and the lower cultivators, except of course in hybrid cultures such as are found in south-eastern Africa; fourth, the conversion of the milk into dairy products which can be conserved for considerable periods; fifth, the use of the animals as beasts of burden or even of draught; sixth, the riding of animals. To us all these well-known practices may appear obvious, but it is important to realize that many pastoralists are completely unaware of some or all of them excepting only the first.

In Africa, south of the Sahara, storable dairy products in the form of cheeses, curds and fermented milk are unknown, while butter is made only in small quantities and as an unguent, not a food. Among cultivating peoples on the forest margin of pastoralism the cattle are not even milked. They are used like the sheep and goats their herders have long possessed, only for meat and hides. Cattle are with few exceptions never used as beasts of burden in Africa, and in south-eastern Africa the eastern Bantu let their women, but not their cattle, carry burdens; they do not possess the donkey kept by the more northern cattle herders and used by them for this purpose. The sacred prohibitions associated with cattle in the north have passed south with that animal and so limit its use. The Hottentot, immune from the associated beliefs and customs have had no hesitation in using them in this way.

In eastern Africa south of Abyssinia riding is also unknown. The absence of the horse and camel is no complete reason for this, for Kazak herders and the Yakut ride bullocks, while the donkey, well known to the pastoralists of equatorial Africa, is ridden in the Mediterranean lands. The explanation undoubtedly lies in the fact that riding is closely associated with the horse and the camel, to which these peoples have never been introduced. Without contact with any riding peoples they have failed to discover the practice for themselves. The Masai, it is true, probably encountered Arab horse riders in the caravans which had penetrated their territory many years before the first Europeans arrived. But apparently only a horseman himself will display the wit, or rather feel the need, to mount a bullock when no other steed is available. In West Africa horse riding did penetrate the savanas at the time of the Islamic conquests, if not earlier, and the use of cavalry as a military weapon has, as has been seen, entered the forest and reached the Guinea coast among non-pastoral peoples like the Yoruba.

The east African uses of live stock are therefore very limited. Indeed, the religious prohibitions surrounding cattle do not even permit the eastern Bantu to make full use of them as food-supply, and they depend on game more than on live stock for their meat; the Dutch, when they established a colony at Capetown in the seventeenth century, were exceptionally fortunate in encountering the Hottentot, a people who would supply abundant, if tough, beef. Nearly everywhere else they would have had considerable difficulty. Even the Peruvians, while not technically pastoral people and ignorant of the practice of milking, nevertheless made good use of the strength, flesh, hides and wool of their llamas and alpacas. Only the most north-easterly reindeer herders of Asia show a more limited use of their live stock, and the situation in that area, which has already been discussed, indicates the importance of diffusion and transference of techniques in accounting for the uses to which live stock is put.

When we pass to Saharan Africa and to south-western and central Asia the pastoral pattern is more complete. The wool of sheep and the hair of goats and camels are woven in the south-west and also felted in central Asia. Rugs are made by elaborate knotting devices. All these are practices completely foreign to the transaharan pastoralists of Africa, where, it must be admitted, they would, in such hot climates, have had far less value. Milking is not confined to cattle, but is extended to horses, goats and sheep; butter, cheeses and fermented drinks are made. The camel herders are rather defective in this respect, but this is due to the properties of camel milk and the rarity of a milk surplus under severely arid conditions, rather than to a complete ignorance of dairying.

Camels, bullocks, and yaks are beasts of burden in central Asia, while horses are the essential riding animals. In the far north these animals are all, however, with few exceptions excluded and the reindeer becomes the sole animal of the pastoralist.

Before proceeding to the consideration of social patterns among pastoral peoples it is necessary to refer briefly to two aspects of pastoralism concerning which exaggerated views have been frequently expressed, namely, the stability and durability of pastoralism among particular peoples and the social and political relations between pastoralist and cultivator.

It has frequently been implied, in the first place, that the pastoralist, in consequence of the specialization and limitations of his economy, is indelibly stamped with psychological attitudes which render his conversion to a settled life extremely difficult. To a certain extent this is true, but it is no more true of the pastoralist than it is of the food-gatherer or the cultivator. To attempt to convert the Nootka or the Haida, or again the Boro or the Yoruba, into cattle herders at short notice would meet with equally poor success. Indeed, we have several very good instances in point. Domestic reindeer have been introduced among some of the Alaskan Eskimo, who were to be trained by Asiatic or Lapp herdsmen. For a long time the herds were neglected and slaughtered indiscriminately for food, and it was only after a considerable period of adaptation on the part of the Eskimo and the introduction of more Asiatic herdsmen who carefully supervised the stock, that the Eskimo were finally persuaded of the advantages of refraining from treating domestic reindeer as wild caribou. The Bergdama, a northern group of Bushmen in south-west Africa, have many of them become servants, if not serfs, of their northern neighbours the pastoral Herero. Although they cultivate sporadically and when among the Herero they herd their masters' cattle, they make little attempt to acquire live stock of their own. They may have watched animals being milked every day for several years, but any cattle they take back to their own settlements are killed for food within a very short time. Some of them have acquired small flocks of goats, but these are kept permanently on remote pastures in charge of a herdsman who takes all the milk. The owners want neither the risks of raids on their settlements nor the interference with hunting that the daily routine of herding entails.

In actual fact pastoralism is often a less stable economy than cultivation. In its more advanced forms it exists on the margins of sedentary areas, with which it has close economic ties. In many places it has existed in areas where agriculture could, if developed, support a denser and more prosperous population, and in such areas where the settled peoples have shown solidarity, or have been given security, the frontiers of agriculture have advanced and pastoralists have been incorporated in settled communities.

Reference has been made to the variable extent of camel and sheep pastoralism as opposed to cultivation in Arabia. There are also in the northern steppes of Syria peoples who are in the act of abandoning 'pastoralism' for 'agriculture'. Still living in black goat-hair tents they raise crops of millet and turn their sheep and camels out into the surrounding pastures under the care of a few herdsmen. The tent, unmoved for a considerable time, is made more snug with a wall of sods or sun-dried clay. Gradually it is abandoned altogether and flat-roofed mud houses like those of the neighbouring villages are built. These peoples have become, for those who have an eye only for types, 'sedentary cultivators with auxiliary herding'. Actually the transition is but a slow gain of one economy at the expense of another, and the point at which the house replaces the tent is but an incident in the process. Grain eating was there from the beginning, and the flock of sheep will remain to the end.

Many of the occupants of the Moroccan Tell live in tents and migrate, but are no longer 'pastoralists'. They keep only small flocks and farm land in several places in this upland country, cultivating their scattered plots one after another throughout the year. The tent is retained, for it still suits their frequent change of abode.

There are also many instances of pastoral Berber groups in the north-western Sahara who, having lost a large proportion of their herds to enemies, have become settlers in oases growing wheat and dates. That their later condition is, in material welfare, often inferior to their first, and that some of them have once more regained herds and resumed a nomadic pastoral life does not invalidate the reality of these changes. These facts merely serve to combat another common fallacy, that a nomadic life is always and by its nature inferior and less comfortable than a sedentary agricultural existence.

In discussing the Khirghiz it was pointed out that at a former period they engaged in agriculture on a considerable scale and now, even more than the Kazak, endeavour to maintain patches of cultivated and irrigated land to supply a small amount of cereals. It is very doubtful indeed whether any of the higher pastoralists of Asia, from the Badawîn to the Mongols of the Gobi, are completely non-agricultural, save where they have suffered adversity or are able to rely on fairly regular supplies of grain from the settled country.

There is little doubt that many pastoral peoples in Asia are to be regarded as denuded agriculturists—communities which have largely or entirely abandoned the raising of crops and have increased and concentrated on the herds of animals which they formerly kept only in small numbers. This process has been associated with unsettled political conditions or with immigration into areas in which agriculture was difficult or impossible as the main basis of subsistence.

Even where agriculture is completely excluded from the activities of a herding people their economy may be by no means exclusively pastoral, for hunting and gathering often remain important. Although hunting is largely a 'sport' among the Kazak and the Badawîn, the gathering of wild products by the women is quite important at certain periods. Among many of the African herding peoples whose 'miserly' attitude to their stock prevents them killing beasts for food, hunting is sometimes actually of greater importance as a source of food. The Tewarik, the Fula and the eastern Bantu are all great hunters of antelope, gazelle, giraffe and other game; their herds are regarded as milk givers and as indices of wealth and prestige. The animals are allowed to grow old, lean and decrepit but are never killed except for ceremonial uses and in real extremity.

The second generalization referred to above, namely, that since the needs and outlook of the pastoralist are alien to those of the cultivator, his attitude towards settled peoples is inveterately hostile and disruptive, also demands considerable qualification. That settled cultivating peoples of higher civilizations have in certain places and at certain times been at great pains to exclude and protect themselves from threatening pastoral peoples need not be denied. The Great Wall of China is a monument to the fact. But the Roman *limes* was also required to exclude barbarians who, for their period, were most efficient cultivators as well as stock breeders. It is not pastoralism and cultivation as such that face each other in hostility, but mobility with poverty as against sessile and vulnerable wealth. That the pastoral nomad who travels light mentally and aesthetically as well as materially may have little immediate appreciation for the intellectual and artistic superstructure that an advanced agricultural economy can support, is also manifest. But the advanced societies themselves, as we well know, are by no means immune from internecine bouts of destructiveness. Moreover, the great pastoral empires, when they have been more than names for a series of successful raids and extortions have, like those of the Mongols and of the Moslems, had a very solid basis of support and maintenance in the settled country. Nomadic peoples have attacked each other as frequently as and more persistently than they have raided settled country. Powerful groups have preyed on the herds of weaker pastoral communities. Masai raiding in East Africa was not directed towards the agricultural wealth of villages but to cattle herds, no matter who possessed them. The northward migration of the Yakut can reasonably be attributed to the attacks of other pastoral communities, while internal feuds and raids are characteristic of the Badawîn, the Kazak and the Kirghiz.

The pastoralist may often scorn cultivation and despise cultivators: such an attitude would be characteristic among the Masai or in a well-born Kazak; but it is often forgotten that this feeling would be reciprocated by a prosperous peasant in a Turkestan oasis and would probably be expressed by a Yoruba towards a Fula herdsman. The northern Chinese, although for centuries in close contact with Mongol pastoralists, have no more seen the glamour of a pastoral life than they have accepted the transferable elements of pastoral economy. When, as has happened, pastoral dynasties have succeeded in installing themselves as rulers they have been rapidly assimilated to the agricultural economy of the Chinese. The pastoralist's repugnance for agriculture and its practitioners is of the same order as an eighteenth-century gentleman's scorn for commerce. Where, for reasons to be discussed shortly, he can express it openly and even brutally, he does not hesitate to do so, but that of itself is no indication that any peculiar psychological factor is involved.

Nomadism is justifiably associated with a pastoral life, but its extent and character are very variable. Eternal wandering in which no spot is deliberately sought a second time is never found. Everywhere a unit community, whether it be a kin group, a larger clan or a whole tribe, has a fairly well-defined territory which it oversteps at its own risk just as invaders transgress it at theirs. Within that territory are more narrowly defined sites which are occupied for a considerable period each year. The Masai continually revisited and refurbished their main kraals. The winter sites of the Kazak with their sod huts were regarded as family property. It is only in symbiotic economies like that of some Badawîn that such foci appear to be absent. The villages of alien or tributary cultivators here take their place.

Moreover, the range of the seasonal movement is extremely variable. While some of the central Asiatic pastoralists, with superior organization and the great mobility made possible by the horse, cover several hundreds of miles regularly every year, they are not wedded to this wanderlust. Where as among the Altai Kalmuck rich and permanent pastures are available, a settlement is deserted only when the site has been fouled by the beasts.

But in times of adversity, after one or a series of very arid years or attacks of more powerful rivals, a pastoral people can and will desert its territory, seeking a less sterile or less dangerous home. They not only can but must, if their herds are not to be almost exterminated, find new pastures. So they may move as a whole people over a great distance within a short space of time. Furthermore, the appearance of an organizing genius can amalgamate, at least for a short time, a great many normally individualist tribes and so forge a weapon of great power against all but the best organized of sedentary peoples.

The essential point, so far as relations with cultivators are concerned, is that a pastoral people, especially if equipped with riding animals, has a superior mobility which, although it may at a given time be latent, is always there as an asset when there is opportunity for gain, and equally when there is need for retreat. Cultivating peoples cannot carry their food-supply with them at a moment's notice; their daily life is not like that of the more nomadic herders, a continuous rehearsal of campaign conditions. But they have achieved military conquests. The sedentary Baganda have been regularly victorious over the pastoral Bakitara. The advances of the settled peoples are less spectacular but more enduring. The memory of a transient but all-conquering horde has a peculiarly vivid quality for the human imagination. Attila ravaged Gaul, but the effect was slighter and less enduring than the slow and almost imperceptible advance of the endless chain of ploughmen who carried a more advanced agriculture to the limits of Europe and Asia. The pastoral nomad is, however, from the nature and limitations of his economy so frequently in the position of having little to lose and so much to gain that the spoliation of weak and sedentary peoples has frequently occurred. The cultivator, although he has superior man-power and greater resources, having little need of the nomad and nothing to gain by pursuing him into the wilderness, is too often content to leave him on the borders until it is too late.

The character and scale of the social and political organization among peoples who rely mainly on live stock for their support varies as widely as among agricultural peoples; it is a far cry from the organization of a Hottentot kraal to that of a large Khirghiz aul. The reindeer herders may, when they are ex-cattle breeders, retain some of the social and ceremonial patterns of their former life, but in general their communities are but little larger or more formal than those of their hunting and fishing neighbours. Pastoral nomadism is popularly associated with an authoritarian system in which the head of a large household wields autocratic powers over a large number of wives, sons, daughters and slaves. This 'patriarchal' system is of course most widely known in connexion with the Biblical Israelites herding sheep, goats and asses on the margins of the settled country. But while this type of organization is widespread among the pastoralists of south-western and central Asia, it is by no means characteristic in Africa south of the Sahara, where the organization of, for instance, a Yoruba compound or a Boloki household is far more 'patriarchal' than is that of a Masai kraal. The importance and prestige of warrior grades of young men in Masai society has been made sufficiently plain. The authoritarian elder in an ancient Israelite or modern Badawîn or Kazak kin group is not, however, the be-all or end-all of social regulation in these pastoral societies. The organization of families into clans and tribes with popularly elected figure-heads among the Kazak and the acknowledgment of a tribal *sheikh* among the Badawîn carry social integration to a considerably higher level.

Polygyny is similarly no prerogative of pastoral peoples. Among the Badawîn or Kazak only the wealthy and socially prominent have a plurality of wives, and polygyny of this type is far more developed among some African cultivating peoples as, for example, the Yoruba. Solomon, it might be remembered, was not a pastoral nomad. Where the tending of live stock is undertaken by women, as among some of the Kalmuck and among the Chuckchi herders, a large number of herds invites the acquisition of several wives to care for them, but female herding is not universal and it is often barred.

The subjection of women in some pastoral communities is often less real and complete than its reiteration might lead the unwary to suspect. The freedom of Kazak women as compared with those of the Sart villages in Turkestan is notorious: Kazak women are neither veiled nor secluded; they participate in most festivals, and their considerable social importance in the household has been sufficiently emphasized in an earlier chapter. While the women among the Altaian Kalmuck have nominally a higher status than among the Kazak and Khirghiz, where a veneer of Mohammedanism has affected their formal status, in point of fact the Kalmuck women undertake practically all the drudgery of milking and the tending of all live stock save mares, and often also cultivate plots of barley, while the women of the Kazak and Khirghiz are not called upon to herd, to gather firewood or to cultivate.

The fallacy of identifying Mohammedan religion, including its attitude to women, with a pastoral economy, should hardly need re-emphasis; the vast majority of Moslems are, and have been from the beginning, sedentary, cultivating peoples. Moreover, Chinese civilization, which has remained continuously antipathetic and impervious to pastoralism for so many centuries, is nevertheless pervaded with the notion of female inferiority in society, in religion and at law.

As Lowie has pointed out, the treatment of women is one thing, the character and extent of their labour another, their legal status still another, while the degree of public prominence and activity is yet a fourth. All of them are distinct, and there may be very different correlations between them, while to confuse any of them with a matrilineal reckoning of kinship and clan membership is to fly in the face of patent and well-known facts. The lot of women is hard and undignified among both the matrilineal and the patrilineal peoples of Australia, although they provide a considerable part of the food-supply. Among the Andamanese and Veddah, where hunting is more prominent, the status of women is decidedly higher in most of the affairs of life. Among the Hopi and other Pueblo peoples where matrilineal descent is associated with female control of land and houses, the women have no official voice in government and very little in ritual. A man may live in the house which his wife has received from her mother, but he is nevertheless the real master. Matrilineal descent and matrilocal residence affect, not the superiority of the wife, but the importance of her kin in the life of her children.

The explanation of the low formal status of women among the Asiatic pastoral peoples generally takes an economic form. The herding of beasts is essentially a man's work, and women, providing so little and being economically so dependent, are relegated to an inferior rank. This may to a certain extent be true, but it must be borne in mind that this formal status may have little relation to actual daily life, and that such behaviour patterns as the relations between the sexes may survive over long periods of time. Their explanation often lies in the remote historical past and not in any present realization of the need for assigning a particular status. The economy may in the present merely play the passive role of permitting the accepted status to survive.

Moreover, an economic argument is also equally applicable among the plough cultivators, where men are again dominant in the production of food. In fact, women are here again quite often just as inferior in their formal ranking. It is worth noting in this connexion that the status of women is lower among the eastern Bantu peoples, where they provide the bulk of the food by cultivation, than among the Hottentot, who are purely pastoral. Economic determinism affords no simple solution of the status of women any more than of any other social pattern or mechanism.

CHAPTER **XXI**

CULTIVATED PLANTS AND THE DEVELOPMENT
OF AGRICULTURE

I. The Root Crops of Forest Cultivators

IT will now be of value to turn to a brief survey of the distributions of the more important plants on which cultivators depend in various parts of the world, and to consider the different technical methods associated with particular crops and regions.

In the tropical forest regions root[1] crops in general provide the staple foods. They are cultivated for their large tuberous growths, which form at the base of the stem (rhizomes), in the root proper deeper underground, or on tuber stalks. The food value of the plant in all cases lies in the starchy material stored up to provide for a new growth in the ensuing season. Of these crops the most widely used are yams, manioc, taro and the sweet potato.

The genus *Dioscorea*, to which belong both the wild and cultivated vines which develop the tuberous roots known as yams, has a world-wide distribution in tropical and sub-tropical climates. Species of wild yam are most numerous in southern and eastern Asia, and they are also found in northern Australia and perhaps in parts of Melanesia. Some of the wild forms are poisonous and, as has been seen, these harmful elements are removed by some collectors of wild yams. The cultivated varieties are not poisonous, but many of them have been satisfactorily related to wild species from which they have diverged under cultivation. Some of the cultivated yams of south-east Asia and Oceania reach over a hundred pounds in weight. In Polynesia cultivated yams are practically universal, but although 'wild' yams grow in the bush in many islands, they are believed to be degenerate relatives of cultivated varieties, rather than native wild species. In tropical Africa there are fewer wild species, but the two or three native

---

[1] The term root is not, of course, used in a strict botanical sense, but is intended to cover plants cultivated for their underground growth, whether rhizomes, tubers or true roots.

cultivated forms are apparently distinct from the Asiatic. In South America wild yams are also found in the Amazon forest area and in the Guianas to the north. None of the few cultivated varieties have, however, so far been shown to derive from particular wild forms, and some of them have certainly been introduced from the Old World in post-Columbian times.

In the New World, however, the native manioc, which provides a food of similar type, appears to have restricted the utilization of yams. Manioc is unknown as an indigenous cultivated plant outside tropical America. The genus *Manihot* consists of shrubs of the *Euphorbiacea* family in which tuberous swellings form on the roots after the first season and continue to develop for two or more years. Nearly fifty species are known, and they are all American, being found mostly in the Brazilian forests, although a few are native to the Guianas and southern Mexico. Some of them contain poisonous juices, which can, however, be removed by methods such as have already been described. The more important cultivated varieties which yield larger growths, in particular *Manihot utilissima*, the most widely grown and possessing this poisonous character, have not been identified with any certainty in a wild form, a situation which suggests considerable antiquity of cultivation.

Unfortunately little botanical and ethnographic work on the cultivation of yams and manioc has been undertaken, but it is clear that these root crops are native tropical forest plants whose cultivation and use have spread over wide areas. While the yams of Melanesia and the central Pacific can with a fair degree of certainty be regarded as derived from Asiatic cultivated varieties, the questions of historical connexions between yam cultivation in Africa and Asia on the one hand and between the Old World and the New remain completely obscure. Yams are, however, everywhere cultivated by the same method, that is, by planting the tops or eyes of the tubers from which new stalks and roots sprout. It is claimed that a stage of incipient yam cultivation was found among some of the Australians of northern Queensland, who, although they cannot be considered as cultivators since they neither cleared the ground nor planted regularly, did nevertheless frequently put back into the ground the tops of the wild yams which they dug up. The women also appear to have claimed individual or family rights over patches of ground in which these wild yams were abundant.

For taro, another cultivated plant flourishing under humid and tropical conditions which provides an edible underground rhizome at the base of the stalk, the botanical and distributional evidence is somewhat more precise. Taro proper (*Colocasia antiquorum*), together with a related species often cultivated with it, is found wild in India, Ceylon and Indonesia. Cultivated varieties clearly derived from this wild species are found in many parts of the same areas, and they were also carried out into the Pacific, where although grown rather sporadically in Melanesia, they have superseded yams as the staple root crop over the greater part of Polynesia. There is apparently fairly good botanical evidence for regarding some part of India as the scene of first cultivation. The method of propagation by planting new stalk shoots is but slightly different from that employed for the yam and is substantially the same wherever it is grown. The close association of taro with elaborate irrigation methods in Polynesia and its more sporadic distribution and secondary importance in Melanesia may suggest that it reached Oceania considerably later than yams. The late date of the earliest literary reference to taro in the West and in China also indicates that its diffusion from India or south-east Asia generally occurred rather late. Pliny's reference to it appears to be the first record of its cultivation in Egypt, where it was grown fairly extensively by irrigation in Roman times and was known by a name similar to the Sanscrit term for taro.

Another root plant of wide cultivation is the sweet potato (*Ipomea batatas*), cultivated in the New World from Chile to the south-eastern United States. This is undoubtedly a plant of New World origin and no wild species are known elsewhere. It was, however, found cultivated in several parts of Oceania and Indonesia by the explorers of the eighteenth century. This extension had, after some investigation, been generally attributed to introductions made by Spanish explorers sailing from South America during and shortly after the end of the sixteenth century. But a recent and more detailed investigation, by R. B. Dixon, of the evidence available in the records of early exploration, has shown that the distribution and relative importance of the plant in Oceania in the later eighteenth century is at many points incompatible with this hypothesis. The early Spanish explorers discovered only a few groups of islands, and the Marquesas is the only one in Polynesia with which they had more than the briefest contact The narratives of the discovery of that group, although ambiguous, may have intended to indicate that the sweet potato was already known there; in any case, there is no suggestion that the Spaniards themselves planted and left behind any sweet potatoes. The plant was, however, in later times always of very minor importance in the Marquesas and also in central Polynesia. But the more extended explorations that began less than two centuries later revealed that the sweet potato was known and cultivated as a secondary and often rather neglected crop in most Polynesian islands, while in the extremities of Polynesia, on the contrary, in Easter Island, Hawaii, and above all in North Island of New Zealand it was of the first importance. In New Zealand, where climatic conditions practically excluded the other Polynesian food plants, at least twenty different varieties were being grown, a greater number than that known in Peru! It is extremely difficult to assume that a food plant introduced into the Marquesas in the late sixteenth century but which failed to acquire any real importance either there or in central Polynesia, was nevertheless carried to the extreme limits of the region to become a food staple in New Zealand and Hawaii within less than two centuries. Although during earlier periods, as has been described in an earlier chapter, many native voyages were made from central Polynesia to the peripheral groups, the evidence of both tradition and material culture indicates that after about the fourteenth century contact between the centre and the peripheries had ceased. Indeed, the neglect of the sweet potato in central Polynesia would have been a more likely occurrence *after* the period of the great voyages and during the decline in agriculture which appears to have accompanied the dominance of the *arii* in that part of Oceania. The case of New Zealand is particularly obstinate. The specialization of Maori culture leaves very little doubt that the great Polynesian migrations to New Zealand must have occurred well before the sixteenth century, and the twelfth or thirteenth century is generally accepted on the internal evidence of mythology and genealogies as the probable time of this movement. After a relatively short period contact with the Northern Island ceased. The theory that the Spaniards first introduced the sweet potato into the Pacific makes it necessary therefore to assume that for three or four centuries after their first arrival in New Zealand the Maori were forced to abandon agriculture in North as well as South Island, save for the northern extremity where yams would grow. Then, early in the seventeenth century, as a result of native voyages of which there is no ethnological trace, they received the sweet potato from elsewhere, at a time when sea contact with other Polynesian groups is generally accepted, on other evidence, as having ceased! They immediately resumed cultivation on a wide scale and either received a great many varieties of this new plant—varieties which were nevertheless many of them unknown a century or two later in the rest of Polynesia—or proceeded to develop them by a most unusual attention to selection.

The evidence for Spanish introduction of the sweet potato into Melanesia is equally meagre and only slightly less improbable. In fact, the only place into which the Spaniards are definitely known to have brought the plant was their great east Asiatic colony, the Philippine Islands, and here they introduced at the same time the Mexican name for that plant —*camote*. In Polynesia, on the other hand, it was universally known as *umara*, a word whose suspicious resemblance to the Kechua (Peruvian) term *kumara* has long been noted.

This problem of the sweet potato has been sketched at some length because it raises in a very specific form the long-debated and much wider question of cultural contacts between the Old World and the New by way of Oceania. Professor Dixon, after long denying the validity of much other evidence on various aspects of the question, is now satisfied that in this fundamental matter of a specific cultivated plant it is impossible to deny that either Polynesian voyagers reached American shores and successfully returned bringing the sweet potato with them, or that Peruvian or other aboriginal Americans sailed westwards with the plant and arrived in some part of Polynesia. The only possible way of evading this conclusion is to assume that several entirely unrecorded visits were made by Europeans to several parts of Oceania in the early seventeenth century and that they bestowed the new food plant on the inhabitants. But this would seem to be a more difficult assumption than that of earlier aboriginal contact.

In only one region of cool climate have root crops been of great importance in native cultivation. The high plateaux within the ranges of the central Andes, although they lie well within the tropics and reach the Equator on the north, have, in consequence of their elevation from nine to over thirteen thousand feet above sea-level, a cool climate in which there is no season of greatly increased temperature, but only a very great diurnal range. While the heat in the sunshine may be considerable, the nights, in consequence of rapid radiation, are severely cold. Maize can be and is grown up to altitudes of eleven thousand feet and even higher in a few places, but it becomes increasingly precarious as a food-supply. An inferior plant, quinoa (*Chenopodium quinoa*), which affords edible seeds and is cultivated only in the Andean region, can be grown as high as thirteen thousand feet, but the greater part of the food-supply at higher altitudes was obtained from the tubers of oca (*Oxalis tuberosa*) and potatoes (*Solanum tuberosum*). Several hundred cultivated varieties of potatoes were being grown in various parts of the Andean plateau from Ecuador to Bolivia at the time of the Spanish conquest. At the higher levels, round Lake Titicaca, for example, where the cold climate made it very difficult to preserve them for food, the potatoes were and are still to-day converted into a flour known as *chunya* by an elaborate process of alternate freezing and warming which breaks down the starch-containing cells. This flour could be stored for long periods if necessary. Although a native plant of the high plateaux, the cultivated potato spread southwards into the sub-tropical coast lands of central Chile and was grown sporadically in the northern parts of the south Chilean forest (see p. 96).

II. TROPICAL FRUITS

The lower cultivators of the tropical forests and woodlands do not, however, depend entirely on root crops, for they have a number of cultivated and semi-cultivated fruits. In the New World the pineapple, tomato, avocado pear and a number of others were grown, while one of the most important crops of the Maya in the forests of Guatemala and Honduras was the cocoa tree. The native cultivated fruits of the New World have not a uniform distribution, and the majority of them were restricted at the time of discovery to the higher cultures of southern Mexico, central America and the flanks of the northern Andes. Some of them were little developed from the wild form, and others were not cultivated in a strict sense; the naturally propagated plants or trees were merely tended. In all cases, however, the precise area in which they first received attention remains unknown.

None of these New World fruits were known in Oceania or Asia, where different cultivated fruits were used, some of them over very wide areas.

The coconut (*Cocos nucifera*), which is found both cultivated and self-propagated as a food plant throughout Oceania and south-eastern Asia, is indeed thought to be of New World origin; for, although the particular palm is not found wild in the Americas and was unknown as a cultivated plant, its close relatives are all found there and none is known in the Old World. But the New World origin of the coconut palm does not, like that of the sweet potato, imply that human inter-ference necessarily accounts for its appearance and development in the Pacific and Indian Oceans, since the ripe nuts of this and related palms could be carried thousands of miles by the westward currents in the equatorial latitudes of the Pacific and still germinate successfully when thrown up on a sandy beach. The coconut is therefore generally regarded by botanists as native to the Pacific, where it developed from a sea-borne South American form. Its distribution has, however, been greatly extended there by man, who has also been responsible for its further diffusion on the mainland of Asia.

The breadfruit tree, the areca nut palm, and several other semi-cultivated trees in Oceania are found both wild and cultivated in south-eastern Asia. Southern India is, indeed, on botanical grounds regarded as the region in which improved varieties of many of these food plants of Indonesia and the Pacific were originally cultivated.

Among these plants is the banana or plantain (*Musa sapientum*) which raises a special problem as it is also widely grown in tropical Africa. The carrying of the cultivated banana from the Asiatic mainland into Oceania by man is practically certain, and all the eastern forms are thought to have come originally from India, where the banana was a very famous fruit in classical times. But since a wild species grows in Africa and since there is a considerable gap in the westward distribution, cultivation in that continent has often been regarded as independent in origin. More detailed study has, however, shown that this cannot be the case. New banana plants are everywhere, both in Africa and Asia, propagated by planting out side-shoots which develop on the old growth; the seeds of the fruit are nearly always sterile. But the wild African banana (*Musa ensete*), which propagates itself from seed, lacks these shoots, so that it could never have been propagated and improved by the technique which is actually used for the cultivated banana. Quite apart, therefore, from the fact that the wild fruit is small, inedible and unlikely to attract attention, the characteristics of the plant indicate that it is not connected with the development of banana cultivation and that the Asiatic species which did form side-shoots must have been introduced. The period at which this occurred is uncertain; both the Malayan colonization of Madagascar and the early medieval expansion of Arab trade down the East African coast have been suggested as likely carriers of the cultivated banana. A date as recent as the latter, about the ninth century A.D., is not rendered improbable by the fact that native knowledge and use of the plant extends not only over the wetter parts of East Africa, but is found nearly everywhere in the Congo Basin and Guinea coast regions. The extremely rapid and equally wide diffusion of maize, manioc and tobacco, after their introduction from the New World into tropical

Africa by the Portuguese and Spaniards from the sixteenth century onwards, provides undoubted examples of the rapidity with which new cultivated plants have been adopted and handed on from one people to another in Africa.

III. THE CEREALS

The root crops and fruits which have so far been considered did not, however, provide the main food basis of the higher civilizations. Although the date palm, for example, has been cultivated from a very remote period in south-western Asia, the seeds of cultivated grasses have played a far more important rôle, and it is undoubtedly in connexion with them that plough cultivation developed in the Old World. The reward of cereal cultivation is greater than that of any other form of agriculture. The gathering and threshing of grain is less laborious than the digging of roots; the food value is considerably greater for a given bulk; further, the product can be stored easily and will remain in perfect condition for very long periods. Surpluses can thus be accumulated to protect dense populations against crop failure.

Some of these cultivated grasses, or cereals, like maize and millets, can be grown in damp, hot forest climates, and one of them, rice, must be grown in such a climate unless irrigation is practised. The early development of cereal cultivation is not, however, associated with the forests, but with drier subtropical areas. Since the Old World cereals, barley and wheat, played so important a part as the food staples of the early civilizations of the Ancient East and still remain the basic food of Western civilization, a great deal more attention has been paid to the problems of their first cultivation and later improvement than is the case with the plants so far discussed.

So far as our present evidence goes, cereal cultivation began considerably earlier than elsewhere, in the riverine lands and oases of the Ancient East, a great sub-tropical arid belt from the Nile to the Indus. It was already being practised some six thousand years ago in the Nile valley and in the Tigris-Euphrates plain, and may prove to be scarcely less remote in the valley of the Indus. These same plants, barley and wheat, which afforded the essential basis of the dense populations established there by 3000 B.C. were already being cultivated at these remote periods.

At several points in the Nile valley small settlements have been found in recent years which almost certainly antedate the longer known in prehistoric civilizations. These are known in Upper Egypt in the neighbourhood of Badari, near Assiut, and in the Fayyum depression, where they lay on the margins of the shrinking Fayyum lake. They were already established before the desiccation of North Africa had deprived the Nile valley of its heavy timber (the roots of large trees have been found in the Badarian settlements), and therefore probably before the Sahara had reached a condition of extreme aridity. There is a growing body of evidence to show that the Sahara in late Palaeolithic times was extensively occupied by peoples who hunted game now long since expelled by drought; and the equipment of the Badarians, particularly their throwing sticks and their extensive use of animal skins, indicates that

FIG. 105. A FAYYUM FLINT BLADED SICKLE, C. 20 IN. LONG
(*After photograph by G. Caton Thompson*)

hunting remained important in their economy. But they were already far advanced beyond the cultural level of the old Stone Age and practised the fundamental crafts of civilization. They made remarkably fine pottery, wove flax or some other fibre and made axes by grinding hard stone. Indeed, a rudimentary knowledge of metals is indicated by the discovery of copper beads and a single pin of copper wire. But above all they cultivated barley and wheat. In the Fayyum, small chipped flints were found fitted into a groove in a straight stick which served as a sickle, and these small flints are among the most characteristic objects found in both these and the Badarian settlements. Still more recently sickles of the same type and mortars have been found on a site in Palestine, which, to judge from the character of the other implements, may be earlier still. The early settlements round the Fayyum lake, which can be tentatively dated by the recessions of the lake margin to between 5500 and 4500 B.C. exhibit so many similarities with those of Tasa and Badari that they are generally accepted as little, if any, later in time. One of the most remarkable discoveries in the Fayyum was the numerous basketry and straw-lined pits which had served as storehouses for grain.

In the lower Tigris-Euphrates plain the settlements of early cultivators have been found at several points many feet below the present ground level, on a surface which had at that time but recently emerged from the shallow lagoons and marshes that fringed the retreating Persian Gulf. The huts of reed matting and plastered clay were sometimes placed on platform of reed bundles laid criss-cross on the marshy ground. A al 'Ubaid near Ur, at abu Shahrein and elsewhere, there hav been found flat grindstones. Large hoe-like tools roughl' fashioned out of chert together with clay sickles into whic short lengths of flint with saw-like edges were probably fitte and others which consisted only of curved blades of bake clay, accompany them. These, like the sickles of early Dynasti Egypt, bear a striking resemblance to half of a ruminant' jaw bone and give an unexpected point to the weapon whic Samson chose to smite the Philistines. So far no actual grain or remains of other cultivated plants have been found at thi early level in Sumeria, but the character of the tools and th great importance of barley and wheat in later times make i fairly certain that one or both were already being cultivated.

It is still uncertain whether the occupants of the wattl huts erected on the dried marsh bottoms were earlier than th people of the ancient settlements in the foothills of the Zagro Mountains to the east. At Susa, in the foothills of the eas of the Gulf-head, a very early walled village occupied a hilloc on the banks of the Kherka about five hundred feet above th level of the plain, and other related sites have been discovere on the eastern tributaries of the Tigris farther north. In th piedmont country of northern Mesopotamia at and nea Nineveh and Assur in later Assyria at Tell Halaf, on th Khabur tributary of the Euphrates, and farther west in Syria in the country round the great bend of the Euphrates, othe very early settlements have been identified. That there wa an underlying cultural unity between all these is indicate by the many similarities in tools, utensils and ornaments, an in particular the styles of the painted pottery. At the firs village of Susa copper was smelted and used extensively fc flat axes, chisels, needles and mirrors, but out on the plain more remote from the ores of the Zagros, metals were at firs unknown or very little used.

At Kish, in the upper part of the alluvial plain, an earl settlement of great interest has been found. It shows n signs of cultivation, potmaking or the use of metals, and th small flint tools characteristic of this site suggest an occupatio of late Palaeolithic hunters, who were living on during th early spread of the cultivating peoples.

Villages of early cultivators have also been found in man of the small alluvial basins in the arid interior of the Irania plateau, especially to the east in Baluchistan. Depending o small, cultivable areas and on the use of minor rivers descending from the high ranges, and isolated one from another and from the outside world by difficult country, these early colonies of cultivators did not go on to the great achievements of the riverine lands. In some parts indeed they appear to have been later abandoned with the failure of their water supply, in consequence of a drier climate.

Still farther east, in the basin of the Lower Indus, physical conditions analagous to those of Mesopotamia again formed the basis of an early civilization which shortly after 3000 B.C. equalled the Sumerian cities of Lower Mesopotamia in density of settlement and wealth. There were undoubtedly cultural contacts and probably also effective trade relations between the Indus cities and Sumer. The early development of this ancient centre of Indian civilization in the Sind and Punjab has not, however, been yet revealed; the ancient oasis villages of Baluchistan, just referred to, appear to be cultural dependants rather than precursors of the developments on the Indus. Here again, however, the same essential food plants, wheat and barley, made the development of higher civilization possible, and they are found again in the one group of early settlements so far discovered north of the mountain barrier at Anau, in the foothill country of southern Turkestan.

It is clear that the cultivation of these grasses underlay the whole development of higher civilization in the Old World. By the fourth millennium B.C. agricultural communities were springing up far and wide, over a wide zone of territory in north-east Africa and south-western Asia. In all of them the two grains were fundamental; their cultivation made possible a rapid increase in population and laid the foundation of the great civilizations of the Ancient East. How did they first come to be grown? Why are they associated with river-flood cultivation and found in this great arid belt? Where did the first stages of this great and revolutionary development take place? To most of these questions only tentative answers can be given. So far as present knowledge goes the record of cultivation goes back considerably further in the Nile and Tigris-Euphrates valleys than elsewhere, but the problem of the rise of the earliest cultivation in these areas is part of the larger question of the growth of the earliest civilizations and the lines of movement in the Ancient East. The relative time of the beginnings of the Badarian and the earliest Mesopotamian settlements remains at present unknown, and detailed consideration of the material from both areas does not at present yield certain or generally agreed results. The fundamental similarity of the new economies and their approximately equal antiquity is, however, clear, and the progress of exploration and excavation may be expected to reveal the development of the early stages. At present there is a strong probability that the Badarian, itself preceded in the Nile Valley by the more primitive Tasian settlements, is older at least than the first village at Susa and the earliest settlements on the drying marshes at the head of the Persian Gulf.

Can we obtain further light on the problem from a study of the distribution of the wild forms of these essential plants? It is necessary, in the first place, to guard against what has been unkindly called the 'Botanists' Fallacy', the assumption that a plant was brought into cultivation in a particular area merely because a wild form of that plant is found there. A well-known instance will show the danger of this. Wild vines occur both in Italy and in China, but viticulture and the use of the grape were discovered in neither of these places; the cultivated vine was in both instances introduced from without. Nevertheless, if we know the distribution of the wild plants, we can at least circumscribe the area. Wild barleys, from which the cultivated varieties were clearly derived, are found sporadically across a wide area from Russian Turkestan to Tunisia. Wild forms of two wheats are known. The cultivated variety of one of these, Emmer wheat (*Triticum dicoccum*) was the wheat of Ancient Egypt, and continued in use until classical times. This has been, up to the present, found growing wild only in Syria and Palestine, and its discovery by Aaronsohn on the slopes of Mount Hermon and elsewhere in this region was the result of a long search. Earlier but less certain reports of wild Emmer come from Mesopotamia and western Persia, while it has very recently been found in a possibly wild state in Armenia and Georgia. The other and the poorer species, Einkorn (*Triticum monococcum*) is known wild in Anatolia, North Syria, the Balkans and elsewhere, but it does not appear to have been cultivated so early, did not assume great importance in the Ancient East and has now almost gone out of cultivation on account of its great inferiority to other wheats.

But a wheat superior to Emmer was developed in early times. This is bread wheat (*Triticum vulgare*), whose improved descendants provide the world's supply of wheat to-day. It was formerly thought to be unknown in the Ancient East before classical times, and the earliest specimens came from early sites in southern Russia and from Anau in Turkestan. But it has recently been claimed, on the evidence of carbonized remains of grains, that bread wheat was being grown by the later prehistoric peoples of Mesopotamia. It was certainly grown there in early historic times, and was also grown by the peoples of the early Indus cities. No wild form of bread wheat has ever been found, and it is now generally regarded as a hybrid, produced perhaps naturally from a crossing of Emmer with Einkorn (as suggested by Ruggles Gates) or with the wild grass *aegilops* (as suggested by Percival).

The Russian botanist Vavilov has recently attempted to define more closely the scene of earliest cultivation of these cereals by a study of the distribution of the many cultivated varieties, making the general assumption that cultivation was first developed in one of the areas where the greatest number of cultivated varieties exist at the present time. He recognizes, however, that 'varietal riches' can occur in secondary areas remote from the original scene, in which, for various reasons, many varieties have been brought together from distinct regions or have been developed by man. But is it not also possible for numerous inferior varieties to disappear from areas of more advanced cultivation as a result of specialization on relatively few superior breeds? Vavilov's conclusions do not agree at all closely with such archaeological indications as we have at present. For cultivated barley he claims Abyssinia as a primary centre of cultivation on account of the large number of varieties found there. There is, however, no archaeological evidence to corroborate this claim that Abyssinia should be regarded as a primary centre of cereal cultivation; the cultural gradient in north-eastern Africa seems almost always to have passed up the Nile and not down it. Further, although Abyssinia is archaeologically practically unexplored the remains of former cultures so far reported are not of great antiquity. There does not appear to be any cogent objection to treating Abyssinia as Vavilov does south-eastern Asia, namely, to regard it as a secondary area owing its 'varietal riches' to a combination of accessibility and economic retardation. His views do, however, favour a north-east African as opposed to a south-west Asiatic centre for the beginnings of barley cultivation. He finds the largest number of cultivated forms of Emmer wheat in the North African coast lands. But again his major centre, Algeria, is archaeologically an unlikely district for the first period of cultivation; no signs of a civilization comparable to that of pre-dynastic Egypt have yet been found in north-west Africa. The bias again is African rather than Syrian and Asiatic, despite the fact that the wild survival of the plant is known in Syria.

There can, however, be little doubt that the wild ancestors of barley and wheat were growing naturally over a considerable area at least, of the more western areas of the arid sub-tropical zone in which ancient civilization developed. It is reasonable to assume that the later Palaeolithic food-gatherers of this region, of whose existence there is abundant evidence, were collecting and using the seeds of these wild grasses after the manner of the Paiute in the Great Basin and other peoples of western North America in recent times. The Badarian and Fayyum settlements reveal to us the situation soon after deliberate cultivation had begun. Although definite evidence is, in the nature of the case, almost impossible to obtain, it would seem probable that the increasing dryness of the Sahara-Arabia region which undoubtedly accompanied the final retreat of the European glaciers, may have stimulated the development of cultivation by reducing both the formerly abundant game and also the wild crop of grasses. Under semi-desert conditions they would grow only where surface water periodically inundated the ground. From the observation and adaptation of such natural flooding the development of true irrigation, culminating in the great basins and canals of Ancient Egypt and Babylonia, must be derived.

Irrigation agriculture might at first sight appear to be a complicated version of ordinary rainy season cultivation undertaken by cultivators who have entered an arid region and adapted their economy to it. It may, however, more properly be regarded as a distinct type of cultivation in which rainfall plays little or no part and it is indeed probable that cereal cultivation, both in the Old World and the New, began with irrigation at first natural and later artificial. Cultivation dependent on rains is, from this point of view, the secondary development. The advantages of arid conditions and dependence on flood water are important both in inducing cultivation and in facilitating its development. The aridity of the region and the limited distribution of the natural crop are combined with opportunities for increasing its extent by expanding the flooded area without the need to clear dense vegetation. On cleared land the seeds of the desired grasses will sprout every season with little interference from weeds. The limited or relatively simple character of the adjustments necessary will have been clear from the description of Hopi and Yuma maize growing in an earlier chapter. Hence the paradox that a manner of cultivation that we, in well-watered, temperate latitudes, regard as a complicated addition to ordinary procedure, was probably the initial stage whereby cereal cultivation became known to man. It was with the spread of these crops to well-watered regions that the selection of naturally flooded areas or the construction of irrigation channels and basins became unnecessary.

Wheat and barley were the first cereals to be cultivated, but they do not stand alone, and in certain areas others came to be of greater importance. Oats and rye can be grown beyond the limits of wheat and barley under colder and damper conditions. But it is unlikely that they were discovered independently of the growing of the others. Both of them are found as 'weeds of cultivation' in crops of wheat and barley. In other words, when gathering a harvest the seeds of other grasses growing wild were and in many areas of backward cultivation are still gathered in and threshed out together with the wheat or barley. Mixed in with the seed corn they are re-sown the next season and are thus maintained. Over the greater part of Asia Minor and Persia rye grows in this way in considerable quantities in the wheat-fields and is regarded as a great nuisance. According to Theophrastus, it was a common notion in classical times that wheat grown on poor soil would turn to rye! What actually happened, of course, was that from the mixed seed the rye alone came to maturity. But at high altitudes its value is appreciated and the planting seed is often deliberately an equal mixture of rye and wheat so that although in a good year space has been wasted on an inferior grain, in bad years of greater cold the rye at least survives and gives a crop. In mountain regions above six thousand feet it is sown pure. Rye is almost certainly a by-product of wheat cultivation, grown and improved at first perhaps unintentionally, but later valued in areas too severe for wheat cultivation. The story of oats, which will support conditions much moister and cooler than wheat, is apparently the same. The species to which cultivated varieties belong (*Avena sativa*) is thought to be a native of eastern Europe and Turkestan. Wild species are found over a wide area from North Africa to Iran, and it is a common 'weed of cultivation' in fields of Emmer. Although there is no direct evidence of its cultivation as a separate crop in early times in south-west Asia and the Mediterranean, it was nevertheless so grown in the Bronze Age Lake Dwellings of Switzerland (*c.* 1000 B.C. or earlier).

Can a process of the same kind be invoked in connexion with the cultivation of rice, the great cereal of south-eastern Asia? All the cultivated forms of rice belong to the species *Oryza sativa*, but they fall into two groups from the point of view of the physical requirements of the plant. The most valuable varieties giving a very high yield and large grains must be grown under swampy conditions, such as have already been described; others, generally referred to as 'hill rice' can, however, be grown on drier ground provided that there is a fair rainfall and a long warm season. Wild species of *Oryza sativa*, closely similar to cultivated varieties, are found both in southern Asia and in tropical Africa, but the greater number of the cultivated varieties are found in India, where at least a thousand are known.

There is no direct evidence to indicate whether rice was first grown as a rain crop from upland wild varieties or whether it began with the cultivation of the swamp varieties; there is, nevertheless, a strong presumption in favour of the latter. India is the probable home of its earliest cultivation. In north-eastern India irrigation on the flood plains of the Indus and its tributaries had been developed on a considerable scale by 3000 B.C. Cultivated wheat and barley grown by irrigation were the food staples of the large cities, such as Mohenjo-daro, Harappa and, earlier still, Amri, established on the banks of these rivers. Some of the cities covered nearly a square mile of ground and their fields must have extended for several miles over the flood plains. That an eastward expansion of this civilization, with its cultivation and plants, took place can hardly be doubted, although little or no direct archaeological evidence is yet available. In the eastern plains of Hindustan, in the middle and lower Ganges valley, it would, however, have encountered a region in which the growing of wheat and barley became increasingly difficult on account of the humidity of the climate, but which at the same time offered a substitute cereal in the rice growing wild along the rivers. The same conditions would hold true of any expansion of agriculture southward from the Indus basin down the western parts of India. Rice growing may, indeed, have begun in the Indus basin itself, as a supplement to barley and wheat, but there is so far no evidence of this from the storehouses of the early cities. It is also necessary to realize that the methods of rice cultivation, although specialized in some areas and for some purposes (for instance, the transplantation of seedlings), are essentially similar to those adopted for wheat and barley. The use of draught animals and the plough, the harrowing and levelling of fields, broadcast sowing, the reaping sickle and the use of beasts for treading out the grain, are all part of the technique of wheat and barley cultivation as found in Egypt and Mesopotamia as early as 3000 B.C. The similarity between the methods of cultivation applied to the two crops is undoubted, and the assumption that they were carried *west* from some early area of rice cultivation would be quite gratuitous, since there is within the Ancient East a continuity and development of cultivation methods going back to the straight sickle sticks and granaries of the Fayyum and to the chert hoes and flint 'jawbone' sickles of al 'Ubaid.

Hill rice is relatively little cultivated in the areas of higher civilization of southern Asia. It has, however, been often adopted by hoe cultivators on the fringes of these areas; and, further, it can often be shown to have superseded, at a relatively recent date, earlier cereals of a group now to be considered, namely, the millets.

The 'millets' actually consist of a number of plants of different genera, and with them are usually grouped the sorghums, which can be grown under conditions similar to most of the millets. These tall, cultivated grasses have several characteristics in common. They afford grains which are both smaller and less nourishing than those so far considered, but they can be cultivated in climates too tropical for wheat or barley and too dry for rice. They combine, as a rule, a tolerance to great humidity with a relative indifference to severe drought during some part of the growing season, so that they can be cultivated under widely diverse conditions; this makes them of prime importance in many regions. Most of them will ripen in a relatively short warm season, but they flourish under tropical conditions.

Concerning the places and periods of their first cultivation very little is known. The botanical evidence suggests that the area of first cultivation of true millet (*Panicum miliaceum*) lay in the same region as that of wheat and barley. It was apparently known in pre-Dynastic Egypt, for traces of millet as well as barley husks have been found in the stomachs of desiccated pre-Dynastic corpses. Whether these grains belong to a cultivated variety is, however, uncertain. This same millet was also grown in the Swiss Lake Dwellings. Another species of *Panicum* (*P. italica*) was one of the most widely spread cereals of ancient times. It too has been found in the Swiss Lake Dwellings, and although it is doubtful whether it was cultivated in Egypt it was well known in the Mediterranean world in classical times. It is one of the six 'Royal Cereals' that were ceremonially sown in early China, and it is grown to-day throughout southern and eastern Asia, from India to Indonesia and in Manchuria and Japan. *Eleusine* (*El. coracana*), which resembles *Panicum* in both appearance and requirements, has an even wider distribution, for, in addition to an equally wide Asiatic distribution, it is much grown as a native crop in north-eastern Africa and a probable wild form has been reported from Abyssinia. The varieties of sorghum (*Holcus sorghum*) are still more widespread in Africa. Ordinary sorghum is the 'Kaffir corn' of the East African cultivators, and it flourishes under tropical conditions both in the forests and on the drier grasslands. In Asia these cultivated grasses of the millet group are the great supplements to, and alternatives of rice cultivation. They are grown during the drier season in the wet areas, as has been seen on the Malabar coast. They replace rice as the staple crop of plough cultivators where the temperature or the water supply from rain or river is insufficient for rice, as for instance, in northern China and on the Deccan plateau in India. Millets are also the crops of the hoe cultivators of remote areas of south-eastern Asia, in such places as Upper Assam, the interior of French Indo-China and among the Savage Malays.

The relative importance of millet and root cultivation in the forests of tropical Africa has already been discussed, and it was seen that millet cultivation spread relatively late from the tropical grasslands into the forests. While the root cultivation of the tropical forests of Africa and Asia has no technical relation to cereal cultivation and may be a distinct development of considerable antiquity, there is little doubt that the cultivation of cereals both with the hoe and the plough is everywhere in the Old World part of a single complex process of accretion. One by one other grasses have been added, and in various areas, to those first cultivated by the people who cleared the useless plants from the first depressions on the banks of some flooding river in order to scatter the seeds of still wild Emmer and barley. By the very act of improving the conditions for plant growth and of selecting the best seeds for scattering in successive seasons, the plants themselves have been improved in their yield and quality of grain.

It is not to be thought that grain cultivation spread rapidly along a few narrow lines in a single direction, or that the utilization of new and more suitable cereals and of superior methods in various regions followed regularly and rapidly. We are dealing rather with a slow creep affected by innumerable vicissitudes in which contact between group and group and the expansion of flourishing communities had nevertheless advanced so far that by the time the Europeans began to know the remote parts of the Old World, cereals were grown nearly everywhere where they were climatically possible. A few remote islands were left in south-eastern Asia and in south-western Africa, and the best cereal known to man for a particular climate and soil was not always actually available or grown.

Cereals, however, had not everywhere ousted roots as the dominant crops, and it may be suspected that the conversion of root growers to cereal cultivators in tropical forest areas was rarely a spontaneous matter, since it involved a radical change in the objectives and methods of cultivation. The plot had to be more carefully cleared, the soil more thoroughly loosened before scattering the grain, the ripening crop had to be guarded against the plundering of birds and animals, and the frequent complaints of the early missionaries in Oceania on the insupportability of the native diet to which they were subjected should remind us how reluctant a people usually is to change its staple food.

One of the areas in which cereal cultivation was not implanted is Oceania. Rice cultivation was carried far east in Indonesia and was introduced into the Philippine Islands, but in New Guinea and the rest of the Pacific it failed to become established. The reasons for this are not clear. Hindu kingdoms were established in Java in medieval times, and there is archaeological evidence of dense population and advanced culture before their advent. It is almost certain that cereal-cultivating peoples reached western New Guinea, for iron working, unknown elsewhere among root cultivators in Asia, was introduced. Finally, a large number of Asiatic mainland plants were introduced into Oceania and were carried to practically every island group. It is arguable that the cultivation of yams and taro and the tending of breadfruit reached Melanesia at a very early period and from areas in which cereals were still unknown. But important elements of the Polynesian racial stock and culture undoubtedly derive from south-eastern Asia at a relatively recent date. On linguistic and other grounds it is generally thought that the important movements cannot be earlier than the beginning of the Christian era and that some of them are considerably later. It is necessary in that case either to assume that the peoples involved in those movements lacked all knowledge of rice cultivation in their Indonesian or Indian homeland, or to adopt the hypothesis that root and fruit cultivation was relatively so much easier in the Pacific that rice growing, if attempted at all, died out leaving no trace. In the former case it is necessary to make the further assumption that rice cultivation had a far more restricted distribution right down to the early centuries of the Christian era than it had in the times of the

Chinese travellers in late medieval times and in the sixteenth century, when the Portuguese and other Europeans first visited this region. Rice may indeed have been largely unknown over the greater part of Indonesia and even southern India at this time, and may have been introduced only for the first time in association with the migrations from India that led to the foundation of the Hindu and Buddhist kingdoms in the Malay peninsula, Java and elsewhere from the fifth to the seventh centuries A.D. To assume the absence previous to this of millet cultivation is more difficult, since the spread of rice growing at the expense of millet is very generally recorded as a recent process in backward areas.

On the other hand, rice or millet cultivation may have been known by some of the ancestral Polynesian groups and abandoned by them. This would be no more surprising than their probable abandonment of both pot-making and weaving. On atolls and other low islands the sandy soil, relatively low rainfall and lack of water would be very unfavourable to rice cultivation. On high islands it could undoubtedly be grown as easily as taro on the irrigated terraces that were built, and it has been adopted in many areas since the beginning of the nineteenth century. But if relatively small immigrant groups were involved, and if they practically everywhere encountered an earlier root-growing and fruit-growing population who could supply a surplus, the lapse of cereal cultivation might easily have occurred. It should in this connexion be remembered that the ruling caste of central Polynesia took no part in agricultural pursuits, which it appears to have despised. If this was an original attitude on the part of the later immigrants from the mainland or Indonesia it would go far to explain their failure to introduce grains. It is possible that a careful examination of the historical, ethnographic and botanical evidence available could throw a great deal of light on this obscure question of the period at which rice cultivation first became important in Indonesia and its relation to the absence of grain growing in Oceania. Although there can be little more than speculation, it is worth while to raise the matter here, since it affords an example of the type of problem which is awaiting attack in many parts of the world.

The only cultivated cereal in the New World was maize. It is true that quinoa was grown for its seeds in the Andean plateaus, but its restricted distribution, encircled by maize cultivation and limited to high altitudes where maize could be grown with difficulty, if at all, indicates quite clearly that it is a local substitute for the climatically excluded grain. Such an adaptation occurred nowhere else, and cereal cultivation was in consequence excluded from the colder temperate areas. As has already been pointed out, the maize growers on the north-eastern margin of cultivation failed to bring into cultivation the swamp grass or 'wild rice' which was gathered by many of the hunting and collecting peoples. In the west maize cultivation did not extend to its climatic limits, for it was not grown west of the Colorado river.

The wild parent of cultivated maize (*Zea mays*) has not been identified, but it is believed to have been closely related to a wild grass ('*teocentli*'), which grows abundantly on the more open southern plateaux of Mexico. Teocentli will hydridize with cultivated maize, and it has been suggested that maize is itself a hybrid of teocentli with another grass as yet unrecognized.

Maize was cultivated from the St. Lawrence river to the Plate. It was grown from sea-level to heights of eleven thousand feet and even higher, but both the habitat of teocentli and the requirements of the cultivated plant whose optimum conditions are a long growing season, warmth both by day and by night, and a moderate rainfall or other water supply especially during the earlier period of growth, suggest that it was first cultivated in the tropical highland climate obtaining on the drier interior plateaux of South Mexico.

Varieties of maize far smaller in the ear or 'cob' than those cultivated by the Pueblo peoples to-day have been found in prehistoric sites. Maize was already being grown in the 'Archaic Culture', the forerunner of the Toltec and later Aztec civilizations of Mexico valley, widespread in southern Mexico and probably extending into the northern Andean region. The early cave-dwelling 'Basket Makers' who occupied the Southwest before the development of Pueblo culture were already growing maize nearly two thousand years ago. It has also been found in coastal Peruvian sites of remote predecessors of the Incaic civilization.

Maize may, as was probably the case with the Old World cereals, have been first brought into cultivation by taking advantage of natural flooding. That its cultivation spread from a single early centre is indicated not only by the continuity of distribution but also by the fact that maize is almost invariably accompanied by beans and squashes; in other words, that there was an arbitrary 'agricultural complex' which was diffused as a whole. It is only in areas severely unfavourable in climate that these companions of maize are not found.

Maize cultivation did not remain restricted to tropical sub-arid regions; it extended into tropical forest. Not only is it grown over the greater part of the Amazon forest, but it was also the food staple of the great Maya civilization of the forested lowlands of Guatemala and Honduras in a region to which it must, in the beginning, have been very unsuited. Carbonized maize cobs and representations of the crop on sculpture have been found in the cities of the Early Empire which were occupied in the first centuries of the Christian era.

In certain areas other staple food plants were cultivated, but all these had a more limited distribution. Manioc, the most widespread of them, was grown nearly everywhere in the humid tropical areas of South America. Manioc cultivation can scarcely have begun in the same region as maize, but whether the cultivation of this root owes anything to the stimulus of maize cultivators, or whether on the other hand maize succeeded manioc as a cultivated plant in the South American forests, remains unknown. In the forests, however, manioc is everywhere of greater importance than maize, although it is often less valued. The cultivation of potatoes on the high Andean plateaux and its expansion to the Pacific coast lands has already been referred to. The sweet potato was also cultivated in company with maize over a very wide area from the lower altitudes in the Andean region to the northern coast lands of South America, the Antilles and the south-eastern United States. A number of other plants, including tomatoes and cocoa, were used by the peoples of the higher civilizations of Mexico and Central America. These may not have been in some cases actually cultivated, but merely protected and encouraged to propagate themselves.

IV. The Digging Stick, the Hoe and the Plough

The agriculture of the Old World is also distinguished from that of the Americas and Oceania in its possession of more efficient means of cultivation, namely, the hoe and the plough.

It is a remarkable and generally unappreciated fact that hoes with blades of wood or stone are among the rarest of ethnographical specimens, and that outside the Old World area of the iron hoe, the primary agricultural implement among the lower cultivators from Senegal to Indo-China, the digging stick alone is found. This simplest of all agricultural implements has, indeed, been improved upon in one or two areas; in some of the Pueblos a crotched stick was used so that the crotch, a foot or so from the point, could be used to

apply further pressure with the foot; a similar result was
obtained by some Maori in New Zealand by lashing a short
transverse piece of wood to the stick; while in Peru, where
copper and bronze were made, the digging stick was sometimes
shod with a socketed metal point or small shovel. The so-called
'foot plough' (*taclla*) of the Peruvian highlands is even further
specialized. It is a gently curved pole some six feet long, to
which a foot-rest and a short handle halfway down are attached;
the foot-rest is prevented from slipping down under pressure
by a rope tied to the upper handle. The curve makes it
possible to drive the point obliquely into the ground. The
early Spanish chronicler, Garcilasso, stated that this implement
was sometimes drawn through the earth by a number of men
pulling on a rope. If this was so the first steps towards the
development of a plough had been taken, but although the
taclla is still used on the Andean plateau to-day, it is not
apparently pulled in this manner. Foot ploughs of a similar
kind were also known in the Old World and survived until
recent times even in Europe; the best-known example is the
'cashcrom' of the Hebrides, in which the foot enters the ground
at a very gentle angle.[1]

The light implement made by hafting an animal blade bone
and used by some if not all the cultivating peoples of the
Eastern Woodlands of North America, was a hoe in form, but
it could not, on account of the weakness of the material, be
used for breaking up the soil, and, as described for the Hidatsa,
was restricted in its use to scraping up the loose surface soil
round the hills in which plants were grown. There is, moreover, no definite evidence, so far as I am aware, that these
'hoes' were used in pre-Columbian times. The possibility
remains that they are copies of European metal hoes introduced
by early colonists.

The use of the hoe, in the sense of a tool used to hack up
the surface of the ground by vertical blows, can however be
traced back to a very early period in the Old World, for it was
employed by the Egyptians from the very beginnings of the
Dynastic period (*c.* 3400 B.C.), and a conventionalized drawing
of a hoe is the Egyptian hieroglyph for agriculture. But this
early Egyptian hoe is of a peculiar type, very different from
the short, broad-bladed iron hoes used by primitive cultivators
in Africa and Asia to-day. As represented in the numerous
paintings and carvings of the Old Kingdom and later Dynasties,
the blade was a curved piece of wood, three or four feet long,

[1] Another type of 'push plough' was reinvented in England in the nineteenth century for deturfing fields. See *Man*, July, 1933.

which tapered to a point or narrow edge. This was fitted at a very steep angle on to a perforated handle shorter than the blade, and was prevented from coming adrift in use by a tie which ran from the lower part of the handle to the middle of the wooden blade. Flint hoe blades of early Dynastic age, six to eight inches long and two to four inches wide at the blade, which is often worn and polished by long use, have been recovered in large numbers from Abydos and elsewhere, but by the Fifth Dynasty at least hoes were also being shod with a copper tip.

That short, broad-bladed hoes may have been used at a very early period is, however, suggested by the numerous rough-shaped tools of chert which have been found in the settlements of the earliest cultivators in Lower Mesopotamia (see p. 420). Unfortunately, few representations of agricultural implements occur among the relics of Sumerian and Babylonian civilization, and the later history of this alleged early hoe of prehistoric Sumeria is unknown. The iron hoe cannot have been developed earlier than the fourteenth century B.C., when iron working began in the Ancient East, but bronze forms may have preceded it.

The more developed agriculture of the Old World which can sustain dense sedentary populations has depended on the invention of a more efficient implement, the plough. It was suggested by several students during the nineteenth century that the plough was developed from the hoe by dragging this through the earth instead of using it to hack at the ground. It does not seem to have been generally recognized that the short and rather broad-bladed hoe would be most unsuitable for this purpose; it would present its broad edge to the line of pull and, even if the blade could be kept in the ground, the strain would certainly cause it to break at the joint in a very short time. Tylor has presented a far more arguable case in claiming that the Egyptian long-bladed pointed hoe was the point of departure. Some of the representations of ploughs in Egyptian drawings undoubtedly suggest that it was but a hoe with a longer main handle, now become the beam, which was pulled forward, and two shorter handles with which the blade was guided and pressed into the soil. The shape of the blade, the angle of the blade to the original handle, and the rope tie between the two are all preserved. The earliest known representation of this ancient plough was made in the Third Dynasty, i.e. very shortly after 3000 B.C. An actual specimen is, however, available. The blade, or share, which is much shorter than in the drawings referred to, here consists of two

ointed pieces of wood which converge to form the point and
re in one piece with the two guiding handles. The beam by
which it is drawn is secondarily attached by a lashing and is
ot socketed to the share itself. The date of this specimen is

FIG. 106. REPRESENTATION OF EARLY DYNASTIC
EGYPTIAN HOE AND PLOUGH
(*After Wilkinson*)

ncertain, but it can be approximately assigned to the begin-
ing of the New Kingdom, after the introduction of the horse,
r about fifteen hundred years later than the date of the
arliest known representation of a plough in Egypt. Now it
obviously arguable that in a thousand years the plough
ould have undergone considerable modification in order to

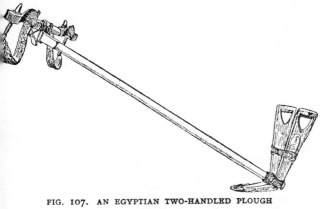

FIG. 107. AN EGYPTIAN TWO-HANDLED PLOUGH
(*After Leser*)

rengthen it and to make it more serviceable, and that the
ppression of the weak joint between blade and beam, for
stance, is only to be expected. This may be the case, but
is noteworthy that the rudimentary ploughs surviving in use
til modern times in various remote parts of Asia do not show

in their structure any surviving indication that the guidin
handle began as an addition to a dragged hoe. The plough
in universal use on the Malabar coast until the present centur
are examples of this type. Simple ploughs of the same kir
from remote parts of western Europe, with the proportions ar
form of the surviving Hebridean 'cashcrom', have been note
and a similar form is found in the prehistoric, probably Bron;
Age, rock carvings in Sweden. Moreover, most rudimentar
ploughs found in Asia to-day, like those of classical times, hav
only a single handle.

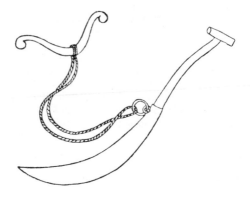

FIG. 108. A JAPANESE REPRESENTATION
OF A DRAW-SPADE
(*After Leser*)

The derivation of the plough from the hoe has recently bee
questioned by Leser, who considers that some form of 'drav
spade', a tool of the type of the 'cashcrom' and the Peruvia
taclla (to which he does not, however, refer) was a more probabl
forerunner. Implements of this type, with ropes attached fo
men to pull them, survive in a few scattered places to-day–
in Korea, Japan, Central Asia, Armenia and southern Arabi;
Some of these tools must, however, be regarded as specialize
and late so far as the form of the blade is concerned, and onl
one of them, apparently, has the narrow blade necessary fo
continuous travel below the surface. This example fror
Japan would, however, provide a good prototype. Dr. Leser'
argument on this point appears to be that the circumstance c
their rare occurrence at a number of widely separated point

ndicates that these tools are to be regarded as sporadic survivals of a very early form extinct nearly everywhere else.
t might be added that they appear to survive in rocky country,
s in the Hindu Kush and Baluchistan, where draught animals
or true ploughs are difficult to use, or in areas of very small
lots, such as Japan, where draught animals are scarce.

That the great majority of the primitive ploughs of to-day
re single-handed and the difference of the earliest actual
Egyptian specimen, which is two-handled, from the early
ictured hoes of that country, suggests that Dr. Leser may
e right in attributing the development of the plough to the
nfluence of some implement of the 'push-plough' type, but
he older Egyptian drawings make it equally probable that
his was preceded at an earlier stage, at least in that country,
y an adaptation of the peculiar Egyptian hoe. Hoes with
ery elongated handles, said to be drawn lengthways through
he earth to make furrows, are found in several parts of the
West African savana to-day, including Senegambia and
orthern Togoland. Certainty can never be attained in these
natters where the materials available for study are so incom-
lete. The development of the plough after the first beginnings
nay well have been complex, and the features of more than one
rimitive tool may have been incorporated.

The ploughs of most Asiatic and North African peoples are
ften, but by no means always, shod with a pointed metal
ole like the later ploughs of the Ancient World, but they lack
coulter to cut the turf, a mould board to turn the clods over
nd a wheel to run more easily over the ground. These are
nuch later and probably European developments. The
ative Asiatic plough, like that of classical times, merely cuts
shallow furrow in the ground, thrusting up clods to either
de which have then to be broken up with the aid of the
rviving digging stick, often still wielded by women who
llow the plough. This shallowness of the furrow is of less
onsequence than might at first appear, for, in the warmer
nd moister monsoon lands at least, ploughing is undertaken
r rice growing, and deep ploughing, if adequate fallowing
allowed, is not required. The seed can be sown within
n inch or so of the surface and the plant is very shallow
ooting.

A seeding tube attached to the plough, through which
rains fell from a bag into the furrow as it was opened, was
nployed before 2000 B.C. in Babylonia. It was not, however,
use in the Mediterranean in classical times. Both in Asia
nd in North Africa to-day seed is sown broadcast, or in

rice-growing areas seedlings are raised in small beds to be planted out by hand.

The devising of an implement that could be drawn through the ground would not, of itself, lead to plough cultivation. Some powerful form of traction is also required. Indeed, the very sporadic distribution and limited use of 'draw-spades' serves to indicate that cultivators could unaided make little use of such an idea even if it occurred. To harness men to a 'draw-spade' by means of ropes is probably in ordinary circumstances a less efficient use of their labour than to give each a 'cashcrom' or hoe of his own.

The use of the plough is inseparably connected with the domestication of large animals that can be harnessed to it. A brief survey of what is known of the domestication of animals will be made later, but in the meantime it is essential to realize that domestic oxen were already known in Egypt and Mesopotamia before the periods for which the first record of ploughing are found. The spread of plough cultivation from its early centre of development also involved the concurrent diffusion of large domestic animals. But the raising of domestic animals to assist in agriculture at one season of the year would not be likely to have any immediate appeal to hoe cultivators, for the change involved is not merely one of tending a single beast, but of raising sufficient live stock to maintain an adequate and continuous supply of draught animals for the whole community. In the African forest cattle diseases would preclude their development, but a consideration of the economy of such peoples as the Melanesians or the Hopi immediately suggests the magnitude of the economic and social change required. It is indeed of the magnitude of that resistance by peasants of to-day who are faced with the problem of mechanizing their agriculture. Furthermore, the possession of domestic cattle does not, in the absence of direct and sympathetic contact with plough cultivators, automatically result in the forging of hoes into ploughshares. The economy of the East African people affords an actual instance, for although they possess cattle often to excess, they make no use of them in cultivation, and indeed, use them for no draught purposes whatever.

In consequence of these and related circumstances, and although the plough is some five thousand years old in the Nile valley and so not much younger than the beginning of cereal cultivation itself, the frontiers of plough cultivation have not advanced coterminously with those of grain growing.

The review of cultivating peoples and this discussion of the problems concerning the development of early and primitive agriculture affords a basis for assessing the significance of agriculture in human life.

Although the thrusting of the great variety of human economies into a series of stages rigidly conceived and assumed to develop one from the other must be abandoned, the cleavage between the gathering of wild fruits and the cultivation of plants has a fundamental validity and is chronologically significant. As we pass backward in time our knowledge of human activities on the earth becomes more and more restricted and uncertain. The areas for which we can reconstruct the succession of peoples are small patches which dwindle to mere islands at the remoter periods. But in Europe and the Near East the record has been roughly charted right back to the Ice Age, and in parts of India and Africa vestiges of remotely prehistoric peoples are slowly taking shape. In a few patches of the New World, in the western deserts of U.S.A., in central America and coastal Peru, settlements which probably go back to the beginning of our Christian era are known. But although our knowledge is patchy in the extreme, there is little probability that any great and fundamental centre of early agricultural civilization remains completely unknown, and where records exist there is, as we go back in time, a progressive shrinkage in the number and extent of such regions. And when we reach the remote period of the later phases of the Ice Age, soon after the appearance of the first modern men, there is no evidence of cultivation or dense population at any point. Palaeolithic man, wherever known to us at all clearly, was quite ignorant of agriculture. The immense periods of time during which hunting and gathering were the sole means of subsistence for *Homo sapiens* and his predecessors, and the evidence in limited areas of the expansion of cultivation in later times leave little room for doubt that the world patterns of human economy have been largely effected by the progressive expansion of cultivation from small beginnings and narrowly circumscribed centres until it has commanded almost the entire earth.

But temperate regions such as we now associate with the complex technical achievements of Western civilization remained on the fringe and often outside this development. Tropical forests and even sub-tropical deserts offered a better opportunity for the early spread of cultivation. Nevertheless there was one region of the world where cereal cultivation advancing from the older centres of the Ancient East painfully established itself in a temperate climate and developed an economy and culture of unique potentialities. Western Europe, the terminus of the early expansion of wheat and barley cultivation, still the 'far West' in classical times, was yet to be transformed into the new hub of the universe of man.

CHAPTER XXII

THE DOMESTICATION AND UTILIZATION OF ANIMALS

THE facts and problems concerning the domestication of animals and the uses of live stock do not relate only to the pastoral economy reviewed in the previous chapter, since domesticated animals are possessed and used by peoples of every way of life, from hunters to plough cultivators.

The Tasmanians and, less certainly, the Andamanese are the only peoples who can be regarded as probably never having known the dog. In north-eastern Asia and in Arctic America dogs draw sledges; on the American plains the travois. A few people use them to carry small packs. Several cultivating peoples in the Congo region raise dogs for food, and the Maori and a few North American peoples formerly did so, while the peoples of the Northwest Coast, the Araucanians of central Chile and the Maori used dog 'wool' for blankets. Apart from these specialized uses the dog is over a wide area the companion and assistant of the hunter, and less often the guardian of the camp or flock. Not infrequently, however, it is put to little use and is, as in Australia and among most African forest peoples, mainly a companion of man or a parasite on the camp group or household. Indeed, it is in this parasitism that Hahn sought the beginnings of its domestication. It is probable that the Capsian hunters, who occupied North Africa and Spain during the last phases of the Ice Age, already had domestic dogs, for their bones have been found in shell middens of this period in Algeria, and they are represented in hunting scenes painted on rock faces in south-eastern Spain. Shortly after this the dog appears to have spread farther into Europe with the northward advance of these peoples in Epipalaeolithic times. Dog-gnawed bones and the bones of dogs themselves have been found in Portuguese and Danish shell middens which may have been formed a thousand years before the first cultivators reached western Europe. The earliest dogs represented in pre-Dynastic Egypt also closely resemble those shown on the Spanish wall paintings.

It is on zoological grounds exceedingly probable that all the domestic dogs in the world, from the Eskimo husky to the toy Pekinese, derive from the domestication of a single species at a very remote date. It was formerly suggested that various breeds of domestic dogs were descended from distinct species of the Canis family which had been domesticated in various areas. An early type of domestic dog, whose remains were found in the Swiss Lake Dwellings of the Bronze Age (*Canis familiaris palustris*), which is probably ancestral to some modern European breeds, including terriers and Pomeranians, was regarded as derived from the northern jackal (*Canis aureus*), while other breeds were derived from the wolf (*Canis lupus*), the coyote and even the fox. The comparative study of the dentition of dogs, wolves, jackals and foxes has, however, excluded the hypothesis of the actual origin of any Old World breed of dog from the jackal or the fox, while the coyote has similarly been eliminated from the ancestry of the dogs of the New World.[1] The dentition of these rejected animals is essentially distinct from those of the wolf and dog, which are closely similar. Moreover, observations on wolves bred in captivity show that the long, narrow skull of the wolf may modify very rapidly in the direction of the dog. A detailed study of aboriginal dogs in North America has convinced Allen of their derivation as a whole from an Asiatic form. The rapidity with which true breeding varieties can be established in dogs also led other zoologists to deny that a plural ancestry from different races of wolf need be assumed. There were, however, several distinct dog breeds in early times. In the early Dynastic period (*c.* 3000 B.C.) the Egyptians already had two breeds, one a short-legged type and the other lightly but strongly built. The latter is the ancestor of the greyhound, which did not reach Europe until classical times. This greyhound type of dog is widespread in Africa, being found not only among the Hamites of north-east Africa, but also among the Fula of the western Sudan and the Hottentot in the far south of the continent. The early breeds of Mesopotamia were distinct from the Egyptian,[2] and the Assyrians by 600 B.C. had a powerful breed of mastiff which they used both in hunting and in war. Dogs are also found in the Indus cities as far back as the present record goes, that is,

---

[1] Hilzneimer, however, remains doubtful about the early Egyptian greyhound breed referred to below. See *Antiquity* 6, 1932, 411 ff.

[2] A dog like the early Sumerian type was carved on the ivory handle of the Egyptian Gebel el Arak knife of late pre-Dynastic date. There has been much discussion as to whether the subjects and styles represented on this knife are derived from Sumer.

to about 3000 B.C. While one type closely resembles the long-faced 'pariah' dog of northern India to-day, a larger breed is more like a mastiff.

The team dogs of the sledge-using peoples of northern Asia and America are a widespread and very homogeneous type. The Eskimo dogs are considered, however, to be closer to the wolf. Like the wolf, and unlike the Asiatic varieties, they do not bark but howl. The Eskimo dog does, however, carry his tail re-curved over one haunch and not, like the tundra or timber wolf, drooping behind. It is entirely possible that Eskimo dogs, and indeed domestic dogs in many parts of the world, have at various times crossed with wild wolves with which they are completely interfertile.

The possession of dogs does not, however, constitute stock breeding. While it will be useful and indeed necessary to consider separately some of the more important animals which have been domesticated as live stock, it is important to realize from the outset that the appearance of these domestic animals is, from the point of view of human history as a whole, a sudden and almost abrupt development. For so far as our present knowledge goes, domestic animals do not appear one by one in widely different areas at long intervals of time. After the tens of thousands of years during which domestic animals were unknown to man, communities appear in the Ancient East from the Nile to the Indus between about 5000 and 3000 B.C., in which not one but several animals are reared. Moreover, the same animals are reared in the different centres of early civilization. Although it is very dangerous to argue *ab ignorantia*, and we still know very little of the early development of civilization in many areas, the juxtaposition in time and space is overwhelmingly in favour of the view that the vitally important area of northern Africa and south-west Asia, which saw the birth of cereal cultivation, was also the scene of the early stages in animal domestication in the Old World. There are indeed physical and in particular climatic factors which would have encouraged such people as the north African Capsians not to rest with the dog which merely helped them hunt their game. With the final melting of the European ice sheets the damp pluvial period which the Sahara-Arabian region had enjoyed came to an end, and the desert conditions, already fully established by 3000 B.C., began to develop. At such a time, as Childe has pointed out, the resources of the hunters would be progressively depleted and at the same time concentrated in a manner more favourable to domestication:

'Enforced concentration in oases or by the banks of ever more precarious springs and streams would require an intensified search for means of nourishment. Animals and men would be herded together round pools and wadis that were growing increasingly isolated by desert tracts, and such enforced juxtaposition might almost of itself promote that sort of symbiosis between man and beast that is expressed in the word "domestication". For the situation thus engendered to produce the desired effects it is clearly necessary that the men who had to cope with the crisis should find at hand the cereals and animals apt for domestication'.[1]

Whatever the process the facts are surprising enough. Deliberate and presumably ritual burials of cattle and sheep have been found in the settlements of the early Badarian cultivators, while pigs, sheep or goats, and cattle have been identified in the settlements of their cultural relatives in the Fayyum. At a somewhat later period clay models of domestic cattle standing quietly in rows were buried in the graves of early pre-Dynastic times together with models of other possessions that they might accompany the dead. Clay figurines of cattle, sheep and swine have also been found in the settlements of the early al Ubaid phase in Lower Mesopotamia. It can be argued that these represent only wild animals, but the use of dung in plastering the wattle huts would seem to belie this. Rows of goats are shown on the painted wares of the early settlements in the Zagros foothills and in northern Mesopotamia. They also appear, but are perhaps later, as decorative motifs on pottery in Baluchistan. In the Indus basin no sites comparable in antiquity to the earliest in Egypt and Sumer have yet been found, but cattle, sheep, swine, water buffalo and fowls were all reared by the occupants of the early cities of the third millennium B.C. The earliest farmers of this wide and pregnant tract of the earth's surface lost no time in adding domestic cattle to their economy.

These important developments must be borne in mind when considering the problems of the time and place at which particular animals were domesticated.

The pig may be considered first, for, although it has played but a humble and limited role, its use is very widespread and it is the only meat-provider of some lower cultivators. The pig is a forest and swamp animal. It does not eat grass but shrubs and roots. In Europe it was being reared in Neolithic

1 Childe, V. G.: *The Most Ancient East*, p. 42.

settlements in south-eastern Europe and Switzerland before 2000 B.C. The domestic pig is, however, of still greater recorded antiquity in Egypt, where wild boars were native to the Nile swamps. Considerable herds of swine were kept in the early Dynastic period, but as in early Babylonia the extent and purpose of domestication is unknown, for the pig appears to have been neither eaten nor put to other economic use in Dynastic times until a quite late period. Attention has already been called to the bones of pigs found in the early Fayyum settlements and to the clay models of swine found in the earliest settlements of Lower Mesopotamia. Pigs of the eastern breed, *Sus cristatus*, were used for food in the Indus, but no evidence of their domestication has yet come to light. In China, where the pig is still the most important meat animal, pig bones have been found in surprising quantities in the early Neolithic sites of the Painted Pottery peoples which probably represented the eastward expansion across Asia of the comparable cultures of Mesopotamia and Iran.

There has been much discussion as to the relation of European domestic pigs to the wild European form (*Sus scrofa*) and to other wild forms, especially the southern Asiatic *Sus indicus* (*cristatus*). While the later pigs of the Swiss lake dwellings are accepted as domestic varieties of the European *Sus scrofa*, it has been generally considered that the earlier form which preceded it, the Turbary pig (*Sus palustris*), was derived from *Sus indicus*, and hence was introduced into Europe from the East. The manner and precise period of such an introduction remain unknown and, in the absence of detailed investigations of early breeds of pig in Egypt and Lower Mesopotamia, cannot be further clarified. Hilzheimer has suggested that the resemblances to *Sus indicus* are misleading, that both the Turbary pig and *Sus indicus* differ from the wild *Sus scrofa* in having more juvenile traits, but that in the former case these can result from domestication and need imply no genetic relations between the two. Nevertheless, the fact that the Ancient East was such a prolific centre of early domestic animals and that *Sus indicus*, found to-day from India to Indonesia, was probably the native wild form in south-west Asia, renders the older view entirely possible. It is in any case practically impossible on general archaeological grounds to assume an introduction of domestic pigs from Europe into Egypt and Mesopotamia before 3000 B.C., for Europe was then only learning of agriculture and the domestication of animals for the first time.

It is of interest to note that a third species of wild pig (*Sus barbatus*), which is found in Indo-China and Indonesia, has never been domesticated although it is said to be easily tamed. The domestic pigs of that region, like those of Oceania, belong to the European and south Asiatic breeds.

The distribution of the domestic pig is to a large extent limited by its requirements. It is unsuited to grasslands, whether tropical or temperate, and can only survive under really arid conditions in riverine marshes. Although tropical and monsoon forests are as favourable as European woodland, the pig is not found in any considerable numbers on the southern side of the Saharan barrier and has never been an important animal among the Congo and Guinea peoples. To many of them indeed it appears to have been unknown until recent times. The spread of Mohammedan religion, which inculcates the idea that the pig is unclean and may not be eaten, has no doubt considerably modified its Asiatic and North African distribution since ancient times, but nowhere is the pig an animal of pastoral peoples. The conditions which they seek for their domestic herbivores are automatically unfavourable for this scavenging forest animal.

It is to be noted that the peccary, the representative of the *Suidae* in the New World, which has a wild distribution extending from northern Mexico to Patagonia and is abundant in the tropical forests, was never domesticated, although it is one of the most important animals hunted in Amazonia.

Another domestic animal that is generally divorced from pastoral economy is the domestic fowl (*Gallus gallus*), which is reared by lower cultivators in south-eastern Asia and Oceania and in forest Africa. The wild race is found to-day from northern India to Indonesia, where it inhabits forest country, living mainly in bamboo thickets and laying its clutch of eight to a dozen eggs on the ground. There are several other wild species of *Gallus*, but this alone was domesticated in early times. The early centre of its domestication has often been placed in Further India, but its early appearance in the Indus civilization suggests that the centre may have lain here. Wild fowl are still abundant in the foothills of the Punjab.

Among many of the more primitive peoples the chicken, to us a bird of real economic importance, raises in an extreme form a problem which must be discussed later, namely, the importance of non-economic factors in the initial domestication and maintenance of domestic animals. In Burma, near the probable centre of its domestication, the chicken is not kept for utilitarian purposes and the eggs are hardly if ever consumed. The main function of the chicken is to supply bones for the purpose of divination. Similar practices occur elsewhere in China and Indonesia, and the antiquity of this use in south-eastern Asia is attested by Chinese records as early as the late second century B.C. In Africa similar ritual uses of the chicken are widespread and frequently outweigh their economic value. The Yoruba appear to use chickens far more frequently for sacrificial purposes than as food. The Fang of the Cameroons eat chickens only during rituals, while the Bakitara eat neither their chickens nor the eggs, but inspect the entrails of slaughtered birds for omens.

Far more important in the history of civilization than any of the animals so far considered are the domestic herbivores, and of these cattle *Bos taurus* have attained the greatest importance and the widest distribution both in the higher civilizations and among Old World pastoral nomads.

The wild ox or urus (*Bos primigenius*), from which domestic cattle are generally considered to be derived, had a wide distribution in Europe and south-western Asia in the late glacial period and survived into medieval times. As their pictures show, it was important among the game of the Capsian hunters in Spain. The remains of urus, or of a closely related form, have been found in Algeria, and there are early Egyptian records of hunting wild cattle in the Nile country. The wild ox of Europe and western Asia, represented in Assyrian bas-reliefs and described by Caesar and others in classical times, was a very large animal with long upcurving horns. But the early varieties of domestic oxen are considerably smaller, and some were short-horned while others had none at all. In early Dynastic times Egyptians were raising both shorthorn and polled cattle as well as the sacred herds with long lyrate horns (*Bos taurus Aegypticus*), which appear to have died out fairly early.

Bryner Jones has recently suggested that the part played by urus in the ancestry of domestic cattle has been exaggerated. The characteristics of *Leptobos*, the Pliocene and early Pleistocene ancestor of *Bos primigenius*, suggest that the latter was a rather specialized development. Moreover, the appearance of short-horned and polled cattle among the herds of very early times cannot be explained by the domestication of urus alone. He therefore considers it necessary to postulate that other smaller species or races descended from *Leptobos* existed in post-glacial times, some of which were hornless and others short-horned, in order to account for the characteristics of early domestic cattle in the Near East and in Europe. The discovery of bones of 'a small ox' in Capsian middens in North Africa may be of great significance in this connexion.[1]

Hilzheimer, basing his argument on the long history and advanced technique of Egyptian cattle raising and on the large number of breeds found there at an early period, considers the Nile Valley to be the most probable scene of the first domestication of cattle. Hahn had earlier attributed it to the Mesopotamian area, largely on the ground that cattle there played such a prominent role as sacred animals. But sacred oxen and offerings of milk to the deities are no Babylonian speciality. Indeed the sanctifying of animals both domestic and wild is one of the most outstanding features of early Egyptian religion. The cow was here peculiarly sacred as the embodiment of the mother-goddess Hathor. Moreover, it is to the very strong development of ritual concepts in early Egypt that the attitude to cattle so widespread in tropical Africa must be attributed. As between a north-east African and south-west Asiatic origin of cattle domestication it is impossible on the existing evidence to decide. The important point is that in both areas it follows very quickly on the heels of the first cultivation. It has frequently been claimed, largely on the basis of exaggerated datings of the settlements at Anau, that cattle were first domesticated in central Asia. The settlements at Anau cannot, however, be dated in any but the most approximate manner: their relations with Babylonia are far too indirect. But there is no reason to regard the culture of Anau as ancestral to Sumerian civilization or as older than the third millennium B.C. The founders of the first settlement here appear to have possessed no domestic animals, and the development of the civilization can best be accounted for by successive periods of contact with the higher cultures to the south. The last phase, with its wheel-made pottery, seals, figurines and beads, bears the unmistakable imprint of south-west Asiatic civilization.

The maintenance of large herds in these hot, dry Nile and Euphrates basins presented considerable difficulties. In Egypt, in Dynastic times, cattle were pastured on clover fields for four months of the year and were stall-fed for the remaining eight months, largely it would appear on aquatic plants such as papyrus reed. In Sumer cattle were fed with grain during a considerable part of the year. The cows were milked, butter and cheeses were made, beef was eaten and in both areas bullocks were used to draw both ploughs and carts.

In the Indus cities cattle were also reared. Furthermore,

[1] *L'Anthropologie* 42, p. 476.

in addition to a breed of *Bos taurus* another genus and another species were domesticated, namely, the humped cattle or zebu (*Bos indicus*), and a species of buffalo (*Bubalus*). The zebu was the most important of the animals here; abundant remains have been found, and zebu bulls are represented on countless seals, while *Bos taurus* is known so far only from figurines.

While little is known of the uses of these animals, model carts have been found. Since the archaeological evidence so far available suggests that the Indus civilization received its first impetus from farther west, the domestication of the zebu and the buffalo is to be regarded as the transference of the domestication of cattle to other animals. No truly wild form of the zebu is known. Rutimeyer's suggestion that it could be derived from the bantin, a member of the bovine family but of a distinct sub-genus *Bibos* found wild and semi-domesticated in Indo-China and Indonesia, is now generally rejected. It is regarded as derived from a variant of *Bos*, and the large, fleshy hump which may weigh as much as fifty pounds is thought to have been developed under domestication.

Although unknown in the West in very early times the zebu begins to appear in Mesopotamia and Egypt during the middle of the second millennium. The zebu and western cattle are completely interfertile and crossing took place at an early period. A zebu strain has spread into Africa, where it has blended with other forms. The so-called Galla cattle of the Sudan, which have very long, lyre-shaped horns, closely resembling those of the ancient *Bos Aegypticus*, are humped like the zebu, although the hump is usually of smaller size, and is sometimes insignificant. Cattle of this type are found from the Upper Nile southwards to the Lakes plateau and westwards beyond Lake Chad. The native herds are, however, very mixed, and shorter horned and humpless forms are also found. The cattle of the more southern pastoralists, although often long-horned, have no hump, which suggests a relatively late and limited diffusion of the zebu strain in Africa. In north-eastern India a large breed of native cattle, the Gayal, is believed to descend from another species of *Bos*, the Gaur, native to that region and still found in a wild state.

The water buffalo (*Bubalus*), found so early as a domestic animal in north-west India, and far better suited than cattle to hot damp regions, very largely replaces other cattle as a draught animal in southern and eastern Asia, and in this area the use of cattle for dairying purposes fades out. The buffalo does, nevertheless, afford a quantity of thick, ropy milk and the Toda of the Nilgiri Hills live an almost exclusively pastoral life dependent on their buffalo herds.

The period at which domestic cattle were carried into central Asia remains unknown, but they reached northern China long before the Christian era. Within central Asia itself on the high Pamir and Tibetan plateaux yet another member of the Bovidae was domesticated—the yak (*Poëphagus grunniens*). As has already been sufficiently indicated it has been put to all the uses found among the cattle breeders of surrounding areas.

The early domestication of *Bos taurus* in the Ancient East has therefore been the starting point for the domestication of several other species and genera of the Bovidae. At the same time the uses of cattle have been diffused with the animals themselves, completely in some areas, particularly in Europe and western Asia, but partially in others. In Sumer cattle were already being used to draw carts soon after 3000 B.C. As in Egypt they were used also for ploughing, threshing and for milking and had at the same time important ritual functions. In India they have retained their sanctity and importance as draught animals, while dairying is of little economic importance; butter is made only for ceremonial purposes. In the pastoral areas of arid Asia the milking and dairying uses are found, but cattle give pride of place to the horse and sheep. In Africa south of the Equator milking is the essential economic use of live stock, but dairying is not found. The ritual prominence of cattle remains and mere possession has acquired great prestige. Although a native species of buffalo is abundant in tropical Africa it has not been domesticated and there is no evidence for the initial domestication of any animal south of the Sahara.

Domestic sheep appear almost as early as cattle in the oldest settlements of the Ancient East. Whether the fragmentary remains in the Fayyum settlements were sheep or goats cannot be decided, but domestic sheep are represented on pots and palettes of the second pre-Dynastic period in Egypt. Figurines of sheep which may have been domesticated were found at al 'Ubaid, and at the beginnings of historic Sumerian civilization (*c.* 3000 B.C.) large flocks were kept and the ewes, as in Egypt, were milked like cattle.

Two species of wild sheep are concerned in the ancestry of the many breeds of early times and of the domestic sheep throughout the world to-day. These are the mouflon (*Ovis musimon*) and the urial (*Ovis longipes* or *vignei*). The former survives in south-western Asia (especially in Persia and

Anatolia) and in southern Europe, where it existed, at least until recently, in Cyprus, Corsica and Sardinia. The mouflon is a heavy animal with a hairy coat. The ram has a mane and long recurved horns which lie close to the head. The domesticated mouflon is represented very early in Sumerian times. The urial, a more lightly built animal with a longer neck, splayed and more slender horns, longer legs and in some varieties a long tail, is found wild over a much wider area in south-western Asia extending east to the Punjab and north to the Ust-urt plateau in Turkestan. It is found in lowland as well as in mountainous country, and it occupies more arid areas than does the mouflon. The early sheep of the Old Kingdom in Dynastic Egypt, and also those represented in pre-Dynastic art, as well as the oldest sheep found in the Swiss Lake Dwellings, are believed to derive from the urial. There is, however, no evidence that wild sheep existed in northern Africa at the dawn of civilization. The so-called Barbary sheep of the Atlas region is a goat-like animal of an entirely different genus (*Ammotragus*). The supposed Palaeolithic age of drawings of 'wild sheep' in Algeria and South Morocco has been disproved by Hilzheimer as well as by Obermaier. They have shown that the animals represented are typical of the domesticated long-legged sheep distinct from any known wild form and have neck-bands whch are not markings but collars and indicate that they were domesticated. There are, however, references to remains of animals which may be sheep in some North African Capsian sites,[1] so that although the wild faunas of North Africa and of Asia appear to have been in general sharply distinct, the possibility remains that wild sheep may have existed in the former area in the moister late glacial period. Should this prove to be so it may afford the explanation of the difference in breed between the early Egyptian and early Sumerian sheep, which were apparently derived from the urial and mouflon respectively.[2] From the twelfth Dynasty onwards a new fat-tailed breed of sheep appeared in Egypt which ousted the earlier long-legged type. The development of heavy fat tails, and also of deposits of fat on the rump, has been satisfactorily shown to be an effect of selective breeding by man. Where this development first occurred is unknown, but domestic fat-tailed and fat-rumped sheep are characteristic of both settled and nomadic pastoral peoples in Asia. The early Egyptian fat-tailed variety appears

[1] *Nature*, 1928, p. 499.
[2] Several distinct breeds of sheep were, however, being reared in Sumer and domestic urials appear to be indicated in some representations.

to be an intrusive breed, and if so it must have come from somewhere on the Asiatic side of Sinai. Fat-tailed sheep are common in the flocks of the North and East African pastoral peoples to-day.

No wild sheep have a thick woolly fleece. The use of wool is a by-product of initial domestication for other purposes. Heavily fleeced sheep were possessed by the Babylonians, who used wool extensively as a textile material, while wool for weaving, felting and rug-making has long been obtained from their flocks by both sedentary and pastoral peoples in south-western Asia. In Africa the development and use of the fleece has received practically no attention: neither the Egyptians nor, at the present time, the pastoral peoples of the grasslands have used the wool of the sheep—yet another instance of the frequent contrasts in the uses of domestic animals in different regions.

In both Asia and Africa the goat accompanies the sheep as a domestic animal. It is put to similar uses in the various areas and is treated as an inferior sheep: Congo peoples milk neither but eat both. The Kazak pasture their goats with their sheep and milk both into the same bucket. The Asiatic and African breeds of domestic goat are generally considered to derive from a single wild species (*Capra aegagrus*) which had formerly a very wide distribution in southern Europe and western Asia. As has been seen, representations of goats that were probably domestic appear as early as sheep in south-western Asia. It is, however, possible that the dwarf goat commonly found among the cultivating peoples of central and West Africa may be descended from a different and perhaps African ancestor. It has a much higher immunity to fly-borne diseases than has the larger brown goat of the African savanas.

While the known distribution of wild sheep and goats has been taken to imply that they were first domesticated in south-western Asia, when we turn to the oldest member of the horse family a north-east African area of domestication is practically certain. All the varieties of the domesticated asses derive from the true wild ass of this region. Several varieties of the species *Equus asinus* probably existed, and two survive to-day in the south-western Sudan, in the Atbara river basin, and in Somaliland. Wild species of the genus *Equus* other than the wild horse do exist in Asia, and some of them have been called 'wild asses': those of the Scriptures are a case in point, but these animals, although one of them, the onager, has a habitat similar in climate and vegetation to that of the wild ass (it ranges from Syria to north-western India and is a truly desert animal), have no share in the ancestry of the donkey and were not themselves domesticated.

There was probably a considerable period in the Ancient East during which the donkey had not yet become the poor relation of the horse. In Egypt a row of asses is shown on a slate palette of late pre-Dynastic date, a period at which the peoples to the east of the Delta already had considerable herds. It was certainly being reared at the beginning of Dynastic times and it appears before the opening of the historic Sumerian period (c. 3000 B.C.) in lower Mesopotamia. Able to thrive on much poorer fodder, it was used as an alternative and supplement to cattle; the she asses were milked and draught donkeys were used to draw both ploughs and chariots.

The first evidences of domestic donkeys are, however, later than those of cattle both in Egypt and Mesopotamia, and, since these animals appear always to have been less numerous and less important than cattle, it is probable that they were domesticated somewhat later. The point of prime importance is that in the early period they were employed in the same way as cattle, and in no new way. The riding of asses appears considerably later and in imitation of the animal next to be considered.

The domestic horse does not assume importance in the ancient civilizations until a relatively late period, and that appearance is associated with a new use for domestic animals, namely, riding. The first explicit literary record of the horse in Mesopotamia occurs only shortly before 2000 B.C. It was introduced into Babylonia, at least in large numbers, only with the Kassite invasion from the Persian plateau in the middle of the eighteenth century. In Egypt the horse also appears with equestrian invaders, 'the shepherd kings' or Hyksos, in about 1700 B.C. There was, however, some knowledge of the horse in the higher civilizations at much earlier times. A rider is apparently portrayed on an object from the 'Royal Tombs' at Ur, while a still earlier representation of what looks like a horse and rider is found on a prehistoric bone carving at Susa. Furthermore, the sign which was used to refer to the horse in Babylonian times, and which means significantly enough 'the ass of the mountains', has now been identified in the ideographic precursor of Sumerian writing in the late prehistoric period (before c. 3000 B.C.). Moreover, temple inventories of the earlier part of the third millennium B.C. refer to an animal similar to but distinct from the ass.

The animal from which the early domestic breeds derive is the steppe horse, or *Equus przewalski*, which still survives in remote parts of the Kobdo plateau, in western Mongolia, where it lives in small herds of six to a dozen mares, each controlled by a stallion. This small, pony-like animal, only twelve hands high, has its native habitat in the dry, open steppe, and it can withstand severely cold conditions. There is every reason to believe that in early post-glacial times it occupied the steppes of south-western Turkestan and the Iranian plateau. Quite recently the remains of wild horses have been found in Epipalaeolithic sites in Palestine. Still earlier during the Ice Age it had occupied Europe at certain periods, and was one of the most important game animals of the Aurignacian hunters in France. Whether the original domestication of the horse was modelled on that of the donkey which may have been carried northwards and eastwards from Babylonia remains unknown, but in some area perhaps outside the orbit of the more advanced civilizations the new art of horse riding was discovered. That it was used for this purpose alone is doubtful in view of the enormously widespread and ancient use of milking mares. The herding of horses for milk and meat more probably came first, although the mare is a far less satisfactory milking animal than the cow, yielding only for a short season and needing to be milked several times a day. In the Ancient East, moreover, the fleetness of the horse in drawing chariots was for a considerable period appreciated far more highly than the new equestrian use. Horse riding and the use of cavalry in war were of no great importance until fairly late Assyrian times, whereas horse chariots are nearly always depicted in battle-scenes after the middle of the second millennium B.C. The horse thus became the driving and riding animal in peace and war and was used for little else. It was with these associations that it penetrated Europe in the Bronze Age, little before 1000 B.C. It is not generally realized that this restricted use of the horse, which is equally true of classical times, continued for a very long period in western Europe. The ox was the animal used to draw both ploughs and carts in England right down to the eighteenth century Horses were reserved for riding and carriages. The milking of mares strikes a European as strange, and its flesh is eaten only to a very limited extent.

While the lightly built horses of the Near East both in ancient and modern times are undoubtedly domesticated forms of Przewalski's horse, it is generally assumed that another but unknown breed, heavier in build and native to the forests, was domesticated in Europe at a later period and is the ancestor of the Shire horses.

As has been seen, the horse attained only a limited distribution in Africa, and may have been unknown there, outside the areas of Roman civilization until the medieval Arab conquests. Both the animal and the art of riding remained unknown to the pastoralists of eastern Africa, but where the horse did penetrate, as in the western Sudan and among the Yoruba on the Guinea coast, the art of riding went with it.

The camel is also a comparatively late-comer in the early civilizations of the Old World. Both the Arabian (*Camelus dromedarius*) and the two-humped (*C. bactrianus*) species are desert animals. A wild form of the Bactrian camel, which is a shorter-legged and heavier-built animal and grows a long, thick winter coat suitable to the continental climate of the interior deserts of Asia, survives in the south-western parts of the Tarim Basin. But the Arabian camel, which was probably the first to be domesticated, is unknown in a wild state. The wild camel existed in North Africa in the late Pleistocene period, but was already extinct there in the earliest historic times.

An early indication of the knowledge of the camel in the Ancient World is afforded by a vase of Egyptian style in the form of a camel found in Syria. This vase comes from an Egyptian colony established at Byblos in early Dynastic times, but it is no certain index of domestication, for theriomorphic jars of this type frequently represented wild animals. A camel-hair rope has also been recovered among early Dynastic remains in the Fayyum.[1] But it is not until the beginning of the Middle Kingdom that domestic camels become common in Egypt. The earliest references to the camel in Babylonia are as late as 1100 B.C., and it does not seem to have made its appearance there in any numbers until the ninth century B.C., by which time the Bactrian camel was also known. Remains of camels have been found in the settlement of the second period at Anau and in the latest levels of Mohenjo-daro on the Indus. The domestication of these animals is not, however, certain. Among the cultivating peoples of the desert areas the camel was soon adopted as a substitute for the ox and donkey in drawing the plough. It is also the essential beast of burden in the arid belt, and is also ridden after the manner of the horse.

This review of the more important domestic animals in the Old World should in the first place serve to dispel the fallacy that each domesticated animal that is biologically distinct has an equally independent cultural history. Transference of

[1] G. Caton Thompson, *Man*, January 1934.

pattern from one animal to another, a process which was considered earlier in connexion with the reindeer (see p. 365), is seen to have played a very important part in the domestication of other animals in early times.

The second point of importance is that the use of the larger domestic animals for draught in pulling ploughs and carts is considerably earlier, at least in the areas of high civilization, than riding. Two and four-wheeled vehicles, both chariots and carts, were used in Sumer by 3000 B.C. At first they are known only in association with ceremonial and warfare. These early vehicles had solid wheels which turned with the axle and were tyred with leather. In the famous 'Royal Tombs' at Ur, belonging to the end of the prehistoric period, the dead sovereigns were carried into their great tombs on biers or chariots drawn by teams of oxen. But already the monuments from these same tombs depict light war-chariots in each of which a driver and a warrior ride, the latter wielding both throwing and thrusting spears. Models of wheeled vehicles have also been found at an early period in the Indus cities. The art of riding is the only important use of a domestic animal in the Old World that appears, at present, to have developed in an area relatively remote from the main centres of civilization. Whether the animal which was the occasion of this development was itself domesticated in the first place by people with no previous knowledge of domestic animals, is much more doubtful, and is on general grounds highly improbable.

It is necessary to consider the extent to which economic factors and deliberate purpose may be considered to underlie the domestication of animals. It is quite obvious that domestic animals have long been of great economic value both as food and as beasts of burden in many parts of the world, and these values were appreciated very early by the agricultural peoples of the Ancient East. Nevertheless, many of these animals were at the same time closely associated with important rituals in early times, while among many of the modern peoples of lower civilization they are rarely regarded as ordinary resources of the environment to be exploited in a purely material way. Not only the chickens of Indonesia but the cattle of southern Asia and Africa and also the pigs of Oceania are limited in their economic value by magical or religious beliefs concerning them. The cat, the only feline to be domesticated, has never served an economic purpose. From Egypt, where it had important religious significance in early Dynastic times, the domestic cat (derived from a wild North African variety *Felis*

ocreata maniculata) has been carried into Europe and Asia.
It has lost its religious significance and has become merely a
pet, which will sometimes keep down vermin. In China alone
is it used to some extent for food.

In many parts of the world other animals are kept, either
truly domestic or as tamed pets, with no thought of economic
use. Many of the South American forest peoples keep and
feed tame macaws, monkeys, lizards and other small animals.
Bates told Galton of no fewer than twenty-two different species
of quadruped as well as many birds that he found in various
Amazon villages. Some of the northern Algonquin Indians
frequently tamed moose, others tamed bear cubs. The Chinese
went to great trouble in breeding crickets, at first to enjoy
their 'music' and, after the ninth century A.D., that they might
witness cricket fights. Veritable menageries, including tame
lions, elephants, leopards and other animals were found by
early travellers in various parts of tropical Africa.

The important religious significance of cattle in early Babylonia led Hahn to claim that their domestication began entirely
for ritual purposes. While there can be no proof of this since
domestic cattle long precede written records, it is important
to realize that until an animal was already domesticated and
available in considerable numbers it would be almost impossible to conceive of such secondary economic uses for it as
providing milk or drawing ploughs. Domestication cannot
have begun with these later values in view.

On the other hand, the ritual importance of an animal does
not necessarily lead to its domestication. Ritual attitudes are
by no means absent towards wild animals, and the elaborate
bear ceremonialism of north-eastern Asia and north-western
America is but a particular instance of a common attitude.
Domestication could therefore begin with a desire to assure a
food-supply from captive game, and the ritual might either
precede or follow domestication for this purpose. Keeping
animals as pets would be expected to conflict with the former
object, since there is a universal reluctance to kill and eat such
animals. Moreover, the important domestic animals contrast
with the majority of 'pets' in their gregarious character, which
both facilitates and increases the value of domestication. The
eating of sacrificed animals affords an easier hypothetical
transition.

Whatever the initial stages through which it passed the
complex of animal domestication in the Old World appears
almost certainly to have begun in the Near East in a period
which may be approximately dated to between 5000 and

4000 B.C. From the first beginnings, which may have been directed towards cattle, other animals were added by a process of accretion, so that within two or three thousand years all the more valuable domestic animals known to man in the Old World were already within human control. Since that time no other of importance has been added to the list; there has only been improvement of the ancient breeds.

The domestication of an animal is no simple process which is easily achieved with patience. After their amazing success with cattle, sheep and other animals an orgy of attempts at domestication appears to have taken place in early Egypt and Sumer. In Egypt early paintings and bas-reliefs show antelopes and other animals being kept in herds, standing in stalls and at the leash. In Sumer leopards are shown drawing chariots, and antelopes are grouped among live stock. But these experiments came to nothing. Galton held the view that so great is the human propensity for taming amenable animals that every beast capable of domestication and worth the trouble of maintaining has long since been domesticated. This view appears to remain substantially as true to-day as when he wrote nearly seventy-five years ago. There is, no doubt, a number of animals that could be still domesticated if it were worth the while. The seal is probably among them, but efforts in the nineteenth century to domesticate the zebra failed, and the ostrich remains only by courtesy a domestic animal.

The conditions that an animal must fulfil if a domestic breed is to be established are, according to Galton, that it should be hardy, that it should have an inborn liking for man, that it should be comfort-loving, that it should prove useful, that it should breed freely in captivity, and that it should be easy to tend. All these conditions appear to be fulfilled completely by very few animals. Nearly all the domestic animals do fulfil them. The elephant has remained only a tamed animal, for it will not readily breed in captivity; elephants are usually caught young and tamed whether for a chiefly menagerie and procession or for piling teak. In both cases the process is long and tedious.

Gregariousness is also a most important quality for animals that are to be herded, and docility is required in beasts that are to be broken for harness, yoke or saddle. Apart from the cat, which breaks every rule and remains domesticated only through its great love of comfort, the reindeer is the only beast which is retained as a domestic animal despite its lack of a strong attachment to man.

This does not imply that the domesticated animals possessed

by man differ in no way from their wild forbears. They are probably as different in their psychological as in their physical characters. For in every generation the tamer beasts in the herd have remained the longest; the wild doubtless escaped under early conditions and were permanently lost, while the vicious were killed for food. Centuries of breeding from the more docile stock have exerted a powerful selection, which has resulted in the unremarked marvel to be seen in every pasture.

Nor can it be assumed that the various uses to which animals have been put have followed automatically from domestication. In the New World, more meagre both in the animals available for domestication and in its accumulation of discovery and invention, and cut off at least from the higher crafts of the Old World, neither wheeled vehicles nor ploughs were known. The arts of milking and riding were neither introduced from the Old World nor independently discovered. Between these two hemispheres there remained the great contrast which is immediately apparent when the chief domestic animals and the uses to which they have been put are listed:

New World

 Dog—hunting and draught (Eskimo and Plains).
 Llama and alpaca—burden, wool and (to a limited extent) food (Andean highlands).
 Turkey—a pet with ceremonial uses, very rarely eaten (Mexico and Pueblo).
 Guinea-pig—tamed as a pet and eaten occasionally (Andean highlands and Guianas).

Old World

 Dog—draught, hunting and occasionally food.
 Pig—ritual and food.
 Chicken—ritual and only occasionally (save in Europe) food.
 Duck, goose—food.
 Pigeon, peacock—pets but rarely eaten.
 Cattle—milk, draught, riding as a substitute for horse, and meat to a limited extent (except in Europe).
 Gayal—draught, to some extent milk.
 Buffalo—draught, burden, milk.
 Yak—burden, riding, milk.
 Sheep—milk, meat, wool.
 Goat—milk, meat, hair.
 Horse—milk, draught, riding, occasionally burden and meat.
 Ass—milk, draught, burden, riding.
 Camel—milk, burden, draught, hair, riding.
 Reindeer—milk, meat, draught, burden, riding.

CHAPTER XXIII

CONCLUSION

THE main object of this book has been to provide a
series of brief but precise studies that may make it
possible to appreciate the complex relations between
the human habitat and the manifold technical and social
devices developed for its exploitation among the peoples who
lie outside the sphere of modern civilization. The economies
depend for their continuance on certain physical conditions,
but at the same time they select and transmute some of the
latent resources into particular values and are the foundations
for particular forms of social organization. Geographers,
economists and sociologists have all on occasion produced a
lay figure, a 'primitive man', stripped of reality and redressed
according to need, with which to portray particular theories as
to the role of physical circumstances in human affairs, as to
the nature of social evolution, or concerning the development
of economic relations in human society. Selecting an instance
here and a generalization there, it is possible to provide a
superficially plausible case for almost any scheme of causation
or any theory of development. Almost equally easy is it to
produce contrary instances, and to give some substance to
contrary generalizations. The reality of human activity
escapes through so coarse a mesh. The study of the interrelations between habitat, economy and society among a number
of particular peoples is needed to afford the material and the
experience for judgment and appreciation of these complex
problems. In some of the earlier chapters comparisons
between societies in generally similar habitats or in adjacent
regions have afforded some comparative basis for discussion,
while in the later part of the book an attempt has been made
to review the conditions found among the particular peoples
against a broader geographical and historical background.

The particular peoples studied in the earlier sections were
for convenience grouped in three broad categories, as food
gatherers, cultivators and pastoralists. The great differences
of economic pattern and social organization to be found within
each of these provisional groupings have been indicated. It

is obvious that while there is little homogeneity within them, there is also no abrupt transition from one to another.

The far-reaching significance of different modes of life was already recognized in classical times, and they were soon endowed with a developmental value as 'economic stages'. In the nineteenth century, when attention was first seriously devoted to the economies of primitive peoples, these hoary economic stages met with little criticism from the ideas of unilinear evolution, themselves transferred uncritically from biology to human culture. Man had begun everywhere, it was suggested, as a hunter, had later learned to domesticate some of his game animals and so became a pastoralist, and finally rose to the stage of agriculture. Little distinction was drawn between the very different kinds of food gathering, or between the rudimentary digging of planted roots and advanced cereal agriculture with the plough. Nor were any valid reasons adduced for supposing that pastoralism everywhere preceded cultivation. Finally, the concept of cultural diffusion and the recognition of the part it played in affecting the economic pattern over vast areas was almost entirely neglected. The ideas of evolution and progress that dominated scientific and social thought produced a vague and abstract 'man' living nowhere in particular, who was always tending to struggle up to a higher stage. Criticism of this three-stage theory is no longer required: its inadequacy has long been realized. The German geographer, Edouard Hahn, performed the valuable service of attacking the dogma of pastoral priority, which archaeological discovery has since done so much to refute, and of indicating the great gulf that usually lies between digging stick and plough cultivation.

Peoples do not live at economic stages. They possess economies; and again we do not find single and exclusive economies but combinations of them. Development is not in one direction along a single line, and some economies have played almost no part in the historical growth of particular cultures. Pastoralism had, for instance, a relatively late and very limited development in the New World.

The essential economies may in the broadest way be termed collecting, hunting, fishing, cultivation and stock rearing. But the adoption and practice of any one does not imply or necessitate the complete abandonment of another, nor has any people been known to rely exclusively on one alone. Different economies may be divided between the sexes, as in south-eastern Africa; they may be undertaken by different social classes, as among the Bakitara; or by specialists in particular localities, as among the Yoruba. Only the densest populations and the most intensive agriculture, as in Cochin, reduce collecting and hunting to negligible proportions, while fishing survives in the most advanced cultures. The hunting of large game is elaborately developed among the south-eastern Bantu, who also cultivate millet and raise cattle. Fishing had greater social prestige than cultivation nearly everywhere in central Polynesia. It remains of great importance in Malabar and indeed in the North Sea. We still gather our blackberries and are, moreover, at great pains to prevent the extinction of wild game, so that a hunting economy, which has outlived its economic value, may continue to afford pleasure and minister to social prestige.

The elaboration and efficiency of equipment for any economy may vary enormously, from the elaborate devices of the Eskimo to the poor weapons of the Yahgan or the Tasmanians, from the digging stick of the Boro to the iron hoes of the Yoruba. The development of co-operative effort is similarly diverse. Moreover, the terms 'cultivation' and 'stock rearing' conceal rather than clarify the realities of mode of life. Between cultivation with the use of ploughs, beasts of burden and manures on the one hand and hoe or digging-stick tillage on the other, there may be fundamental differences of the greatest importance for the division and specialization of labour and the density of population. But the simple terms 'hoe cultivation' and 'plough cultivation' are not, as has been seen, completely adequate to express these categories. Intensive and highly productive agriculture may not, as in southern China, involve the use of the plough. The implement may be neglected, even though it has long been known. An extensive use of manures and irrigation may exist, as in Peru, where an elaborated digging stick is nevertheless the only agricultural implement. Indeed, it is impossible to separate a series of peoples such as the Boro, the Solomon Islanders, the Yoruba, the Hopi, the Ifugao, the southern Chinese and the people of Cochin into two sharply distinct groups.

Moreover, while among stock raisers there is an obvious cleavage between people who raise a few sheep, goats and chickens (as in the Congo-Guinea region), or pigs and chickens (as in Oceania), and those who rely almost entirely on considerable herds of herbivorous animals, the gradation through Kavirondo, Baganda, Bakitara and Masai in eastern Africa presents similar overlaps, and shows the difficulty of simple classification. In Asia the transitions in the character, number and uses of the live stock are equally gradual as one passes from Kazak through Kalmuck, Yakut and Tungus to the Chuckchi.

Neither the world distributions of the various economies, nor their development and relative importance among particular peoples, can be regarded as simple functions of physical conditions and natural resources. Between the physical environment and human activity there is always a middle term, a collection of specific objectives and values, a body of knowledge and belief: in other words, a cultural pattern. That the culture itself is not static, that it is adaptable and modifiable in relation to physical conditions, must not be allowed to obscure the fact that adaptation proceeds by discoveries and inventions which are themselves in no sense inevitable and which are, in any individual community, nearly all of them acquisitions or impositions from without. The peoples of whole continents have failed to make discoveries that might at first blush seem obvious. Equally important are the restrictions placed by social patterns and religious concepts on the utilization of certain resources or on adaptations to physical conditions. As Febvre has recognized:

> 'wherever "man" and natural products are concerned, the "idea" intervenes. This last often has nothing utilitarian about it and governs not only the food of men but their dress also, and the construction of their dwellings, and in fact, all their physical and material well-being. . . . Between the desires and the needs of man and everything in nature that can be utilized by him, beliefs, ideas and customs interpose . . . [moreover] we are never concerned with "man" but with human society and its organized groups.'[1]

Although the adaptation of culture, and particularly of crafts and economy to the habitat exists everywhere, and is usually (in its outlines) obvious enough, the whole complex of the physical environment does not affect human activity in any single and comprehensive way. It is necessary to distinguish negative conditions that are limiting factors at all stages of culture, and which demand special efforts and unusual costs if they are to be overcome (such are, for instance, difficulties of terrain, climatic restrictions on particular plants and animals), from those which acquire positive significance only in connexion with specific cultural achievements. This distinction may be expressed by saying that physical conditions have both restrictive and permissive relations to human activities.

[1] Febvre, L., *A Geographical Introduction to History*, p. 168.

Furthermore, the relations between culture and habitat may be direct or indirect. The tools, utensils, houses and indeed the greater part of the material equipment in the lower cultures will show a direct relation, not inasmuch as they exist but in materials and in some aspects of their specific forms, to the available resources. This relationship will often extend also to the modification of imported forms. But the social concomitants of physical conditions (such as the poverty or wealth in supplies of particular foods or materials) operate only at several removes from those physical conditions, and many other factors intervene. The more indirect the relation to the habitat, the more important are the intervening historical and sociological factors. The habitat at one and the same time circumscribes and affords scope for cultural development in relation to the pre-existing equipment and tendency of a particular society, and to any new concepts and equipment that may reach it from without.

Moreover, broad general classifications of climatic or vegetational regions are quite inadequate for the analysis of cultural possibilities, and the occupants of regions similar in their general geographical conditions often show great divergencies in cultural achievement. The term tropical rain forest (applicable to Amazonia, the Solomons, the central Congo and to the Malabar coast) does not express the reality of these areas as human habitats, nor does it adequately define their resources for cultural development. The limitations of tropical forests in general have to be qualified by the multifarious and specific restrictions and possibilities of any one such area in the hands of any particular culture. Between any two broadly similar regions the contrasts in detail in the precise conditions that are effective in the culture, to say nothing of the great importance of relations in space to other and contrasted physical and cultural regions, outweigh the significance of any generalization concerning them all.

Physical conditions enter intimately into every cultural development and pattern, not excluding the most abstract and non-material; they enter not as determinants, however, but as one category of the raw material of cultural elaboration. The study of the relations between cultural patterns and physical conditions is of the greatest importance for an understanding of human society, but it cannot be undertaken in terms of simple geographical controls alleged to be identifiable on sight. It must proceed inductively from the minute analysis of each actual society. The culture must in the first place be studied as an entity and as an historical development; there can be no other effective approach to interrelations of such complexity. The most meticulous knowledge of physical geography, whether of great regions or of small areas, will not serve to elucidate these problems unless the nature of cultural development is grasped. The geographer who is unversed in the culture of the people of the land he studies, or in the lessons which ethnology as a whole has to teach, will, as soon as he begins to consider the mainsprings of human activity, find himself groping uncertainly for geographical factors whose significance he cannot truly assess. Human geography demands as much knowledge of humanity as of geography.

But if geographical determinism fails to account for the existence and distribution of economies, economic determinism is equally inadequate in accounting for the social and political organizations, the religious beliefs and the psychological attitudes, which may be found in the cultures based on those economies. Indeed, the economy may owe as much to the social and ritual pattern as does the character of society to the economy. The possession of particular methods of hunting or cultivating, of certain cultivated plants or domestic animals, in no wise defines the pattern of society. Again there is interaction and on a new plane. As physical conditions may limit the possibilities of the economy, so the economy may in turn be a limiting or stimulating factor in relation to the size, density and stability of human settlement, and to the scale of the social and political unit. But it is only one such factor, and advantage may not be taken of the opportunities it affords. The tenure and transmission of land and other property, the development and relations of social classes, the nature of government, the religious and ceremonial life—all these are parts of a social superstructure, the development of which is conditioned not only by the foundations of habitat and economy, but by complex interactions within its own fabric and by external contacts, often largely indifferent to both the physical background and to the basic economy alike.

It will, I think, be clear that the economic and social activities of any community are the products of long and intricate processes of cultural accumulation and integration, extending far back in time to the emergence of man himself. Since we are concerned with peoples of whom historical evidence is generally lacking for all but the briefest of periods, the details, and often even the major sequences of the cultural changes cannot with certainty be known. Nevertheless, some of the factors which enter into and direct the course of this process of accumulation or accretion can be estimated. The mere fact that there should be such a wide range of variation in the character and development of craft, economy and society—between not only diverse habitats but those very similar in their general conditions—makes it obvious that much has depended on particular discoveries in particular areas, and on special trends of development in particular societies.

The differences in character and content between particular cultures have, as has been said, often been ascribed to one or more of a number of general factors, and especially to differences of race and physical environment, or to differences in the alleged stage of social or even psychological evolution. No one of these general factors can alone explain anything, nor can their significance be analysed in isolation; for they do not operate singly nor in a vacuum. They fail both singly and collectively because they ignore the fact that the culture of every single human community has had a specific history. How far that history is known will make all the difference to the degree of our understanding; but unless there is realization of the existence of that specific history, both of internal change and external contact in one or several specific environments, understanding cannot begin.

No human community has lived in prolonged and absolute isolation. Man has both a greater effective mobility, and a wider distribution on the earth's surface than any other species of animal. In his ability to acquire and to impart knowledge and belief, he is able not only to develop a particular cultural pattern and to transmit it from generation to generation within a particular society, but also, despite the confusion of tongues, to transfer such knowledge to other societies. Any and every single item of knowledge or belief could theoretically be transmitted to, and be acquired by any people anywhere in the world; and of the reality and great importance of this transmission or diffusion of culture there can be no doubt. Not only is it taking place on a world-wide scale to-day, and can also be studied in detail in any historical period, but the precise and arbitrary parallels between many details of the cultures of different peoples establish its existence in the absence of historical knowledge. The fundamental homogeneity of Polynesian culture or the distribution of food plants in the Pacific, the distribution of particular domestic animals and the ways in which they are used and raised, are but broad instances. Language is a very ineffective barrier to cultural transference, nor is the linguistic unit the cultural unit.

The world can be empirically divided into a number of culture areas, or territories, over which certain crafts, economies and social patterns dominate human activity. The number and size of such areas will depend to some extent on the refinement of discrimination, but Polynesia, the Northwest Coast or the south-east African cattle-rearing area are obvious examples. Within such culture areas, if defined in broad terms, there are often great and important variations in detail. There may be geographical discontinuities, such as the presence of the pastoral Herero on the western coast of southern Africa. Sharp frontiers can almost never be drawn, and there is an unequal fading towards the margins. Indeed, it is sometimes not the cultural elements themselves—no one of which may be exclusive to the area—but rather their combination in a particular pattern, that is significant. A close relation is often observable between a culture area and a particular habitat in which it finds favourable physical conditions. The south-east African cattle area, the Eskimo territory, or the Northwest Coast afford instances. Such correlations are never, however, completely precise, for other cultural patterns are competing at the fringes. Such may have been in previous occupation of a part of the suitable habitat and have resisted assimilation. The concept of culture areas is a valuable one, for it expresses briefly the local diffusion of a number of elements, and their integration in a basically similar pattern. But its abstract character must be realized. It cannot replace the reality of cultural variation in time and space, and must not be allowed to obscure the individuality of particular societies.

The mobility of man is not such as to nullify obstacles of physical difficulty or distance, nor is his receptivity such that the process of cultural accretion is mechanical and in practice unlimited. So far as physical barriers and mere distance affect the establishment of contact, it is extremely difficult to make any safe generalization; for barriers and distances have no absolute value—they are relative to the impetus which attacks them. It is, moreover, not as a rule a question of individual men travelling over immense distances or traversing wide tracts of sea or difficult country, although such things have been done at quite low cultural levels; but of the slower transmission from community to community.

Just as a given culture is an integration of many and diverse elements acquired in different ways and at different times, so when diffusion and borrowing occurs cultural elements of the most diverse character may be transferred together. These *adhesions* (that is, groups of tools or practices which have no functional relation one to another, but co-exist over a wide area at different times) form arbitrary complexes whose distributions are often very extensive. The use of the dog-sledge and of tailored fur clothing throughout the Arctic, from Lapland to Greenland; the use of magical pearl shell ornaments and domestic pigs in Oceania; the growing of corn and the making of pottery in the New World; the maintenance of an advanced pastoral economy and the recital of epic poetry in central Asia—are all instances of these juxtapositions.

A cultural current may, as it were, travel through and along a chain of human societies, each of which in turn becomes recipient and transmitter. Such a current will, however, meet with varying resistances. The resistances will vary not only from community to community according to the pre-existing cultural pattern, but also according to the nature of the cultural element itself. Such differences may be studied in detail among peoples who have come for the first time into contact with European civilization. While some resist the invasion of Western manners, beliefs and even tools very strongly and for a considerable time, others show a surprising rapidity of assimilation. These differences in a large measure express the relativity of the invading and the invaded culture. Much also depends on the manner in which contact is effected. The extraordinary and outstanding contrasts between the reaction of the Japanese and Chinese to Western influence suffice to indicate the reality and great extent of such differences.

Moreover, the ease and rapidity with which cultural elements are transferred depends very greatly, as has been said, on the character of those elements. A more efficient or more useful tool obtainable by barter—as, say, a steel knife for a flint blade—will generally be seized upon with alacrity; a new source of food-supply which can be grown easily with no important change of cultivating methods may—like cassava and maize in Central Africa, or the potato in New Zealand—be adopted with almost equal rapidity. But more complex technical devices—the learning of metal working for instance, or the making of more elaborate equipment, for which more instruction is needed and less urgent need may be felt—are less readily acquired. New practices which involve serious changes in the social institutions and in belief and ritual are still more difficult to adopt and meet more resistance in the community; for they serve little or no obvious and immediate need and will conflict with a coherent body of social and religious tradition.

The aspects of human culture with which we have been particularly concerned, namely, the methods and organizations associated with getting a livelihood under particular physical conditions with a particular equipment and standards, might seem at first sight to fall largely into the more easily assimilated categories; but the intricate interrelations between craft and social pattern are such that apparently simple transfers may meet unexpected obstacles, or may set up repercussions which affect the whole fabric of society. The use of the plough and the yoking of bullocks are not easily introduced into the type of society characteristic of south-eastern Africa, in which agriculture is exclusively women's work, and cattle (which are in the charge of men) are the centre of complex rituals and prohibitions.

The enormous supremacy in wealth and physical power enjoyed by Western civilization in comparison with the lower cultures leads to changes and even to forcible disruptions on a more overwhelming scale than ever before. That is not to suggest, however, that 'Westernization' is different in its nature from the 'Romanization' of western Europe in the early centuries of the Christian era, or from the 'Indianization' of much of western Indonesia by Hindu princes and their retainers at about the same period. Violent and temporarily disruptive cultural change as a result of alien dominance is nothing new. Did we but know in detail the early history of East Africa, of Oceania, or indeed of any area of complex culture, there can be little doubt that many events of this character would be revealed. The differences between culture contacts and transmissions in the past and the Westernization of the world to-day, however great they may be in scale and rapidity, are differences only of degree.

So long as a culture can retain in some measure its own autonomy, there is obviously a process of selection by which new techniques and social forms are adopted; not in relation to any absolute standards of utility, but according to the extent to which the new can find a place in the fabric of the old. That complex of activities in any human society which we call its culture is a going concern. It has its own momentum, its dogmas, its habits, its efficiencies and its weaknesses. The elements which go to make it are of very different antiquity; some are old and moribund, but others as old may be vigorous; some borrowings or developments of yesterday are already almost forgotten, others have become strongly entrenched. To appreciate the quality of a particular culture at a particular time; to understand why one new custom or technique is adopted and another rejected, despite persistent external efforts at introduction; to get behind the general and abstract terms which label such somewhat arbitrarily divided categories of activity and interest as arts and crafts, social organization, religion and so forth; and to see the culture as a living whole —for all these purposes it is necessary to inquire minutely into the relations between the multifarious activities of a community and to discover where and how they buttress or conflict with one another. Nothing that happens, whether it is the mere whittling of a child's toy or the concentration of energy on some major economy, operates in isolation or fails to react in some degree on many other activities. The careful exploration of what have been called 'functional', or 'dynamic', relations within a society may disclose much that was unexpected in the processes of interaction between one aspect of culture and another. It may reveal, to cite a much-quoted case, the great psychological and ultimately economic value of magic in hunting, fishing and agriculture which stimulates both individual and collective effort in the group by giving confidence in the face of unknown hazards.

While the investigation of the relations between different elements and activities within a single culture is essential for the appreciation of its individuality and internal structure, it cannot alone reveal the processes whereby the elements as such have actually come to exist. The content of a culture is not merely the result of a local elaboration of a series of satisfactory and mutually congenial activities with their associated equipment. The study of the ways in which pigs are tended, used and regarded in Melanesia, for instance, or of the uses of cattle in eastern Africa, can account neither for the presence of the animals in those areas, nor for the regard in which they are held. Nor are the modes of their acquisition and their associations in earlier cultures irrelevant to their present functions. The assumption of the local origin of any element of cultural equipment and of the attitudes expressed towards it is never a safe one. Comparative and historical studies are essential for the elucidation of these aspects of culture.

There has grown up in recent times a false quarrel between sociological and comparative studies in ethnology. Enthusiasm over the discovery that the internal complexities of lower cultures are as far-reaching in scope, if not in magnitude, as are those of Western civilization, has led to the implication that these alone are of importance, and even that all the significant elements of the culture concerned are spontaneous developments created in order to give an opportunity for the working of the sociological processes discovered, or, alternatively, that their sources and manner of derivation are of no social significance. But the briefest comparative survey makes it plain that the cultural capital of any given community is almost entirely borrowed. The functions of the reindeer, for example, among various Asiatic herders—including, that is to say, the part they play in social and religious life as well as in the direct supply of food—are not to be accounted for by any innate or immutable needs, aptitudes or social tendencies existing among the particular peoples. Important and intricate social relations among the particular peoples proceed from the fact that reindeer pull sledges for one people and are ridden by another; that in one case they are milked and in another live as half-wild herds exploited only for their meat and skins. But these differences in use are not purely questions of native genius or internal social needs. As has been seen, their distribution and their external relations with dog driving on the one hand and cattle breeding on the other indicate that fundamental processes of transference are involved. The processes of cultural accumulation by contact and conquest have operated everywhere. The extent to which transmission and reintegration of cultural elements have proceeded among a particular people, and the directions from which new elements and impulses have come can only be studied (where documentary evidence of earlier time is entirely or largely absent) by means of careful comparative investigations. Such studies are important not only from an historical point of view; they are also as essential for the understanding of the existing social and economic relations as is a monographic analysis of the particular people. That they are often more difficult, require more laborious sifting of scattered evidence and the temporary abandonment of the ethnographer's tent for the library, is irrelevant to their importance. A functional analysis of the culture of a people does not complete, it initiates the scientific study of that culture. A comparative analysis of other cultures, both past and present, and of both the material elements and the sociological patterns associated with them, is required before any approach to a full understanding of the presence and implications of the observed practices can be approached. When information concerning the practices of earlier peoples of higher civilizations is known to have a probable bearing on living cultures, such evidence must be examined and interpreted. That such comparative studies have sometimes been uncritical is no argument against the scientific urgency of such work. The same charge can be levelled against much functional and psychological interpretation, and indeed against any branch of human inquiry. These two aspects of study—we might call them the physiology and the comparative anatomy of cultures—are not only complementary, they are mutually essential.

To approach the study of human society from an exclusively internal point of view may result in a very serious failure to appreciate the strength of cultural inertia. The belief that functional relations owe their existence to the needs they now fulfil, when they may be secondary by-products; the assumption that of two related elements neither could exist apart; in brief, the ascription of genetical significance to the existing functions of cultural traits and the neglect of any attempt to trace their history, can lead to a sociological determinism as invalid as environmentalism.

No culture is ever a complete and finished wnole. However stable and even rigid it may appear at a moment of time, its integrative capacity is never entirely lost. Just as it has been built up by the accretion and assimilation of new elements, so it can continue to change; and so too, by the loss of elements, can it be impoverished. Neither process is of necessity felt as an irreparable loss or as a miraculous gain. The fact that Western civilization stands at so far higher a level of technical equipment and political organization, that its equipment is so alien and so much more powerful, and can overwhelm a weaker culture so rapidly, has resulted in the last few centuries in wholesale destruction or mutilation of the lower cultures. But this process is different only in the degree of its intensity from other great cultural diffusions; and its distinctiveness is no brief either for regarding the lower cultures as formerly static and functionally completely integrated, or for the belief that interference with the life of a people by a culturally superior (that is, more powerful) group is a new-found curse of Western civilization.

On the other hand, the last two centuries have shown only too often that there are limits to the rate of cultural change, and that beyond a certain point the pressure of alien culture results in the internal collapse of the native life without assimilation of the new. The change is all in the direction suited to the more powerful culture, which thus suffers less derangement even when in alien territory; while the plasticity of the victim is strained to the breaking point.

From the practical point of view, a civilization as dominant and powerful as that of the Western world needs to watch self-consciously the advance of its influence, to limit the fronts on which it invades, and to draw back at signs of disintegration. Since, however, this cultural pressure is only rarely exercised by an organized and self-conscious body, but is rather the resultant of conflicting forces within the Western world itself —governments, traders, planters, colonists and missionaries— such a plan is very difficult of achievement and the dangers are too often unseen until too late.

CHAPTER REFERENCES

ABBREVIATIONS USED

Af.	Africa, Journal of the International Institute for African Languages and Cultures, London.
A	Anthropos, Vienna.
AA	American Anthropologist (New Series unless otherwise stated), Menasha, Wis.
A de G	Annales de Géographie, Paris.
AAAG	Annals of the Association of American Geographers.
AM–AMNH	Anthropological Memoirs, American Museum of Natural History, New York.
AP–AMNH	Anthropological Papers, American Museum of Natural History, New York.
ARBAE	Annual Report of the Bureau of American Ethnology, Washington, D.C.
AS	Année Sociologique, Paris.
BAR	British Association for the Advancement of Science, Report (annual), London.
BBAE	Bulletin of the Bureau of American Ethnology, Washington, D.C.
BPBM	Bernice P. Bishop Museum, Honolulu, Hawaii.
FMNH	Field Museum of Natural History, Chicago.
G	Geography (formerly the 'Geographical Teacher'), Geographical Association, Manchester.
GR	Geographical Review, American Geographical Society, New York.
ICA	International Congress of Americanists.
JRAI	Journal of the Royal Anthropological Institute, London.
MAAA	Memoirs of the American Anthropological Association, Menasha, Wis.
MAI–HF	Museum of the American Indian, Heye Foundation, New York.
Man	Man, a monthly record of the Royal Anthropological Institute, London.
MoG	Meddelelser om Grønland, Copenhagen.
PZ	Prähistorische Zeitschrift, Berlin.
RCAE	Report of the Canadian Arctic Expedition, Ottawa.
TRSC	Transactions of the Royal Society of Canada.
UC–PAAE	University of California Publications in American Archaeology and Ethnology, Berkeley.

474   HABITAT, ECONOMY AND SOCIETY

UC–PG   University of California Publications in Geography,
                Berkeley.
UMSSS   University of Minnesota Studies in the Social Sciences,
                Minneapolis.
UPAP   University of Pennsylvania Anthropological Papers,
                Philadelphia.
USNM   United States National Museum, Washington, D.C.

[NOTE.—Periodical references are cited by volume, page and year
in that order.]

CHAPTER II

SKEAT, W. W., and C. O. BLAGDEN: *Pagan Races of the Malay
    Peninsula.* London, 1906, 2 vols. Is the most important
    source of material on the peoples of Malay. The introduction
    contains a fine account of the equatorial forest itself.
MARTIN, R.: *Die Inlandstämme der Malayischen Halbinsel.* Jena,
    1905. Contains valuable material on the Semang and Sakai.
ANNANDALE, N., and H. C. ROBINSON: *Fasciculi Malayenses.*
    Liverpool University Press, Anthropology, Part I, 1903; and
    DE MORGAN, J.: *Négritos de la presqu'île Malaise,* L'Homme,
    2, 1885, afford further details on the Semang and Sakai.
SCHEBESTA, P.: *Among the Forest Dwarfs of Malaya.* London, n.d.
    A popular account of an expedition recently undertaken to
    investigate religious beliefs among the Semang. It includes
    some vivid descriptions of the country and of particular
    Semang groups.
MAN, H. T.: *The Andaman Islands.* Royal Anthropological
    Institute, 1932. The most systematic account of Andaman
    culture, which is also discussed from the point of view of
    sociological theory by A. R. BROWN, *The Andaman Islands*
    (new edition), 1932.

CHAPTER III

SCHAPERA, I.: *The Khoisan Peoples of South Africa.* London,
    1930. A recent and full ethnography of the Bushmen and
    Hottentot. With an extensive bibliography.
BLEEK, D.: *The Naron, a Bushman Tribe of the Central Kalahari.*
    Cambridge, 1928. A brief but very useful account of a single
    Bushman group.
  See also PASSARGE, S.: *Die Buschmänner der Kalahari,* Berlin,
    1907; BLEEK, D.: *Bushmen of Central Angola,* Bantu Studies,
    iii, pp. 105–25, 1928; FOURIE, L.: *The Bushmen of South-West
    Africa* in *The Native Tribes of South-West Africa,* pp. 79–105,
    Capetown, 1928; DORNAN, S. S.: *Notes on the Bushmen of
    Basutoland.* Transactions of the South African Philosophical
    Society, xviii, pp. 437–50, 1909; SCHAPERA, I.: *A Preliminary
    Consideration of the Relationship Between the Hottentots and*

the Bushmen, South African Journ. Science, 23, pp. 833-66, 1926.

CHAPTER IV

For the Northern Paiute or Paviotso see:

STEWARD, J. H.: *The Owen's Valley Paiute.* UC–PAAE, 33, 3, 1933.

KELLY, I. T.: *Ethnography of the Surprise Valley Paiute.* UC–PAAE, 31, 3, 1932.

HOPKINS, S. W.: *Life Among the Piutes.* Boston, 1883. An account by a native women with many details of daily life.

CURTIS, E. S.: *The North American Indian.* Vols. 15 and 16. Cambridge, Mass., 1908.

For more general questions see:

LOWIE, R. H.: *Notes on Shoshonean Ethnography.* AP–AMNH, 20, 3, 1924.

LOWIE, R. H.: *Cultural Connections of California and Plateau Shoshoneans.* UC–PAAE, 20, 1923.

For the Yokuts:

KROEBER, A. L.: *Handbook of the Indians of California:* s.v. Yokuts. BBAE, 78, Washington, 1925.

CHAPTER V

WISSLER, C.: *The North American Indians of the Plains.* AMNH, Handbook Series, No. 1, 1927. Affords a short and very well illustrated sketch of Plains culture.

JENNESS, D.: *The Indians of Canada.* National Museum of Canada, Bull. 65, 1932. Also contains a well-illustrated survey of the northern Plains tribes.

WISSLER, C.: *The Material Culture of the Blackfoot Indians,* AP–AMNH, 5, 1910; *The Social Life of the Blackfoot Indians,* AP–AMNH, 7, 1912; and *Blackfoot Societies,* AP–AMNH, 9, 1914, provide unusually full materials for the study of the people considered in this chapter. GRINNELL, G. B.: *Blackfoot Lodge Tales,* New York, 1904, is also useful.

WISSLER, C.: *The Influence of the Horse in the Development of Plains Culture.* AA, 16, 1–25, 1914.

WISSLER, C.: *Ethnographical Problems of the Missouri-Saskatchewan Area.* AA, 10, 197–207, 1908.

KROEBER, A. L.: *Native Cultures of the Southwest,* UC–PAAE, 23, 1928, and STRONG, W. D.: *The Plains Culture Area in the Light of Archaeology,* AA, 35, 2, 271–288, 1933, are important considerations of the development and modification of Plains culture.

LOWIE, R. H.: *Plains Indians Age-Societies.* AP–AMNH, 2, 13,

1916. Gives a full comparative analysis of these institutions which is of great methodological importance.

ALLEN, J. A.: *The American Bisons.* Memoirs Geological Survey: Kentucky, 1, pt. 2. Cambridge, Mass., 1876.

The scientific and exploration literature of the Plains Indians is very extensive. The former is mainly to be found in the Reports, Bulletins and Papers of the Bureau of American Ethnology, the American Museum of Natural History and the Field Museum of Natural History (Chicago). Of the latter the following are of great importance:

MAXIMILIAN, PRINCE OF WIED: *Travels in the Interior of North America.* Trans. H. Evans Lloyd. London, 1843.

WINSHIP, G. P. (trans. and ed.): *The Journey of Coronado, 1540–1542.* New York, 1904.

LEWIS and CLARK: *History of the Expedition . . . to the Sources of the Missouri, etc., 1804–6.* 3 vols. New York, 1902. Also *Original Journals.* New York, 1904.

CATLIN, G.: *Illustrations of the Manners, Customs and Conditions of the North American Indians.* London, 1848.

HENRY and THOMPSON: *New Light on the Early History of the Great North West.* New York, 1897.

HENRY, A.: *Travels and Adventures in Canada . . ., 1760–1776.* New York, 1809.

CHAPTER VI

GODDARD, P. E.: *Indians of the Northwest Coast.* AMNH, Handbook Series, No. 10, 1924. Affords a general and well-illustrated short account of the area.

JENNESS, D.: *Indians of Canada.* Ottawa, 1932. Much fuller on the economic life; is also well illustrated and referenced.

For particular peoples see:

BOAS, F.: *Social Organization and Secret Societies of the Kwakiutl Indians.* Report USNM, pp. 311–737. Washington, 1897.

BOAS, F.: *Ethnology of the Kwakiutl.* ARBAE, 35. Washington, 1921.

BOAS, F.: BAR, 1890 (Nootka); 1894 (Lower Frazer Region); 1899 (Kwakiutl).

SWANTON, J. R.: *The Haida of Queen Charlotte Islands.* Jesup North Pacific Expedition, AM–AMNH, 5, 1, 1905.

SWANTON, J. R.: *Social Conditions of the Tlingit Indians.* ARBAE, 26, pp. 391–512. 1908.

KRAUSE, A.: *Die Tlingit-Indianer.* Jena, 1885.

Valuable accounts by early explorers are:

JEWITT, J. R.: *Narrative of the Adventures and Sufferings of John R. Jewitt . . . during a Captivity of nearly Three Years among the Savages of Nootka Sound.* Reprinted Edinburgh, 1924.

VANCOUVER, G.: *A Voyage of Discovery to the North Pacific Ocean . . . 1790-95.* 3 vol s. London, 1798.

SPROAT, G. M.: *Scenes and Studies of Savage Life.* London, 1868 (for the Nootka).

COOK, J.: *A Voyage to the Pacific Ocean.* Vol. 2. London, 1785 (for the Nootka).

On special aspects and problems see:

SAPIR, E.: *Social Organization of the West Coast Tribes.* TRSC, Section III, 9, 355 ff., 1915.

WATERMAN, T. T.: *Native Houses of Western North America.* MAI–HF, Indian Notes and Monographs, 1921.

DAVIDSON, D. S.: *Family Hunting Territories in Northwestern North America* [Tlingit]. MAI–HF, Indian Notes and Monographs, 1921.

DIXON, R. B.: *Tobacco Chewing on the Northwest Coast.* AA, 35, 146-150, 1933.

OLSON, R.: *The Possible Middle American Origin of Northwest Coast Weaving.* AA, 31, 114 ff. 1929.

OLSON, R.: *Adze, Canoe and House Types of the Northwest Coast.* University of Washington Publications in Anthropology, 2, 1, 1927.

KROEBER, A. L.: *American Culture and the Northwest Coast.* AA, 25, 1–20, 1923.

For southern Chile see:

COOPER, J. M.: *Analytical and Critical Bibliography of the Tribes of Tierra del Fuego and Adjacent Territory.* BBAE, 63. Washington, 1917.

COOPER, J. M.: *Fuegian and Chonoan Tribal Relations.* In XIX ICA, Washington, 1917.

COOPER, J. M.: *Cultural Diffusion and Culture Areas in Southern South America.* In XXI ICA, Göteborg, 1925.

KOPPERS, W.: *Unter Feuerland-Indianern,* Stuttgart, 1924; and also *Die geheime Jugendweihe der Yagan und Alakaluf* and *Mythologie und Weltanschauung der Yagan* in ICA, 21. Göteborg, 1925.

A full and well-illustrated account of Yahgan technology will be found in:

LOTHROP, S. K.: *Indians of Tierra del Fuego.* Contributions from the Museum of the American Indian, Heye Foundation, vol. 10, 1928. See also: MASON, O. T.: *Aboriginal American Harpoons.* Report USNM (1900), pp. 189–304. Washington, 1902.

On other areas only meagre data are available:

FITZROY, R.: *Narrative of the Surveying Voyages of His Majesty's Ships 'Adventure' and 'Beagle' between the years 1826 and 1836.*

Vol. II. Proceedings of the Second Expedition, London, 1839, is, however, valuable for the Alakaluf and Chono.

LING ROTH, H.: *Aborigines of Tasmania*. London, 1890. Covers practically all that is known of the Tasmanians.

CHAPTER VII

The only extended account of the Yukaghir is to be found in the memoir:

JOCHELSON, W.: *The Yukaghir and the Yukaghirized Tungus* Jesup North Pacific Expedition, AM–AMNH, 9, 1910. For a vivid account of the tundra and taiga see HAVILAND, M. D.: *Forest, Steppe and Tundra*. Cambridge, 1926.

CHAPTER VIII

The literature on the Eskimo is vast; for an extensive bibliography and a full account of the habitat and social life see:

WEYER, E. M.: *The Eskimos: Their Environment and Folkways* Yale, 1932.

Important monographs dealing with Eskimo in the Central area are

BOAS, F.: *The Eskimo of Baffin Land and Hudson Bay*. Bulletin AMNH, 15, 1907.

BOAS, F.: *The Central Eskimo*. ARBAE, 6, 1888.

JENNESS, D.: *Life of the Copper Eskimos*. RCAE, 12, pt. A Ottawa, 1923.

MATHIASSEN, T.: *Material Culture of the Iglulik Eskimos*. Repor of the fifth Thule Expedition, 6, No. 1. Copenhagen, 1928.

RASMUSSEN, K.: *Intellectual Culture of the Iglulik Eskimos*. Repor of the fifth Thule Expedition, 7, No. 1. Copenhagen, 1929.

For other areas, more general accounts and particular problems see

BIRKET SMITH, KAJ: *The Caribou Eskimo*. Report of the fift Thule Expedition, 5, pts. 1 and 2. Copenhagen, 1929.

EKBLAW, W. E.: *Material Responses of the Polar Eskimo to thei far Arctic Environment*. AAAG, 18, 1, 1928.

STEENSBY, H. P.: *Contributions to the Ethnology and Anthrope geography of the Polar Eskimos*. MoG, 14, 1910.

STEENSBY, H. P.: *An Anthropogeographical Study of the Origi of the Eskimo Culture*. MoG, 53, 1917.

JENNESS, D.: *The Problem of the Eskimo*, in *The American Abor gines*. . . . 5th Pacific Science Congress, 373–96. Toronte 1933.

RASMUSSEN, K.: *The People of the Polar North*. London, 1908.

STEFANSSON, V.: *My Life with the Eskimos*. New York, 1919.

MATHIASSEN and FREUCHEN: *Contributions to the Physical Geo graphy of the Regions North of Hudson Bay*. GR, 15, 1925.

On the racial affinities of the Eskimo, see:

SHAPIRO, H. L.: *The Alaskan Eskimo*. AP–AMNH, 31, 1931.

CHAPTER IX

WHIFFEN, T.: *The North-west Amazons*. London, 1915. An extremely well-written account of an expedition to the Japura river country, with a fairly full account of the Boro and neighbouring peoples. See also:

KOCH-GRUNBERG, T.: *Zwei Jahre unter den Indianern. Reisen in Nord-westbrasilien*, Berlin, 1910; KIRCHHOFF, P.: *Die Verwandtschaftsorganisation der Urwaldstämme Südamerikas*. Zeitschrift für Ethnologie, 63, 1931; TESSMAN, G.: *Die Indianer Nordost-Perus*, Hamburg, 1930; WALLACE, A. R.: *Travels on the Amazon and Rio Negro*, London, 1854; BATES, H. W.: *A Naturalist on the River Amazons*, London, 1892.

CHAPTER X

For the Yoruba:

TALBOT, A. P.: *The Peoples of Southern Nigeria*, 4 vols., Oxford, 1921; AJISAFE, A. K.: *The Laws and Customs of the Yoruba People*, London, 1924; DENNETT, R. E.: *Nigerian Studies*, London, 1910; JOHNSON, S.: *History of the Yorubas*, London, 1921; ELLIS, A. B.: *The Yoruba Speaking Peoples of the Slave Coast of West Africa*, London, 1894.

WARD PRICE, H. L.: *Land Tenure in the Yoruba Provinces*. Lagos, 1933. Has become available since this chapter was written. It contains valuable material on the economic organization past and present among the Yoruba.

For the Boloki:

WEEKS, J.: *Notes on the Bangala*. JRAI, 39, 45 ff., 97 ff., 1909, and *Among Congo Cannibals*, London, 1913.

On the division of labour in hoe culture, and its distribution in Africa:

FORDE, C. DARYLL: *Land and Labour in a Cross River Village, Southern Nigeria*, Geog. Journ., 90, 24 ff., 1937.

BAUMANN, H.: *The Division of Work according to Sex in African Hoe Culture*. Af., 1, 3, 1928.

SCHMIDT, MAX.: *Die materielle Wirtschaft der Naturvölker*. Leipzig, 1923.

SCHWEINFURTH, G.: *Im Herzen von Africa* (Eng. trans, as *The Heart of Africa*. 2 vols. London), 1873.

CHAPTER XI

For Melanesia:

CODRINGTON, R. H.: *The Melanesians*. London, 1891. A classic of great and permanent value. It does not, however, deal in any detail with physical conditions, economic life or crafts.

IVENS, W. G.: *Melanesians of the S.E. Solomon Islands.* London, 1927. Is unusually full on the aspects referred to above and on it the account of S. Mala and Ulawa is based.

GUPPY, H. B.: *The Solomon Islands and their Natives*, London, 1887, and BRENCHLEY, J. L.: *The Cruise of the 'Curacao'*, London, 1873, also provide valuable material on the Solomons.

SELIGMAN, C. G.: *The Melanesians of British New Guinea.* Cambridge, 1910. Especially Chapter VIII on Motu voyages for sago in return for pottery (Barton). See also WILLIAMS, F. E.: *Trading Voyages from the Gulf of Papua*, Oceania, 3, p. 139 ff., 1932; and MALINOWSKI, B.: *Argonauts of the Western Pacific*, London, 1922, should be consulted for northern Melanesia and the development of the Kula in this area.

On Melanesian shell money see especially:

DANKS, B.: *Shell Money of New Britain*, JRAI, 17, p. 305 ff., 1888: and LEWIS, A. B.: *Melanesian Shell Money*, FMNH, Anthrop, Publications, No. 268, 1929; and for Mala: WOODFORD, C. M.. *Notes on the Manufacture of Malaita Shell Bead Money*, Man; 8, 43, pp. 81–83, 1908.

For Polynesia the literature is very extensive and scattered. Only a few sources relative to the aspects raised here can be cited:

LINTON, R.: *Ethnology of Polynesia and Micronesia*, FMNH, Chicago, 1926, is a very useful general sketch of Polynesian culture. Unfortunately no detailed account of the economic life and its relation to habitat, crafts and social organization is available for Central Polynesia.

ELLIS, W.: *Polynesian Researches.* London, 1830–36. An account of the Society Islands' culture by an early missionary which gives unusually full accounts of the exploitation of resources.

HANDY, E. S. C.: *History and Culture in the Society Islands.* BPBM, Bulletin 79, 1930. An analysis of the culture and economy into newer and older elements. It affords a useful study of the role of the *arii* in Tahiti.

HANDY, E. S. C.: *Houses, Boats and Fishing in the Society Islands.* BPBM, Bulletin 90, 1932. Gives a technical account of these important crafts.

HENRY, T.: *Ancient Tahiti.* BPBM, Bulletin 48, 1928. A native account of Tahitian life before native crafts and institutions disintegrated under European influence.

FORSTER, J. R.: *Observations Made During a Voyage Round the World in the 'Resolution'.* London, 1779.

BANKS, J.: *Journal of Sir Joseph Banks.* Ed. J. D. Hooker. London, 1896. Both the above give good accounts of Society Islands' crafts.

DRIVER, H. E., and A. L. KROEBER: *Quantitive Expression of Cultural Relationships.* UC–PAAE, 31, 4, 1932.

BEST, E.: *Polynesian Navigators.* Geographical Review, 3, p. 177 ff., 1918; *Polynesian Voyagers.* N.Z. Journal of Science and Technology, Wellington, 1923; *Maori Agriculture,* Dominion Mus. Bull., 9, 1925.

For other areas in Polynesia see:

MARINER, W.: *An Account of the Natives of the Tonga Islands.* London, 1817. A magnificent account by an English seaman.

GIFFORD, E. W.: *Tongan Society.* BPBM, Bulletin 61, 1929. One of the few detailed and comprehensive studies of social organization.

KRAMER, A.: *Die Samoa Inseln.* Stuttgart, 1902.

FIRTH, R.: *The Primitive Economics of the New Zealand Maori.* London, 1929. Has brought together widely scattered material and enables the peculiar developments of Polynesian culture in New Zealand to be more fully grasped.

Numerous vivid accounts of various aspects of Tahiti and other parts of Polynesia are contained in *The Journal and Voyages of Captain Cook* (London, 1773, 1777, 1784), while the Atlas contains many illustrations, but these were unfortunately drawn by artists who had not seen the country or who introduced European conventions.

CHAPTER XII

For the Hopi:

GODDARD, P. E.: *Indians of the Southwest.* AMNH, Handbook Series, No. 2. New York, 1927. A well-illustrated introduction to the culture of the Southwest.

GREGORY, H.: *The Navaho Country.* U.S. Geological Survey, Water Supply Paper, No. 380, 1917. An extended account of the physical geography of the area in which the Hopi Pueblos are situated.

FORDE, C. D.: *Hopi Agriculture and Land Ownership.* JRAI, 41, 357–405, 1931. A fuller account of the physical conditions, methods and social aspects of Hopi agriculture.

BRYAN, K.: *Flood Water Farming in Southern New Mexico.* Geographical Review, 19, 453 ff, 1929. Summarises the general distribution and character of flood water farming in the south-western United States and discusses the physiographic problem of arroyo cutting in recent times.

HOUGH, W.: *The Hopi Indian Collection in the U.S. National Museum.* Proc. USNM, 54, 235–96, 1918. A useful summary of Hopi material culture.

MINDELEFF, V.: *A Study in Pueblo Architecture.* ARBAE, 8, Washington, 1891. Should be consulted for the details of Hopi house construction and Pueblo architecture generally.

PARSONS, E. C.: *A Pueblo Indian Journal*. MAAA, 32, 1925. The diary of a Hopi (Tewa) which gives many details of the agricultural and social life as it proceeds from day to day.

LOWIE, R. H.: *Notes on Hopi Clans*. AP–AMNH 33, 1929. Important for both the development and functions of Hopi clans.

STEWARD, J.: *Notes on Hopi Ceremonies in their Initiatory Form in 1927–28*. AA, 33, 1931. An account of the ritual referred to on p. 244.

BENEDICT, R.: *Psychological Types in the Cultures of the Southwest*. ICA, XXIII, 572 ff., 1928. A study of the great contrast between the cultural bias and mental outlook of the Pueblo peoples and those of the surrounding non-agricultural peoples.

For other peoples referred to:

SPIER, L.: *Havasupai Ethnography*. AP–AMNH, 29, 1928. A full account of the economy and society of this people.

FORDE, C. D.: *Ethnography of the Yuma Indians*. UC–PAAE, 28, 4, 1931. Records the results of a recent field study of this Lower Colorado people and gives as full an account of the economic life as can be recovered to-day. See also GIFFORD, E. W.: *The Cocopa*, UC–PAAE, 31, 5, 1933, for a study of the southern neighbours and enemies of the Yuma, while the results of a study of their northern allies, the Mohave, are briefly sketched in KROEBER, A. L.: *Handbook of the Indians of California*, BBAE, 78, 1925.

KNIFFEN, F.: *The Natural Landscape of the Lower Colorado*. UCPG, 5, 1931. For an account of the physical geography of this area.

WILSON, G. I.: *Agriculture of the Hidatsa Indians*. UMSSS, No. 9, 1917. An account as recovered from a native woman of her own agricultural practice.

JENNESS, D.: *Indians of Canada*. Ottawa, 1932. Includes a short account of Iroquois economy and organization. More detailed studies and early authorities are there cited. Particularly important are: WAUGH, F. W.: *Iroquois Foods and Food Preparation*. Geol. Survey of Canada, Memoir 86, Ottawa, 1916; STITES, S. H.: *Economics of the Iroquois*. Bryn Mawr College Monographs, vol. 1, Bryn Mawr, 1905; and PARKER, A. C.: *Iroquois Uses of Maize and Other Food Plants*. New York State Museum, Bulletin 144, Albany, 1910.

JENKS, A. E.: *The Wild Rice Gatherers of the Upper Lakes*. ARBAE, 19, 2, Washington, 1900, and BLAIR, E. H.: *Indian Tribes of the Upper Mississippi Region*, Cleveland, 1911, give details of the wild rice gathering peoples beyond the limits of cultivation.

SPECK, F. G.: *Ethnology of the Yuchi Indians*. UPAP, 1, Philadelphia, 1909. One of the few comprehensive accounts of a south-east Woodland people.

KROEBER, A. L.: *Native American Population*, AA, 36, 1–25, 1934, includes a most suggestive discussion of the significance and importance of agriculture in different regions of aboriginal North America.

CHAPTER XIII

ACHYUTA MENON, C.: *The Cochin State Manual.* Cochin Govt. Press, Ernakulam, 1911.

ANANDAKRISHNA IYER, L. K.: *The Cochin Tribes and Castes.* 2 vols. Madras, 1909–12.

SANKARA MENON, T. K.: Census of India 1931, Vol. 21; Cochin. Ernakulam, 1933; see also the volumes on Travancore and Madras for other parts of the Malabar coast.

PADMANABHA MENON, K. P.: *History of Kerala*, n.d.

SUBBARAMA IYER, S.: *Economic Life in a Malabar Village.* University of Madras, Economic Series, 11, 1925.

SLATER, G.: *Some South Indian Villages.* University of Madras, Economic Series, Oxford, 1918, and *The Dravidian Element in Indian Culture*, London, 1926.

MOORE, L.: *Malabar Law and Custom.* Madras, 1905.

LOGAN, W.: *Malabar*, 2 vols. Madras, 1887.

THURSTON, E.: *Castes and Tribes of Southern India.* 7 vols. Madras, 1909.

CHAPTER XIV

No full and critical account of the Masai is available, and the authorities are contradictory on many points concerning the social organization. The character and size of the districts which organize the Age groups and their relations to the clans are particularly obscure.

THOMSON, J.: *Through Masai Land.* London, n.d. A vivid if necessarily superficial account of an early expedition before European interference had restricted the military organization and rinderpest had reduced the live stock.

MERKER, M.: *Die Masai.* Berlin, 1910. A lengthy study based mainly on information obtained among the more southern groups in Tanganyika. The accounts of crafts and economic activities are good, but it is extremely difficult to reconcile much of the data on social organization and tribal divisions with the comparable material of other writers.

HOLLIS, A.C.: *The Masai.* Oxford, 1905. Primarily an account of Masai language, but the translated texts contain valuable material on the social and economic life.

LEAKEY, L. S. B.: *Some Notes on the Masai of Kenya Colony.* JRAI, 60, 186–209, 1930. Gives a more complete account of the social structure and the Age groups.

STORRS FOX, D.: *Further Notes on the Masai of Kenya Colony.*

JRAI, 60, 447–65, 1930. Based on lengthy observations as a District Officer. It corrects the above in several particulars and gives a concrete account of the operation of the Age group system in recent years.

For other pastoral areas and peoples referred to:

ROSCOE, J.: *Immigrants and their Influence in the Lake Region of Central Africa*, Frazer Lecture for 1923. Cambridge, 1924; and DRIBERG, J. H.: *The East African Problem*, London, 1930, afford brief sketches of the influence of pastoral invasions on the economy and social organization of these areas.

PAULITSCHKE, P.: *Ethnographie Nordost-Afrikas*. Berlin, 1893.

ROSCOE, J.: *The Bakitara*, Cambridge, 1923; *The Banyankole*, Cambridge, 1923; and *The Baganda*, London, 1911.

MAIR, L. P.: *Baganda Land Tenure*. Africa, 6, p. 187 ff., 1933.

SMITH, E., and DALE, A. M.: *The Ila-speaking Peoples of Northern Rhodesia*. London, 1920.

RICHARDS, A. I.: *Hunger and Work in a Savage Tribe* [Southern Bantu]. London, 1932.

SCHAPERA, I. *The Khoisan Peoples of South Africa*. London, 1930. The only comprehensive account of Hottentot culture.

HOERNLE, A. W.: *The Social Organization of the Nama Hottentots of South-west Africa*. AA, 27, 1925.

HERSKOVITS, M.: *The Cattle Complex in East Africa*. AA, 28, 1926.

CHAPTER XV

MUSIL, A.: *Manners and Customs of the Rwala Bedouins*. American Geographical Society, New York, 1928; and *Arabia Deserta*, American Geographical Society, 1927.

These full accounts by Professor Alois Musil of his expeditions in the territory of the Ruwala provide the most detailed material available for the systematic study of a Badawîn tribe, and on them this brief analysis of Badawîn life is largely based. Many characteristic features of Badawîn society are also described with a wealth of detail in the accounts of English explorers, especially:

PALGRAVE, W. G.: *Narrative of a Year's Journey Through Central and Eastern Arabia* (1862–3). 2 vols. London, 1865.

DOUGHTY, C. M.: *Travels in Arabia Deserta*. London, 1908.

PHILBY, H. ST. J. B.: *The Heart of Arabia*, 2 vols., London, 1922; *Arabia of the Wahabis*, London, 1928; and *The Empty Quarter*, London, 1933.

CHAPTER XVI

RADLOFF, A.: *Aus Siberien*. Leipzig, 1884. By far the best and, indeed, the only fairly comprehensive account of the peoples considered in this chapter. See also:

ROCKHILL, W. W., ed.: *The Journey of William of Rubruck* Hakluyt Society, London, 1900.

PALLAS, P. S.: *Reise durch verschiedene Provinzen des russischen Reiches.* 3 vols. St. Petersburg, 1771–6.

LEVSHIN, A. I.: *Description des hordes et des steppes des Kirghiz-Kazaks.* Paris, 1840.

HUC, M.: *Travels in Tartary, Thibet and China,* 1844–6 (trans. W. Hazlett).

SKRINE, F. H. B., and ROSS, E. D.: *The Heart of Asia, a History of Russian Turkestan and the Central Khanates from the Earliest Times.* London, 1899.

CARRUTHERS, D.: *Unknown Mongolia.* 2 vols. London, 1913.

BADDLEY, J. F.: *Russia, Mongolia, China.* 2 vols. London, 1919.

SYKES, E. and P.: *Through Deserts and Oases of Central Asia.* London, 1920.

LATTIMORE, O.: *The Desert Road to Turkestan.* London, 1928.

PARKER, E. H.: *A Thousand Years of the Tartars.* London, 1924.

CZAPLICKA, M. A.: *The Turks of Central Asia.* Oxford, 1916.

CHAPTER XVII

SHIROKOGOROFF, S. M.: *Social Organization of the Northern Tungus* Shanghai, 1929.

JOCHELSON, W.: *Peoples of Asiatic Russia.* AMNH, New York, 1928.

CZAPLICKA, M. A.: *Aboriginal Siberia.* Oxford, 1914.

BOGORAS, W.: *The Chuckchee.* AM–AMNH, 11, pts. 1–3, 1904–9.

JOCHELSON, W.: *The Koryak.* AM–AMNH, 10, 1905–8.

HAVILAND, M. D.: *Forest, Steppe and Tundra.* Cambridge, 1926

For the reindeer see:

JOCHELSON, W.: *The Koryak,* AM–AMNH, 10, pt. 2, 1905.

SIRELIUS, U. T.: *Über die Art und Zeit der Zähmung des Renntiers* Journal de la Societé Finno-Ougrienne. Helsingfors, 1916.

LAUFER, B.: *The Reindeer and its Domestication.* MAAA, 4, 1917.

HATT, G.: *Notes on Reindeer Domestication.* MAAA, 6, 1919.

On the Yakut see:

JOCHELSON, W.: *The Yakut.* AP–AMNH, 33, 1933.

CHAPTER XVIII

In addition to the works cited in connexion with the chapters in Part I, the following are of importance:

LOWIE, R. H.: *Primitive Society,* New York, 1920; and *The Origin of the State,* New York, 1927.

HOBHOUSE, L. T., WHEELER, G. C., and M. GINSBERG: *The Material Culture and Social Institutions of the Simpler Peoples.* London, 1930.

THURNWALD, R.: *Die menschliche Gesellschaft in ihren ethno-soziologischen Grundlagen.* Vol. I: *Repräsentative Lebensbilder von Naturvölkern,* Berlin, 1931; and *Economics in Primitive Communities,* Oxford, 1932.

These works deal with primitive societies of all grades. Of the last two the first is an extended treatment of social, political and economic relations, containing many short sketches of particular peoples; the second, although covering much the same ground, is very condensed.

On the aspect of Australian culture discussed see: RIVERS, W. H. R.: *The Contact of Peoples in Psychology and Ethnology.* London, 1926.

CHAPTER XIX

In addition to the references given in the various chapters of Part II, see for Chinese and Japanese agriculture:

KING, F. H.: *Farmers of Forty Centuries,* London, 1927; and WAGNER, A.: *Chinesische Landwirtschaft,* Berlin, 1926; and KULP, D. H.: *Country Life in South China,* New York, 1925.

For the Philippines see:

JENKS, A. E.: *The Bontoc Igorot,* Ethnol. Survey Pubns.; Philippines, vol. I, 1905; and BARTON, R. F.: *Ifugao Economics,* UC–PAAE, 15, 5, 1922.

On iron-working see:

RICKARD, T.: *Man and Metals,* 2 vols, New York, 1933 ; also, idem, *The Antiquity of Metal-working,* Journ. Iron and Steel Institute, London, 120, 323, 1930.

LOUIS, H.: *Iron Manufacture and Heat Generation.* Nature, 1929, vol. 123, pp. 762–5.

CHAPTER XX

In addition to the references cited for the chapters in Part III, the following are important for the topics raised in this chapter:

For oscillations between pastoral and settled life in the north-western Sahara see:

BERNARD, A., and H. LACROIX: *L'Évolution du nomadisme en Algérie.* Annales de Géographie, 15, 1906; and BERNARD, A.: *Le Maroc,* Paris, 1906; and GAUTIER, E.: *Mission au Sahara,* vol. I (algérien), Paris, 1908.

For the French Sudan see:

CHUDEAU, R.: *Mission au Sahara,* vol. 2 (*soudanais*), Paris, 1908; CHEVALIER, A.: *L'Afrique centrale française* (1902–4), Paris, 1908 (account of the Chari-Tchad Mission); and MENIAUD, J.:

Haut Sénégal, Niger (Soudan français), Géographie Économique, 2 vols., Paris, 1912. A valuable account of the pastoral peoples of the West African savanas.

For contrasts between Asiatic and African (transaharan) pastoralism see:

HAHN, E.: *Die Hirtenvölker in Asien und Africa*. Geog. Zeitschrift, 19, 1913.

On pastoralism in Abyssinia, Somaliland, etc., see:

PAULITSCHKE: *Ethnographie Nordost-Afrikas*. Berlin, 1893.

For an account of a Sudan arab tribe see:

SELIGMAN, C. G. and B. Z.: *The Kababish*. Harvard African Studies, 2, 1918.

For a short but brilliant polemic against exaggerated and stereotyped descriptions of pastoral nomadism see:

FEBVRE, L.: *Geographical Introduction to History*, Part III, Chapter 4. London, 1925.

On the northern Bushman of Damaraland see:

VEDDER, N.: *Die Bergdama*. Hamburg, 1923.

On the status of women in pastoral and other societies see:

LOWIE, R. H.: *Primitive Society*, Chapter 9. London, 1920.

For instances of Egyptian traits in the Upper Nile region see:

SELIGMAN, C. G.: *Egyptian Influence in Negro Africa*. In Studies presented to F. Ll. Griffith (Egypt Exploration Fund). London, 1932.

CHAPTER XXI

CANDOLLE, A. DE: *Origin of Cultivated Plants*. 3rd ed. London, 1909, remains the only general work dealing with the distribution and history of cultivated plants. Both the distributions and conclusions often require modification as a result of more recent work.

WILLIS, J. C.: *Agriculture in the Tropics*. Cambridge, 1909. Contains much valuable material.

On particular problems raised see:

LING ROTH, H.: *On the Origin of Agriculture*. JRAI, 16, 103, 1887.

TYLOR, E. B.: *Origin of the Plough*. JRAI, 10, 77, 1881.

LESER, P.: *Entstehung und Verbreitung des Pfluges*. Münster, 1933.

DIXON, R. B.: *The Problem of the Sweet Potato in Polynesia*. AA, 34, pp. 40–67, 1932.

RIVERS, W. H. R.: *Irrigation and the Cultivation of Taro*, in *Psychology and Ethnology*. London, 1926.

For the beginnings of agriculture in the Ancient East see:

CHILDE, V. G.: *New Light on the Most Ancient East*. London, 1934. A precise but vivid survey of all aspects of early civilization in this region.

BRUNTON, G., CATON THOMPSON, G., and PETRIE, F.: *The Badarian Civilization*. London, 1930.

CATON THOMPSON, G.: *Reports on Excavations in the Fayyum*, Antiquity, I, 1927; JRAI, 56, 1926; Man, 80, 1928.

ELLIOT SMITH, G.: *The Ancient Egyptians*. London, 1925.

PEAKE, H. J.: *The Beginnings of Agriculture*. Presidential Address. JRAI, 61, 1927.

NEWBERRY, T.: *Egypt as a Field for Anthropological Research*. Presidential Address. BAR, 1924.

CHERRY, T.: *The Origin of Agriculture*. Australian Association for the Advancement of Science, 1921.

MARSHALL, SIR J.: *Mohenjo daro and the Indus civilization*. 3 vols. London, 1932.

PERCIVAL, J.: *The Wheat Plant*. London, 1921.

VAVILOV, N.: *Studies in the Origin of Cultivated Plants*, Bulletin Applied Botany . . . 1926, 196–209, Leningrad; and *The Role of Central Asia in the Origin of Cultivated Plants*, Bulletin Applied Botany . . . 26, 1–44, Leningrad, 1931. Contain résumés in English.

On agriculture in the New World see:

SPINDEN, H. J.: *The Origin and Distribution of Agriculture in America*. ICA XIX, 269–76, 1917.

VAVILOV, N.: *Mexico and Central America as the Principal Centre of the Origin of Cultivated Plants in the New World*. Bulletin Applied Botany, 135–99, 1931, Leningrad.

THOMPSON, J. E.: *The Civilization of the Maya*, FMNH, Anthropology Handbook, 23, 1927; and *Mexico before Cortez*, London, 1933.

MEANS, P. A.: *Ancient Civilizations of the Andes*. New York, 1931.

CHAPTER XXII

For general problems of domestication see:

GALTON, F.: *The First Steps towards the Domestication of Animals*, Trans. Ethnological Soc., 3, 1865; also in *Inquiries into Human Faculty*, London, 1883.

HAHN, E.: *Die Haustiere*. Leipzig, 1896.

ANTONIUS, O.: *Grundzuge einer Stammegeschichte der Haustiere*. Jena, 1922.

HILZHEIMER, M.: *Die altesten Haustiere Vorderasiens*, Sitz. Ber.

Ges. Naturforschung, Berlin, 1931 ; also *Säugertierkunde und Archaeologie*, Zeit. f. Säugertierkunde, 1, 1926, Berlin.

Concerning particular animals see:

ALLEN, G. M.: *Domestic Dogs of the North American Indians.* Bulletin Harvard Museum of Comparative Zoology, 63, 1920.

HILZHEIMER, M.: *Dogs.* Antiquity, 6, 1932.

LYDDEKER, R.: *The Ox and its Kindred.* London, 1912.

JONES, C. B.: *The Origin and Development of British Cattle.* Proc. First International Congress of Prehistoric Sciences (London, 1932). London, pp. 151–4, 1934.

HILZHEIMER, M.: Article *'Rind'* in Ebert's Reallexikon der Vorgeschichte. (See also articles on other domestic animals under their several titles.)

LYDDEKER, R.: *The Sheep and its Cousins.* London, 1912.

SUSCHKIN, P. P.: *The Wild Sheep of the Old World.* Journal of Mammalogy, 6, 1925. New York.

HILZHEIMER, M. *Nord-afrikanische Schafe und ihre Bedeutung für die Besiedlungsfrage Nord-afrikas.* Zeit. f. Säugertierkunde, 3, 1928.

LYDDEKER, R.: *The Horse and its Relatives.* London, 1912.

For early evidence of the domestication and use of animals see:

CATON THOMPSON, G.: *The Neolithic Industry of the North Fayyum Desert*, JRAI, 56, 1926; and Man, Jan., 1934.

PETRIE, SIR F.: *Prehistoric Egypt.* London, 1920.

WILKINSON, SIR J. G.: *The Ancient Egyptians.* 1878.

CAPART, J.: *Les débuts de l'art en Égypte.* Brussels, 1904.

HILZHEIMER, M.: *Die Anschurung bei den alten Sumeren.* PZ, 22, 34, 1931.

MACKAY, E.: *Report on the Excavation of the 'A' Cemetery at Kish.* Anthrop. Mem., 1, FMNH. Chicago, 1925.

SCHNEIDER, A.: *Die sumerische Tempelstadt.* Leipsig, 1920.

LAUFER, B.: *Insect Musicians and Cricket Champions of China.* FMNH, 1927.

LAUFER, B.: *The Domestication of the Cormorant in China and Japan.* Anthropological series, FMNH, 18, 1931.

HALLOWELL, I.: *Bear Ceremonialism in the Northern Hemisphere.* AA., 28, 1926.

CHAPTER XXIII

On economic organization and development see:

HAHN, E.: *Demeter und Baubo. Versuch einer Theorie der Entstehung unseres Ackerbaus*, Lubeck, 1896; *Das Alter der wirtschaftlichen Arbeit*, Heidelberg, 1908; *Die Entstehung der Pflugkultur*, Heidelberg, 1909.

BÜCHER, K.: *Die Wirtschaft der Naturvölker*, Leipzig, 1898; *Die Entstehung der Volkswirtschaft*, Tubingen, 1920 (trans. as Industrial Evolution, London, 1901.)

LEROY, O.: *Essai d'introduction critique à l'étude de l'économie primitive.* Paris, 1925.

KOPPERS, P. W.: *Die ethnologische Wirtforschung.* A, 10-11, 1915-6.

MAUSS, M.: *Essai sur le don.* AS, n.s., 1, 1923.

SCHMIDT, M.: *Grundriss der ethnologischen Volkswirtschaftslehre,* 2 vols. (Stuttgart, 1920); and *Die materielle Wirtschaft bei den Naturvolkern,* Leipzig, 1923.

STEINMETZ, R.: *Classification des types sociaux.* AS, 3, 1900.

FIRTH, R.: *Primitive Economics of the New Zealand Maori,* London, 1929; *Some Features of Primitive Industry* [among the Maori], Econ. Journ., Economic History Suppt., 1926.

THURNWALD, R.: *Die menschliche Gesellschaft,* vol. 1, Berlin, 1931; *Economics in Primitive Communities,* Oxford, 1932.

On environmental relations see:

FEBVRE, L.: *A Geographical Introduction to History,* London, 1925. By far the most masterly critique of the whole problem.

VIDAL DE LA BLACHE, P.: *Les conditions géographiques des faits sociaux,* A de G., 11, 1902; and *Les genres de la vie dans la géographie humaine,* A de G., 20, 1911.

WISSLER, C.: *The Relation of Nature and Man in Aboriginal America.* New York, 1928.

FORDE, C. D.: *Values in Human Geography.* G., 13, 215, 1925.

AHRENS, R.: *Wirtschaftsformen und Landschaft.* Hamburg, 1927.

On discovery and invention see:

HARRISON, H. S.: *Opportunism and the Factors of Invention,* AA, 32, 1930; *Evolution in Material Culture.* Presidential Address, Section H, BAR., 1930; and also Man, 1926, Nos. 74, 101, 143, and 1927, No. 28.

INDEX

491